OUR MARTYR PRESIDENTS.

Memorial Edition

COMPLETE LIFE OF

William McKinley

AND

Story of His Assassination

AN AUTHENTIC AND OFFICIAL MEMORIAL EDITION, CONTAINING
EVERY INCIDENT IN THE CAREER OF THE IMMORTAL
STATESMAN, SOLDIER, ORATOR AND PATRIOT

BY

MARSHALL EVERETT

The Great Descriptive Writer and Friend of the Martyr President

---

PROFUSELY ILLUSTRATED WITH FULL-PAGE
PHOTOGRAPHS OF

THE ASSASSINATION SCENE

Portraits of President McKinley, His Cabinet, Famous Men of His
Adminstration and Vivid Life-Like Pictures of Eventful
Scenes in His Great and Grand Career

PREFACE.

No figure of modern American history appeals so strongly to the patriotism and love of the American people as William McKinley, and no volume can have greater interest and value at the present day, or be more dearly prized, than a history of his life in which every event of his great career as a noble youth, a gallant soldier, an able lawyer, a brilliant orator, a grand statesman, a brave patriot and an heroic martyr is set forth accurately, and in a spirit of love and reverence.

The author of this memorial edition has produced exactly the volume described.

In graphic words he has described the assassination of President McKinley. It is a word picture that will linger forever in the memory of every reader, calling forth sympathy and patriotism on behalf of the martyr President and undying contempt and horror of the assassin and the foul and cowardly thing called anarchy. Every detail of that now historic scene is told so vividly that the reader sees it as if he were an eye-witness.

McKinley's gallant fight for life, his cheerfulness, his patience, his tender solicitude for his invalid wife, his trust in God and all the beautiful attributes of his grand Christian spirit are recorded with fidelity to truth and a just appreciation of the nobility of such a grand character.

Nothing in history is more touching and beautiful than the author's description of the death-bed scene of President McKinley—the tender parting of devoted husband and loving, clinging wife, and the noble resignation of the dying man to the will of the Creator as expressed in the last words he uttered, addressed to his sorrowing wife: "God's will, not ours, be done!"

Another chapter describes the efforts of surgical and medical science to save and prolong the life so dear to the nation.

With the closing of the last chapters of that fearful scene at Buffalo, the painless death and the national funeral services, the author takes up the boyhood life of William McKinley and follows it step by step, up, up and ever upward to the very summit of his greatness when he fell a martyr to liberty and lawful government.

His early Christian training by his noble mother—"Mother McKinley"

3

as the whole nation learned to call her—who lived to see her boy in the White House, and all the events which went to shape his character are depicted with interest.

Next in order is his career as a soldier in the Civil War—in which the author gives every thrilling incident and exciting experience in which William McKinley figured during that great struggle. Later, it is told how in after years he did so much to reunite the sections of his country and wipe out all bitter memory of that war between brothers.

As a congressman, governor and President, nothing is omitted in this history that is a part of the life of this great American statesman. The history of his campaigns and administrations is given in full, together with his management of the Spanish war, the policy of expansion, the growth of national commerce and all the other great achievements and policies that were a part of his life work.

In other words, this volume is exactly what it purports to be, a COMPLETE life of William McKinley.

The beautiful illustrations in this volume have been made from actual photographs, and reproduced by the well-known half-tone process. There are hundreds of scenes of interest in the life, death and funeral of President McKinley. The pictures of the assassination, the death-bed scene and the places and people of the great tragedy are true to life in every particular and have an historic interest and value for every American citizen.

This volume is in every respect truly a memorial edition of the Complete Life of William McKinley, whose memory will ever remain in the minds of loyal Americans inseparably associated with his two fellow martyr-Presidents, Lincoln and Garfield, and the record of whose patriotic and noble life is contained herein.

TABLE OF CONTENTS.

CHAPTER I.

THE ASSASSINATION OF PRESIDENT McKINLEY.

A graphic and vivid description of the Shooting of the President by Leon Czolgosz, an Anarchist, at the Pan-American Exposition, Buffalo—Two shots fired from a derringer concealed by the assassin under a handkerchief which looked like a bandage—Different accounts by eye-witnesses—Assassin seized by James F. Parker, a colored man—Saved from the mob by the President's words, "Let no one hurt him"—Scenes among the horror-stricken crowds in the Temple of Music—The President taken on a gallop to the Emergency Hospital—Description of his wounds—How the great man bore the ordeal...................................... 33

CHAPTER II.

PRESIDENT McKINLEY'S FIGHT FOR LIFE.

The fateful week at the house of President Milburn of the Exposition where President McKinley lay wounded—His coolness, bravery and cheerfulness—Physicians and country hopeful—President shows signs of recovery—How he was nourished—Scenes in the President's apartment—His sudden relapse—Hopes of the nation dashed by the news.. 41

CHAPTER III.

DEATHBED SCENE OF PRESIDENT McKINLEY.

Friends and officials called back—President regains consciousness after first relapse—Pathetic parting between the President and Mrs. McKinley—The farewell Kiss—"God's will, not ours, be done," his last words to her—"Nearer My God to Thee" Dr. Rixey remains to the end—Unconscious for hours before dissolution—A Christian deathbed scene that will remain forever, a beautiful and inspiring memory 57

CHAPTER IV.

THE STORY OF THE ASSASSIN.

Description of Czolgosz the assassin—A Pole by birth—Boasted that he was an Anarchist and believed in killing the rulers of all nations—Became an Anarchist under the teachings of Emma Goldman—How and why he went to Buffalo—Followed the President for three days seeking an opportunity to kill him—A monstrous confession—His father and mother found in Cleveland—Poor and ignorant, but nothing known against them—People who knew the assassin tell of his belonging to Anarchist clubs and always preaching Anarchy.................. 65

5

CHAPTER V.

EMMA GOLDMAN, WOMAN LEADER OF ANARCHISTS.

Description of the woman from whom the assassin learned the teachings of Anarchy —Text of Emma Goldman's speech which Czolgosz says inflamed him to commit assassination—Emma Goldman's career as an Anarchist in New York and Europe —Her arrest in Chicago—Arrest of the "Free Society" branch of Anarchists in Chicago 76

CHAPTER VI.

ANARCHISM AND ITS OBJECTS.

Definition of anarchy—No two Anarchists agree—Some of the leaders who have talked, written and acted anarchy in this country and in Europe—A hellish doctrine that has caused many of the world's greatest men to fall by the hands of assassins— Complete history of anarchy from Proudhon to the present day—Review of anarchistic agitation and murder—Story of the Haymarket assassinations in Chicago.. 89

CHAPTER VII.

SCENES AT BUFFALO FOLLOWING THE ASSASSINATION.

Wild anger of the people at the appalling crime—How the assassin was guarded against the popular wrath—Grief and anger mingled—The location of the Milburn house— The President's clothes—What he had in his pockets—Senator Hanna's remarkable dream of warning—The devotion of Private Secretary Cortelyou................... 99

CHAPTER VIII.

DAYS OF ANXIETY AND SORROW.

How the American people watched and waited, hoped and prayed while the President lay ill—All the civilized world shared in the sorrow and anxiety—World-wide grief at the President's death—Rulers of the world eulogize the dead President—Their messages of sympathy... 107

CHAPTER IX.

PRESIDENT McKINLEY'S LAST SPEECH.

Greatest speech ever made by the President delivered on the day before the assassination—World-wide in its influence and uniting the American people in praise of his wise statesmanship—Great honors shown the nation's chief on the day before his assassination—Events of a day to be memorable in American history............ 115

CHAPTER X.

WILLIAM McKINLEY'S BOYHOOD.

His Scotch-Irish ancestry—His sturdy sire, William McKinley, Sr.—The Christian influence of Mother McKinley, who lived to see her boy in the White House—Early occupations of the future President—Supporter of Fremont and Lincoln—Early days at Niles and Poland, Ohio.. 123

CHAPTER XI.

McKINLEY AS A SOLDIER IN THE CIVIL WAR.

Enlisted as a private and won a commission by gallant and heroic conduct—Under fire at Antietam and other historic battles—Promoted by General, afterwards President, Hayes—Brave and modest—Stories of his experiences in battle.................. 129

CHAPTER XII.

McKINLEY IN CONGRESS.

Elected in the Centennial year—Soon gave evidence of legislative ability—Chairman of the Ways and Means Committee and leader of his party in the Lower House of Congress—Fourteen years of memorable work—Some of his memorable speeches and debates—How his district was "gerrymandered" in order to defeat him—A marvelous legislative record... 141

CHAPTER XIII.

McKINLEY'S LIFE WAS PROTECTION'S ERA.

First champion of Protection for Protection's sake—Made his policy the policy of his party and the nation—Growth of the country's industry—His last speech substituted Reciprocity for Protection.. 161

CHAPTER XIV.

McKINLEY AS GOVERNOR OF OHIO.

Twice chosen as chief executive of his state—First nomination by acclamation—A campaign that carried the people with him—Governor McKinley and the labor troubles—Always stood for law and order and sympathized with honest labor.... 169

CHAPTER XV.

McKINLEY AS A CAMPAIGNER.

His winning personality in politics—Believed in the people and knew how to convert men to his way of thinking—His methods of campaigning—His wonderful knowledge of politics—Campaigns of education—McKinley a wonderful speechmaker—Talks to workingmen and business men on the lawn at Canton.................... 177

CHAPTER XVI.

GOVERNOR McKINLEY'S FINANCIAL TROUBLES.

In trying to assist a friend his small fortune is swept away—Governor McKinley and his wife turn over all of their property to meet his obligation—Friends come to the rescue and he is relieved from owing any man a cent—The story of how W. R. Day, H. H. Kohlsaat, Myron T. Herrick and Marcus A. Hanna stood by Governor McKinley in his hour of need—Governor McKinley's attitude above criticism.... 185

CHAPTER XVII.

McKINLEY'S LOYALTY TO SHERMAN, BLAINE AND HARRISON.

Friendship between three great statesmen—McKinley always an enthusiastic Blaine man—His honorable attitude toward the Ohio statesman—Thrilling scene in a

National convention when delegates attempt to stampede to McKinley—How he
stopped his own nomination for President and brought about the nomination of
General Harrison by acclamation... 189

CHAPTER XVIII.

FIRST NOMINATION FOR PRESIDENT.

The sentiment of the people strong for McKinley's nomination in 1896—The other
candidates—History of the great National Republican Convention at St. Louis in
1896—Foraker set the delegates wild with his speech nominating McKinley—First
ballot secures his nomination—Historic political scenes and characters—Hobart
named for the second place.. 195

CHAPTER XIX.

THE GREAT CAMPAIGN OF 1896.

Men and issues of a memorable national campaign—William Jennings Bryan as Mc-
Kinley's opponent—Gold vs. Silver—How the issues were stated by leading de-
baters—Bryan's speech-making tour—Pilgrimages of the people to Canton—
McKinley receives thousands of voters at his home............................ 213

CHAPTER XX.

THE SPANISH WAR CLOUD.

How President McKinley exhausted every means in his power to honorably settle the
Cuban trouble and avert war with Spain—Brief history of the causes leading to the
war with Spain—Wisdom and patriotism of President McKinley—A war for
humanity 221

CHAPTER XXI.

McKINLEY'S OWN STORY OF THE SPANISH-AMERICAN WAR.

In a celebrated state paper the President reviews the entire history of the Spanish war
—His able conduct of the war—Every great historical detail of the struggle for
humanity set forth by President McKinley—An historical document that will
remain forever as a true record of President McKinley's humane and wise statesmanship 227

CHAPTER XXII.

McKINLEY AND EXPANSION.

Great amount of territory acquired by the United States under President McKinley—
The story of American expansion—President's policy toward the people of our new
possessions—The greatness of President McKinley's Expansion policy—What it
meant to the nation.. 251

CHAPTER XXIII.

SECOND PRESIDENTIAL NOMINATION AND ELECTION OF McKINLEY.

Complete history of the Philadelphia convention of 1900—McKinley's renomination a
foregone conclusion—Senator Wolcott's great eulogy of President McKinley—
Theodore Roosevelt named for Vice-President.................................. 263

CHAPTER XXIV.

PRESIDENT McKINLEY AND THE CHINESE CRISIS.

Prompt action by the President following the boxer uprising—Cause of the trouble—
The siege of Peking—The United States joins the powers to rescue the besieged
legations—China appeals to the United States to prevent the powers from dividing
the Empire—President McKinley's attitude results in a just settlement of the
trouble—A remarkable chapter on President McKinley's wise diplomacy........ 271

CHAPTER XXV.

McKINLEY: BUILDER OF A WORLD POWER.

A complete history of the foreign policy of President McKinley during his two administrations—How he built up the nation to be one of the great powers of the world
—The master work of his life was in giving the United States its proper place in
the family of nations—Results that will rank with those of Washington and Lincoln
in adding to the greatness of the American nation................................ 281

CHAPTER XXVI.

PRIVATE LIFE OF WILLIAM McKINLEY.

A model son and husband—His courtship of Ida Saxton—Their marriage—Two children bless the union, only to die in infancy—Mrs. McKinley's health shattered—
The "Major's" devotion to his invalid wife—William McKinley, the highest type
of American manhood, and a model for every American boy and man............ 293

CHAPTER XXVII.

McKINLEY'S EULOGY OF LINCOLN.

Full text of an address delivered by President McKinley on President Lincoln's Birthday anniversary... 298

CHAPTER XVIII.

PRESIDENT ROOSEVELT TAKES THE OATH OF OFFICE.

The new President sworn in at Buffalo—A simple ceremony tinged with the gloom of
tragedy—Biography of President Roosevelt, soldier, author, statesman—A review
of one of the most remarkable careers in history................................. 304

CHAPTER XXIX.

GREAT EVENTS OF THE WORLD DURING PRESIDENT McKINLEY'S ADMINISTRATION.

A chapter of happenings of world-wide importance, many of which were influenced by
the late President... 321

CHAPTER XXX.

THE FUNERAL SERVICE AT BUFFALO.

Private funeral of William McKinley, the man and citizen, held at the Milburn house
—Touching scenes of last farewell—Simple but beautiful services................. 330

CHAPTER XXXI.

LYING IN STATE AT BUFFALO.

Body of the President viewed by thousands in the city hall—All classes of people present—Italian women remove the shawls from their heads—Indians drop flowers on the casket—Eloquent tributes of Indian chiefs—Thousands brave a storm and drenching rain to gaze on the features of the nation's beloved dead.............. 339

CHAPTER XXXII.

THE FUNERAL TRAIN TO WASHINGTON.

Thousands line the route—Bells toll, choral societies sing, people stand uncovered and reverently bow their heads as the train passes—Outward signs and emblems of a nation's grief such as were never before witnessed in the world—Complete story of the journey to the National Capital... 345

CHAPTER XXXIII.

THE LAST NIGHT IN THE WHITE HOUSE.

President's body taken to the White House from the funeral train—Awe-inspiring scenes at the station—President McKinley's happy departure for Buffalo recalled—Body placed in the great East Room... 349

CHAPTER XXXIV.

FUNERAL SERVICES AND PROCESSION AT WASHINGTON.

National funeral services held in the rotunda of the Capitol, directly under the dome—Body brought from the White House—Description of the procession—Rev. Dr. Naylor's eloquent prayer—Bishop Andrews' funeral sermon...................... 357

CHAPTER XXXV.

LYING IN STATE AT THE CAPITOL.

Crowds throng the Capitol building at Washington for a last look at the martyr-President—Complete description of the scene—A panic caused by immense crush—Beautiful floral designs—The last day at the seat of national government........ 367

CHAPTER XXXVI.

THE ASSASSIN ARRAIGNED.

While the President's body was lying in state in the National Capitol, the assassin was arraigned in court and attorneys enter plea of "not guilty"—Text of the indictment 375

CHAPTER XXXVII.

THE SAD JOURNEY TO CANTON.

Route of the funeral train from the National Capital to the Ohio home lined with mourners—Journey through Maryland and Pennsylvania—Touching incidents on the way—Through Ohio—Arrival at Canton, a city of sorrow.................... 381

CHAPTER XXXVIII.

CANTON BATHED IN TEARS.

How the people of Canton received the body of their fellow townsman—Grief in every heart 387

CHAPTER XXXIX.

FUNERAL SERVICES IN ALL CHURCHES.

First Sunday after the death of President McKinley—All sects and creeds unite in eulogy—Sad and impressive scenes... 395

CHAPTER XL.

CANTON'S FAREWELL TO McKINLEY.

Friends and neighbors take their last view of the dead President—Many pathetic and beautiful incidents mark the final leave-taking................................... 404

CHAPTER XLI.

McKINLEY LAID AT REST.

Complete account of the funeral and burial of President McKinley—Beautiful and impressive ceremonies—Soldiers guard the tomb.................................... 415

CHAPTER XLII.

NATION OBSERVES BURIAL DAY.

Services held in every part of the United States—The old world joins in observing McKinley's burial day—Five minutes of silence................................... 425

CHAPTER XLIII.

ASSASSINATIONS OF LINCOLN AND GARFIELD.

Complete story of the manner in which our other two martyr-presidents were shot down by assassins 431

NOTABLE ASSASSINATIONS AND ATTEMPTS OF RECENT TIMES.

George III. of England, attempt by Margaret Nicholson on August 2, 1786, and by James Hatfield on May 15, 1800.

Napoleon I. of France, attempt by use of an infernal machine on December 24, 1800.

Czar Paul of Russia, killed by nobles of his court on March 24, 1801.

Spencer Percival, Premier of England, killed by Bellingham on May 11, 1812.

George IV. of England, attempt on January 28, 1817.

August Kotzebue of Germany, killed by Earl Sand for political motives on March 23, 1819.

Charles duc de Berri, killed on February 13, 1820.

Andrew Jackson, President of the United States, attempt on January 30, 1835.

Louis Philippe of France, six attempts: By Fieschi, on July 28, 1835; by Alibaud, on June 25, 1836; by Miunier, on December 27, 1836; by Darmos, on October 16, 1840; by Lecompte, on April 14, 1846; by Henry, on July 19, 1846.

Denis Affre, Archbishop of Paris, on June 27, 1848.

Rossi, Comte Pellegrino, Roman statesman, on November 15, 1848.

Frederick William IV. of Prussia, attempt by Sofelage on May 22, 1850.

Francis Joseph of Austria, attempt by Libenyi on February 18, 1853.

Ferdinand, Charles III., Duke of Parma, on March 27, 1854.

Isabella II. of Spain, attempts by La Riva on May 4, 1847; by Merino on February 2, 1852; by Raymond Fuentes on May 28, 1856.

Napoleon III., attempts by Pianori on April 28, 1855; by Bellemarre on September 8, 1855; by Orsini and others (France) on January 14, 1858.

Daniel, Prince of Montenegro, on August 13, 1860.

Abraham Lincoln, President of the United States, at Ford's Theater, Washington, by John Wilkes Booth, on the evening of April 14; died on April 15, 1865.

Michael, Prince of Servia, on June 10, 1868.

Prim, Marshal of Spain, on December 28; died on December 30, 1870.

George Darboy, Archbishop of Paris, by communists, on May 24, 1871.

Richard, Earl of Mayo, Governor General of India, by Shere Ali, a convict, in Andaman Islands, on February 8, 1872.

Amadeus, Duke of Aosta, when King of Spain, attempt on July 19, 1872.

Prince Bismarck, attempt by Blind on May 7, 1866; by Kullman on July 13, 1874.

Abdul Aziz, Sultan of Turkey, on June 4, 1876.

Hussein Avni and other Turkish Ministers, by Hassan, a Circassian officer, on June 15, 1876.

William I. of Prussia and Germany, attempts by Oscar Becker on July 14, 1861; by Hodel on May 11, 1878; by Dr. Nobiling on June 2, 1878.

Mehemet Ali, Pasha, by Albanians on September 7, 1878.

Lord Lytton, Viceroy of India, attempt by Busa on December 12, 1878.

Alfonso XII. of Spain, attempts by J. O. Moncasi on October 25, 1878; by Francisco Otero Gonzalez on December 30, 1879.

Loris Melikoff, Russian General, attempt on March 4, 1880.

Bratiano, Premier of Roumania, attempt by J. Pietraro on December 14, 1880.

Alexander II. of Russia, attempts by Karakozow at St. Petersburg on April 16, 1866; by Berezowski at Paris on June 6, 1867; by Alexander Solovieff on April 14, 1879; by undermining a railway train on December 1, 1879; by explosion of Winter Palace, St. Petersburg, on February 17, 1880; killed by explosion of a bomb thrown by a man who was himself killed, St. Petersburg, on March 13, 1881.

James A. Garfield, President of the United States, shot by Charles J. Guiteau on July 2, 1881.

Mayor Carter H. Harrison of Chicago, shot by Prendergast on October 28, 1893.

Marie Francois Carnot, President of France, stabbed mortally at Lyons by Cesare Santo, an Anarchist, on Sunday, June 24, 1894.

Stanislaus Stambuloff, ex-Premier of Bulgaria, killed by four persons, armed with revolvers and knives, on July 25, 1895.

Nasr-ed-din, Shah of Persia, was assassinated on May 1, 1896, as he was entering a shrine near his palace. The man who shot him was disguised as a woman and is believed to have been the tool of a band of conspirators. He was caught and suffered the most horrible death that Persian ingenuity could invent.

Antonio Canovas del Castillo, Prime Minister of Spain, shot to death by Michel Angolillo, alias Golli, an Italian Anarchist, at Santa Agueda, Spain, while going to the baths, on August 8, 1897.

Juan Idiarte Borda, President of Uruguay, killed on August 25, 1897, at Montevideo by Avelino Arredondo, officer in Uruguayan army.

President Diaz, attempt in the City of Mexico by M. Arnulfo on September 20, 1897.

Jose Maria Reyna Barrios, President of Guatemala, killed at Guatemala City on February 8, 1898, by Oscar Solinger.

Empress Elizabeth of Austria, stabbed by Luchini, a French-Italian Anarchist, at Geneva, Switzerland, on September 10, 1898.

William Goebel, Democratic claimant to the Governorship of Kentucky, shot by a person unknown on Tuesday, January 30, 1900, while on his way to the State Capitol in Frankfort, Ky.

Humbert, King of Italy, shot to death on July 29, 1900, at Monza, Italy, by Angelo Bresci.

Albert Edward, then Prince of Wales, now King of England, attempt by Brussels Anarchist on April 4, 1900.

William McKinley, President of the United States, shot at Buffalo on September 6, 1901. Died September 14, 1901.

Chronology

OF

President William McKinley

Born Niles, Ohio, January 29, 1843.

School-teacher, Poland, Ohio, 1860.

Enlisted Union Army June, 1861.

Second Lieutenant September 24, 1862.

First Lieutenant February 7, 1863.

Captain July 25, 1864.

Brevet Major for gallantry, 1865.

Admitted to the Ohio bar 1867.

Elected state's attorney 1869.

Elected first to Congress 1876.

Re-elected 1878, 1880, 1882, 1884 to 1890.

Elected Governor of Ohio 1891.

Re-elected Governor of Ohio 1893.

Elected President United States 1896.

Re-elected President United States 1900.

Shot by an assassin September 6, 1901.

Died Buffalo, N. Y., September 14, 1901.

William McKinley

CHARACTERISTIC POSE OF PRESIDENT McKINLEY.

PRESIDENT McKINLEY AND HIS WAR CABINET OF 1898.

PRESIDENT, WM. McKINLEY.

MRS. WILLIAM McKINLEY.

MR. AND MRS. McKINLEY AND THEIR HOME AT
CANTON, OHIO.

MRS. McKINLEY, MOTHER OF THE PRESIDENT.

MRS. McKINLEY, MOTHER OF THE PRESIDENT.

WILLIAM McKINLEY IN HIS CANTON HOME.

MISS HELEN McKINLEY.

MR. ABNER McKINLEY, BROTHER OF THE
PRESIDENT.

PRESIDENT McKINLEY AND MARSHALL EVERETT IN CONSUL-
TATION DURING THE SPANISH-AMERICAN WAR.

HEARSE BEARING PRESIDENT McKINLEY'S REMAINS PASSING THE TREASURY DEPARTMENT, WASHINGTON, D. C.

U. S. MARINES IN THE McKINLEY FUNERAL PROCESSION, WASHINGTON, D. C.

U. S. SENATORS AND REPRESENTATIVES IN THE McKINLEY FUNERAL PROCESSION, WASHINGTON, D. C.

PRESIDENT THEODORE ROOSEVELT.

BUILDING IN WHICH PRESIDENT McKINLEY WAS SHOT, TEMPLE OF MUSIC, PAN-AMERICAN EXPOSITION, BUFFALO, N. Y.

LEON CZOLGOSZ, THE ASSASSIN OF PRESIDENT McKINLEY.

ASSASSINATION OF PRESIDENT McKINLEY.

...*The Life*...

OF

President William McKinley

CHAPTER I.

THE ASSASSINATION OF PRESIDENT McKINLEY.

On Friday, September 6, 1901, the blackest Friday in American history, the American people were shocked and stunned by the news that their beloved President, William McKinley, had been shot down by a cowardly assassin, while attending the Pan-American Exposition at Buffalo.

It was like a flash of lightning from a clear sky. The people were stunned into momentary silence. The sign of grief was on the face of every loyal American, and the hearts of the people beat as one in sympathy for the stricken chief.

The horror of the tragic event grew when it was learned that the assassin was an anarchist, and not an insane man as was first supposed.

Then came the full realization that the murderous bullet of the assassin was aimed not only at the foremost citizen of the Republic, but that the Red Thing called Anarchy had raised its blood-stained hand against government, against all peaceable authority and law. It was a blow struck at all the institutions of society that men hold dear and sacred.

With that wonderful self-control that distinguishes the American people, loyal citizens restrained the rising passion in their breasts, and their suppressed rage was further held in check by the word of hope which followed that the President was yet alive.

Alas! it was but a hope, destined to linger but a few days.

The scene of the assassination was the Temple of Music, at the Exposition grounds. The day previous was President's day at the Exposition, and President McKinley had delivered what many believed to be the greatest

33

speech of his life. Praises for his wisdom and statesmanship were ringing around the world.

On the fateful day the President attended the Exposition as a visitor, and in the afternoon held a reception in the Temple of Music.

The reception to the President was one to which the general public had been invited. President John G. Milburn of the Exposition had introduced the President to the great crowd in the Temple, and men, women and children came forward for a personal greeting.

Among those in line was Leon Czolgosz, whose right hand was wrapped in a handkerchief. Folded in the handkerchief was a 32-caliber self-acting revolver holding five bullets.

A little girl was led up by her father and the President shook hands with her. As she passed along to the right the President looked after her smilingly and waved his hand in a pleasant adieu.

Next in line came a boyish-featured man about 26 years old, preceded by a short Italian who leaned backward against the bandaged hand of his follower. The officers, who attended the President, noted this man, their attention being first attracted by the Italian, whose dark, shaggy brows and black mustache caused the professional protectors to regard him with suspicion.

The man with the bandaged hand and innocent face received no attention from the detectives beyond the mental observation that his right hand was apparently injured, and that he would present his left hand to the President.

The Italian stood before the palm bower. He held the President's right hand so long that the officers stepped forward to break the clasp, and make room for the man with the bandaged hand, who extended the left hand towards the President's right.

THE FATAL SHOTS.

The President smiled and presented his right hand in a position to meet the left of the approaching man. Hardly a foot of space intervened between the bodies of the two men. Before their hands met two pistol shots rang out, and the President turned slightly to the left and reeled.

The bandage on the hand of the tall, innocent looking young man had concealed a revolver. He had fired through the bandage without removing any portion of the handkerchief.

The first bullet entered too high for the purpose of the assassin, who had fired again as soon as his finger could move the trigger.

On receiving the first shot President McKinley lifted himself on his toes with something of a gasp. His movement caused the second shot to enter just below the navel. With the second shot the President doubled slightly forward and then sank back. Secret Service Detective Geary caught the President in his arms and President Milburn helped to support him.

ASKS IF HE IS SHOT.

When the President fell into the arms of Detective Geary he coolly asked: "Am I shot?"

Geary unbuttoned the President's vest, and, seeing blood, replied: "I fear you are, Mr. President."

It had all happened in an instant. Almost before the noise of the second shot sounded a negro waiter, James F. Parker, leaped upon the assassin, striking him a terrific blow and crushing him to the floor. Soldiers of the United States artillery detailed at the reception sprang upon them, and he was surrounded by a squad of exposition police and secret service detectives. Detective Gallagher seized Czolgosz's hand, tore away the handkerchief and took the revolver.

The artillerymen, seeing the revolver in Gallagher's hand, rushed at the assassin and handled him rather roughly. Meanwhile Detective Ireland and the negro held the assassin, endeavoring to shield him from the attacks of the infuriated artillerymen and the blows of the policemen's clubs.

Supported by Detective Geary and President of the Exposition Milburn, and surrounded by Secretary George B. Cortelyou and half a dozen exposition officials, the President was assisted to a chair. His face was white, but he made no outcry.

When the second shot struck the President he sank back with one hand holding his abdomen, the other fumbling at his breast. His eyes were open and he was clearly conscious of all that had transpired. He looked up into President Milburn's face and gasped: "Cortelyou," the name of his private secretary. The President's secretary bent over him. "Cortelyou," said the President, "my wife, be careful about her; don't let her know."

Moved by a paroxysm he writhed to the left and then his eyes fell on the prostrate form of the assassin, Czolgosz, lying on the floor bloody and helpless beneath the blows of the guard.

The President raised his right hand, red with his own blood, and placed it on the shoulder of his secretary. "Let no one hurt him," he gasped, and sank back in the chair, while the guards carried Czolgosz out of his sight.

The ambulance from the exposition hospital was summoned immediately and the President, still conscious, sank upon the stretcher. Secretary Cortelyou and Mr. Milburn rode with him in the ambulance, and in nine minutes after the shooting the President was awaiting the arrival of surgeons, who had been summoned from all sections of the city, and by special train from Niagara Falls.

The President continued conscious and conversed with Mr. Cortelyou and Mr. Milburn on his way to the hospital. "I am sorry," he said, "to have been the cause of trouble to the exposition."

Three thoughts had found expression with the President—first, that the news should be kept from his wife; second, that the would-be assassin should not be harmed; and, third, regret that the tragedy might hurt the exposition.

The news that the President had been shot passed across the exposition grounds with almost incredible speed, and the crowd around the Temple grew until it counted 50,000 persons. This big crowd followed the ambulance respectfully to the hospital, then divided itself into two parts, one anxious to learn the condition of the President and to catch every rumor that came from the hospital; the other eager to find the assassin and to punish him.

Certain it is that if the officials had not used remarkable diligence in taking Czolgosz out of the way of the crowd he would have been mobbed and beaten to death.

Czolgosz had been carried into a side room at the northwest corner of the Temple. There he was searched, but nothing was found upon him except a letter relating to lodging. The officers washed the blood from his face and asked him who he was and why he had tried to kill the President. He made no answer at first, but finally gave the name of Nieman. He offered no explanation of the deed except that he was an Anarchist and had done his duty.

A detail of exposition guards was sent for a company of soldiers. A carriage was summoned. South of the Temple a space had been roped off. The crowd tore out the iron stanchion holding the ropes and carried the ropes to the flagpole standing near by on the esplanade.

"Lynch him," cried a hundred voices, and a start was made for one of the entrances of the Temple. Soldiers and police beat back the crowd. Guards and people were wrangling, shouting and fighting.

In this confusion, Czolgosz, still bleeding, his clothes torn, and scarcely able to walk, was led out by Captain James F. Vallaly, chief of the exposition detectives; Commandant Robinson, and a squad of secret service men.

Czolgosz was thrown into a carriage and three detectives jumped in with him. Captain Vallaly jumped on the driver's seat and lashed the horses into a gallop.

Six doctors were at the President's side within thirty seconds after his arrival at the hospital, among them the President's family physician, Dr. P. M. Rixey. Dr. Roswell Park, a surgeon of national reputation, was summoned from Niagara Falls, where he was performing an operation, and Dr. Herman Mynter arrived soon after.

The surgeons consulted and hesitated about performing an operation. The President reassured them by expressing his confidence, but no decision was reached when Dr. Mann of the exposition hospital staff arrived. After another consultation Dr. Mann informed the President that an operation was necessary.

"All right," replied the President. "Go ahead. Do whatever is proper."

The anesthetic administered was ether, and for two and a half hours the President was under the influence of this.

The wound in the breast proved to be only a flesh wound. The bullet struck a button and was somewhat deflected. It entered the middle of the breast above the breast bone, but did not penetrate far. When the President was undressed for the operation the bullet fell from his clothing upon the table.

The second and serious wound was a bullet hole in the abdomen, about five inches below the left nipple and an inch and a half to the left of the median line. The bullet which caused that wound penetrated both the interior and posterior walls of the stomach, going completely through that organ.

It was found also that as a consequence of the perforation the stomach fluid had circulated about the abdominal cavity.

Further examination disclosed that the hole made by the entrance of the bullet was small and clean cut, while that on the other side of the stomach was large and ragged.

A five-inch incision was made and through that aperture the physicians were enabled to turn the organ about so as to suture the larger bullet hole. After that had been sewed the abdominal cavity was washed with a salt solution.

The operation performed on President McKinley at the emergency hospital left no need for a second operation to follow it almost immediately. Dr. Mann, who performed the operation, had for his first assistant Dr. Herman Mynter. His second assistant was Dr. John Parmenter. His third assistant was Dr. Lee of St. Louis, who happened to be on the exposition grounds at the time of the tragedy, and placed his services at the disposal of the President. Dr. Nelson W. Wilson noted the time of the operation, and took notes. Dr. Eugene Wasdin of the marine hospital gave the anesthetic. Dr. Rixey arrived at the latter part of the operation, and held the light. Dr. Park arrived at the close of the operation. It was Dr. Mann who wielded the knife.

The operation lasted almost an hour. A cut about five inches long was made. It was found necessary to turn up the stomach of the President in order to trace the course of the bullet. The bullet's opening in the front wall of the stomach was small and it was carefully closed with sutures, after which a search was made for the hole in the back wall of the stomach.

This hole, where the bullet went out of the stomach, was larger than the hole in the front wall of the stomach; in fact, it was a wound over an inch in diameter, jagged and ragged. It was sewed up in three layers. This wound was larger than the wound where the bullet entered the stomach, because the bullet, in its course, forced tissues through ahead of it.

In turning up the stomach, an act that was absolutely necessary, and was performed by Dr. Mann with rare skill, the danger was that some of the contents of the stomach might go into the abdominal cavity, and as a result cause peritonitis. It so happened that there was little in the President's stomach at the time of the operation. Moreover, subsequent developments tended to show that this feature of the operation was successful and that none of the contents of the stomach entered the abdominal cavity. If any of the contents had entered the cavity the probability is that peritonitis would have set in.

The weapon used by the assassin proved to be a five-barreled double-action revolver of 32 caliber. Every chamber contained a bullet, and three remained in the weapon after the shooting.

It was at first reported that the weapon was a derringer, but this proved to be incorrect.

Many of the accounts of the assassination vary in detail, which is quite natural under the excitement of the moment, and the fact that no two persons see and hear alike. One account, given by an eye-witness, which differs in some respects from the one with which this chapter begins, is as follows:

"It was about four o'clock, near the close of the reception in the Temple of Music, and the President, in his customary cordial manner, was reaching forward, with a pleasant smile, to take the hands of the good-natured crowd that was pushing forward. A six-foot colored man, who proved to be a waiter in the Plaza, named James F. Parker, had just shaken hands with the President and was smiling all over with enjoyment, when suddenly, behind him, pressed forward the slight figure of a smooth-faced but muscular young man, whose eyes were wild and glaring, whose head was drooping, and who seemed to me to have sprung up from the floor, as I had not observed him before. The President took no special notice of him, but simply stooped over to shake his hand, without looking, apparently, at the individual.

"Their palms had hardly touched before I heard two shots in quick succession. A hush and quiet instantly followed. The President straightened up for a moment and stepped back five or six feet. Secretary Cortelyou, who had been standing at his side, burst into tears, and exclaimed, 'You're shot!' The President murmured, 'Oh, no, it cannot be!' But Secretary Cortelyou and Mr. Milburn had torn open the President's vest, and the telltale blood, flowing from the wound in the abdomen, revealed the fearful truth. The President had dropped into a chair and now turned deathly pale. Meanwhile, the other wound in the breast had been uncovered and both Mr. Milburn and Secretary Cortelyou were in tears. The President, seeing their emotion, put up his hand and gently murmured that he was all right, or some reassuring words, and appeared to faint away.

"The Secret Service men, Foster and Ireland, at one bound seized the assassin, before the smoke had cleared away, and, in fact, before the sound of the second shot was heard. The negro, Parker, also turned instantly and confronted Czolgosz, whose right hand was being tightly held behind him by the detectives and whose face was thrust forward. Parker, with his clenched fist, smashed the assassin three times squarely in the face, and was apparently wild to kill the creature, while all the crowd of artillerymen, policemen, and others, also set upon the object of their wrath.

"The women in the vast audience were hysterical, and the men were little less than crazy. The transformation from the scene of smiles and gladness of a moment before, to the wild, rushing, mighty roar of an infuriated crowd, was simply awful. The police and military at once set about the task of clearing the building, which they accomplished with amazing celerity and good judgment, considering the fact that a crowd of 50,000 at the outside was pressing into the entrance."

A third narrative is still somewhat different. The narrator recites that the President, after he had been shot, was calm, seemed to grow taller, and had a look of half reproach and half indignation in his eyes as he turned and started toward a chair unassisted. Then Secretary Cortelyou and Mr. Milburn went to his help. Secret Service Agent S. R. Ireland and George F. Foster had grappled with the assassin, but, quicker than both, was a gigantic negro, James F. Parker, a waiter in a restaurant in the Plaza, who had been standing behind Czolgosz, awaiting an opportunity, in joyous expectation, to shake the President's hand. He stood there, six feet four inches tall, with two hundred and fifty pounds of muscular enthusiasm, grinning happily, until he heard the pistol shots. With one quick shift of his clenched fist he knocked the pistol from the assassin's hand. With another he spun the man around like a top, and, with a third, he broke Czolgosz's nose. A fourth split the assassin's lip and knocked out several teeth, and when the officers tore him away from Parker the latter, crying like a baby, exclaimed, "Oh, for only ten seconds more!"

CHAPTER II.

McKINLEY'S FIGHT FOR LIFE.

The courage exhibited on the battlefield, when the whole being is aroused and the nerves are tingling with a thrill of excitement, is worthy of the highest praise, but to show fortitude and resigned courage in a battle for life, when the approach of death is heralded by unfailing signs, requires a hero. Such was the lamented Chief Executive in the trying hours following the attack of the assassin. Few of those about President McKinley on that memorable day expected to see him survive the night.

Prompt work on the part of the surgeons and a rugged constitution prevailed over wounds considered mortal. The President was under the care of the most skillful practitioners, who were encouraged by the favorable turn, and they, by their bulletins, which were full of hopefulness and buoyancy, led the nation and the entire world to believe that their distinguished patient would soon be back at his desk. All realized the gravity of the situation; nevertheless few anticipated any but a favorable outcome.

Beginning on the eventful Friday night, the official statements sent out were encouraging. While the normal pulse is about 80, the fact that McKinley's was from 120 to 128 was not considered cause for alarm. In all cases where an operation is undergone, a high pulse follows for some days. During the week the President lay wounded his averaged 120, high under normal conditions, but not alarming in the case of a wounded man.

Dr. P. M. Rixey, the family physician, was the most constant watcher at the bedside of the wounded man. After McKinley had recovered sufficiently to talk, which was on the third day, he would ask regarding the condition of Mrs. McKinley. The assurance that she was bearing up bravely seemed to act beneficially on the President.

Mrs. McKinley was permitted to see her husband daily, but only for a few minutes at a time. As was his wont in former days to cheer his invalid wife, so it was a pleasure for her to show a reciprocal spirit, which she did. The daily meetings were those of true lovers, and every eye in the sick room would be wet ere the parting kiss of the day would be given.

These visits, at all times brief, were still a source of deep satisfaction to the stricken President. The outcome of the struggle vitally interested Mc-

Kinley, more because of the effect his death would have on his wife and on the nation than for personal reasons.

A man of sterling Christian character, pious and devout, he did not fear death. The end had no terrors for him, but he felt it would leave a void, a vacancy, which none other could fill. The invalid who for 30 years had relied on him alone as her support and protector, her aid and comfort, still needed him. It was parting from her that made him feel reluctant to lay down his life's work.

Cares of state engrossed little of his attention during that week spent in the Milburn residence. He had builded well, and the dedication, as it were, of his noble edifice of national policy, in which all culminated, was in the memorable speech of the day preceding the fateful Friday. Several times during his last days he smiled upon being complimented for that truly great oration, but he did not live to learn how thoroughly it was appreciated throughout the length and breadth of the land.

Dr. Charles McBurney, the eminent New York specialist, was summoned to Buffalo the evening of the shooting. He did not arrive until Sunday morning, however.

The President passed the first night after the shooting fairly comfortably. His temperature increased from 100° to 100.6° between 1 and 3 a. m., and fears were entertained that peritonitis might set in. The doctors chosen to care for the case—P. M. Rixey, M. B. Mann, Roswell Park, H. Mynter and Eugene Wasdin—were in attendance at the President's bedside all night, watching carefully each symptom.

At 10:40 p. m. the doctors issued this bulletin: "The President is rallying satisfactorily and is resting comfortably. Temperature, 100.4°; pulse, 124; respiration, 24."

At 1:30 a .m. the bulletin read: "The President is free from pain and resting well. Temperature, 100.2°; pulse, 120; respiration, 24."

Saturday, the day following the shooting, was one of grave anxiety. The President, while holding his own, was approaching, so the doctors said, a crisis. It was thought that Sunday would decide what effect the shots fired by Czolgosz would be. Dr. Rixey gave it as his opinion that the President would recover. The other physicians refused to commit themselves, saying that they could not make promises until further developments.

An X-ray apparatus was brought from Thomas A. Edison's laboratory with which it was intended to locate the bullet which lodged in the back. It was not used. On Sunday morning at 5 o'clock the physicians issued this bulletin: "The President has passed a fairly good night. Pulse, 122; temperature, 102.4°; respiration, 24."

Sunday proved a rather uneventful day after all. The anticipated crisis did not materialize. The news was good throughout the day. It was not merely negative good news, but news of a distinct improvement. The President's temperature on Sunday evening was a degree lower than it was during the morning, the pulse was slower and the respiration easier.

Dr. McBurney arrived during the day and held a consultation with the other doctors at 3 o'clock Sunday afternoon.

Immediately following the consultation this bulletin was issued: "The President since the last bulletin (3 p. m.) has slept quietly, four hours altogether, since 9 o'clock. His condition is satisfactory to all the physicians present. Pulse, 128; temperature, 101°; respiration, 28." This bulletin was signed by Drs. Rixey, Mann, Park, Mynter, Wasdin and McBurney.

DR. McBURNEY'S STATEMENT.

Later Dr. McBurney said in an interview:

"The fact that there is no unfavorable symptom is a most favorable sign. What we are all waiting for is the lapse of time without the occurrence of inflammation or septic conditions.

"I want to say right here that in my opinion everything has been done for him that could and should have been done. The case has been most handsomely handled. If he lives he will owe his life to the promptness and skill of the physicians here.

"The question of time is of the greatest importance in a case of this kind. An operation could not have been performed too soon. It was performed in one of the quickest times on record. It will be famous in the history of surgery."

This report from so eminent a surgeon served to allay all doubts, and the reports sent out from Buffalo cheered millions of Americans, who had spent a sorrowing Sunday. Prayers had gone up for the President from thousands of hearts and their invocations seemed to be answered by a divine Providence.

Telegrams of sympathy and condolence were changed to congratulations over the good tidings. Hopes rose high, and the somber spirits which had pervaded the land for three days changed to those of a brighter hue. Intimate friends were permitted to see the President for a few moments at a time, and each one on leaving the Milburn home brought cheering news. The bulletins were optimistic, and the members of the Cabinet who had been hastily summoned began to discuss returning.

Vice-President Roosevelt had hurried to Buffalo from Vermont. Senator Hanna had come from Cleveland, his home, and Abner McKinley sped from Denver, with Dr. and Mrs. Herman Baer, the latter being the favorite niece of the stricken President. Roosevelt soon departed for the Adirondack regions on a hunting trip. Hanna returned to Cleveland and hopes ran high, for the departure of these men was taken as proof positive that no serious results were apprehended by the corps of physicians.

The President improved so rapidly on Monday that his friends declared he would be able to attend the duties of his office, at least to a moderate extent, within a month. The worst danger was regarded as past, peritonitis seemed no longer probable, and the only cause for fear was the possibility of a sinking spell. The X-ray instrument was still in the house, but had not been used. It was decided by the doctors that so long as the bullet did not prove immediately dangerous, no serious attempt should be made to locate it, much less to remove it. If it were imbedded in a muscle, or was even loose in the abdominal cavity, it was not regarded as likely to cause much trouble for the time being.

There seemed only one contingency which would necessitate its immediate removal; if it should press against the spinal column it might cause paralysis sooner or later, and would have to be removed to save life. This contingency, however, was remote.

The bulletins throughout Monday were hopeful. One said the President has passed a somewhat restless night, sleeping fairly well; and another declared the President's condition was "becoming more and more satisfactory," and adding that "untoward incidents are less likely to occur." One issued at 3 p. m. stated: "The President's condition steadily improves and he is comfortable, without pain or unfavorable symptoms. Bowel and kidney functions normally performed."

The last bulletin for the day, issued at 9:30 p. m., said: "The President's condition continues favorable. Pulse, 112; temperature, 101; respiration, 27."

Mrs. McKinley felt so encouraged that she took a drive during the afternoon. She had just left the President, after an interview in which she displayed quite as much fortitude as the President. She seated herself beside his bed and took his hand. They said little. In each other's eyes they seemed to read what each would say. Then the President remarked quietly: "We must bear up. It will be better for both."

There were tears in her eyes as Mrs. McKinley bowed her head in assent. Soon afterward Dr. Rixey lead her gently from the room.

Mrs. McKinley paid another brief visit to the President that evening. They were alone for a moment only, barely sufficient for her to kiss him good night and murmur a few words of cheer.

The way Mrs. McKinley is regarded in the Presidential circle is well expressed by Secretary Wilson.

"It is a little less than wonderful," he said, "how remarkably well the noble woman bore her trial. She was shocked and frightened, but never for a moment did she show the slightest sign of collapse. Tears came to her relief, and perhaps it is fortunate for her that they did, as such an expression of grief undoubtedly lessened the strain."

News from the bedside on Tuesday was more favorable than on the preceding day. The danger point was regarded as past, and fast recovery was the general prediction. The doctors had only two services—aside, of course, from careful watching—to perform. One was to open in part the President's outside wound to remove some foreign substances, and the other was to give him food for the first time. It developed that a portion of the President's clothing had been carried into the wound by the bullet, and this had not all been removed at the first operation. As slight irritation was caused by the cloth, the surgeons removed it. The operation caused no harm, and little annoyance to the patient.

The President felt so well that he asked for some newspapers to read. The request was denied. The President enjoyed the food given him—beef extract. At 10:30 o'clock on Tuesday night the physicians issued this bulletin: "The condition of the President unchanged in all important particulars. His temperature is 100.6; pulse, 114; respiration, 28."

Whenever the physicians would permit the wounded man to talk, he would show his hopefulness. Jokingly he assured the constant watchers that his wants were all filled except one—his desire to smoke. McKinley loved a good cigar and smoked from ten to twenty each day. The craving for a cigar was constant and only by great self-denial did he keep from demanding one. The weakness of his heart, which later was one of the contributing causes of his death, was in part due to the sudden change from free use of cigars to the absolute prohibition which the doctors imposed.

The consultation held by the physicians in attendance upon President

McKinley lasted from 9:20 until 11:20 o'clock Tuesday night. Half an hour after they left the Milburn residence the following bulletin was issued:

"The condition of the President is unchanged in all important particulars. His temperature is 100.6, pulse 114, respiration 28. When the operation was done on Friday last it was noted that the bullet had carried with it a short distance beneath the skin a fragment of the President's coat. This foreign material was, of course, removed, but a slight irritation of the tissues was produced, the evidence of which has appeared only to-night. It has been necessary on account of this slight disturbance to remove a few stitches and partially open the skin wound. This incident cannot give rise to other complications, but it is communicated to the public, as the surgeons in attendance wish to make their bulletins entirely frank. In consequence of this separation of the edges of the surface wound the healing of the same will be somewhat delayed. The President is now well enough to begin to take nourishment by the mouth in the form of pure beef juice.

"P. M. Rixey.
"M. D. Mann.
"Roswell Park.
"Herman Mynter.
"Charles McBurney.
"George B. Cortelyou,
"Secretary to the President."

Before the doctors appeared, Secretaries Smith, Wilson, and Hitchcock came out of the house, followed by Secretaries Hay and Root. They said the doctors were still engaged in their consultation, and had not come down stairs. They had been informed, though, they said, that the satisfactory conditions still continued.

Very soon after the doctors had left the morning visitors began coming. First came Comptroller Charles G. Dawes, Senator Fairbanks, and Judge Day. They went into the house about 10:50 o'clock. They were only there a few minutes when Senator Hanna and Secretary Hitchcock, Postmaster-General Smith and Congressman Grosvenor of Ohio appeared. They all expressed themselves as confident of the outcome. The bulletin of the physicians was not taken to indicate anything serious, and the visitors confirmed the hopefulness of the situation. The President showed so much improvement in his condition the people began to send flowers to him. Shortly before noon Tuesday a wagon load of flowers arrived at the Milburn house, the gift of Governor Gregory of Rhode Island to the President. They were accompanied by a message of the tenderest sympathy and encouragement. The flowers, which were in baskets, were placed on the lawn and were photographed before being taken into the house. Two large bouquets came from the First Signal corps, and some of the friends of the Milburns sent other baskets.

While interest at Buffalo materially centered at the Milburn house, the prison in which Czolgosz was confined received attention from many. The President was interested in the assassin, and asked for information a number of times. The physicians would not enter into details, but stated that the man was undoubtedly insane, and that the general public attached no meaning to the attack further than to attribute it to a diseased mind.

Roosevelt left Buffalo for the Adirondack woods Tuesday night. He planned to hunt for a few days and then proceed to his home at Oyster Bay. Senator Hanna and most of the members of the Cabinet left Tuesday or Wednesday.

Wednesday was another day full of hopeful signs. The President continued to show remarkable recuperative powers and passed the day without the slightest unfavorable symptom. He was able to retain food on his stomach, and surprised and amused his doctors by again asking for a cigar. He was not allowed to smoke, but he was placed in a new bed. He was also given a bath. His highest temperature on Wednesday was 100.4. That was at ten o'clock in the evening. The highest point reached by his pulse was 120—at six o'clock a. m.—and his respiration remained normal at 26.

Mrs. McKinley saw the President on Wednesday morning. When the doctors arrived at the house for the consultation they passed her sitting in the upper corridor of the residence at work on her knitting. She was in good spirits, and after the visit of the doctors they gave their assent to her entering the sick room again. She remained only a minute, as the physicians were avoiding any sapping of the President's strength by prolonged visits, even by those nearest to him.

Governor Yates of Illinois and State Senator Templeton, chairman of the Exposition Commission of Illinois, called to pay their respects and advise with Secretary Cortelyou as to the propriety of proceeding with the arrangements for Illinois Day at the Exposition, which was set for the following Monday.

Secretary Cortelyou told them that it was the President's own desire that none of the features of the Exposition should be disturbed by his illness, and assured them that there would not be the slightest impropriety in going ahead with the arrangements.   Such was the confidence displayed forty-eight hours before McKinley's death.

The physicians announced that there was no intention of hurrying Mr. McKinley away from Buffalo, which city is much cooler than either Canton or Washington, and the home of the President of the Buffalo Exposition is a first-class modern residence, admirably equipped for taking care of the patient.   It is in a residence part of town, and by utilizing the police and the infantry had been completely isolated.

It was Mrs. McKinley's wish that they remain at Buffalo until the President had recovered and then spend a month at the home at Canton in final recuperation, after which they were to proceed to Washington.   The President favored going to Washington and the Cabinet officers favored this plan. There was no pressing public business, but the routine duties are numerous. Plans were under preparation for the journey to Washington when the distinguished patient began to show signs of a relapse.

It was on Thursday, just six days after the shooting, that the President suffered a relapse.   Everybody was still full of hopes until 8:30 oclock in the evening, when the physicians announced officially that the President's condition was not so good.   The problem of disposing of the food in the stomach was becoming a serious one, and the danger of heart failure increased. At midnight the situation was critical.   Calomel and oil were given to flush the bowels and digitalis to quiet the heart.   The bowels moved soon afterwards, and the patient improved.   The pulse dropped to 120, and the prospect was regarded as brighter.

Secretary Cortelyou announced that there would be no more bulletins during the night, and the physicians departed.

Shortly after two o'clock, after a heavy thunderstorm, the physicians and nurses who were left on watch detected a weakening of the heart action.   The pulse fluttered and weakened and the President sank toward a collapse.   The end appeared at hand.   Restoratives were applied speedily, but they did not at once prove effective.   It was then decided to send for the other physicians, relatives, members of the Cabinet, and close personal friends of the President.

Trouble began on Thursday afternoon through the failure of the digestive organs to perform their functions.   The necessity for nourishment had been pressing for several days, and the partial failure of artificial means had led to the adoption of natural means.   The rectum, through which nourishment had been injected previously to Wednesday, became irritated and rejected the enemas.

PRESIDENT McKINLEY FALLING INTO ARMS OF CORTELYOU,
SAYING: "AM I SHOT?"

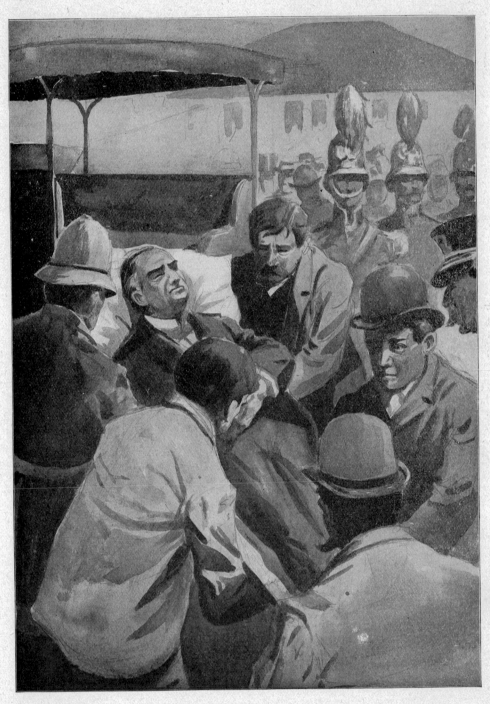

PRESIDENT McKINLEY BEING PUT IN THE AMBULANCE
AFTER BEING SHOT.

The physicians tried to feed him through the mouth, probably before the stomach was prepared. The first administration of beef juice through the mouth, however, seemed to agree with the patient, and the physicians were highly gratified at the way the stomach seemed to receive the food.

Dr. McBurney was especially jubilant over the action of the stomach and before his departure for New York dwelt upon the fact that the stomach seemed to have resumed its normal functions. The breakfast of chicken broth and toast given Thursday morning was spoken of by all the physicians as strong evidence of the President's marked improvement. It was only when it became apparent late in the morning that this food had not agreed with the President that the first genuine anxiety appeared. The first note of alarm was sounded in the official bulletin Thursday afternoon, which spoke of the President's fatigue.

President McKinley, already weak from the ordeal of the tragedy and suffering, complained of an increasing feeling of fatigue. He had heretofore been so buoyant and cheerful that his complaints were regarded seriously. The pulse was then also abnormally high, 126 beats to the minute. With a temperature of 100.2 it should have been thirty beats lower.

The weakness of the heart began to arouse serious concern. Instead of growing better, the President's condition after that grew steadily worse.

The staff of physicians, augmented by Dr. Stockton, who had temporarily taken the place of Dr. McBurney, was summoned early in the evening, and there was a conference.

At 8:30 the physicians announced officially that the President's condition was not so good. The problem of disposing of the food in the stomach was becoming a serious one and the danger of heart failure increased.

It was believed then that the opening of the bowels, which was effected, would have the effect of allaying the wild pulsations of the heart. His pulse did drop to 120 and the prospect was slightly brighter. But owing to the President's extreme weakness and his fatigue no attempt was made to conceal the serious apprehension which was felt. The feeling of depression increased in volume and intensity.

Secretary Cortelyou insisted that the truth should be made public by the doctors and the bulletins themselves were telling their unfortunate story all too plainly. There was still hope that the worn and weary patient would be better in the morning, and at midnight Secretary Cortelyou said it was not probable that another bulletin would be issued until morning.

Hope came once more to the breasts of those who had waited for hours in anxiety. The physicians parted for the night and every sign was a cheering one. There had been disquieting pulse action for several hours, but practically all of the unfavorable symptoms had been linked with the stomach trouble, and it was thought they would probably disappear with the removal of the cause which was supposed to have created them.

The unofficial reports at one o'clock and 1:30 o'clock were both of a satisfactory nature and the watchers gathered about the house prepared for an uninterrupted night.

Another thunderstorm came out of the north and a few minutes' play of the lightning brought rain in a heavy downpour. A bluster wind blew up from the west to complete the cheerlessness of the night.

Shortly after two o'clock the physicians and nurses detected a weakening of the heart action. The pulse fluttered and weakened and the President sank toward collapse. The end appeared to be at hand.

Restoratives were speedily applied and the physicians fought the battle with all the reserve forces of science. Action was immediate and decisive. Digitalis and strychnia were administered, and as a last resort saline solution was injected into the veins.

A general alarm went speeding to the consulting physicians and trained nurses as fast as messengers, the telegraph and telephone could carry it.

The restoratives did not at once prove effective and it was realized that the President was in an extremely critical condition.

That realization, with the shadow of death behind it, led to another call, and that a summons to the Cabinet, relatives and close personal friends of the President.

The messengers who returned with the doctors and nurses were hurried off after those within reach, and to those who were absent from the city telegrams conveying the painful tidings were quickly transmitted.

The scene about the house and in the storm-swept street was dramatic in its action and setting, and the spirit of the tragedy was on those who looked upon it. A messenger who darted into the rain and was whisked away in an electric cab gave the outside watchers the first intimation of the ill news from within.

At the same moment new lights burned within the windows of the Milburn residence. Soon the word was passed out that the President had partly collapsed and was critically ill. It was a confirmation that was hardly needed, for the fact had been established by action that needed no words.

Mrs. McKinley went through the long night of sorrow as only the thoroughbred woman does. She slept, but that she could have slept much was impossible. But no traces of the night's agony showed as she turned her serene face upon early callers next morning.

Mrs. Barber, Mrs. McKinley's sister, was present, and with her the Misses Barber, her daughters, and her son, Assistant Paymaster Barber of the Navy. When the two sisters met, Mrs. McKinley came nearer to breaking down than she had at any time. Her eyes overflowed and her voice broke. But she soon recovered and was again the strong, consoling wife of a stricken mate.

When the serious condition of the President was realized, early Friday morning, Secretaries Hitchcock and Wilson, the only Cabinet officers in the city, were summoned at once and came in a short time. Drs. Mann and Mynter and Dr. Park, who had been present at the consultations held during the night, arrived just after them. The first two were together in an automobile. They leaped from it before it stopped and ran up to the house. Dr. Park showed the same haste.

Miss Mackenzie, one of the nurses, arrived at 3:10 in a cab. She jumped from her cab and ran up the steps. Mrs. Newell, another of the nurses, followed her in five minutes in an automobile.

Secret Service men, summoned by Operator Foster, came and took possession of the Western Union telegraph wires leading to the Milburn house. Communication was attempted with Vice-President Roosevelt. The Cabinet ministers who were not in Buffalo were sent word to come at once. Senator Hanna was summoned from Cleveland, and answered that he would come as fast as a chartered train could bring him.

Mrs. Lafayette McWilliams drove up to the house at 3:35 and went directly to Mrs. McKinley, who at that time was still sleeping. Then the procession of carriages arriving at the Milburn house at a gallop grew thicker, bringing state dignitaries and friends of the President with their anxiety marked on their faces.

When the immediate danger of death was considered passed the visitors at the house began to depart, and some of the physicians left. At eight o'clock the only person at the house besides doctors and regular attendants were Secretaries Hitchcock and Wilson, Abner McKinley, Colonel Brown of Fostoria, Ohio, John G. Milburn, Miss Alice Barber and Mrs. Lafayette McWilliams.

Crowds of the curious had surrounded the house by that time, the news of the President's extremity having circulated rapidly through the city. The lines of police and soldiers were doubled, but the crowd grew and seemed content to wait for news from the physicians.

Shortly after eight o'clock the physicians began to arrive at the house again, some of them having gone home for breakfast and rest. Abner McKinley did not go to his breakfast. Mrs. McKinley was still sleeping at eight o'clock and Secretary Cortelyou had lain down to rest, as the strain and anxiety of the night had exhausted him.

Major Diehl called at 9:30 and with him was former Postmaster-General Bissel. They were informed by Dr. Mann that if the President survived the day there was hope for him. The President was in a collapse, he said, although his heart action was slightly strengthened.

A clergyman, Arthur O. Sykes, arrived soon after and caused much excitement among the watchers, as his presence was interpreted as a sign of extremity. It was learned, however, that he only came to bring messages of sympathy from the citizens of Portsmouth, Va.

Senator Hanna arrived at the house in an automobile at 9:35. He arrived at the Central Station on his special train but a few minutes before, after a record-breaking run from Cleveland in a chartered train. Detective Ireland met him at the train and the automobile brought him to the President as fast as possible.

At eleven o'clock the President fell into a slumber. While he slept the sun, whose beams had dispelled the rain clouds of the night, was again overcast. A chilling rain began to fall. Visitors still came into the house, inquired of the President's condition and departed.

Governor Yates of Illinois was among them. He arrived shortly after eleven o'clock. When he left he said the surgeons had informed him there was a slight improvement in the President's condition, but not sufficient to remove the grave apprehension felt.

Senator Chauncey M. Depew arrived shortly after noon with Colonel Myron T. Herrick, who had gone to the depot to meet him. Senator Depew had been summoned during the night. Colonel Herrick arrived on the same train that brought Senator Hanna.

The news that came from the house at this time was still of the gravest kind. Nothing more than a fighting chance was conceded by the physicians. That was the news that Colonel Herrick brought out when he left the house at 12:18 to go to dinner.

By far the most hopeful of the watchers was Senator Hanna, who declared his belief that the President had a good chance for his life. He sent for Dr. Rixey and questioned him and the doctor replied:

"The President is gaining strength and has a good fighting chance but for his heart. God knows what it will do."

The most noted heart specialist in the country, Dr. Janeway of Washington, was summoned during the morning.

The advance of death may be read in the bulletins which were issued by the physicians and others and sent by the newspaper reporters to their respective papers.

Beginning at 10:28 a. m. Dr. Mynter announced that the President had a fighting chance. Then came, at 1:45, "The President is sleeping and an examination will be postponed until later."

Then for a time no information came which would give the watchers outside any clew as to the positive condition of the patient within. Suddenly a carriage came up at a rapid speed and Dr. Stockton jumped out. He bore what appeared to be a case of surgical instruments.

It was not until after this that the information came that during the morning Mrs. McKinley had been in the room for a brief time, but the fact that her husband was dying was not imparted to her, and every effort was made to keep any suspicion of the true condition from her.

Colonel Alexander came from the house at 2:20 and declared the President had just awakened from a sound sleep which lasted an hour and a half. It was rumored, however, that the sleep was caused by the use of drugs and that Mr. McKinley was really dying.

At 4:45 p. m. Secretary Hitchcock and Secretary Wilson arrived and passed hurriedly into the house. They would answer no questions.

The anxiety of the watchers outside was abated somewhat immediately after this, however, by the appearance from the house of Mrs. Abner McKinley and her daughter, Mrs. Herman Baer. The women drove away, and, it was argued that, were the President in any immediate danger, they would not have left the house.

The President's physicians issued a bulletin at 4:50 which stated that there had been but a slight improvement since the last official bulletin was issued. This notice said the pulse and temperature were practically the same.

A few minutes after the posting of this bulletin Harry Hamlin came from the house. He would not speak, and, summoning a carriage, he drove away at full speed.

Though no statement was given out, the appearance of every one about the Milburn house indicated that the President's death was expected any moment. Figures moved about swiftly but noiselessly within the house.

The end seemed at hand when the physicians announced at 5:25 that the condition of the President was very bad—in fact, could not be worse.

The news was flashed to the White House from an official source at Buffalo that at 5:45 the President's condition was most grave. That his heart was responding but poorly to stimulants. Secretary Root, accompanied by Carlton Sprague, reached the Milburn residence a few minutes after five o'clock. It was said that Secretary Long would arrive at 11:40 o'clock.

To those who were so anxiously waiting for Vice-President Roosevelt or knowledge of his whereabouts, word came from the train dispatcher at Saratoga that at 7:30 p. m. Mr. Roosevelt had not been found, so far as he knew, by the guides who were scouring the Adirondack woods for him. The Vice-President had not reached North Creek, fifty-nine miles north of Saratoga.

At eight o'clock word came that under the influence of oxygen the President regained consciousness for a moment. Dr. McBurney arrived at the house at eight o'clock, and a moment later a guard was placed around the tent in which was located the direct wire to the White House.

CHAPTER III.

DEATHBED OF PRESIDENT McKINLEY.

William McKinley, twenty-fifth President of the United States, died at fifteen minutes past two o'clock on the morning of Saturday, September 14, 1901, at the age of fifty-eight years. He had lived just six and a half days after receiving his wound at the hands of Leon Czolgosz, the anarchist.

From the time President McKinley was carried to the bed in the Milburn home, at Buffalo, there had been a continually rising barometer of hope. Frightful as had been the shock of his wound, serious as were the consequences in a bullet necessarily retained in his body, the great reserves of courage and of strength had come to the President's rescue, and he had seemed to mend from the start. As the days passed following the assault, the whole nation emerged from that black pall of gloom which fell in the hour when men first whispered: "The President is shot!" Usual vocations were taken up again. Social activities were renewed. The people in general, scarcely pausing from the pressure of a necessary labor, caught the note of encouragement, and were happy as they worked. Apprehension almost faded away as the days of the week followed each other, and every succeeding bulletin painted but brighter the scene in the sick room. By Wednesday the millions of Americans who were watching with eyes of love at that bedside—however near or remote they might be—had quite dismissed the thought of a fatal ending to the President's case. They accepted his speedy recovery as a fact to be shared with jubilation, and had forgotten the grip of dismay and fear which seized them when the first news came.

And out of this rising glow of happiness came, late Thursday night, another shock—the bitterer for the hope which had preceded it.

"The President is worse." That was the message men whispered to each other. After bulletins which exhausted the possibility of variety in statement came one which chilled the warm heart of the nation, and frightened far away the hope which had seemed so certain. The Thursday morning statement of physicians and secretary reported all that could be argued from the sanguine statements of preceding days.

At three o'clock in the afternoon there was a note of distress in the reporting. The country had already been apprised, through the watchful

57

press, of such "hurryings to and fro" as presaged a return of peril, and of fear. There were drawn, white faces at the windows of the Milburn house. The calm of preceding days was disturbed. Messengers were sent flying to various destinations. Carriages and automobiles rolled up or rolled away in a haste which could mean but burning anxiety. And in the evening hours came that carefully considered bulletin which was the more portentous for the very vagueness of its terms:

Milburn House, Buffalo, N. Y., September 12.—The following bulletin was issued by the President's physicians at 8:30 p. m.:

> The President's condition this evening is not quite so good. His food has not agreed with him and has been stopped. Excretion has not yet been properly established. The kidneys are acting well. His pulse is not satisfactory, but has improved in the last two hours. The wound is doing well. He is resting quietly. Temperature, 100.2; pulse, 128.
>
> P. M. Rixey,
M. D. Mann,
Roswell Park,
Herman Mynter,
Eugene Wasdin,
Charles D. Stockton.
George B. Cortelyou,
Secretary to the President.

Little by little the people learned. Early on Thursday there were signs of pain. There were alarming developments. The physicians, carefully scanning every evidence, breathlessly watching their patient's every moment, learned that a relapse had come. They battled against it. They called up all the known agencies for assisting nature in opposing the grim enemy that threatened.

But the President was sinking. That was the truth about it.

All through Thursday night, all through Friday that battling for life went on, the patient, brave and uncomplaining victim of a reasonless shot, was subjecting himself utterly to the control of the medical men. And they were exhausting the possibilities of medicine and of surgery. They were doing all that man could do. They were rendering such service as king's can not command. But the baffling difficulty continued. They could not understand.

Down through the body, hidden from their eyes, ran the channel which a murderous bullet had plowed. And in every inch of its course the fatal gangrene had settled. Death was at his feast in the President's body!

Nothing could check that devastation. Nothing could spur the heart to combat longer. Nothing could restore those pulses to normal beating.

The President was dying!

All through the early hours of Friday night it was known he could not live to another sunrise. Friends, relatives, cabinet officers, the Vice President—all were summoned; and they were hastening to the bedside in the hush of an awful sorrow.

At three o'clock Friday morning all of the physicians were gathered at the bedside of the President. It was stated that digitalis was being administered. Drs. Mynter and Mann arrived at the house at 2:40, having been sent for hurriedly.

Dr. Park reached the house at 2:50, and shortly after him came Secretaries Hitchcock and Wilson.

Several messengers were hurried from the house and it was understood that they carried dispatches to the absent members of the Cabinet and the kin of the President.

Additional lights burned. The household was astir. It was manifest that the wounded President faced a grave and menacing crisis.

Alarm could be read in the faces of those to whose nursing and care he was committed.

Mrs. Newell, one of the trained nurses suddenly called, arrived at 3:15. She sprang from an electric carriage and ran down the sidewalk to the house.

The scene about the house was dramatic. The attendants could be seen hurrying about behind the unshaded and brightly lighted windows, and messengers came and went hastily through the guarded door.

Outside half a hundred newspaper correspondents were assembled awaiting news.

Meanwhile the nation—the world—stood watching for the final word. Buffalo, where the President was assassinated, stood agape with horror and rage.

It was past midday when he had entered upon his final struggle. The thousands gathered at the Pan-American Exposition, the nation and the outside world were not prepared even then for a realization that the worst was at hand.

A furious rainstorm was sweeping the city when the first ominous announcement came from the Milburn house:

"President McKinley is dying. He can live but a few moments."

Then signal service operators took possession of the telegraph wires leading to the house of death. Cabinet officers and members of the President's family began to arrive, and the beginning of the end had come.

Then it was announced that the President might live for several hours. But even then his limbs were growing cold and his pulse was fluttering with the feeble efforts of his will alone. He was conscious. Every light in the house was aglow.

Within, the wife had paid her last tribute to her dying sweetheart of thirty years. Dr. Rixey led her into the room, and as she laid her head alongside his she sobbed:

"I cannot let him go."

She knew that the President was dying then, and in the dim silence of her adjoining room she waited and wept as the hours sped and the doctors wondered at the mighty battle of the dying man.

It was midnight when Secretary Long of the Navy arrived. He found his beloved chief alive, but unconscious, and Dr. Mann told him, as he stood in the hallway, "The President is pulseless and dying, but he may live an hour."

At half an hour past midnight Coroner Wilson arrived at the Milburn house, and an unfounded announcement of McKinley's death was quickly telegraphed to all parts of the country. He left as soon as he found that the order summoning him was a mistake.

But the President, now finally unconscious, and breathing but faintly, struggled on. Midnight, 1 and 2 o'clock, found him wavering on the verge, and the men of science could but stand and marvel at the wondrous but hopeless fight which he had maintained so long. Intervals of apparent consciousness came upon him. Sometimes he opened his fading eyes and gazed calmly around.

At 2 o'clock the dim, gray light began to fall across his shrunken face, and then—death won!

He had been unconscious, the doctors said, for nearly six hours. During all this time he had been gradually sinking. For the last half hour he had been in such condition that it was difficult to tell when he breathed.

With him at the time of his death was Dr. Rixey, alone of all the physicians, and by the side of the bed were grouped Senator Hanna and members of the President's family.

He died unattended by a minister of the gospel, but his last words were an humble submission to the will of God, in whom he believed. He was reconciled to the cruel fate to which an assassin's bullet had condemned him, and faced death in the same spirit of calmness and poise which has marked his long and honorable career.

His last conscious words, reduced to writing by Dr. Mann, who stood at his bedside when they were uttered, were as follows:

"Good-by, all; good-by. It is God's way. His will be done, not ours."

His relatives and the members of his official family were at the Milburn house, except Secretary Wilson, who did not avail himself of the opportunity and some of his personal and political friends took leave of him. This painful ceremony was simple. His friends came to the door of the sick room, took a longing glance at him and turned tearfully away.

He was practically unconscious during this time, but the powerful heart stimulants, including oxygen, were employed to restore him to consciousness for his final parting with his wife. He asked for her and she sat at his side and held his hand. He consoled her and bade her good-by.

She went through the heart-trying scene with the same bravery and fortitude with which she had borne the grief of the tragedy which ended his life.

That last day on earth had tried him severely. He had commenced wearing away a little before 3 o'clock Friday morning. Throughout the day and evening the expectations of attendants, physicians and friends oscillated as a pendulum between hope and despair. Hopeless bulletins followed encouraging reports from the sick room, and they in turn gave way to recurrent hope.

The truth was too evident to be passed over or concealed. The President's life was hanging in the balance. The watchers felt that at any moment might come the announcement of a change which would foreshadow the end.

When it was learned that the President was taking small quantities of nourishment hope rose that he would pass the crisis in safety. Everybody knew, though—and no attempt was made to conceal it—that the coming night would in all human probability be his last on earth. It was known that he was being kept alive by the strongest of heart stimulants, and that the physicians had obtained a supply of oxygen to be administered if the worse came.

During the day President McKinley was conscious when he was not sleeping. Early in the morning when he awoke he looked out of the window and saw that the sky was overcast with heavy clouds.

"It is not so bright as it was yesterday," said he.

His eyes then caught the waving branches of the trees, glistening with rain, and their bright green evidently made an agreeable impression upon him.

"It is pleasant to see them," said he, feebly.

Mrs. McKinley did not take her usual drive. She saw the President once before night, and then only for a moment. No words passed between them. The physicians led her to the bedside of her husband, and after she had looked at him for a moment they led her away.

While Mrs. McKinley was told that the President was not so well the physicians deemed it best not to attempt to explain to her fully the nature of the complications which had arisen or the real gravity of his condition.

As fast as steam could bring them the President's secretaries, the members of his family and the physicians who had left convinced that the President would recover, were whirled back to Buffalo. They went at once to the house in which he was lying, and the information which they obtained there was of a nature to heighten rather than to relieve their fears.

All night the doctors worked to keep the President alive. The day broke with a gloomy sky and a pouring rain, broken by frequent bursts of gusty downpours. It seemed as though nature was sympathizing with the gloom which surrounded the ivy-clad house about which the sentries were steadily marching.

The 2 o'clock bulletin, issued at 2:30, swung the pendulum away over on the side of confidence. It stated that the President had more than held his own since morning, and that his condition justified the expectation of further improvement. It added: "He is better than at this time yesterday."

Faces up and down the street brightened. Telegraph messenger boys, in their youthful spirits, restrained all the day by the gloom around the Milburn house, whooped as they ran and nobody reproved. The sun shone again.

But the news was too good to last. Secretary Cortelyou walked across the street to the press and telegraph tents and explained that the sentence, "He is better than at this time yesterday," should be stricken out. Then the sky was black again.

The bravery of Mrs. McKinley in this last moment was only paralleled by the heroism with which the President himself, murmuring the words of

"Nearer, My God, to Thee," turned his face away from all so dear to him in life, and passed into the last and eternal sleep.

All through the struggle of Friday when the erratic heart of the President leaped and then failed, Mrs. McKinley's courage had been at the highest point. The beautiful womanhood within her, the memories of thirty years of perfect married life, the recollections of the tender devotions of the dying President, rose and gave her the strength needed to face the worst.

She remained in her apartments surrounded by friends, anxious to be by the President's side, but obedient to Dr. Rixey's wishes that she should not come until she was called.

Oxygen had been given the President, and under its influence he had slightly revived. He told Dr. Rixey that he realized he was about to die, and he asked for Mrs. McKinley.

She came and knelt down by his bed and his eyes rested lovingly upon her. His first solicitude was for her—her care, her happiness. All the love of three decades shone in his face as he feebly put out his hands and covered her own with his.

He knew that he was dying, she only half apprehended it. But even in such a trial she kept herself up most bravely, lifting her tear-stained face to Dr. Rixey's and exclaiming:

"I know that you will save him. I cannot let him go. The country cannot spare him."

The President's strength did not last long. Unconsciousness returned to him, and they led Mrs. McKinley away.

When she was without the room Mr. Milburn told her that the President could hardly live until morning.

Herbert P. Bissell came to her side as she wavered, and Dr. Wasdin hurried from the President's chamber and administered a restorative.

Little by little Mrs. McKinley gained new strength, and in half an hour was in full control of herself. Several ladies sat beside her, and to one of these she turned and whispered:

"I will be strong for his sake."

An invalid herself, racked for twenty years with pain, almost helpless at times, since the years in which her children passed from her, the wife and sweetheart of the dying President conquered herself.

And so the heavy hours hurried away. Midnight had come, and gone. The dawn was lingering far in the east, and not even the edge of the world glowed with the promise of day. It had rained on Friday, and a storm had raged which will long be remembered by those who were called abroad in the troubled city. As at the close of Napoleon's life the elements warred tumultuously, so on the last day of this gentler ruler, the winds and the clouds filled the earth with tears and the sounds of weeping.

They did not know, but his physicians were helpless from the start. The demon who had struck so surely, might well make mockery of them. Six days of pain, six days of agony, six days of hovering at the slippery brink of death—and on the seventh he was at rest.

The great heart of the President was still forever. The man who had confessed his God in childhood, bade farewell to earth with the words: "Thy will be done!" The man who had helped his parents and his brothers and his sisters, who had periled his life freely in the defense of his country, who had made an honorable name and given the blessing of a husband's love to one good woman, the man who had never harmed a human being purposely, who had lived at peace with God and man almost for three-score years, had drifted across the bar. His heart had throbbed lightly, and was still. The varying pulse had ceased, and the calm eyes that had fronted life and death and destiny without ever flinching—this Man was dead. The head of a nation, the chief executive of eighty millions of people, the statesman who had guided his country so wisely and so well, had been thrust from earth by an assassin who had no cause of complaint, who had no wrongs to avenge, no advantage to secure, no benefit to hope.

And into the silent room where all need for silence had passed, where footfalls need not be guided lightly, where bated breath were no more known, the night wind came through wide-flung windows, and touched the lips and brow and nerveless hands. And the sound of unchecked weeping waited for the dawn.

CHAPTER IV.

THE STORY OF THE ASSASSIN.

Leon F. Czolgosz, the assassin of President McKinley, was born of Polish parents, who resided in Cleveland at the time he committed the terrible crime. Twenty-six years of age, born in Detroit, of medium height, smooth-shaven, brown hair, and dressed like a workingman completes all the description necessary.

After the shooting he made a confession, in which he told how he had followed the President from the time of the latter's arrival at the exposition until the fatal shots were fired. All of this time, like a prowling wild beast, he sought the life of President McKinley.

He received some education in the common schools of Detroit, but left school and went to work when a boy as a blacksmith's apprentice. Later he went to work at Cleveland and then went to Chicago.

While in Chicago he became interested in the Socialist movement. When he went back to Cleveland his interest in the movement increased. He read all the Socialist literature he could lay his hands on, and finally began to take part in Socialistic matters. In time he became well known among Anarchists in Chicago, Cleveland and Detroit, not only as a Socialist, but as an Anarchist of the most bitter type.

After returning to Cleveland from Chicago he went to work in the wire mills in Newburg, a suburb of Cleveland.

About two weeks previous to his fearful crime, Czolgosz attended a meeting of Socialists in Cleveland, at which a lecture was given by Emma Goldman, the woman whose anarchistic doctrines have made her notorious all over the country. The extermination of rulers of people is part of her creed.

It was this lecture and others heard in Chicago prior to that time that instilled in the heart of the Pole the poison of assassination. He went back to his lodging from the lecture with fever in his brain. His mind was filled with the preaching of this woman. The doctrine that rulers had no right to live was burned into his soul. He awoke in the morning with the lecture of Emma Goldman running through his mind.

A few days afterward he read in a Chicago paper that President McKinley was to visit the Pan-American Exposition and to remain in Buffalo for several days. The lecture of Emma Goldman and the projected visit of the President to Buffalo were linked in his every thought.

Eight days before the tragedy he packed a small telescope valise with a few of his belongings and took an early train for Buffalo. At that time there was no well-formed purpose in his mind. The plot to murder had not crystallized, but the thought that in Buffalo he would be able, perhaps, to reach the President's side was what led him to start for the East, and with it was the dim conviction that his mission was one of blood.

Upon arriving in Buffalo he went at once to an hotel kept by one John Nowak. He went there because he knew Nowak was a Pole. He told Nowak he had come to see the exposition, and that his stay would be indefinite. He inquired of Nowak about the visit of the President, when he would arrive, how long he would be in the city, what he was to do there, and whether the people would be able to see much of him. Nowak told him what the plans were.

The next day Czolgosz went to the exposition. He went there on the following day, and the day following. The idea that he might kill the President when he came was in his mind, but the purpose was but half formed. At that time it might have been possible to have diverted his mind from the thought of such a mission. But he was alone in the city. He had no friends there. There was nothing to check the fever burning deeper and deeper into his mind.

On Wednesday morning, the day of the President's arrival, Czolgosz had his mind made up. His mission to Buffalo was clear to him then. He determined to shoot the President. The first thing he did was to get a revolver.

He arrived on the grounds shortly before noon. He knew the President would not arrive before the early evening. He had read the papers carefully and knew every detail of the plans. But he was anxious to be on the scene where the assassination was to be committed. He remained at the exposition all day.

In the afternoon he took up his position close to the railroad gate. He knew the President would enter the grounds that way. After a time other people began to assemble there until there was a crowd that hedged him in on all sides. He came to the conclusion that the place for him to be was outside of the railroad station, close to the tracks.

He feared that inside the grounds the crush might be so great that he would be brushed aside and prevented from reaching the President. He tried to pass through the gate to the station, but he was too late. Guards had

"LET ME SEE THE TREES; THEY ARE SO BEAUTIFUL," SAID PRESIDENT McKINLEY.

MRS. McKINLEY BIDDING HER HUSBAND THE LAST FAREWELL.

just closed the exit. The President was to arrive soon, and the police did not desire to have the station crowded, so they pushed Czolgosz back into the crowd.

He was in the forefront of the throng when the President came through the gate. The exhibition of tenderness and affection for his wife which the President unconsciously gave her as he led her through the entrance thrilled every one in the throng but Czolgosz. He alone felt no pity for the pale, sweet-faced, suffering woman. He pressed forward with the rest of the crowd as the President approached the carriage. He was gripping the weapon in his pocket in his right hand.

Several times, as the figure of the Chief Executive came into full view as the guards drew aside, the impulse to rush forward and shoot took possession of him, but each time he changed his mind. He feared that he would be discovered before he could reach the President. He was afraid that the glint of the revolver, if he drew it from his pocket, might attract the attention of a detective or a soldier or a citizen before he could put his plan into execution, and in that event the assassin knew that all hope of killing the President would be over. He saw the President enter the carriage and drive away. He followed, but the crowd closed in front of him and held him back.

The next morning he was at the exposition early. He took up his position close to the stand beneath the Pylon of Liberty, where the President was to speak. When the time came for the President to arrive the guards pushed him back. He saw the President arrive and mount to the stand. He stood there in the front row of the hurrahing people, mute, with a single thought in his mind.

He heard Mr. McKinley speak. He reckoned up the chances in his mind of stealing closer and shooting down the President where he stood. Once he fully determined to make the attempt, but just then a stalwart guard appeared in front of him. He concluded to wait a better opportunity. After the address he was among those who attempted to crowd up to the President's carriage. One of the detectives caught him by the shoulder and shoved him back into the crowd.

He saw the President drive away and followed. He tried to pass through the entrance after the President, but the guards halted him and sent him away. He entered the stadium by another entrance, but was not permitted to get within reach of the President.

The next morning he was at the exposition again and was in the crowd at the railroad gate when the President arrived at that point after crossing the grounds from the Lincoln Park entrance. But with the rest of the crowd he was driven back when the President's carriage arrived. He saw the President pass through the gate to the special train which was to take him to the falls.

Czolgosz waited for the President's return. In the afternoon he went to the Temple of Music and was one of the first of the throng to enter. He crowded well forward, as close to the stage as possible. He was there when the President entered through the side door. He was one of the first to hurry forward when the President took his position and prepared to shake hands with the people.

Czolgosz had his revolver gripped in his right hand, and about both the hand and the revolver was wrapped a handkerchief. He held the weapon to his breast, so that any one who noticed him might suppose that the hand was injured.

He reached the President finally. He did not look into the President's face. He extended his left hand, pressed the revolver against the President's breast with his right hand and fired twice.

That was all there was to his story.

"Did you mean to kill the President?" asked the District Attorney.

"I did," was the reply.

"What was the motive that induced you to commit this crime?" he was asked.

"I am a disciple of Emma Goldman," he replied.

The following is Czolgosz's signed confession to the police. It agrees with the above, but we give it in his exact words:

"I was born in Detroit nearly twenty-nine years ago. My parents were Russian Poles. They came here forty-two years ago. I got my education in the public schools of Detroit and then went to Cleveland, where I got work. In Cleveland I read books on socialism and met a great many Socialists. I was pretty well known as a Socialist in the West. After being in Cleveland for several years I went to Chicago, where I remained seven months, after which I went to Newburg, on the outskirt of Cleveland, and went to work in the Newburg wire mills.

"During the last five years I have had as friends Anarchists in Chicago, Cleveland, Detroit, and other Western cities, and I suppose I became more or less bitter. Yes, I know I was bitter. I never had much luck at anything and this preyed upon me. It made me morose and envious, but what started the craze to kill was a lecture I heard some little time ago by Emma Goldman.

She was in Cleveland and I and other Anarchists went to hear her. She set me on fire.

"Her doctrine that all rulers should be exterminated was what set me to thinking so that my head nearly split with the pain. Miss Goldman's words went right through me and when I left the lecture I had made up my mind that I would have to do something heroic for the cause I loved.

"Eight days ago, while I was in Chicago, I read in a Chicago newspaper of President McKinley's visit to the Pan-American Exposition at Buffalo. That day I bought a ticket for Buffalo and got there with the determination to do something, but I did not know just what. I thought of shooting the President, but I had not formed a plan.

"I went to live at 1078 Broadway, which is a saloon and hotel. John Nowak, a Pole, a sort of politician who has led his people here for years, owns it. I told Nowak that I came to see the fair. He knew nothing about what was setting me crazy. I went to the Exposition grounds a couple of times a day.

"Not until Tuesday morning did the resolution to shoot the President take a hold of me. It was in my heart; there was no escape for me. I could not have conquered it had my life been at stake. There were thousands of people in town on Tuesday. I heard it was President's Day. All these people seemed bowing to the great ruler. I made up my mind to kill that ruler. I bought a 32-caliber revolver and loaded it.

"On Tuesday night I went to the Fair grounds and was near the railroad gate when the Presidential party arrived. I tried to get near him, but the police forced me back. They forced everybody back so that the great ruler could pass. I was close to the President when he got into the grounds, but was afraid to attempt the assassination because there were so many men in the bodyguard that watched him. I was not afraid of them or that I should get hurt, but afraid I might be seized and that my chance would be gone forever.

"Well, he went away that time and I went home. On Wednesday I went to the grounds and stood right near the President, right under him near the stand from which he spoke.

"I thought half a dozen times of shooting while he was speaking, but I could not get close enough. I was afraid I might miss, and then the great crowd was always jostling, and I was afraid lest my aim fail. I waited on Wednesday, and the President got into his carriage again, and a lot of men were about him and formed a cordon that I could not get through. I was tossed about by the crowd, and my spirits were getting pretty low.   I was almost hopeless that night as I went home.

"Yesterday morning I went again to the Exposition grounds.   Emma Goldman's speech was still burning me up.   I waited near the central entrance for the President, who was to board his special train from that gate, but the police allowed nobody but the President's party to pass where the train waited, so I stayed at the grounds all day waiting.

"During yesterday I first thought of hiding my pistol under my hand- kerchief.   I was afraid if I had to draw it from my pocket I would be seen and seized by the guards.   I got to the Temple of Music the first one and waited at the spot where the reception was to be held.

"Then he came, the President—the ruler— and I got in line and trembled and trembled until I got right up to him, and then I shot him twice, through my white handkerchief.   I would have fired more, but I was stunned by a blow in the face—a frightful blow that knocked me down—and then every- body jumped on me.   I thought I would be killed and was surprised the way they treated me."

Czolgosz ended his story in utter exhaustion.   When he had about con- cluded he was asked : "Did you really mean to kill the President ?"

"I did," was the reply.

"What was your motive, what good could it do you?" he was asked.

"I am an Anarchist.   I am a disciple of Emma Goldman.   Her words set me on fire," he replied, with not the slightest tremor.

"I deny that I have had an accomplice at any time," Czolgosz told District Attorney Penny.   "I don't regret my act, because I was doing what I could for the great cause.   I am not connected with the Paterson group or with those Anarchists who sent Bresci to Italy to kill Humbert.   I had no con- fidants; no one to help me.   I was alone absolutely."

Czolgosz, the assassin, was the son of Paul Czolgosz, who lived at 306 Fleet street, Cleveland, Ohio, at the time of the assassination, having moved there from Warrensburg, Ohio, in search of work.   Other members of the family were John, who lived at home with his father and stepmother; Mike, a soldier serving in the Philippines; Vladiolan, who was on his father's farm, located on the Chagrin Falls Suburban line; and Jacob, of Marcelline avenue. There were two uncles living on Hosmer street.

The family was Polish and evidently poor.

Czolgosz's father talked of his son's crime.   He said his son should be hanged, and that there was no excuse for the crime.   At first he appeared not to realize the enormity of the crime, but when aroused he denounced his son, saying he must have been mad.

The stepmother could not speak English, but gave out the following interview through the medium of an interpreter. She said:

"Leon left home sixty days before this terrible affair. We heard from him a few weeks ago. He was then in Indiana and wrote to us that he was going away, stating that in all probability we would not see him again."

The family had not heard from him since. The stepmother denies Leon was a disciple of Emma Goldman or in any way interested in her doctrines. She said he was not interested in such matters and scarcely intelligent enough to understand them. They had always considered the boy partly demented. Up to three years ago he had worked at the Cleveland rolling mill, but had to quit on account of poor health. Since that time he has been idle. While living on the farm near Warrensville his father had not asked Leon to work, having always considered him too weak for manual labor.

Regarding the shooting of the President, Mrs. Czolgosz said:

"I can't believe Leon is the one. He was such a timid boy, so afraid of everything. Why, he was the biggest coward you ever saw in your life."

Leon Czolgosz was born in Alpena County, Michigan, and spent his early life there. Although the family was well known but little was known of Czolgosz, he being only thirteen years of age when the family moved away.

The family is Polish and was strict in religious observances, but the record does not show that Leon Czolgosz was baptized either at Alpena or at Posen, where the family lived a short time before moving to Alpena.

Czolgosz, the father, was born in the Province of Posen, Krais Schubin, County of Bromberg, Village of Haido, near Barin, and came directly to Alpena County from Germany about thirty years ago. He worked on the docks and was regarded as a peaceful, inoffensive, ignorant foreigner. The father of Leon Czolgosz raised ten children, of which the assassin was one of the youngest.

After leaving Alpena the family was only heard of a few times, and that indirectly, but they were known to be in Cleveland, where several of the children were living with them. Valentine Misgalski, a prominent and intelligent Pole, and former friend of the Czolgosz family, said that he never saw any evidences of viciousness in the family. He remembers Leon and said there was nothing unusual about him as a boy. He attended the parochial school, was devoted to his church, and remembers him as in every way an ordinary boy.

Andrew Czolgosz, uncle of the assassin, lived in Metz Township, thirty miles from Alpena, the most of which distance has to be made overland. He was unable to talk English and conversation had to be carried on through his sons. This family lived in a thickly populated Polish settlement, where the people were ignorant and not always to be trusted, and inquiries had to be made with great care. These people quarrelled and fought among themselves, but at a signal that any one of their members was in danger from any one from the outside, as they call it, a man's life was in great danger.

It was in this settlement that Paul Czolgosz lived for a short time after coming to this country before settling in Alpena.

During the conversation with Andrew Czolgosz a significant remark was made by one of the sons. Inquiry was made as to where Paul Czolgosz could be found, and also his son Leon, without giving a reason for the inquiry. The old man said his brother was in Cleveland, that he had heard from him occasionally, but he did not know what had become of Leon. He had kept track of some of the boys, but he denied any knowledge of where Leon was.

When the interviewer started to return he asked the boys, who talk English well, if they had heard President McKinley was shot. One of them spoke up quickly, "Did Leon shoot him?" He was told there was a report current to that effect, to which the boy made no reply. An effort was made to resume the conversation, but they would answer no questions, nor would they ask any more questions of their father.

Leon Czolgosz has an aunt living in Alpena, but she would answer no questions. Czolgosz also had a brother living in the Polish settlement.

On the rolls of the Pension Office was the name of Jacob F. Czolgosz. A pension of $30 a month was paid to Jacob because of a wound in the right hand and forearm. The wound was received through the explosion of a shell at Sandy Hook in 1899. Czolgosz enlisted from Cleveland, Ohio (giving his address at 199 Hosmer street), first in Battery M, Sixth Artillery, on September 15, 1898. He was afterward discharged on January 22, 1899, and then re-enlisted in the ordnance branch, in Captain Babbitt's company, and was serving there when wounded.

He was born at Alpena, Michigan, and was twenty-two years and ten months old when he first enlisted.

Leon Czolgosz was a member of several Anarchist clubs in Cleveland, one of which was named "Sila," which means "force." The club met at the corner of Tod street and Third avenue, over a saloon which, it is said, Czolgosz once owned. Three years before the assassination the club disbanded and he left it, but joined another.

"Czolgosz made no secret of the fact that he was an Anarchist," said Anton Zwolinski, a Cleveland Pole. "He was always talking about it and trying to force Anarchists' principles on every one whom he talked with. He was a great coward, however, and I am surprised he had the nerve to do as he did. It would not surprise me to learn that he is merely the tool of some other persons. When the Sila Club broke up Czolgosz joined another one."

Several years previous to his crime, Czolgosz was employed in a Newburg mill, where he was known as Fred Nieman. He was a member of Forest City Castle Lodge No. 22 of the Golden Eagles. His former associates said he was a queer man, but was known to have a most violent temper. It is said that the assassin was a strong infidel and a red-hot Socialist. He was last seen by his Cleveland friends around Newburg the previous spring, when he was living on a farm with his father near Warrensville, Ohio.

John Ginder, an employe of the Newburg wire mill, where Czolgosz formerly worked, and who was also a member of the Golden Eagle Lodge, received a letter from Czolgosz in July, dated West Seneca, N. Y.

The letter, which was taken by the police, was written in red ink and contained a strange reference to the fare to Buffalo. It read as follows:

"West Seneca, N. Y., July 30, 1901.—John Ginder—Dear Sir and Brother: Inclosed you will find $1 to pay my lodge dues. I paid $1 to Brother George Coonish to pay the assessment sent out on account of the death of Brother David Jones.

"Brother Ginder, please send my book to me at my cost, and also send password if you can do so.

"I left Cleveland Thursday, July 11. I am working here and will stay for some time. *The fare from here to Buffalo is $5.15.*

"Hoping this finds you well, as it leaves me, I remain

FRED C. NIEMAN."

Czolgosz was placed on trial before Justice Truman C. White of the State Supreme Bench, at Buffalo, on Monday, September 23. On the following day the jury found him guilty, and on Thursday, September 26, he was sentenced to death by electrocution in the week beginning October 28. He refused to consult with the attorneys appointed to defend him, and practically made no defense.

CHAPTER V.

EMMA GOLDMAN, THE ANARCHIST LEADER.

Russia, the land of the nihilists, and the home of the "propaganda of action"—which means assassination—was the birthplace of Emma Goldman. Though still a young woman, she is recognized as a radical among radicals, when it comes to expounding the principles of her faith. For more than ten years she has been known as an enemy of government.

Miss Goldman's contempt for the present system of law is pronounced, bitter, and unrelenting, yet she never fails to deny that she is an advocate of violence.

"I have never advocated violence," she asserted some time ago, in an interview, "but neither do I condemn the Anarchist who resorts to it. I look behind him for the conditions that made him possible, and my horror is swallowed up in pity. Perhaps under the same conditions I would have done the same."

Miss Goldman says she was born a revolutionist, but that her belief in anarchy was not actually crystallized until after the hanging of the Chicago Anarchists in 1887. Then she became what she describes as an active Anarchist, and her activity has never flagged since then. She has been a prolific writer for all publications in this country that would give space to her articles upon anarchy, and has devoted much of her time to lecturing.

Miss Goldman had frequently lectured in Chicago, but until the attack on President McKinley, the police found no reason to arrest her.

The lectures in Chicago attracted little attention, seldom having been announced in an obtrusive manner. Her reputation was such, however, that the management of Hull House refused to permit her to speak in that establishment.

In 1893 the New York police arrested Miss Goldman on a warrant charging her with "inciting to riot." The arrest was a result of her activity during the famous Debs strike, and it was followed by her imprisonment on Blackwell's Island for a term of one year, which was shortened to seven months on account of good behavior. She formerly had led a strike of the Waist and Shirt Maker Girls' union in New York, but without attracting much attention.

In an extended interview which Miss Goldman gave out a few months ago while in New York she told many things about her life and her views on social and political questions which have a special interest at the present moment. She said:

"I am a Russian through and through, although little of my life was spent there. I was born in Russia, but was brought up in Germany and graduated from a German school. All that didn't make a German of me. I went back to Russia when I was 15 years old, and felt that I was returning to my home. My family was orthodox. None of my revolutionary tendencies was inherited—at least my parents were not responsible for them and were horrified by them.

"While I was in Germany I did not think much about anarchy, but when I went back to St. Petersburg my whole attitude toward life changed, and I went into radicalism with all my heart and soul. You see, things are different in Russia from what they are here or anywhere else. One breathes a revolutionary thought with the air, and without being definitely interested in anarchy one learns its principles. There was discussion and thought and enthusiasm all around me, and something within me responded to it all.

WOMAN'S EQUALITY IN RUSSIA.

"There is no other place in the world where woman has what she has in Russia. There the women have not only the same rights in law as the men, they have the same liberties and the same social and intellectual freedom. There man respects woman, looks upon her as his equal, is her good chum— yes, that is the word. Nowhere are men and women chums as they are in Russia.

"A woman student in Russia may receive visitors all day and most of the night, discuss all vital subjects with them, go with men when and where she pleases, and yet she will not be criticised, and no landlady would dream of insinuating that there was anything wrong with her morals. What is more, there wouldn't be anything wrong with them. The standard of morals in the student class is phenomenally high, and the average intelligent Russian woman's mind is as pure as it is broad.

"The relation between the sexes in Russia is the most ideal of any I know about. That is why young Russian women learn to think. And because they think they become Anarchists.

"I was an Anarchist when I left Russia to come to America, but I had hardly formulated my belief. The final influence that crystallized my views was the hanging of the Chicago Anarchists in 1887. I followed that case carefully and it made me an active Anarchist. I was living with my family in Rochester then, and the nearest thing to a radical society the town had was a Social Democratic society, tame as a house cat. I came away to New York and went to work in a factory. That showed me a new side of life. My family had been well-to-do, and I hadn't come in actual contact with the want and suffering of the world until I joined the wage-earners.

"Of course the experience strengthened my revolutionary ideas. When the Waist and Shirtmaker Girls' union went out in 1888 I led the strike. That is, in a way I led it. I have never been an Anarchist leader. I cannot afford it. A leader must be a diplomat. I am not a diplomat. A leader of a party makes concessions to his party, for the sake of holding his power. He must give way to his followers in order to be sure they will sustain him. I can't do all that, I am an Anarchist because I love individual freedom and I will not surrender that freedom.

"You know I am a professional nurse. It has always been the dream of my life to be a doctor, but I never could manage it—could not get means for the study. My factory work undermined my health, so I thought that if I couldn't be a doctor I could at least be a little part of the profession. I went through the training for a nurse, did the hospital work, and now nurse private cases.

"When I came out of prison on Blackwell's Island I was nervous. I decided to try a change and go to Europe for a year. I could lecture for the cause and take a course in massage and in midwifery in Vienna. There is no good training for either here, though we have the best training schools for nurses in the world.

"Well, I went and did my studying and then went to Paris to study and wait for the Anarchists' congress. You know the government prohibited the congress. We had it all the same, but the meetings were secret. I received the honor or dishonor of especially strict surveillance. I was to give a series of lectures, but after the third the authorities warned me that if I gave any more I must leave France, and as I wanted to attend the congress I kept quiet.

"Finally, detectives escorted me to the station and saw my luggage checked to the steamer and then notified the government that the dangerous woman was on her way out of France."

Leon Czolgosz, the murderer of President McKinley, asserted immediately after his arrest, that he was led to undertake the assassination of the President by a speech delivered by Emma Goldman, the leader of the Anarchist propaganda in America. This speech was delivered in Cleveland, O., the home of Czolgosz, May 6. In it Miss Goldman outlined the principles of anarchy, and detailed the methods whereby she expected to secure the establishment of anarchy throughout the world. Her talk was full of forceful passages, in some cases more notable for their strength than for their elegance.

"Men under the present state of society," she said, "are mere products of circumstances. Under the galling yoke of government, ecclesiasticism, and a bond of custom and prejudice, it is impossible for the individual to work out his own career as he could wish. Anarchism aims at a new and complete freedom. It strives to bring about the freedom which is not only the freedom from within but a freedom from without, which will prevent any man from having a desire to interfere in any way with the liberty of his neighbor.

"Vanderbilt says, 'I am a free man within myself, but the others be damned.' This is not the freedom we are striving for. We merely desire complete individual liberty, and this can never be obtained as long as there is an existing government.

"We do not favor the socialistic idea of converting men and women into mere producing machines under the eye of a paternal government. We go to the opposite extreme and demand the fullest and most complete liberty for each and every person to work out his own salvation upon any line that he pleases. The degrading notion of men and women as machines is far from our ideals of life.

"Anarchism has nothing to do with future governments or economic arrangements. We do not favor any particular settlement in this line, but merely ask to do away with the present evils. The future will provide these arrangements after our work has been done. Anarchism deals merely with social relations, and not with economic arrangement."

The speaker then deprecated the idea that all Anarchists were in favor of violence or bomb throwing. She declared that nothing was further from the principles they support. She went on, however, into a detailed explanation of the different crimes committed by Anarchists lately, declaring that the motive was good in each case, and that these acts were merely a matter of temperament.

Some men were so constituted, she said, that they were unable to stand idly by and see the wrong that was being endured by their fellow-mortals.

She herself did not believe in these methods, but she did not think they should be condemned in view of the high and noble motives which prompted their perpetration. She continued: "Some believe we should first obtain by force and let the intelligence and education come afterwards."

Miss Goldman did not hesitate to put forward a number of sentiments far more radical and sensational than any ever publicly advanced here. During Miss Goldman's lecture a strong detail of police was in the hall to keep her from uttering sentiments which were regarded as too radical. This accounts for the fact that the speaker did not give free rein to her thoughts on that occasion. Because of anarchistic uprisings elsewhere it was thought best by the city officials to curb the utterances of the woman.

As soon as it was known that Czolgosz admitted being a disciple of Emma Goldman, the police of a score of cities began an active hunt for her, in the belief that the President's assassination was the result of a conspiracy, of which she was the head. It was known that Miss Goldman had been in Chicago in July, and that she had visited Buffalo in July and August. But her whereabouts immediately following the crime, could not easily be traced. The arrest of a number of anarchists in Chicago, and the capture of a number of letters, gave the police a clue that Miss Goldman was in St. Louis, and the police of that city made active search for her. She was not found, however, though the fact that she was in that city after the attack of Czolgosz on the President, was established. It was then surmised that she had gone to Chicago, and the police of that city redoubled their vigilance. Through a telegram sent to a man living on Oakdale avenue, the Chicago police learned that Miss Goldman had made inquiries concerning the arrest of the Anarchists in that city, and announced her purpose of going to Chicago, and would arrive on Sunday night, Sept. 8. The police watched the house in Oakdale avenue all Sunday night, but no one entered it. The watch was continued, however, and Monday morning the vigilance of the officers was rewarded. A woman approached the house and rang the front door bell. There was no response, and she went around the house to the back door, where she knocked. No one opened the door, nor was there any response. The woman then walked to Sheffield avenue and rang the bell at No. 303, the third flat in which is the home of Charles G. Norris. Here she was admitted, and while one of the detectives watched the house, the other reported to his superior officers. Captain Herman Schuettler, who had considerable experience with the Chicago Anarchists in 1886, prior to and after the Haymarket riot, immediately went to the Sheffield avenue house. The officer on duty there reported that no one had entered or left the house since the woman had disappeared behind its doors. The police officers tried the usual mode of securing admittance, but no response came to their signals. Then Detective Charles K. Hertz climbed in through a window, and opening the door, admitted Captain Schuettler. Sitting in the parlor, dressed in a light wrapper, with two partly filled valises in front of her, was Emma Goldman. She turned pale when the policemen confronted her and denied her identity, which was established by a fountain pen box, on which her name was written. The woman had said that she was a servant.

Miss Goldman was taken to the office of Chief of Police O'Neill and served with a warrant charging her with having conspired with other Anarchists then under arrest, to kill the President.

She detailed her meeting with the assassin in Chicago.

"I was at the house of Abraham Isaak. Yes, the house at 515 Carroll street. I was preparing to take the Nickel Plate train for the East with Miss Isaak. A ring came at the door. I answered the bell and found a young man there. He asked for Mr. Isaak. The latter had left the house, promising to meet us at the station and say good-by. I so told the young man and I further told him that he might go to the station with us and meet Mr. Isaak there. So you see," she asserted, "he would not even have been with me for thirty-five minutes had I not asked him to go to the train.

"The young man—yes, it was Czolgosz, who shot the President—said that he had met me before. He said he had heard me lecture in Cleveland. I had delivered a lecture there on May 6, but I can't remember all the people who shake hands with me, can I? I had no remembrance of him. We went to the station on the elevated train and this man accompanied us. I asked him where he had heard of Mr. Isaak. He said he had read the latter's paper, Free Society. He did not talk to me about a plot. I never heard of him from that time until McKinley was shot."

Emma Goldman's ideas on anarchy are contained in an interview had with her some months before President McKinley's assassination. She said:

"If a man came to me and told me he was planning an assassination I would think him an utter fool and refuse to pay any attention to him. The man who has such a plan, if he is earnest and honest, knows no secret is safe when told. He does the deed himself, runs the risk himself, pays the penalty himself. I honor him for the spirit that prompts him. It is no small thing for a man to be willing to lay down his life for the cause of humanity. The act is noble, but it is mistaken. While I do not advocate violence, neither do I condemn the anarchist who resorts to it.

"I was an anarchist when I left Russia to come to America," she continued, "but I had hardly formulated my belief. The final influence that crystallized my views was the hanging of the Chicago anarchists in 1887.

"I am an anarchist because I love individual freedom, and I will not surrender that freedom. A leader must sooner or later be the victim of the masses he thinks he controls. When I definitely entered the work I gave myself a solemn pledge that I would study, that I would make passion bow to reason, that I would not be carried away from the truth by sentiment. I soon saw that the safest and wisest way to keep myself free was not to be a leader. That is why I am connected with no party. I am a member of no group. Individual freedom and responsibility—there is the basis of true anarchy.

"No, I have never advocated violence, nor do I know a single truly great anarchist leader who ever did advocate violence. Where violence comes with anarchy it is a result of the conditions, not of anarchy. The biggest fallacy going is the idea that anarchists as a body band together and order violence, assassinations of rulers and all that. I ought to know something about anarchy, and I tell you that is false—absolutely false.

"There is ignorance, cruelty, starvation, poverty, suffering, and some victim grows tired of waiting. He believes a decisive blow will call public attention to the wrongs of his country, and may hasten the remedy. He and perhaps one or two intimate friends or relatives make a plan. They do not have orders. They do not consult other anarchists.

"Perhaps under the same conditions I would do the same. If I had been starving in Milan, and had raised my starving baby in the air as an appeal for justice, and had that baby shot in my arms by a brutal soldiery, who knows what I might have done? I might have changed from a philosophical anarchist to a fighting anarchist. Do you suppose if Santo Caserio had had anarchist organization back of him he would have tramped all the weary way to Paris, without money, in order to kill Carnot? If Bresci had been sent out from us, would he have had to scrape together every cent he could, even forcing one of his anarchist friends to pawn some of his clothes in order to repay a loan Bresci had made him? The friend curses Bresci for a hard-hearted creditor, but Bresci never told why he needed the money so desperately.

"Anarchy's best future lies in America. We in America haven't yet reached conditions—economic conditions, I mean—that necessarily breed violence. I am thankful for that; but we are much nearer such conditions than the old-time American ever dreamed we would be, and unless something is done to stop it, the time will come.

"It's all too absolutely silly, this talk about my being dangerous. Half my fellow believers think me a fool because I am always talking against violence and advocating individual work. I believe that the next ten years will see a wonderful spreading of the true principles of anarchy in this country."

Emma Goldman, at the time of the assassination, was a woman thirty-two years old, with coarse features, thick lips, a square jaw and prominent nose. She wore glasses on account of nearsightedness, and her hair was light, almost red—the color of the doctrine she teaches.

She was held without bail, but afterwards released.

After Czolgosz, the first arrests for complicity in the attempt on President McKinley's life were made in the city of Chicago. The metropolis of Illinois, with its cosmopolitan population, has always been a hotbed of anarchy, and it was there the police instantly looked for traces of the movements of the assassin. The police learned from Czolgosz himself that he had recently been in Chicago, and had visited at the house of Abraham Isaak, Sr., 515 Carroll avenue. Isaak was known as an anarchist and the publisher of a paper called Free Society. The police procured warrants for the arrest of Isaak and others on a charge of conspiracy to kill and assassinate the President of the United States, William McKinley, and on visiting Isaak's house Saturday, September 7, found nine persons there, all of whom were arrested. They were:

Abraham Isaak, Sr., publisher of the Free Society and former publisher of the Firebrand, the organ of anarchy, which was suppressed; Abraham Isaak, Jr., Clemence Pfuetzner, Alfred Schneider, Hippolyte Havel, Henry Travaglio, Julia Mechanic, Marie Isaak, mother; Marie Isaak, daughter.

The same day three other men were arrested at 100 Newberry avenue, Chicago, for the same crime. These men were: Martin Raznick, cloakmaker, who rented the premises; Maurice Fox, Michael Raz.

In the house the detectives found box after box heaped with the literature of anarchy and socialism. There were pictures of Emma Goldman and other leaders and many copies of the Firebrand, Isaak's old paper.

The arrests were decided on thus early because of the receipt by the

Chicago police of a telegram from the chief of police at Buffalo, reading as follows:

"We have in custody Leon Czolgosz, alias Fred Nieman, the President's assassin. Locate and arrest E. J. Isaak, who is editor of a socialistic paper and a follower of Emma Goldman, from whom Nieman is said to have taken instructions. It looks as if there might be a plot, and that these people may be implicated."

After being taken to the police station the prisoners were taken before Chief O'Neill and questioned. Isaak, Sr., was the first to be brought in, and he told his story without any suggestion of reticence, occasionally punctuating his answers with anarchistic utterances, angry nods of his head or emphatic gestures with his clenched fists. When asked if he knew Emma Goldman he answered:

"Yes, she was at my house during the latter part of June and the first two weeks of July. The last time I saw her was on the twelfth of July. On that day she left Chicago for Buffalo. I met her at the Lake Shore depot as she was leaving. When I reached the depot I found her talking to a strange man, who appeared about 25 years old, was well dressed and smooth shaven. Miss Goldman told me that the fellow had been following her around wanting to talk to her, but she had no time to devote to him. She asked me to find out what the fellow wanted.

"The man made a bad impression on me from the first, and when he called me aside and asked me about the secret meetings of Chicago anarchists I was sure he was a spy. I despised the man as soon as I saw him and was positive he was a spy.

"Emma Goldman went away on a train which left in about half an hour after my meeting with this stranger, who gave his name as Czlosz (Czolgosz). I wanted to learn more about the stranger, so, when I went home, I asked him to accompany me. On the way to my house he asked me again and again about the secret meetings of our societies, and the impression grew on me that he was a spy. He asked me if we would give him money, and I told him no, but added that if he wanted to stay in Chicago I would help him get work.

"When we reached my house we sat out on the porch for about ten minutes, and his talk during that time was radical. He said he had been a Socialist for many years, but was looking for something more active than socialism. I was sure then that the fellow was a spy, and I wanted to search

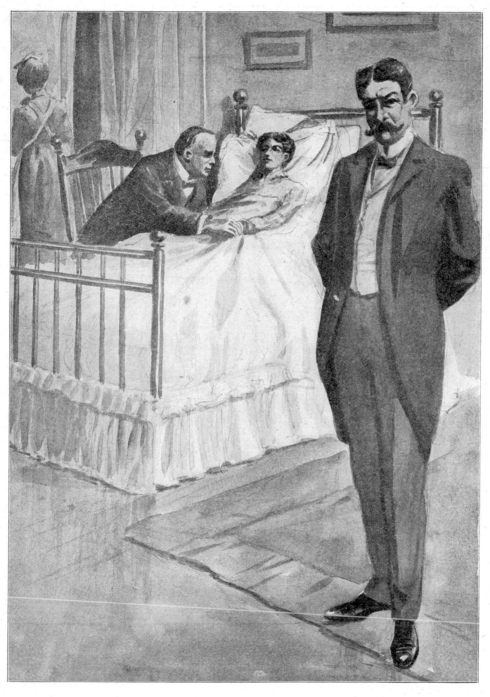

PRESIDENT McKINLEY AT THE BEDSIDE OF HIS WIFE WHEN
SHE WAS ILL IN SAN FRANCISCO.

Secretary Root   Judge Hitchcock   Senator Depew   Private Secretary Cortelyou
Judge Hazel   President Roosevelt   Secretary Wilson   Mr. Milburn

and unmask him, so I arranged with him to come to my house on the following morning for breakfast.

"I took him over to Mrs. Esther Wolfson's rooming-house, at 425 Carroll avenue, and engaged a room for him. Mrs. Wolfson has since moved to New York.

"I didn't see Czolgosz again after that night. He failed to come to my house for breakfast, and when I went over to Mrs. Wolfson's to inquire about him I was told that he had slipped away without saying where he was going. I was suspicious of him all the time, so I wrote to E. Schilling, one of our comrades in Cleveland, Ohio, and asked him if he knew of such a man.

"Schilling replied that a fellow answering his description had called on him, and that he believed the man was a spy in the employ of the police. He said he wanted to 'search' the stranger, but was alone when he called and did not care to attempt the job. Schilling arranged a meeting for another night, but Czolgosz didn't show up, and all trace of him was lost. I wrote to Cleveland because Czolgosz had told me he once lived there.

"After I received Schilling's letter I printed an article in my paper denouncing the fellow as a spy and warning my people against him."

The article renouncing Czolgosz, alluded to by Isaak, was published in the issue of Free Society September 1, and was couched in the following language:

ATTENTION!

The attention of the comrades is called to another spy. He is well dressed, of medium height, rather narrow shoulders, blond and about 25 years of age. Up to the present he has made his appearance in Chicago and Cleveland. In the former place he remained but a short time, while in Cleveland he disappeared when the comrades had confirmed themselves of his identity and were on the point of exposing him. His demeanor is of the usual sort, pretending to be greatly interested in the cause, asking for names or soliciting aid for acts of contemplated violence. If this same individual makes his appearance elsewhere the comrades are warned in advance, and can act accordingly.

The police were suspicious of this alleged fear of Czolgosz, and asserted that the publication of the notice might have been done for the purpose of exculpating the Chicago Anarchists in case they were accused of being parties to the conspiracy.

In his further examination Isaak answered proudly that he was an Anarchist, and when asked what he meant by anarchy, replied:

"I mean a country without government. We recognize neither law nor the right of one man to govern another. The trouble with the world is that it is struggling to abolish effect without seeking to get at the cause. Yes, I am an Anarchist, and there are 10,000 people in Chicago who think and believe as I do. You don't hear about them because they are not organized.

"Assassination is nothing but a natural phenomenon. It always has existed and will exist as long as this tyrannical system of government prevails. However, we don't believe tyranny can be abolished by the killing of one man. Yet there will be absolute anarchy.

"In Russia I was a Nihilist. There are secret meetings there, and I want to tell you that as soon as you attempt to suppress anarchy here there will be secret meetings in the United States.

"I don't believe in killing rulers, but I do believe in self-defense. As long as you let Anarchists talk their creed openly in this country the conservatives will not be in favor of assassinating executives."

Isaak had had an eventful career and had been a socialist and anarchistic agitator for years. He was born in Southern Russia and came to Chicago seven months ago. In Russia, he says, he was a bookkeeper. He was forced to leave the country, and after traveling over South America he came to this country and located first in San Francisco. There he worked as a gardener. Later he removed to Portland, Ore., and began the publication of a rabid anarchistic paper called the Firebrand, but the publication was suppressed by the United States postal authorities.

Then Isaak came to Chicago and started Free Society, a paper devoted to the interests of local Anarchists. Isaak talked intelligently but rabidly on matters pertaining to sociological questions.

Hippolyte Havel, the next in importance to Isaak in the anarchistic group, was also examined by the chief. He proved to be an excitable Bohemian, 35 years of age. In appearance he was the opposite of Isaak. Dwarfed of stature, narrow-eyed, with jet black hair hanging in a confused mass over his low forehead, and a manner of talking that brought into play both hands, he looked the part when he boldly told Chief O'Neill that he was an Anarchist. In Bohemia he was an agitator, and in 1894 was sentenced to two years' confinement in the prison at Plzen for making incendiary speeches. He admitted that he knew Emma Goldman and Czolgosz, and said that if he had known the latter was going to Buffalo to kill the President, he would not have notified the police.

Later, these anarchists were released, as there was no evidence to prove a conspiracy.

CHAPTER VI.

ANARCHISM AND ITS OBJECTS.

Within a few minutes after the shooting of President McKinley at Buffalo, and before anything was known of the identity of the assailant, news of the affair was in every American town and village to which the telegraph reaches. Probably in every town those to whom this first report came exclaimed: "An Anarchist!" and many thousands added bitter denunciation of all anarchists.

When later news arrived it was established definitely by the confession of the would-be slayer that he was an anarchist and fired the shots in a desire to further the cause of those who believe as he does.

What, then, is anarchism, and who are the anarchists that the destruction of the head of a republican government can further their cause? What do they aim at, and what have they accomplished to stand in their account against the long list of murders, of attempted assassinations, and of destruction of property with which they are charged? The questions are asked on every hand, but the answers are hard to find.

When, at the World's Fair in Chicago in October, 1893, an international congress of anarchists was held and representative anarchists were here from every civilized country, an attempt was made to answer some of the questions. A proposition was made that, for the information of the people and the furtherance of anarchism, a document should be drawn up setting forth just what the belief is and what its followers are doing. The proposition almost brought the congress to an end, for it was found that there were as many different ideas of anarchism as there were delegates present, and no definition could be made satisfactory to more than one or two.

Yet in behalf of this doctrine, which is in itself the anarchy of belief, there have been sacrificed in the last quarter of a century more than a hundred human lives and hundreds of thousands of dollars' worth of property by the most violent means. And, as far as can be judged by an outsider, and as is admitted by the leading thinkers of the cult, anarchism is not one whit the gainer by it.

According to Zenker, himself an anarchistic theorist, "anarchism means, in its ideal sense, the perfect, unfettered self-government of the individual, and consequently the absence of any kind of external government."

That such a state is possible not one of the anarchistic philosophers has contended, and each has been eager to hold up his neighbor's plan, if not also his own, as a Utopia. Its realization, said Proudhon, pioneer of the cult, would be an entirely new world, a new Eden, a land of the perfect idealization of freedom and of equality. Yet Proudhon wrote many books and made many addresses in behalf of his doctrine. Like every other anarchist, he found his theory ending in a contradiction—as soon as there was anarchy a new state would be built up.

For anarchy is of two classes, individualistic and communistic. The first is the philosophy of the thinker, which has advanced as the object of its being the attainment of "Liberty, not the daughter but the mother of order." That other anarchy is that which through the influence of terrorism shall crumble empires and republics alike, while from their dust shall rise a free people who shall be in no need of restraints at the hands of their fellow-men. Disciples of this philosophy would build communistic centers upon the ruins of government which violence should have brought about.

Beginning with Proudhon, anarchy had no relationship to the secret society of the assassin. Proudhon simply had criticised a society which "seeks, in formula after formula, institution after institution, that equilibrium which always escapes it, and at every attempt always causes its luxury and its poverty to grow in equal proportion." He had no retributive bomb or dagger for the heads of state under which such inequalities existed. He said, only: "Since equilibrium has never yet been reached, it only remains for us to hope something from a complete solution which synthetically unites theories, which gives back to labor its effectiveness and to each of its organs its power. Hitherto pauperism has been so inextricably connected with labor and want with idleness that all our accusations against Providence only prove our weakness."

Pierre Joseph Proudhon was born in Besancon, France, in 1809. He was a poor man and became a printer, but in 1837 won a scholarship at the academy in his native town, secured an education, and became a philosopher. He followed the teachings of Hegel, the German philosopher, and going beyond them founded the modern cult of anarchist individualism. He became famous from a question and an answer. "What is property?" he demanded, and himself replied: "Property is theft."

Later he came to regret the saying and endeavored to assert his belief in property. "Individual possession is the fundamental condition of social life," he said. He maintained that profit was unjust and that every trade should be an equal exchange.

Proudhon was seeking some means by which the pauper workmen of Europe could be brought to an equality with the aristocracy. In it he came near socialism, but kept the boundary fixed, maintaining that the individual should have his property, should produce as much as he could, have the benefit of his product, and be rich or poor according to it.

Not until the movement started by Proudhon had reached Russia did the "propaganda of action" come into it. In Russia the government, controlling the military, was able to check instantly any movement which might appear in any of the few big cities. In the country no movement could have effect.

"Terrorism arose," says Stepniak, "because of the necessity of taking the great governmental organization in the flank before it could discover that an attack was planned. Nurtured in hatred, it grew up in an electric atmosphere filled by the enthusiasm that is awakened by a noble deed." The "great subterranean stream" of nihilism thus had its rise. From nihilism and its necessary sudden outbreaks anarchism borrowed terrorism, the propaganda of action.

Prince Peter Kropotkin of Russia was the founder of the violent school of anarchists. Banished from Russia, he set about organizing in various countries bands of propagandists. Instead of the individualism of Proudhon he proclaimed anarchist communism, which is now the doctrine of force and is the branch of the cult most followed in Italy, France, Spain and among the Poles.

That form of anarchy to-day is giving great concern to the police and military power of the world. It has its hotbed in continental Europe. Vienna, beyond all the other capitals on the continent, is said to harbor its doctrinaires. Switzerland has contended with its "propaganda of action," which Kropotkin stood for in 1879. Italy, France, Spain, Russia, and nearly every other continental country has felt its force. London itself has been a nest of anarchistic vipers in times past. From all this territory, too, the gradual closing in of the police power has forced both leaders and tools of anarchy to seek asylums in America. The problem of anarchy as now presented to the United States government has to deal almost wholly with this foreign born element.

Its principles, as voiced by the manifesto of the Geneva conference in 1882, stand in great measure for the propaganda of action of to-day:

"Our ruler is our enemy. We anarchists are men without any rulers, fighting against all those who have usurped any power or who wish to usurp it.

"Our enemy is the owner of the land who keeps it for himself and makes the peasant work for his advantage.

"Our enemy is the manufacturer who fills his factory with wage slaves; our enemy is the state, whether monarchical, oligarchical, or democratic, with its officials and staff officers, magistrates, and police spies.

"Our enemy is every thought of authority, whether men call it God or devil, in whose name the priests have so long ruled honest people.

"Our enemy is the law which always oppresses the weak by the strong to the justification and apotheosis of crime.

"But if the landowners, the manufacturers, the heads of the state, the priests, and the law are our enemies, we are also theirs, and we boldly oppose them. We intend to reconquer the land and the factory from the land-owner and the manufacturer; we mean to annihilate the state under whatever name it may be concealed; and we mean to get our freedom back again in spite of priest or law.

"According to our strength we will work for the humiliation of all legal institutions, and are in accord with every one who defies the law by a revolutionary act. We despise all legal means because they are the negation of our rights; we do not want so-called universal suffrage since we cannot get away from our own personal sovereignty and cannot make ourselves accomplices in the crimes committed by our so-called representatives.

"Between us anarchists and all political parties, whether conservatives or moderates, whether they fight for freedom or recognize it by their admissions, a deep gulf is fixed. We wish to remain our own masters, and he among us who strives to become a chief or leader is a traitor to our cause. Of course we know that individual freedom cannot exist without a union with other free associates. We all live by the support of one another; that is the social life which has created us; that it is the work of all which gives to each the consciousness of his rights and the power to defend them. Every social product is the work of the whole community, to which all have a claim in equal manner.

"For we are all communists. It is ours to conquer and defend common property and to overthrow governments by whatever name they may be called."

Johann Most followed Kropotkin, and in pamphlets and papers urged death to rulers and leaders of the people. He published explicit directions for making bombs, placing them in public places; a dictionary of poisons and the means of getting them into the food of Ministers and other government officials. "Extirpate the miserable brood," he said, "extirpate the wretches."

All these leaders and many other theorists, German philosophers, Englishmen and Americans as well, have published books showing why they believe anarchy to be the ideal condition of the human race. None of them believes it possible. It is only the less brilliant followers who attempt to carry out their teachings and thus bring bloodshed. How this is done the psychologists, the students of criminology explain.

"Anarchism is a pathological phenomenon," says Cæsar Lombroso, the Italian criminologist. "Unhealthy and criminal persons adopt anarchism. In every city, in nearly every factory, there are men with active minds but little education. These men stand, day after day, before a machine handling a tool, doing some mechanical action. Their minds must work. They have little to work upon. They are starved for proper food and air and for the mental food which is necessary to a proper understanding of society and of the duties of men. Into the hands of these fall the writings of the anarchists with subtly-worded arguments. Conditions which are apparent everywhere are shown forth, the evils of the city and of industrial conditions are set forth plainly, so that the reader gets an idea that the writer is truthful and impartial. Then the writer sets forth how anarchism can remedy these things. Later on comes the suggestion of violence. Then 'strike down the rulers.'

"The workman may not be moved in the least by the first perusal. He may even be amused. But later, little by little, as he stands at his work, they come back to him, and he broods over them again and again until they become part of his mind and his belief, and sooner or later he becomes a violent anarchist. For such men Johann Most and his followers form little groups which can hold secret meetings, and through them deeds of violence are plotted and accomplished."

In connection with the philosophy of anarchy, it may be interesting to examine the causes which various leaders in the movement have given for espousing the doctrine. August Spies, one of the men executed in Chicago for complicity in the Haymarket conspiracy, replied, when asked what made him an anarchist:

"I became an anarchist on that very day that a policeman seized me by the collar and flung me from a sidewalk into the gutter."

"Probably," wrote this questioner, "the whole history of anarchy could be traced to these petty causes. The sore develops violent action in the uncouth; the finer and thriftier spirits are moved to ventilate their wrongs in print."

There is a suggestion in the point which has been voiced by anarchists everywhere. When Emma Goldman was arrested she complained bitterly that it was the police department of Chicago rather than her teachings which was making anarchists.

The story has been told of Zo d'Axa that at a time when he was hesitating between becoming an anarchist or a religious missionary he was traveling in Italy. One day he was accused—as he contended, wrongfully—of insulting the Empress of Germany, and the legal efforts to call him to account made an anarchist of him. He was a man of fortune and he devoted that fortune to the cause, establishing En Dehors, a journal of revolt, against everything that could limit individualism.

Thus, in these later types the relations of cause and effect have been established. As to the earlier ones, only speculation may fasten the probable truth to them. As to Proudhon, the sting that often comes to one lacking in caste might easily have been his inspiration. He was sent to prison in 1848 for political offenses, just at the moment when his People's Bank had been started upon its brief period of existence, as one of the great ameliorating institutions of French society.

Out of prison again at the end of a long confinement, Proudhon begged permission to issue his paper, Justice, but Napoleon refused the plea. A book, lacking much of the fire of his youth, caused Proudhon to be sentenced to prison a second time, for a period of three years. He escaped by flight, however, and went to Belgium. In the general amnesty granted in 1859 he was excepted, and when, as a special favor, the Emperor, in 1861, granted him permission to return home, Proudhon refused, not returning to Paris until 1863. But troubles and persecutions had told upon him, and on June 19, 1865, he died in the arms of his wife, who had been a helpmeet, and for whom he had always shown loyalty and love.

Caspar Schmidt, better known by the pseudonym of Max Stirner, was a German pupil of Proudhon and was born at Baireuth on October 25, 1806. He became a teacher in a high school, and afterwards in a girls' school in Berlin. In 1844 appeared the book, "The Individual and His Property," acknowledged by Max Stirner. It was meteoric, causing a momentary sensation and then sinking into oblivion until the rejuvenating of anarchism ten years later brought it again to notice. Stirner departs radically from Proudhon. On June 26, 1856, he died, as some one has observed, "Poor in external circumstances, rich in want and bitterness."

Jean Jacques Elisee Reclus is one of the later French apostles of anarchism, a deep student of such prominence that the sentence of transportation in 1871 caused such an outcry from scientific men that banishment was substituted therefor. He has written of anarchism:

"The idea is beautiful, is great, but these miscreants sully our teachings. He who calls himself an anarchist should be one of a good and gentle sort. It is a mistake to believe that the anarchistic idea can be promoted by acts of barbarity."

Of the influence of this man and his type it has been said by a critic.

"They are poets, painters, novelists, or critics. Most of them are men of fortune and family. Their art has brought them fame. They are idealists, and dreamers, and philanthropists. They turn from a dark and troubled present to a future all rose. In a tragic night they await the sunrise of fraternal love.

"And yet, by their sincerity and their eloquence, they are the most dangerous men of to-day. They have made anarchy a splendid ideal, instead of the brutal and meaningless discontent that it was. They have gilded plain ruffians like Ravachol and Caserio with the halo of martyrdom. For them anarchy is a literary toy. But what of the feather-brained wretches who believe in all these fine phrases and carry out the doctrine of social warfare to its logical and bloody conclusion? Whose is the responsibility? Who is the greater criminal? Luccheni or the silken poet who set him on?"

And behind these more or less gentle and philosophic pathfinders in anarchism have come the "doers of the word"—the redhanded assassins of history.

Not long ago Count Malesta, leader of the Italian anarchists, in his suave, gentle, aristocratic attitudes, deplored the use of bombs, pistol, and knife. Yet who will question that Herr Most has drawn inspiration from this teacher, and this schooling was behind that rabid creature's utterance, following the assassination of Carnot, when Most said:

"Whosoever wants to undertake an assassination should at first learn to use the weapon with which he desires to accomplish his purpose before he brings that weapon definitely into play. Attempts by means of the revolver are utterly played out, because out of twenty-five attempts only one is successful, as experience has thoroughly shown. Only expert dead shots may thoroughly rely on their ability to kill. No more child's play! Serious labor! Long live the torch and bomb!"

This is the pupil of the school. Of its tutors, even Kropotkin has been described as a "gentle, courtly, aristocratic patriarch of revolt." He was wealthy, famous, and furiously aristocratic when, in 1872, studying the Swiss glaciers, he stumbled upon the Geneva convention of internationalists and became an anarchist. He returned to the Russian court. His work on the glaciers of Finland became a classic. His lectures on geology and geography were attracting crowds, even while a red revolutionist, Borodin, was stirring police and military with his utterances to workingmen. One night the police trapped Borodin—and Kropotkin. For three years he was confined in prison until he escaped, making his way to London and to the world, which still listens to his voice.

Louise Michel, even, is described as an eager, enthusiastic old woman of much gentleness of manner. She is credited with an unselfishness and self-abnegation that would fit the character of a sister of charity. Virile and keen of intellect, her presence is said to attract, rather than repel, and yet her cry is for freedom, based on force against the machinery of law.

Johann Most has been recognized as the link between the German and English anarchism and the representative of the "propaganda of action." He is the avowed patron of the bomb, and in the present case of Czolgosz some of the instructions which he has vouchsafed to readers of his journal, Freedom, may have a bearing, as for instance, the rule that "never more than one anarchist should take charge of the attempt, so that in case of discovery the anarchist party may suffer as little harm as possible."

France has been especially active in this scrutiny of the followers of the red flag. The government's spy system is almost perfect. Scarcely a meeting may be held on French soil that a government shadow is not somewhere in the background.

In Russia both the police and military arms keep watch upon suspects. London for years has been a hotbed of anarchistic talk and scheming, and even there the system of secret espionage is maintained. Regent's Park on a Sunday afternoon may be full of inflammatory speechmaking, but it is regarded as a harmless venting of spleen in most cases; the actual movements of dangerous anarchists are closely observed.

The United States government at Washington has a list of names and photographs of all the known anarchists of the world.

No city in America has had more experience in dealing with dangerous anarchists than Chicago. As early as 1850 there were disciples of anarchy among the foreign element there, but no attention was paid to them until as late as 1873, when they formed a political party and were more or less noisy for several years. In 1877, during the great railroad strike, they had their first clash with the police and several were killed, and many wounded. Thanksgiving Day, 1884, under the leadership of Albert R. Parsons, August Spies, Sam Fielden, and others they hoisted the black flag and marched through the fashionable residence district of the city, uttering groans and using threatening language. Subsequently they threatened to blow up the new Board of Trade building, and marched past the edifice one night, but were headed off by the police. Parsons, when asked afterward why they had not blown up the Board of Trade building, replied that they had not looked for police interference and were not prepared. "The next time," he said, "we will be prepared to meet them with bombs and dynamite." Fielden reiterated the same sentiments and expressed the opinion that in the course of a year they might be ready for the police.

During all these years the anarchist leaders had openly preached violence, and had taught their followers how to make dynamite bombs. They went so far as to give in detail their plans for fighting the police and militia, and caused more or less consternation among the timid residents of the city.

The local authorities made no effort to stop any of these proceedings. Mayor Harrison believed that repressive measures would be useless and considered that to allow the anarchists to talk would gratify their vanity and preclude the possibility of riot. That such a belief was fallacious, subsequent events proved.

In 1886 came the agitation for the establishment of the eight-hour day, and the anarchist leaders were prominent therein. The first collision between the anarchists and the police came at the McCormick reaper works. There was a sharp fight and the police dispersed the rioters. It was said that many workingmen were killed in that fight, but the story was exaggerated, no one being killed. The anarchists held secret meetings at once and devised a plan to revenge themselves on the police, and to burn and sack the city. As a first step, and for the purpose of demoralizing the police force, a public meeting was called to be held in the Haymarket Square on the night of May 4. The meeting was really held on Desplaines street, between Randolph and Lake streets. Parsons, Spies and Fielden spoke from a wagon in front of Crane's foundry, until the police came up to disperse the meeting, on account of the violent character of the utterances. Inspector Bonfield and Captain Ward were in charge of the police, and no sooner had Captain Ward called upon the crowd to disperse than a bomb was hurled into the midst of the unsuspecting policemen. It burst with a loud report, knocking down nearly every one of the one hundred and twenty-five men in the detail and badly wounding many.

Inspector Bonfield at once rallied his men, and charged the mob with a resistless rush that carried everything before them. After the square had been cleared the officers began to attend to their wounded comrades. Only one, M. J. Degan, had been instantly killed, although seven died afterward from their injuries. Sixty-eight others were injured, some so badly that they were maimed for life, and incapacitated for work.

Of all the men who were subsequently arrested for this crime, only eight were placed on trial. These were August Spies, Michael Schwab, Samuel Fielden, Albert R. Parsons, Adolph Fischer, George Engel, and Louis Lingg, who were found guilty and sentenced to death, and Oscar Neebe, who was sentenced to fifteen years in the penitentiary. Lingg committed suicide by blowing his head to pieces with a bomb while confined in the jail awaiting execution. The sentences of Schwab and Fielden were commuted to imprisonment for life by Governor Oglesby. The other four were hanged in the county jail on November 11, 1887. They were buried at Waldheim cemetery the following Sunday, November 13, and this occasion was made memorable by the honors shown the dead by the anarchist societies of Chicago. It was the last great outpouring of anarchy that the city has seen. Schwab, Fielden, and Neebe were afterward pardoned by Governor Altgeld, and released from the penitentiary.

Looking back upon the work of anarchy in the last fifty years or more its results should be discouraging to any but the most hair-brained of the type. Its violence has not altered or unsettled the course of a single government against which it has been directed. If individuals here and there have been murdered the crimes have reacted upon the tools of butchery, most frequently sending the assassin to a dishonored grave, leaving the name of his kinsman a reproach for all time. The seed of ideal anarchy still is being sown, however, and its crop of crimes and criminals may be expected to be harvested in the future, as in the past, unless, by some concerted, radical efforts of civilization its bloody sophistries are to be wiped from the world.

CHAPTER VII.

SCENES AT BUFFALO FOLLOWING THE ASSASSINATION.

The people of Buffalo and the visitors within their gates behaved admirably during all the weary days and nights after the shooting of the President. That spirit of mob law, which pervaded the multitude that surged about the Temple of Music in the Exposition grounds at the time of the shooting, speedily gave way to one of obedience to law. The knowledge that the President's life had not ebbed away, and that eminent physicians said he would recover, had a tendency to restore men's minds to the normal, and soon the question which passed from man to man was "what news from the President?"

Even the thought of wreaking vengeance on the assassin seemed to have fallen into abeyance. The people became quiet in demeanor, but there was constant anxiety that the physicians had not told all, and that the Nation might at any time be called on to mourn the death of its Chief Executive. This feeling was intensified by the hurrying to the city of members of the Cabinet who were not in attendance on the President at the time he faced the assassin. The first trains brought Vice-President Roosevelt, Secretaries Hay, Gage, Root, Long and Hitchcock, Attorney-General Knox and Postmaster-General Smith. Senator Mark Hanna and other close friends of the President also started hastily for Buffalo, and many of them remained there until the end. The presence of these personages, perhaps, had a tendency to quiet public feeling, inasmuch as they one and all bore themselves with marked dignity during the trying time.

When the President was moved from the Exposition grounds to the residence of Mr. Milburn, there were thousands of people in the streets, but there was no disturbance. Only the tenderest sympathy for the stricken President was manifested, and never, during the President's gallant fight for life, was there aught to complain of on the part of the people.

The Milburn home is situated in the center of a large lot on which stand magnificent trees. As it became, from the time the President was taken there, the center of interest for the civilized world, special preparations were made to meet the exigencies of the case. It was necessary that only those should have ingress and egress who had business there, and hence the premises were surrounded with police and soldiers.   Ropes were stretched so that the crowds which were irresistibly drawn to the scene could be more easily kept back, and the most complete arrangements were made to enable the newspaper men to secure and send broadcast the news of the President's condition.   A huge tent was erected on the lawn and there, from day to day, the doctors, members of the Cabinet, the Vice-President and others were importuned by the reporters for hopeful tidings, which they knew not only the people of Buffalo but the world at large so eagerly awaited.

During all this period the police of Buffalo were working desperately to learn the antecedents of Czolgosz, the assassin; to trace his movements, and to ascertain, if possible, whether he had accomplices.   The villainous wretch, whose brutal act had caused all right thinking people to regard him with horror, remained safely in the police station at Buffalo, where he had been taken by the police after the first struggle to keep the people from lynching him.   After recovering from the fright occasioned by his first contact with the outraged people, he became flippant and tried to glorify his terrible crime and invest it with the halo of a service to humanity.   All these facts were promptly conveyed to the people by the newspapers, and served to intensify the feeling against Czolgosz.

When the fact became known that the President was growing worse, and the physicians became guarded in the expressions as to whether he would recover, the people began to gather on the streets and discuss the punishment of the assassin.   As the bulletins became more and more ominous, the feeling rose to fever heat, and there was a rush toward the police station where Czolgosz was confined.   Thousands of excited citizens clamored for the life of the criminal, but the police forced them back.   Two regiments of the National Guard, the Sixty-fifth and Seventy-fourth, were ordered to assemble in their armories to meet any emergency that might arise.

"We do not propose to allow our prisoner to be taken from us," said Superintendent Bull, of the police force.   "We are able to protect him, and we have the Sixty-fifth and Seventy-fourth Regiments under arms if we need them.   No matter how dastardly this man's crime is, we intend for the good name of American people to keep him safe for the vengeance of the law."

The fact that the President lingered until early in the morning, before death ensued, probably prevented any real conflict between the police and the indignant people.

The members of the two regiments were summoned to their armories by messenger, telegraph, and proclamation in theaters and public places.

This news only helped to direct attention from the dying President to the cell which held his assassin.

That these preparations were quite necessary became apparent by 8:30 o'clock Friday night, when the people had assembled in the vicinity of police headquarters in such numbers that the streets were blocked and impassable.

The police roped off all the streets at a distance of three hundred to four hundred feet from the nearest of the buildings and refused to admit any one within that limit. One hundred patrolmen guarded the ropes and fought back the crowds, while ten mounted men galloped to and fro, holding the crowds in repression.

New details of police from the outside stations came in from time to time, and Superintendent Bull kept in constant touch on the telephone with Colonel Welch, who was at the Sixty-fifth armory, less than a mile away.

In order to divert the attention of the excited crowds, the false report that Czolgosz had been spirited away was sent out. While the source cannot be traced, it is believed the report emanated from the police headquarters. The mob was also informed, whenever possible, that there was no reason to believe that there would be a miscarriage of justice, whether through the pretext that the assassin was insanely irresponsible for his act or through the possibility that he might die before justice could be meted out to him.

It was learned indirectly that Superintendent Bull had asked the insanity experts, who have had Czolgosz under their observation for a week, and Police Surgeon Dr. Fowler, who has had charge of the prisoner's physical health, to prepare a statement of the exact truth about the prisoner's health of mind and body.

The President's clothes, which were removed at the Exposition Hospital, were later sent to the Milburn residence, where the pockets were emptied. The attendant told what he found.

In his right-hand trousers pocket was some $1.80 in currency. With these coins was a small silver nugget, well worn, as if the President had carried it as a pocket piece for a long time.

Three small penknives, pearl-handled, were in the pockets of his trousers. Evidently they were gifts that he prized and was in the habit of carrying all of them. Another battered coin, presumably a pocket piece, was in the left-hand pocket.

The President's wallet was well worn and of black leather, about four inches by five. It was marked with his name. In it was $45 in bills. A number of cards, which evidently had rested in the wallet for some time, were in one of the compartments.

In a vest pocket was a silver-shell lead pencil. Three cigars were found. They were not the black perfectos which the President likes, but were short ones which had been given to him at Niagara Falls that day. On two of them he had chewed, much as General Grant used to bite a cigar.

The President's watch was an open-faced gold case American-made time-keeper. Attached to it was the gold chain which the President always wore. No letters, telegrams or papers were found. There was not on the President's person a single clew to his identity, unless it was to be found in the cards in his wallet, which were not examined.

One of the most striking features of the fateful week at Buffalo was the exclusive use of automobiles by the public officials, friends, relatives and physicians on their trips to and from the Milburn residence. Heretofore the modern vehicles were used chiefly for pleasure and many doubted their utility, but on the well-paved streets of Buffalo they were found to have many advantages over carriages drawn by horses. Lines of the motor cabs were stationed a short distance from the house and whenever a call for one was sent out it approached speedily but noiselessly. No sound as loud as a horse's hoof on the pavement was made by the vehicles.

The wounded President was transferred from the Emergency Hospital on the Exposition grounds to the Milburn residence in an automobile, and the horseless carriages were sent to the railroad stations to meet officials and relatives coming to the bedside of the stricken man.

When the startling report of the assassination first sped along the wires, causing grief and consternation everywhere, Senator Hanna was at his home in Cleveland. Hanna was undoubtedly McKinley's most intimate friend in public life, as well as the President's adviser. Hanna was intensely excited by the news and at once began to make plans for reaching Buffalo as soon as possible. A special train could have been made up, but the time to reach the station would have been considerable.

Some one suggested that the Lake Shore Limited, which is the fastest train between Chicago and New York, be flagged near Hanna's home, and this was at once done. The railway officials gave their consent by telephone, and when the train approached near the house—the railroad is but a few rods from the Hanna residence—it slacked up and the Senator boarded it. Steam was put on and the delay made up in a few hours. The train reached Buffalo on time.

MRS. McKINLEY ALONE WITH HER BELOVED DEAD.

PRESIDENT McKINLEY'S BODY LYING IN STATE AT BUFFALO.

Senator Hanna took a hopeful view of the situation, and assured everyone with whom he conversed of the ultimate recovery of the President. He remained at Buffalo until Tuesday, and then returned to Cleveland, where the G. A. R. Encampment was being held. When he parted from the President he stated that in his opinion, for which he relied chiefly on the physicians, McKinley would be well in a month. Hanna spent Wednesday and Thursday in Cleveland, leaving for Buffalo on a special train when notified of the relapse of the patient. The death of McKinley touched Hanna deeply. He had to be led from the bedside on the occasion of the last interview between the two men. He was almost a total collapse, his face was drawn and his entire form trembled.

On Sunday night, September 8th, two days after the President had been shot, and at a time when it was believed he would recover, Senator Hanna had a remarkable dream, prophetic of the fatal end.

On Monday a newspaper correspondent asked him if he had any fears of a relapse, when he replied:

"That reminds me of a dream I had last night. You know dreams go by contraries. Well, sir, in this dream I was up at the Milburn house waiting to hear how the President was getting along, and everybody was feeling very good. We thought the danger was all past. I was sitting there talking with General Brooke and Mr. Cortelyou, and we were felicitating ourselves on how well the physicians had been carrying the case.

"Suddenly, in my dream, Dr. McBurney entered the room through the door leading to the sick room with a look of the utmost horror and distress on his face. I rushed up to him, and putting a hand on either shoulder, said: 'What is it, Doctor? what is it? let us know the worst.'

"Dr. McBurney replied: 'My dear Senator, it is absolutely the worst that could happen. The President has had a tremendous change for the worse; his temperature is now 440 degrees.' I fell back in my chair in utter collapse, and then I awoke. But, do you know, I could not rest easy until I saw the early bulletins this morning?"

Everyone thought of Mrs. McKinley and the hearts of all went out to her in sympathy when it was known that the end was near. They had tried all day to keep the fatal news from her, but it is probable that when she saw the President she divined something of his serious condition. Mrs. McWilliams, Mrs. Barber, Miss Mary McKinley, and Mrs. Duncan were with her and gave her the most tender and loving ministration. The crowds eagerly scanning the bulletin boards feared for her. It was a matter of current belief that the wife never would survive the shock. There were plenty who said and believed that she would not live through the night; that the papers would tell the world that Emma Goldman's disciple had murdered a woman and a frail invalid as well as the President of the United States.

It was recalled that the President had several times spoken of his assassin and that he had expressed satisfaction when he learned that the man had not been injured by the crowd. All this was gratifying, but it failed to alleviate the sorrow of that Friday night and the few hours of Saturday in which the President continued alive. All Buffalo, all the Nation, watched with deepest anxiety hoping against hope.

The devotion to duty of Private Secretary George B. Cortelyou during the long painful days that came between the shooting and the death of President McKinley offers one of the most striking features of the historic tragedy.

When the chief fell wounded Secretary Cortelyou was practically forced to fill a part of the vacant place and assume all of its responsibilities. He was at the side of the President when Leon Czolgosz fired the murderous shots, and upon him rested the immediate responsibility of issuing the order for the surgical operation that was performed at the emergency hospital.

When Mr. McKinley came from the operating table it fell to Mr. Cortelyou to make the arrangements for his shelter and care, and from that time to the end he was called upon to pass judgment upon every grave question that arose except the technical medical and surgical matters in connection with the care of the wounded chieftain.

He stood between the sickroom and the world as far as information on the progress of the case was concerned, and the place called for the most delicate judgment. In addition to his official connection with the dying President it was his duty to supervise all of the private personal affairs of his superior.

In addition to the work which he could do by verbal direction the executive correspondence by mail and wire trebled and quadrupled. It exceeded that of any other period in the public life of Mr. McKinley, including the days that succeeded both his first and second elections. It seemed that Mr. Cortelyou must fail in the mere physical task of handling it, but no physical exaction seemed too great for him.

His personal affection for his chief was complete, and the President's death was a grievous shock to him. He has not faltered, however, and still stands in the place that he must occupy until the last offices have been performed at the grave of Mr. McKinley.

CHAPTER VIII.

DAYS OF ANXIETY AND SORROW.

The Nation was thrown into a state of grief and indignation never before approached at the terrible news from Buffalo Friday, September 6th. Methods for transmitting intelligence have been vastly improved since the assassination of Garfield, since which time no such national calamity has befallen the United States. Poignant regret, intense indignation, and a feeling of dismay mingled in the hearts of the eighty million Americans who stood appalled at the news which swept like wild fire and reached every part of the world in an incredibly short time.

It was an appalling thought that this great republic, with all its promises and all its deeds for oppressed humanity, exposed its chief magistrates to more deadly chances than does any empire or kingdom. But seven men regularly elected Presidents in the last thirty-six years, and three of them brought low with the assassin's bullet!

The news of the attempt on the life of the President was received from one end of the country to the other first with horrified amazement and then with the deepest grief. In every city in the United States men and women gathered and waited for hours to get every scrap of information that came over the wires. In thousands of small towns the whole population stood about the local telegraph offices and watched tearfully and anxiously for bulletins.

Telegraph offices everywhere were swamped with business, messages of sympathy for the President and his wife from almost every man of prominence in the nation, and for hours after the shooting telephone trunk lines were so overburdened that only a small percentage of subscribers were able to secure service.

Dispatches from every State in the Union showed how widespread and intense was the feeling of dismay and the sense of personal affliction with which the news was received. Public men of all shades of political opinion and social status alike shared the anxiety and found themselves grasping hands with one another and praying that Mr. McKinley's life might be spared. All the details of the tragedy were sought for with trembling eagerness, and in all the large centers of population every effort was made to supply this demand by the newspapers, which issued extras at intervals till far into the night.

Early Saturday morning began arrangements for public prayer in many of the churches on Sunday. Archbishop Ireland of the Catholic Church, Bishop Potter, the Episcopal prelate; Cardinal Gibbons of Baltimore, and high church dignitaries of all denominations joined in the universal supplication to the Heavenly Father to spare the life of the stricken President. Fervent were the invocations and the hopeful news of the following days seemed to portend a favorable answer to the prayers of a nation.

Political lines were forgotten and Democrat and Populist was as eager to show respect for the head of the government as the Republicans. It was respect shown a good man; it was also respect shown the Chief Executive occupying an exalted position by the suffrage of the people.

At the moment when the country was enshrouded in the gloom of the awful tragedy, when it was bowed with its own sorrow and overflowing with sympathy for the bereaved widow, consideration of the dead statesman's career and of the political controversies to which it gave rise, was not attempted. So quick had been the revulsion of feeling, so terrible the shock, that the one emotion of grief was overmastering and all-absorbing.

It had been said many times during the era of alternate hope and fear that Mr. McKinley was the most beloved of our Presidents since Lincoln, and the frequency of the assertion in every quarter and among all classes of people is excellent evidence of its truth. Nor are the reasons for his exceptional hold on the affections of the people far to seek. He had to begin with that sweet and winning personality which captivated everyone who saw him. Thousands felt its influence at Buffalo on the day when the wretched murderer committed his deadly assault, and they responded to it with an affectionate regard, as other thousands had done among the many crowded assemblages with which the President had so freely mingled.

A feeling of tenderest love and veneration was excited also by the knowledge of the beautiful life's devotion of the most thoughtful, considerate and gentlest of husbands. Toward the wife, whom he had ever near him, the President was a ministering angel. In caring for her he evinced the delicacy of a woman, the strength of the strongest of men. May she find resignation in that submission which he taught her, saying: "God's will, not ours, be done."

That such a noble, true soul, such a high-minded man should have been struck down in the very fullness of his powers, when his great abilities were receiving a broadening recognition and he was still growing in the affectionate esteem of his countrymen, caused universal lamentation.

Ex-President Grover Cleveland was fishing at Darling Lake, in Tyringham, Mass., when he received the news regarding the shooting of President McKinley. He at once started for the shore in order to hear more details in regard to the matter, and anxiously asked for the latest advices from Mr. McKinley's bedside. Mr. Cleveland was horrified at the news and said:

"With all American citizens, I am greatly shocked at this news. I cannot conceive of a motive. It must have been the act of a crazy man."

Following receipt of the news of the attempt on his life, W. J. Bryan sent a brief message to President McKinley expressing his concern. Mr. Bryan gave out the following statement:

"The attempted assassination of the President is a shock to the entire country, and he and his wife are the recipients of universal sympathy. The dispatches say that the shot was fired by an insane man, and it is hoped that this is true, for while it is a terrible thing for a President to be the victim of the act of a maniac, it would be even worse for him to be fired upon by a sane person prompted by malice or revenge.

"In a republic where the people elect their officials and can remove them there can be no excuse for a resort to violence. If our President were in constant fear of plots and conspiracies we would soon sink to the level of those nations in which force is the only weapon of the government, and the only weapon of the government's enemies."

An intensity of sympathy was manifested in Canton, for 30 years the home of the McKinleys, for President and Mrs. McKinley, rarely equalled. Cantonians who have so long known them felt that the life of the President meant the life of Mrs. McKinley; his death, they believed, would likely mean the death of Mrs. McKinley in a short time. Eager residents of all classes surrounded telegraph and newspaper offices and watched for bulletins from the bedside of the patient.

In addition to the private expressions of deepest regret and sympathy, public action was taken by many organizations. The commander of Canton Post, G. A. R., of which Mr. McKinley was a member, telegraphed Secretary Cortelyou:

"The President's comrades of Post No. 25 desire to tender him their profoundest sympathy and to express earnest hopes for his safe recovery."

The official body of the First Methodist Episcopal Church, of which the President was a member, adopted resolutions, which say:

"Dear Brother McKinley:—The fourth quarterly conference in this church, now in session, has learned with unspeakable sorrow of the most deplorable incident of which you are the victim. The brethren are deeply concerned and unite

in agonizing importunities that God may intervene to avert serious consequences and graciously minister to you all needed spiritual comfort and grant
you speedy and complete physical recovery. We also extend to your dear wife
assurances of our profoundest and most prayerful sympathy, trusting God may
comfort her in the great trial through which you are passing."

Life at Washington was enveloped in sadness during the fateful week. In
every quarter expressions of the profoundest sympathy were heard. The wish
foremost in the minds of all was that the President be spared, and whenever
encouraging advices were received from Buffalo there was a general feeling of
rejoicing.

Officials of the government who were too affected by the news first received
to discuss the crime talked more freely later and gave expressions of great indignation at the atrocious act. At the Executive Mansion messages poured in
constantly. There were few callers.

Bulletins were received at the White House hourly announcing Mr. Mc-
Kinley's condition, and those reporting an increase in the President's temperature occasioned concern.

In a mechanical way the executive departments opened on the day following
the assassination, but the employes had no heart to work, and the corridors
were filled with knots of eager seekers after the latest bulletins from the President's sick bed. The excitement in the streets was continuous and crowds lingered around the newspaper bulletin boards, while people walked along with
sober faces and with frequent expressions of sorrow and many anxious inquiries.

At the State Department were received an accumulation of cablegrams and
telegraph messages, all expressing the gravest concern and condolence. These
messages were from all parts of the world. They continued to flow in upon the
department. They came from crowned heads, from foreign ministers, from
resident ministers of foreign countries in the United States and from individuals of distinction. Some of them follow :

Rambouillet, September 7.—With keen affliction I learn the news of
the heinous attempt of which your excellency has just been a victim. I take
it to heart to join with the people of the United States in wishing the early recovery of your excellency, and I earnestly desire in this sorrowful juncture to
renew to you the assurance of my sentiments of constant and cordial friendship.

                                                              Emil Loubet.

Koenigsberg, September 7, 1901.—The Emperor and I, horrified at the attempt planned against your husband, express our deep-felt sympathy, hoping that God may restore to health Mr. McKinley.

William, I. R.
Victoria, I. R.

Rome, September 7, 1901.—Deeply grieved, terrible crime. Trust President will be spared to his country and friends.   Baron Fava.

London, September 7.—Secretary of State, Washington:—Following messages of condolence received:

From His Majesty, the King, to American Ambassador—Offer my deepest sympathy at the dastardly attempt on the President's life. Have telegraphed direct to President.

From the Lord Mayor of London—The citizens of London have received with profound regret and great indignation intelligence of the dastardly attack on the life of the distinguished President of the United States and desire to convey through your excellency their sincere sympathy with your country in this melancholy event. They trust that so valuable a life as President McKinley's may be spared for the welfare of the American people.

From Vice Dean of Canterbury Cathedral—Accept expression of deep sorrow at outrage upon President. Prayers offered for his recovery at all services in Canterbury Cathedral.

From Lord Provost of Edinburgh—In the name of the citizens of Edinburgh I beg to express horror at the dastardly outrage upon President McKinley and to assure him and Mrs. McKinley and the government and people of the United States of our sympathy with them and prayers for President's recovery.

From Field Marshal Lord Roberts—Please convey to President and Mrs. McKinley on behalf of myself and the British army our profound regret at what has occurred and our earnest hope that Mr. McKinley's valuable life may be spared.   Choate, Ambassador.

London and all England received the news of the attempt on Mr. McKinley's life with incredulity. Every newspaper and every hotel was besieged with anxious Americans inquiring for the latest intelligence of the reported assassination.

King Edward VII. and Queen Alexandra were traveling in Germany when the news of the assassination reached them. They were greatly shocked. Police guards on the train and along the route were at once ordered increased, as it was feared the shooting of the President at Buffalo might induce some European anarchist to make an attempt on the life of King Edward.

In spite of the late hour at which the news of the attempted assassination of President McKinley reached Paris the report that the American President had been fatally wounded caused the greatest excitement on the boulevards. The occupants of the cafes left their late suppers, rushing in hot haste from the tables to the newspaper offices to verify the news.

Immediately the outburst of sorrow over the attempt on President McKinley's life was spent, comment in Berlin was universally directed against what was termed America's guilty lenity toward the anarchistic fraternity.

The tenderest sympathy and praise of McKinley mingled with deep abhorrence of the crime and vehement denunciation of the teachings that inspired it from every part of the South prove conclusively that the love for the martyr President was as great there as in the North.

It is significant that much of this laudatory comment was coupled with grateful recognition of the work done by the President in unifying the two sections of the country. It is doubtful if the President's most zealous admirers in the North can surpass in fervor of affectionate regard many of the editorial tributes in the Southern press.

A few discordant notes—not sufficient to merit more than passing notice, however—marred the general voice of sympathy and condolence. In an interview regarding the attempt to take the President's life, Senator Wellington of Maryland was reported as saying:

"McKinley and I are enemies. I have nothing good to say about him, and under the circumstances do not care to say anything bad. I am indifferent to the whole matter."

The Senator subsequently refused to deny the interview, and his silence was construed as an affirmation of it. For this unpatriotic utterance the Atlanta Journal editorially called upon the United States Senate to expel him from that body as being unfit to represent the people of Maryland in the highest council of the nation.

In various parts of the country reflections on the President or expression of pleasure at the crime led to rough treatment by indignant crowds. Only cool heads saved several detractors of McKinley from being lynched. Here and there an anarchist would attempt to incite the crowd in behalf of the assassin, but all such attempts were repulsed and the demagogues arrested or driven from the town.

After the first great wave of sorrow and despair had swept the land, the bulletins from Buffalo brought back hope. From Sunday on to Thursday the indication grew more favorable and the fact that recovery seemed assured led many churches to arrange thanksgiving services.

The day of prayer seemed to have passed, the prayer granted and the hearts of a grateful people were set on a day of thanksgiving. Among earnest Christian men and women the desire to anticipate the regular annual thanksgiving festival was universal, and even such persons as have little faith in the efficacy of prayer approved the suggestion that there should be some common recognition of our national good fortune in the escape of the President from death.

Messages of congratulation poured in on the relatives and friends at Buffalo by the hundreds, hope rose high, and cheerful faces shone where all had been gloom. This buoyant feeling continued until Thursday night at Buffalo, and only on Friday morning did the nation learn of the change for the worse.

Among the cablegrams of congratulations sent by European rulers were those from the King of England, the Czar of Russia, the King of Greece and the Emperor of Austria.

The following dispatch was received at the American Embassy at London:

"I am delighted to hear your last most satisfactory account of your President. I sincerely trust that his convalescence may soon be completed.
                                                    "Edward, R."

The following message was received from the Czar of Russia:

"Fredensborg—To President McKinley, Buffalo, N. Y:—I am happy to hear you are feeling better after the ignominious attempt on your life. I join with the American people and the universal world for your speedy recovery.
                                                    "Nicholas."

The following message was received from King George of Greece at Fredensborg:

"I rejoice to hear that you so happily escaped the terrible attempt on your precious life, which has horrified the civilized world, but hope to God that you recover for the good and glory of the American people."

Emperor Francis Joseph of Austria sent an expression of his sympathy at the probable recovery of the President to the United States government to-day. The dispatch was sent through the American Embassy.

On Thursday all was hopefulness; on Friday gloom and fear; on Saturday heads bowed in mourning. Death came with an awful suddenness, notwithstanding the week of suffering. The passionate hope that the President would recover had been followed by a feeling of perfect assurance that he was out of danger, when the wholly unexpected news of Friday put the people on the rack again. There was another torturing day, and when it ended hope and confidence had yielded to universal grief and to a fruitless questioning of the impenetrable ways of Providence. It seemed inexplicably strange that a man so beloved and unoffending and so rich in good works should have been made the victim of the assassin's bullet.

All day long the bulletin boards in every city were surrounded by crowds waiting in suppressed excitement for the latest word from the Milburn home, and numerous newspaper extras were eagerly snapped up.

Every household in Washington was in mourning. The sorrow was complete. Large crowds assembled about the bulletin boards early in the evening of the memorable day, eagerly awaiting the latest news, hoping against hope that something would happen, in the mysterious workings of the Almighty, to spare the President.

The oldest citizens cannot remember when a calamity brought to the national capital such profound grief. The excitement was more intense when Lincoln succumbed to the bullets of the assassin, Booth, and the people sincerely mourned him, but while he was widely loved, his death did not so afflict the people. Garfield was generally admired, and the calamity that overtook him awakened the sympathy of the people, but he was not mourned as was McKinley.

If the precedents set by President Arthur are followed by President Roosevelt, the coming winter will be entirely devoid of official gayety. The official mourning will extend over six months and will be rigorously observed. This period will include New Year's and the usual courtesies extended to the diplomatic corps, the Congress, the judiciary and the army and navy. The official mourning will end on March 14, 1902, and as this date falls after Shrove Tuesday, the official social season will be allowed to lapse. Therefore the New Year's reception of 1903 will in all probability be the first formal gathering of the official and social world at the White House.

Half-masted flags and black column rules mutely proclaimed England's sentiments touching the death of President McKinley. These symbols of mourning, countless in their multitudes, visibly recalled the country's grief at the loss of Queen Victoria. Not only on land, but also at sea, the British honored the martyr President. Thousands of buildings, both public and private, and all the shipping around the coast, flew the Union Jack half-way up the staff. Every British war ship within reach of the telegraph displayed its ensign of sorrow.

The Pope prayed an hour to-day for the soul of President McKinley. The pontiff wept with uncontrollable emotion on receiving the news of the President's death. All audiences at the vatican were suspended.

CHAPTER IX.

PRESIDENT McKINLEY'S LAST SPEECH.

President McKinley's last speech, delivered on President's Day at the Pan-American Exposition, September 5, the day before he was shot, was the greatest speech of his life. It was a message to all the world, robust in its Americanism, and fraught with good will for all nations and all mankind. It was as follows:

"President Milburn, Director General Buchanan, Commissioners, Ladies and Gentlemen:—I am glad to be again in the city of Buffalo and exchange greetings with her people, to whose generous hospitality I am not a stranger, and with whose good will I have been repeatedly and signally honored.

"To-day I have additional satisfaction in meeting and giving welcome to the foreign representatives assembled here, whose presence and participation in this exposition have contributed in so marked a degree to its interests and success. To the commissioners of the Dominion of Canada and the British colonies, the French colonies, the republics of Mexico and of Central and South America and the commissioners of Cuba and Porto Rico, who share with us in this undertaking, we give the hand of fellowship and felicitate with them upon the triumphs of art, science, education and manufacture which the old has bequeathed to the new century.

"Expositions are the timekeepers of progress. They record the world's advancement. They stimulate the energy, enterprise and intellect of the people and quicken human genius. They go into the home. They broaden and brighten the daily life of the people. They open mighty storehouses of information to the student.

BENEFIT IN EXPOSITIONS.

"Every exposition, great or small, has helped to some onward step. Comparison of ideas is always educational, and as such instructs the brain and hand of man. Friendly rivalry follows, which is the spur to industrial improvement, the inspiration to useful invention and to high endeavor in all departments of human activity. It exacts a study of the wants, comforts, and even the whims of the people and recognizes the efficacy of high quality and low prices to win their favor.

"The quest for trade is an incentive to men of business to devise, invent, improve and economize in the cost of production. Business life, whether among ourselves or with other people, is ever a sharp struggle for success. It will be none the less so in the future. Without competition we would be clinging to the clumsy and antiquated processes of farming and manufacture and the methods of business of long ago, and the twentieth would be no further advanced than the eighteenth century. But though commercial competitors we are, commercial enemies we must not be.

INVITES FRIENDLY RIVALRY.

"The Pan-American Exposition has done its work thoroughly, presenting in its exhibits evidences of the highest skill and illustrating the progress of the human family in the western hemisphere. This portion of the earth has no cause for humiliation for the part it has performed in the march of civilization. It has not accomplished everything; far from it. It has simply done its best, and without vanity or boastfulness and recognizing the manifold achievements of others, it invites the friendly rivalry of all the powers in the peaceful pursuits of trade and commerce, and will co-operate with all in advancing the highest and best interests of humanity.

"The wisdom and energy of all the nations are none too great for the world's work. The success of art, science, industry and invention is an international asset and a common glory. After all, how near one to the other is every part of the world. Modern inventions have brought into close relation widely separated peoples, and made them better acquainted. Geographic and political divisions will continue to exist, but distances have been effaced.

ANNIHILATION OF SPACE.

"Swift ships and fast trains are becoming cosmopolitan. They invade fields which a few years ago were impenetrable. The world's products are exchanged as never before, and with increasing transportation facilities come increasing knowledge and trade. Prices are fixed with mathematical precision by supply and demand. The world's selling prices are regulated by market and crop reports. We travel greater distances in a shorter space of time, and with more ease than was ever dreamed of by the fathers.

"Isolation is no longer possible or desirable. The same important news is read, though in different languages, the same day in all Christendom.

The telegraph keeps us advised of what is occurring everywhere, and the press foreshadows, with more or less accuracy, the plans and purposes of the nations.   Market prices of products and of securities are hourly known in every commercial mart, and the investments of the people extend beyond their own national boundaries into the remotest parts of the earth.   Vast transactions are conducted and international exchanges are made by the tick of the cable.   Every event of interest is immediately bulletined.

COMPARISON IS DRAWN.

"The quick gathering and transmission of news, like rapid transit, are of recent origin, and are only made possible by the genius of the inventor and the courage of the investor.   It took a special messenger of the government, with every facility known at the time for rapid travel, nineteen days to go from the City of Washington to New Orleans with a message to General Jackson that the war with England had ceased and a treaty of peace had been signed.

"How different now! We reached General Miles in Porto Rico by cable, and he was able through the military telegraph to stop his army on the firing line with the message that the United States and Spain had signed a protocol suspending hostilities. We knew almost instantly of the first shots fired at Santiago, and the subsequent surrender of the Spanish forces was known at Washington within less than an hour of its consummation.   The first ship of Cervera's fleet had hardly emerged from that historic harbor when the fact was flashed to our capital and the swift destruction that followed was announced immediately through the wonderful medium of telegraphy.

DARK DAYS AT PEKING.

"So accustomed are we to safe and easy communication with distant lands that its temporary interruption, even in ordinary times, results in loss and inconvenience. We shall never forget the days of anxious waiting and awful suspense when no information was permitted to be sent from Peking, and the diplomatic representatives of the nations in China, cut off from all communication inside and outside of the walled capital, were surrounded by an angry and misguided mob that threatened their lives; nor the joy that thrilled the world when a single message from the government of the United States brought through our minister the first news of the safety of the besieged diplomats.

"At the beginning of the nineteenth century there was not a mile ö steam railroad on the globe. Now there are enough miles to make its circuit many times. Then there was not a line of electric telegraph; now we have vast mileage traversing all lands and all seas.

"God and man have linked the nations together. No nation can longer be indifferent to any other. And as we are brought more and more in touch with each other the less occasion is there for misunderstandings and the stronger the disposition, when we have differences, to adjust them in the court of arbitration, which is the noblest forum for the settlement of international disputes.

PROSPERITY OF THE NATION.

"My fellow citizens, trade statistics indicate that this country is in a state of unexampled prosperity. The figures are almost appalling. They show that we are utilizing our fields and forests and mines and that we are furnishing profitable employment to the millions of workingmen through-out the United States, bringing comfort and happiness to their homes and making it possible to lay by savings for old age and disability.

"That all the people are participating in this great prosperity is seen in every American community and shown by the enormous and unprecedented deposits in our savings banks. Our duty is the care and security of these deposits, and their safe investment demands the highest integrity and the best business capacity of those in charge of these depositories of the people's earnings.

"We have a vast and intricate business, built up through years of toil and struggle, in which every part of the country has its stake, which will not permit of either neglect or of undue selfishness. No narrow, sordid policy will subserve it. The greatest skill and wisdom on the part of the manufacturers and producers will be required to hold and increase it. Our industrial enterprises, which have grown to such great proportions, affect the homes and occupations of the people and the welfare of the country. Our capacity to produce has developed so enormously and our products have so multiplied that the problem of more markets requires our urgent and immediate attention.

FOR ENLIGHTENED POLICY.

"Only a broad and enlightened policy will keep what we have. No other policy will get more. In these times of marvelous business energy and gain we ought to be looking to the future, strengthening the weak places in our industrial and commercial systems, so that we may be ready for any storm or strain.

"By sensible trade arrangements which will not interrupt our home production we shall extend the outlets for our increasing surplus. A system which provides a mutual exchange of commodities is manifestly essential to the continued healthful growth of our export trade. We must not repose in fancied security that we can forever sell everything and buy little or nothing. If such a thing were possible it would not be best for us or for those with whom we deal. We should take from our customers such of their products as we can use without harm to our industries and labor.

"Reciprocity is the natural outgrowth of our wonderful industrial development under the domestic policy now firmly established. What we produce beyond our domestic consumption must have a vent abroad. The excess must be relieved through a foreign outlet and we should sell everywhere we can and buy wherever the buying will enlarge our sales and productions, and thereby make a greater demand for home labor.

NEED OF EXPANSION.

"The period of exclusiveness is past. The expansion of our trade and commerce is the pressing problem. Commercial wars are unprofitable. A policy of good will and friendly trade relations will prevent reprisals. Reciprocity treaties are in harmony with the spirit of the times; measures of retaliation are not. If perchance some of our tariffs are no longer needed for revenue or to encourage and protect our industries at home, why should they not be employed to extend and promote our markets abroad?

"Then, too, we have inadequate steamship service. New lines of steamers have already been put in commission between the Pacific coast ports of the United States and those on the western coasts of Mexico and Central and South America. These should be followed up with direct steamship lines between the eastern coast of the United States and South American ports. One of the needs of the times is direct commercial lines from our vast fields of production to the fields of consumption that we have but barely touched. Next in advantage to having the thing to sell is to have the convenience to carry it to the buyer.

"We must encourage our merchant marine. We must have more ships. They must be under the American flag, built and manned and owned by

Americans. These will not be profitable in a commercial sense; they will be messengers of peace and amity wherever they go.

"We must build the isthmian canal, which will unite the two oceans and give a straight line of water communication with the western coasts of Central America, South America and Mexico. The construction of a Pacific cable cannot be longer postponed.

GIVES BLAINE CREDIT.

"In furtherance of these objects of national interest and concern you are performing an important part. This exposition would have touched the heart of that American statesman whose mind was ever alert and thought ever constant for a larger commerce and a truer fraternity of the republics of the new world. His broad American spirit is felt and manifested here. He needs no identification to an assemblage of Americans anywhere, for the name of Blaine is inseparably associated with the Pan-American movement, which finds this practical and substantial expression, and which we all hope will be firmly advanced by the Pan-American congress that assembles this autumn in the capital of Mexico.

"The good work will go on. It cannot be stopped. These buildings will disappear, this creation of art and beauty and industry will perish from sight, but their influence will remain to

"Make it live beyond its too short living
With praises and thanksgiving.

"Who can tell the new thoughts that have been awakened, the ambitions fired and the high achievements that will be wrought through this exposition?

"Gentlemen, let us ever remember that our interest is in concord, not conflict, and that our real eminence rests in the victories of peace, not those of war. We hope that all who are represented here may be moved to higher and nobler effort for their own and the world's good, and that out of this city may come not only greater commerce and trade for us all, but, more essential than these, relations of mutual respect, confidence and friendship, which will deepen and endure.

"Our earnest prayer is that God will graciously vouchsafe prosperity, happiness and peace to all our neighbors and like blessings to all the peoples and powers of earth."

SECRETARY OF STATE, JOHN HAY.

THE U. S. CAPITOL BUILDING, WASHINGTON, D. C.

CHAPTER X.

WILLIAM McKINLEY'S BOYHOOD.

William McKinley was born in Ohio, his ancestors having emigrated to the United States from County Antrim, Ireland. In that ancestry, also, was mingled some of the sterling blood of the Scottish race, and it seems the child who was destined to become twenty-fifth President of the United States combined in his nature the choicest qualities of both races, enriched and broadened by generations of American life. His great-grandfather, David McKinley, was the son of a Revolutionary soldier, and was born in Pennsylvania the year before peace with England was declared.

After the independence of the United States had been achieved, this David McKinley was brought by his soldier father from York to Westmoreland County, Pa., and the lad himself, as he grew to manhood, chose the new State of Ohio as a place of residence, and established there the fortunes and the hopes of the McKinley family.

His grandson, William McKinley, the father of the President, was the second child in a family **of** thirteen, and was born at New Lisbon, Ohio. He was engaged in the iron and foundry business, and resided successively at New Lisbon, Niles, Poland and finally Canton. It was while engaged in the iron industry, then in a primitive stage of development, at Niles, Ohio, that William McKinley, the elder, met and married Miss Nancy Campbell Allison, daughter of a well-to-do business man in the growing Ohio town. And there was born, on January 29, 1843, William McKinley, subject of this biography, and a third martyr President of the United States. The father was at that time manager and part owner of an iron furnace. But seeing greater possibilities in the newer region about Poland, he disposed of his interests at Niles, and removed thither, where he again established a forge.

Surrounding the rising town of Poland lies a fine agricultural country, and in the healthful environment of rural scenes and labor's activities the earliest years of the life of William McKinley, Jr., were spent. Through his mother's family he traced his lineage back to the substantial middle classes of England. And this excellent woman must have possessed in mind and soul and bodily frame the better qualities of the Anglo-Saxon race. Her influence upon this son was pronounced from the beginning; and it seems that an almost prophetic power was given her, for if the whole of the future had been revealed to her she could have guided him no more wisely, could have laid with no more sagacious skill the foundations which his career as statesman and as man required.

And no mother was ever more devotedly loved by son than was this American matron by William McKinley. Throughout her life he made her comfort his own care, and maintained with an increasing tenderness the gentle bearing which, as a child, had been part of his life. In her age, when she had lived to see her son elevated to the chiefest office in the Nation, the beauty of that filial attachment appealed to the people, and untold thousands proved their appreciation when they lovingly bestowed upon her the title, "Mother McKinley."

One of the reasons for the elder McKinley's removal to Poland was that his children might have the advantages of the better schools which— oddly enough—flourished in the younger city. An academy had been established there; and when young William passed through the preparatory years, he was admitted to that institution. As he passed from childhood to youth's estate, he filled the months of vacation in productive labor. At times he worked upon the farms which surrounded the growing, thriving town. At other times he engaged as a clerk in one or other of the stores. But he was never apt at a trade, and really had not the faculty to "buy, and sell, and get gain," as had his younger brother Abner. And as a consequence he maintained that attitude of balance which left him free in his development, and permitted that ripening and broadening of his mind in all directions which the early adoption of a mercantile life would almost certainly have prevented. And it was proof of still another virtue on the lad's part that he preferred, of all the industries that came to his hand, the heavy labor of the forge and foundry. Those years of healthful life, when native powers were developed by bodily industry, when regular hours, plain but abundant food, and long hours of restful sleep were adding to brain and brawn, when the wise mother was guiding him so gently in morals and manners—in those years the character of the future President, the statesman, the soldier and the American patriot, was formed.

As he acquired more of the learning which the academy placed within his reach, young William employed portions of his vacations in teaching school. Not only did this occupation furnish him admirable discipline and training in the process of his development, but it provided him with rather more money for the further prosecution of his studies.

For it was one of the characteristics of the "McKinley boys" that they PAID THEIR WAY. Although the father might have provided them with all needful books and clothing, paid all their school expenses and provided them with spending money, thus encouraging them in idleness, the wise plan of the iron founder, and of that "Mother McKinley," whom a nation has delighted to honor, did not contemplate such a system. They did plan to encourage independence and self-reliance in their children; and they succeeded in achieving that end.

The first term of school taught by William McKinley, Jr., was in the Kerr District, about four miles from Poland, where he presided over the studies of nearly half a hundred pupils through the winter months of 1859-60. With the money secured he not only assisted in defraying the expenses of his sisters and brother at the academy, for which they were by this time prepared, but he was enabled to enter Alexander College, in the autumn of 1860. Two years before that date he had united with the Methodist Church, and had been received into full communion with the society of that denomination in Poland. And through all the years of his life, to the very end, he maintained that relation. In his later years he had been a regular attendant at the forms of worship, a frequent guest at the conferences of his church; and his counsels have been continually at the service of those high in the management of the affairs of Methodism.

It is told of him with a good deal of interest that in the years following the revival at which his conversion was confessed, he was at once a consistent Christian and a happy young man. He delighted in healthful sports, in games which tested muscle, skill and endurance, and took the heartiest possible interest in life. Those were the years under the calm guidance of the wise mother, when stores of power were laying up against the day of need that should come as manhood brought its duties. He was passing through his formative period under the most normal and healthy conditions possible. And that was the best preparation for the broad requirements, the heavy burdens which the future was to lay upon him.

His brother Abner has said that William was a general favorite; that he had no enemies. And one can well believe it, for throughout his adult life he has gone with friends. No one ever hated him. No one ever received an affront at his hands. There is a foolish adage that a man is weak and inconsequential who makes no enemies; that such a character can not be positive, yet that would be a perverse or an ill-informed man who would say William McKinley was either weak or of the negative type of life. And as he has been in manhood, so he was in the early days about the town of Poland. He knew all the workmen in the iron mills, and all the farmers for miles around. He understood them perfectly, and the bond of sympathy for them which was planted in his breast while yet a lad was one of the guides by which he shaped legislation when he came to be a man. His boyish frankness and simplicity and generosity remained permanent traits in his character to the end.

William McKinley, Sr., was a whig, and one of the thousands who marched from that old party into the ranks of the Republicans. Young William had read a great deal. His youthful fancy had been stirred with the stories of California gold, and the Overland Trail. His home was fairly supplied with such reading as is good for a boy, and a part of it dealt with the adventures and the activities of Colonel John C. Fremont. That "Pathfinder," as his friends called him, was a hero to young William. More impressive far than the stories of wealth in the mines were the reports of Fremont's expeditions. More attractive than the magnet which drew adventurers to the new Eldorado was the unspoken yearning to become a member of one of Colonel Fremont's bands of explorers.

And so it is small wonder that his heart glowed with enthusiasm when Fremont was made the nominee of the young Republican party in 1856. He was thirteen years old then, and a stout, healthy boy, with a healthy American boy's appetite for politics. So he shouted the campaign cries of the party, and sang the songs which lauded Fremont to the skies—as well as those less amiable songs which had for their motive the prophesying of defeat for Buchanan.

The result of the election in 1856 was never much in doubt, except to the sanguine youths who mistook their own earnestness for "indications." But the defeat of his champion did not weigh heavily on the lad's heart; and before the next national election came around he was almost man grown, with something of education, with four more years of activity and helpfulness for his family. But it would be impossible for a lad to enter with more earnestness into a cause than he gave to the hosts who were rallying to the support of Lincoln in 1860.

Young William had already taken an active interest in politics. He had "supported" Fremont because that explorer, traveler and soldier had won his honest admiration through many deeds of heroism. But he gave his allegiance to Lincoln because he had read, and because he understood the issues of the day, and believed the "Railsplitter of Illinois" was right. He could not vote for Lincoln that first time, but he could give the aid which politicians know is of value in campaigns. And so he was a member of the circles that marched and sang for the candidate—for freedom's champion.

And he was given to debating, even in those early days. He was naturally a public speaker. He could arrange his argument, marshal his points and present them; and he could thrill his hearers with the genuine eloquence which is not learned, but comes spontaneous from the lips that have been touched with the wand of genius.

He was a reader at all times. And one of the books that made an indelible impression upon him was "Uncle Tom's Cabin." It came in his most impressionable years, and did much to fill his soul with a hatred of human slavery—did much to prepare him for the services of those later years, when he seconded to the limit of his powers the work of the Great Liberator. He had followed the fortunes of Uncle Tom and of Eliza, and regarded them as types. And he was quite certain the horrors of human slavery were fairly depicted in the story.

Among the few but excellent books in his father's possession was one called "Noble Deeds of American Women;" and the reading of it in that period of his youth impressed upon him vividly the struggles and sacrifices of the maids and matrons of the earlier day. The book had not many companions, for libraries were not large in those days; and it will be remembered that the house where William McKinley's boyhood was spent was the home of a workingman.

It was a foreman of workingmen, to be sure, and one who had from time to time an interest in the modest business which he conducted. But yet it was a home where actual toil was by no means unknown; where the mother was the housekeeper, performing with her own hands much of the domestic labor, and where not one of the family was brought up with a contempt for industry.

In those years of transition from boyhood to youth, young William McKinley passed through a period of ill health. It interfered a good deal with his labors at home, and was the cause of cutting short his attendance at the college in Alexandria. It is by no means an unusual phase of a young man's life, and it vanished as he advanced to the years of maturity. Throughout his life, with that exception, he has been a healthy person; and the season of delicate health at the threshold of manhood left no harmful consequences.

In 1896, when one of the enterprising publishers was hurrying to issue a "Campaign Life of William McKinley," he sent a writer into Mahoning and Stark counties, and elsewhere throughout that portion of the Buckeye State, with instructions to find some record of the boyish escapades of young William. The writer found a number of men who had known the nominee in his boyhood, and asked one of them:

"Was he never in mischief—like robbing orchards, or stealing watermelons, or carrying away gates on 'Hallowe'en?'"

The old man thought for a moment, apparently passed the lad's life in review before the judge that abided in his memory, and then he said:

"I don't remember that William was ever in any scrape of any kind."

Then he waited for a moment, filled his pipe, lighted it reflectively and added as he pinched out the flame before throwing the match away:

"And if I did I wouldn't tell it."

The incident proves one of two things. Either young William had all his life the studious regard for the rights of others which has marked his manhood, or he had unconsciously enrolled this staunch old man among the friends who could not possibly be induced to "tell on him." And either view shows the subject of their conversation in a very creditable light.

From infancy until he had attained the age of ten years, the family lived at Niles. The removal from there to Poland, where the Academy could offer better educational advantages to the children, was the last breaking up of home the boy knew. He retained the latter city as his home until after his return from the army, until after the completion of his law studies, when he cast about for a location that promised best for the life he had planned for himself.

But about the old town of Poland are still resident many men and women who knew him as a child, who watched him grow up to sturdy boyhood, and who learned to love him through the years that were adding to his stature and his wisdom. Those friendships he held to the very end. And there is no place in the United States where the blow that came with the news of his assassination fell more heavily than in the boyhood home of William McKinley.

CHAPTER XI.

McKINLEY AS A SOLDIER IN THE CIVIL WAR.

William McKinley was but eighteen years old when the war of the rebellion began.

His enlistment was in every way typical of the man, and representative of the motive and action of the American volunteer. With his cousin, William McKinley Osborne, now United States Consul General at London, he drove to Youngstown, Ohio, in the early summer of 1861, to watch a recently enlisted company of infantrymen at their drill, preparatory to marching away for the field of battle. William McKinley, Sr., was a union man, a Republican, and had been a supporter of both Fremont and Lincoln at the polls. Of course the son had voted for neither, as he still lacked several years of that age at which American youth may exercise the elective franchise. But no man, of any age, had taken a more intense interest in the progress of affairs. He felt the need of supporting the President, and the necessity of preserving the integrity of the nation in all its borders. Nothing could exceed the avidity with which he watched the swiftly accumulating clouds of war and disaster. The love of human freedom, of personal liberty and loyalty to his country were cardinal virtues in the young man's composition. And when war really began he felt a strong desire to give his labor and even his life, if necessary, in the cause which he was certain was the right.

The streets of Youngstown were filled with people, who had gathered to watch the soldiers at their drill, nearly the entire company had been recruited at Poland, and young McKinley personally knew every one of them. After the little band of recruits had gone through their evolutions, and had marched away from Youngstown to the state rendezvous, young William and his cousin Osborne returned to Poland, sobered and inspired to a heroic deed.

The former stated, calmly but firmly, that he felt his duty was to enlist.

"It seems to me the country needs every man who can go," he said, "and I can."

He laid the matter before his mother, and she did not oppose him. That wise woman understood the nature of her son too well to thwart in this day of his greatest experience that advance which she herself had so notably assisted him in making.

So that he, with his cousin Osborne, went to Columbus, as soon as they could set their little affairs in order, and at Camp Chase—named in honor of a man whose genius had already made him famous and powerful —they enlisted in Company E, of the Twenty-third Ohio Volunteer Infantry. When one reflects how promptly Ohio sprang to arms in response to President Lincoln's call for troops, it will be observed that William McKinley embraced a very early opportunity to serve his country. For he enlisted July 30, 1861.

W. S. Rosecrans was the first Colonel of that Twenty-third Ohio, and it had such men as Rutherford B. Hayes and Stanley Matthews on its roster.

Here in the camp, on the march, and in battle young William found the value of his earlier training. His splendid strength, his calm self-control —which made him capable of controlling other men; his better education, and his manly, honorable bearing were all elements in the guaranty of his advancement. At the very first he was chosen a corporal. And at the time of the battle of Antietam, Sept. 17, 1862, he had been promoted to the position of sergeant, and had received the added honor of selection to have charge of the commissary stores. So high an authority as General Rutherford B. Hayes, later Governor of Ohio, and still later President of the United States, has left the following tribute upon record:

"Young as he was, we soon found that in business, in executive ability, young McKinley was a man of rare capacity, of unusual and unsurpassed capacity, especially for a boy of his age. When battles were fought or service was to be performed in warlike things he always took his place. The night was never too dark; the weather was never too cold; there was no sleet, or storm, or hail, or snow, or rain that was in the way of his prompt and efficient performance of every duty."

The bloodiest day of the war, the day on which more men were killed or wounded than on any other one day—was Sept. 17, 1862, in the battle of Antietam.

The battle began at daylight. Before daylight men were in the ranks and preparing for it. Without breakfast, without coffee, they went into the fight, and it continued until after the sun had set. The commissary department of that brigade was under Sergeant McKinley's administration and personal supervision. From his hands every man in the regiment was served with hot coffee and warm meats, a thing that had never occurred under similar circumstances in any other army in the world. He passed under fire and delivered, with his own hands, these things, so essential for the men for whom he was laboring. General Hayes, then a Lieutenant Colonel, was himself wounded at Antietam, and went home on sick leave to recover. While there he related to Governor Tod that circumstance illustrating the cool courage and genuine heroism, and said to the Governor: "Let McKinley be promoted from Sergeant to Lieutenant." And it was done without a moment's delay. When Colonel Hayes returned to the field he assigned Lieutenant McKinley to duty on his staff, and the young man looked back at eighteen months of active service in the ranks as of the greatest possible value to him.

McKinley was still on General Hayes' staff when the battle of Kernstown, July 24, 1864, was fought. Crook's corps had been expecting an easy time when it appeared that the enemy was in force at Kernstown, about four miles from Winchester, where Crook's troops were. There had been some misinformation regarding the Confederate General Early's movements, and the force about to be met was that of Early, which outnumbered Crook's corps three to one. When the battle began one of the regiments was not in position, and Lieutenant McKinley was ordered to bring it in. The road to the regiment needed was through open fields and right in the enemy's line of fire. Shells were bursting on his right and left, but the boy soldier rode on. He reached the regiment, gave the orders to them, and at his suggestion the regiment fired on the enemy and slowly withdrew to take the position where they were assigned. It was a gallant act of the boy soldier, and General Hayes had not expected him to come back alive.

He distinguished himself for gallantry, for good judgment, and military skill at the battle of Opequan. He had been ordered to bring General Duval's troops to join the first division, which was getting into the battle. There was a question of which route to take, and upon the choice depended the very existence of General Duval and his brave men. Lieutenant McKinley weighed the chances swiftly, decided instantly, and on his own responsibility pointed out the direction as he gave his superior officer's command to move. The troops followed his instructions, and came up gallantly and in excellent style, with the smallest possible loss or injury. His own regiment, the Twenty-third Ohio, was less skillfully directed, and suffered the very severe loss of 150 men and officers.

The work accomplished on that day marked young Lieutenant McKinley as both modest and brave.

Early in 1863, William McKinley, Jr., was promoted to the rank of first lieutenant, but was retained on staff duty, as his superior ability, coolness and rare judgment made him invaluable to the regimental commander. That year the regiment saw service almost exclusively in West Virginia, engaged in the scouting duty which alone preserved that territory from falling into the possession of the enemy. It was a wearying year, trying on the men without giving them opportunity to share the glory that more active soldiering would have brought. They were marched east and west, north and south. It was a year of inaction, so far as achieving results were concerned. And in this severer test Lieutenant McKinley proved himself a soldier of the best ability. He kept up that esprit du corps throughout the regiment, without which it would have been ill prepared for service when the time for action came.

This hour—this opportunity—came in late midsummer, when Morgan's raiders swept that terrifying march to the north of the Ohio river—that raid which struck the great North with the shock of a war experience which they had so happily escaped. The Twenty-third was just near enough to hear the summons and fly to the confronting of Morgan and his men. And it was his engagement with McKinley's regiment at Buffington's Island, Ohio, which so crippled the raiders as to completely disarrange their entire plan of campaign, and pave the way for that hopeless march from which they never returned. In that engagement the young Ohio officer bore himself with all bravery, and won a generous share in the honor of crushing the advance of a force which was seriously affecting the moral tone of the whole loyal North.

In the spring of 1864 the Twenty-third marched to Brownstown, on the Kanawha river, where it became a part of the force of General Crook, who was then preparing for his celebrated raid on the Virginia and Tennessee Railroad. The expedition differed little in experience, in danger and in hardship from the everyday service in West Virginia through the previous year. On June 20 the rear of the Union forces, consisting of Hayes' brigade, held Buford Gap against the enemy's advance, and then made a hasty night retreat for the van, supposed to be at Salem. But Hunter was not at Salem. The enemy had attacked and cut off his trains, and had forced him beyond the city. Crook's rear guard was in a manner surrounded, and it was only by rare strategy and brave fighting that he extricated his command from the dilemma. There can be no question the service of Lieutenant William McKinley that day saved the little army, and prevented, in a time when reverses were costly, the recurrence of a Confederate victory.

The retreat before a superior force was kept up without opportunity for rest, and with an insufficient supply of food and ammunition till June 27th, when a safe spot was reached on Big Sewell Mountain. It had been a continuous fight and march for nearly 180 miles. It need not be recited here how General Early's success in the Shenandoah Valley at this time emboldened him to carry his invasion to the very front of Washington, and to challenge a fight for the national capital. It was all too plain that the Union forces under command of Hunter in the valley were unable to cope with the augmented forces of Early. So General ———— sent two corps from the James River country to the rescue of the capital. And it was on that trip that William McKinley, Jr., got his first glimpse of the city of Washington, the capital of the country for which he hoped and prayed, for which he cheerfully imperiled his life.

But Lee had withdrawn from Early's support a body of reinforcements, and the dashing commander of the threatening force was compelled to retreat southward into farther Virginia. It was Lee's one mistake, for he had the capital captured, and might have watched the stars and bars in temporarily triumphal progress down Pennsylvania avenue had he backed up the advance on the Potomac. And the glance which Lieutenant McKinley had of the capitol dome that morning in 1864 would have been the last; for an army of invasion, checked and forced to retire, finds fighting from cover and the consequent burning of buildings one of the inescapable incidents of war.

After the battle of Kernstown—less accurately known as the battle of Winchester—the young soldier from Poland, Ohio, was again promoted, this time to the rank of captain. The document dates his advance from July 25, the day after his wise and heroic conduct in delivering orders under fire, and in piloting the imperiled regiment to its place in the battle formation.

His last battle of importance, and one in which he fittingly crowned a career of gallantry and devotion to duty, was that of Cedar Creek, October 19, 1864. Toward the close of that month the regiment was ordered to Martinsburg. On its march to that point the men voted at the Presidential election. The votes were collected by the judges of election as the column was in march, from among the wagons. It was there McKinley cast his first vote. An ambulance was used as an election booth, and an empty candle-

box did duty as a ballot-box. At the same time and place Generals Sheridan,
Crook and Hayes cast their ballots, and it was the first vote ever cast by
Sheridan or Crook.

Early the following spring the Twenty-third returned to Camp Cumberland and on July 26, 1865, a little more than four years from the time of
enlistment, the regiment was mustered out and the scarred veterans who
had experienced four years of dangers and hardships returned to their homes.

The records show that William McKinley, Jr., enlisted as a private in
Company E of the Twenty-third Ohio Volunteer Infantry on June 11, 1861;
that he was promoted to commissary sergeant on April 15, 1862; that he was
promoted to Second Lieutenant of Company D on September 23, 1862;
that he was promoted to First Lieutenant of Company E on February 7,
1863; that he was promoted to Captain of Company G on July 25, 1864; that
he was detailed as Acting Assistant Adjutant General of the First Division,
First Army Corps, on the staff of General Carroll; that he was brevetted
Major on March 13, 1865, and that he was mustered out of service on July
26, 1865.

"For gallant and meritorious services at the battles of Opequan, Cedar
Creek and Fisher's Hill," reads the document commissioning young McKinley as Brevet Major, signed "A. Lincoln."

This is the brief statement of four years of such activity as are hardly
comprehensible by the sedate citizen in these "piping times of peace;" but
they were years which tried and tested the material of which William Mc-
Kinley was formed, and years in which that symmetrical development of his
whole being went majestically on. As it ripened and quickened his judgment, teaching him self-confidence and the power of rallying resources; as
it planted deep in his nature the love of country and the sense of sacrifice
which proves all patriotism; as it brought him into closer communion with
his fellow men in camp and battle, on the march or in the agonies of the
field hospital—so it developed the physical powers of the vigorous young
man. He has since said, looking at some photographs of himself, taken at
the time of his enlistment: "I was, indeed, a raw recruit."

And he was. The portrait shows him rather slender, and with features
which indicate a certain delicacy and refinement which were far from the
appearance of the ideal soldier of books—the powerful frame, the flashing
eye, the weatherbeaten cheeks "bearded like a pard." And yet he stood that
day of his enlistment, a raw recruit, as the type of millions of his countrymen, as the expression of the best that was in the nation either for peace or

war. And the four years of his slow advance to a major's commission was the most necessary and the most valuable process of development that could possibly have come.

And whether for peace or war, it was the work his nature needed for the service of his nation, for the labors of most value to his people. The beardless boy, delicate in physique, grew to be a rugged, powerful man. The outdoor life, the exposure and hardship, the struggles and suffering and self-control, the planning, the quick decisions, the control of other men had all worked together for the development of a splendid citizen. So that he was mustered out of the service at the end of the war with beard on the lips that had been smooth when he took up the musket of a private soldier, and called back to President Lincoln, in the chorus of marching Americans: "We are coming, Father Abraham—three hundred thousand strong!" And his shoulders were broader, and his muscles were harder, and his view of the whole world was essentially that of a man who had been tried by fire and not found wanting.

It is fair and proper in this connection to present the testimony of those who occupied position above him, and who related in after years the impressions which young McKinley made upon them in his army days. For one thing, he was is no sense an ambitious man. Had he been stung with the asp of ambition he might easily have passed those who commanded at the beginning. His was the education, the training of the brain and the body, the judgment and the patriotic zeal out of which great leaders are made. But he was not a self-seeker. He simply accepted his duty when it presented, and discharged it perfectly. Nothing was illy done. Nothing was half accomplished. His task was fully discharged in every instance, and he was never the man to thirst for power, to maneuver for promotion. The advances which marked his soldier life came to him unsought, the well-earned rewards of a merit which none could deny, coupled with a modesty which all could admire.

General Russell Hastings watched him through a number of battles, and at Cedar Creek saw him tried beyond all ordinary measure. General Hastings, then with the rank of captain, was on the same staff with young Lieutenant McKinley, a member of the same regiment, the Twenty-third Ohio. They were close friends through the war, and remained so throughout their later life. They ate at the same mess, slept under the same blanket, and—when they had a tent—occupied the same tent together. It was in 1892, when William McKinley loomed large because of his loyalty to a friend in political life, that General Hastings placed upon record his recollections—forever stamped upon the pages of his memory,—of an incident from the soldier life of his friend in that battle which began with "Sheridan twenty miles away."

On the Union side was only Crook's corps, some 6,000 strong, while opposed to it was the full force of Early's army. The odds were too great; so, after some severe fighting, Hayes' brigade, which was engaged, drew back in the direction of Winchester. "Just at that moment," says General Hastings, "it was discovered that one of the regiments was still in an orchard where it had been posted at the beginning of the battle. General Hayes, turning to Lieutenant McKinley, directed him to go forward and bring away that regiment, if it had not already fallen. McKinley turned his horse and, keenly spurring it, pushed it at a fierce gallop obliquely toward the advancing enemy.

"A sad look came over Hayes' face as he saw the young, gallant boy riding rapidly forward to almost certain death. * * * None of us expected to see him again, as we watched him push his horse through the open fields, over fences, through ditches, while a well-directed fire from the enemy was poured upon him, with shells exploding around, about, and over him.

"Once he was completely enveloped in the smoke of an exploding shell, and we thought he had gone down. But no, he was saved for better work for his country in his future years. Out of this smoke emerged his wiry little brown horse, with McKinley still firmly seated, and as erect as a hussar.

"McKinley gave the Colonel the orders from Hayes to fall back, saying, in addition, 'He supposed you would have gone to the rear without orders.' The Colonel's reply was, 'I was about concluding I would retire without waiting any longer for orders. I am now ready to go wherever you shall lead, but, Lieutenant, I "pintedly" believe I ought to give those fellows a volley or two before I go.' McKinley's reply was, 'Then up and at them as quickly as possible,' and as the regiment arose to its feet the enemy came on into full view. Colonel Brown's boys gave the enemy a crushing volley, following it up with a rattling fire, and then slowly retreated toward some woods directly in their rear. At this time the enemy halted all along Brown's immediate front and for some distance to his right and left, no doubt feeling he was touching a secondary line, which should be approached with all due caution. During this hesitancy of the enemy McKinley led the regiment through these woods on toward Winchester.

"As Hayes and Crook saw this regiment safely off, they turned, and, following the column, with it moved slowly to the rear, down the Winchester pike. At a point near Winchester, McKinley brought the regiment to the column and to its place in the brigade. McKinley greeted us all with a happy, contented smile—no effusion, no gushing palaver of words, though all of us felt and knew one of the most gallant acts of the war had been performed.

"As McKinley drew up by the side of Hayes to make his verbal report, I heard Hayes say to him, 'I never expected to see you in life again.'"

And when Sheridann galloped along the "good broad highway leading down" from Winchester, shouting his jubilant order: "Face the other way, boys. We're going back!" the whole of Hayes' brigade, thanks to young Lieutenant William McKinley, was in position, and ready for that advance which ended in another splendid Union victory.

Rutherford B. Hayes, once his colonel, then his general and later his President, has declared of William McKinley: "At once it was found that he had unusual character for the mere business of war. There is a quartermaster's department, which is a very necessary and important department in every regiment, in every brigade, in every division, in every army. Young as he was, we soon found that in business, in executive ability, young McKinley was a man of rare capacity, of unusual and unsurpassed capacity, especially for a boy of his age. When battles were fought or service was to be performed in warlike things, he always took his place. The night was never too dark; the weather was never too cold; there was no sleet or storm, or hail or snow, or rain that was in the way of his prompt and efficient performance of every duty."

In an old note book of the war-time period, kept by General Hayes, is another interesting entry which was given to the world in the course of an address at a political meeting in Ohio in 1891. By way of premise it should be stated that General George Crook in 1862 called Lieutenant McKinley to service on his staff, where he remained through the activities of the summer campaign, and until the Union army went into winter quarters. In the last month of the year General Hayes made that entry which seemed like a prophecy. Here it is:

"Saturday, December 13, 1862.—Our new Second Lieutenant, McKinley, returned to-day—an exceedingly bright, intelligent, and gentlemanly young officer. He promises to be one of the best."

And he added, while the thousands broke forth in tumultuous applause:

"He has kept the promise in every sense of the word."

That famous battle of Cedar Creek virtually ended the active military career of Captain McKinley. On March 13, 1865, he was brevetted major. In the spring of 1865 the Twenty-third Ohio was ordered to Camp Cumberland, where it was mustered out of service, July 26, 1865, closing a four-year career of war with honor, leaving a host of brave comrades beneath the turf of the battlefields, returning home to receive the congratulations of loyal friends and to enter once more the occupations of peace. The soldier boy of eighteen years was now a man of twenty-two. The private of 1861 was now a major. The education and aspirations of youth had been supplemented by such an experience in the cause of country as few could claim at his age, and such as would meet the most exalted purposes of after life.

JOHN D. LONG, SECRETARY OF THE NAVY.

NEW CONGRESSIONAL LIBRARY BUILDING AT THE CAPITAL.

CHAPTER XII.

McKINLEY IN CONGRESS.

No man ever approached the gates of public life under circumstances more discouraging than those which confronted William McKinley when, in 1876, his friends suggested him as a candidate for congress. Yet no man ever achieved a more signal triumph at the polls, nor a more glorious career in the halls of legislation. He served fourteen years in Congress. In that time he passed from the modest position of a "first termer"—one of the majority which never returns—to the chairmanship of the Ways and Means committee, a place that has been described as more powerful than that of the President of the United States. Certainly in the effecting of legislation, in the expression of national policy, in raising revenues and shaping the course of government there is no position comparable to it in the United States—probably in any country on earth.

It is interesting to observe in the beginning that Major McKinley's start in congressional life was in itself a tribute to his popularity. When he first launched into the profession of the law at Canton he won early prominence among his brethren of the bar, and a position of influence in his party. And when the managers of that party came to make up their county ticket in 1868, they selected William McKinley, Jr., as their candidate for prosecuting attorney. The county was strongly Democratic, and it was only on occasion, even through the years of the war, that Republicans could capture a county office. Anything like sagacity on the part of the county Democrats in naming their candidates had been certain to preclude the possibility of electing a Republican. It seemed quite hopeless that young McKinley could capture the office of prosecuting attorney from his opponent—a man of experience and ability.

But in the few years Major McKinley had lived in Stark county he had been constantly winning friends. And one reason he won them was that he deserved them. And the chief reason that he held them was because he deserved their adhesion. For while he was making acquaintances all over the county, widening his circle of acquaintance in the city, always urbane, courteous, affable and yet dignified, he was preparing to discharge the duties they would lay upon him.

It has been stated in another part of this work that Major McKinley won in the election. He became prosecuting attorney, though not another man on his ticket was elected. His victory surprised most of the people; but there were some, both in his own party and in the opposition, who recognized the promise of a man of power, and prepared the way for him.

So, in 1876, when his friends cast about for a congressional candidate, this man who had led a forlorn hope for them in a less notable fight eight years before seemed the man most likely to make a creditable showing.

There was little hope of electing him. The district, the old Ohio Eighteenth, was 1,800 strong Democratic. The Democratic nominee was the then incumbent, and he had made a record which pleased his constituents. Besides, the tariff was largely the issue of the campaign and Mr. Tilden's slogan: "A tariff for revenue only" was regarded as expressing a popular sentiment. That other slogan, "Tilden and Reform" had lost some of its effectiveness in the light of the Erie canal investigation at Albany; but the tariff had more than taken its place in the popular thought.

Besides, Major McKinley was one of the very few men in the nation who boldly, and without apology or subterfuge, contended for the principle of protection. It has been said elsewhere in this book that he engaged in a debate on the tariff shortly after returning from the army, and before he left his old home town of Poland. He had studied the question even then, and had become convinced that the present prosperity and future welfare of the nation demanded a policy of high tariff, and would for a number of years.

He lost that debate because the judges, smarting under the burden of war taxes, accepted the popular clamor for a reduction—and decided, without regard to the facts presented or argument deduced, that Major McKinley's opponent had won.

It had been observed in Stark county, since his location at Canton, that Major McKinley held to his daring theory of protection in all his political speeches. Most other Republicans felt the need of trimming, and conceded that protection was bad in policy, if not wrong in morals; and promised the people that it would be abolished.

That was the condition in the Eighteenth District in the summer of 1876, when Major William McKinley was nominated to run against Judge L. D. Woodsworth, a wheelhorse of Democracy in Ohio.

As in 1868, when he was candidate for prosecuting attorney of Stark county, so now, there was little hope of his election. The majority seemed too great to be overcome. But it was overcome. And when the votes were counted it was found that the Republican nominee had a clear majority of 1,300—a change of 3,100 votes from the preceding congressional election.

And it will be remembered that this was in the face of Major McKinley's contention for the policy of protection. He met every sophistry of his opponents with arguments which showed him a thorough master of his subject, and with a skill in debate which disarmed enmity even among his opposers.

So significant a victory won for the young man the attention of the nation; and the arrival in Washington of this strong, courageous champion of a great public policy was occasion for gratulation among the men who saw beyond the immediate present, and were building for the future of the nation—preparing the Republic for that day when it must abandon its hermitage, and take place among the mighty nations of the earth. And they gave him every encouragement. But even they—even Judge Kelley, of Pennsylvania, whose protectionism was less genuine because more a matter of personal interest—found at the very beginning that they could give William McKinley nothing, and that they would shortly be asking favors of him.

Sociologists may interest themselves with speculations on the influences which contributed to William McKinley's success as a statesman. But it is doubtful if they find anything more significant than the sorrow which came to him at this period. His two daughters were dead. His wife had suffered the blow from which she was never to recover; and this man's entry upon national legislation was through the gates of a great sorrow. Maybe it refined him, and purified his nature of whatever dross it contained. Maybe it intensified his thought, and added the sense of a sacred responsibility to him as a public man. He had no children. He knew he never again would hear the lisping call of "Father." And in the holy bereavement of that hour, he must—perhaps unconsciously—have devoted himself to the service of his country. There was no need to "trim," to—

> "Crook the pregnant hinges of the knee,
>   That thrift might follow fawning."

He had but one ambition now, and that was so to live as a public man that the verdict of the nation might be: "Well done, good and faithful servant."

That first term in Congress was judiciously utilized by William Mc-

Kinley. He knew, with that prescience which belongs to the truly great, that this was his field, that he would return to it, that no small considerations of oppositions and repeated elections could keep him from the fulfillment of that duty, the discharge of that task, for which all his life had been but pre- paration.

In the first session he made no speech. He was not even on a committee of importance. But his known position as a protectionist made him a man to be consulted, and his quickly recognized ability made him—a first termer—share in the shaping of legislation.

That was a Democratic Congress, with Samuel J. Randall in the speaker's chair. And the young man from Ohio waited at the portals of opportunity, making himself ready for the day when they should open and admit him.

He made a speech on the floor of the house. He was little considered by the superficial and unthinking. Yet they confessed in committee the influ- ence of his quiet power. He made himself master of every detail. He knew all that was to be known about the subjects that came before him and his confreres. And in a courteous, dignified but effective manner he said the right word in due season, and every man of them felt the presence of great- ness.

His first speech was delivered in the spring of 1878. The question of tariff had loomed large in the eyes of the nation. It had been made an issue. No man could escape it. Seekers for popular applause, for the pres- ent profits that might be secured, exhausted themselves coining verbal as- saults on the policy of protection. The men on the Democratic side, east and west, were almost a unit for a revision which meant a repeal. The time came later when most eastern Democrats took issue with their brothers from the West, as to the wisdom of protection. But in that day the strongest assault was made by a New York man—Fernando Wood.

He was one of the ablest Democrats in Congress. A sharp, shrewd man, plausible in his address, skillful in his arraignment, and attractive as a de- bater. He had, in his bill, reflected well the popular clamor of demagogues throughout the country who could not see the demands or the possibilities of the future. And the Wood tariff bill was sailing serene through the lower house, its friends jubilant, its supporters becoming jealous of the lucky New Yorker—when, one day William McKinley, of Ohio, got the floor, and be- gan an argument against the bill. That frightened no one. They wanted some opposition. They wanted the sport of a game fight, since they were sure they could not be defeated.

But when they had listened fifteen minutes they saw this young man, this unconsidered legislator, was master of the province upon which they had entered. He knew far more about the industrial and commercial conditions of the country than did they. He was infinitely better equipped than they in the matter of economics. And he coined his ideas in sentences so impressive that the jealous men were comforted. They were not frightened on account of the bill, for they were confident in the possession of an invincible majority. But they saw Fernando Wood at last had a foeman worthy of his steel.

At the end of half an hour a movement was made to silence him.. But other debaters on the Republican side saw an advocate had arisen more powerful than they. They gave him their time and he went on. Friends of the bill tried to badger him with questions. But he met every thrust with a dignity which disarmed and a reply which silenced them.

And when William McKinley sat down, the Wood bill was defeated, and nothing like it was ever again offered in the American House of Representatives.

It was a significant part of his work that day—a characteristic of his labors through life—that results were felt in the future. From that day the freetrade army was divided. The West, neither possessing considerable industries nor at the time appreciating their value, found itself divided from the East. From that day no great opponent of protection has come from the East to the halls of Congress. And—what is more to the point—no strong popular sentiment supporting free trade has flourished in the populous Atlantic states.

"A house divided against itself can not stand." How then shall an army divided against itself hope to march victorious?

But "tariff reform" still looked good as an issue, and the opponents of protection continued their crusade against it. They could not believe they would be defeated. They insisted that three thousand miles of ocean was enough protection for the American manufacturer. They pointed out that the price of each protected article was increased to the American consumer by just the amount of the protection tax. They refused to see that the consumer would, under a national policy which should strengthen industries, be better able to pay the increased price than the lower price under free trade. They were short-sighted. And they were confident the masses of the people were as short-sighted as themselves, and would overwhelmingly sustain them.

So their clamor continued.

So the Republicans in 1882, advised and counselled by Congressman McKinley, provided for a tariff commission which should investigate the whole question and recommend legislation that should settle the national policy once and for all. The commission was appointed by President Arthur, but before it could report the tacit agreement was broken, and William R. Morrison, of Illinois, brought forward, in 1884, his remarkable bill for a 20 per cent "horizontal reduction" of the tariff. The house was again Democratic, but William McKinley, overcoming successive gerrymanders in Ohio, was still in the house, now advanced to a position of influence and importance; and no "horizontal reduction" could take place while he was there, no matter what the political complexion of the House might be. Against a hostile majority, he led the forces of protection's friends. A part of his address on that occasion is as follows:

"What can be said of the capacity of the majority of the Committee on Ways and Means as evidenced by the bill now before us? It is a confession upon its face of absolute incapacity to grapple with the great subject. The Morrison bill will never be suspected of having passed the scrutiny of intelligent experts like the Tariff Commission. This is a revision by the cross-cut process. It gives no evidences of the expert's skill. It is the invention of indolence—I will not say of ignorance, for the gentlemen of the majority of the Committee on Ways and Means are competent to prepare a tariff bill. I repeat, it is not only the invention of indolence, but it is the mechanism of a botch workman. A thousand times better refer the question to an intelligent Commission, which will study the question in its relations to the revenues and industries of the country, than to submit to a bill like this.

"They have determined upon doing something, no matter how mischievous, that looks to the reduction of import duties; and doing it, too, in spite of the fact that not a single request has come either from the great producing or great consuming classes of the United States for any change in the direction proposed. With the power in their hands they have determined to put the knife in, no matter where it cuts nor how much blood it draws. It is the volunteer surgeon, unbidden, insisting upon using the knife upon a body that is strong and healthy; needing only rest and release from the quack whose skill is limited to the horizontal amputation, and whose science is barren of either knowledge or discrimination. And then it is not to stop with one horizontal slash; it is to be followed by another and still another, until there is nothing left either of life or hope. And the doctrinaires will then have seen an exemplification of their pet science in the destruction of the great productive interests of the country, and "the starving poor," as denominated by the majority, will be found without work, shelter or food. The sentiment of this country is against any such indiscriminate proposition. The petitions before the Ways and Means Committee from twenty to thirty States of this Union appeal to Congress to let the tariff rest where it is, in general, while others are equally importunate to have the duties on two or three classes of American products raised. The laboring men are unanimous against this bill. These appeals should not go unheeded. The farmers for whom you talk so eloquently, have not asked for it. There is no appeal from any American interest for this legislation.

"It is well, if this bill is to go into force, that on yesterday the other branch of Congress, the Senate, passed a Bankruptcy bill. It is a fitting corollary to the Morrison bill; it is a proper and a necessary companion. The Senate has done wisely, in anticipation of our action here, in providing legal means for settling with creditors, for wiping out balances, and rolling from the shoulders of our people the crushing burdens which this bill will impose."

And in spite of a Democratic majority the Morrison bill failed. That thrust—"the invention of indolence"—went home; and the nation resented the slipshod manner in which its public servants had done their work. And the Representative from Illinois brought from the wreck of his losing battle no more than the comfort of realizing that to the end of his life he would be known by the appropriate title, "Horizontal Bill Morrison."

But the crusade against protection was too attractive to abandon. In 1888, the House being again Democratic, Roger Q. Mills of Texas, was made chairman of the Ways and Means Committee, and he brought in a bill that expressed really all that was best in the opposition's case. But he made the fatal mistake of presenting a bill prepared by his political associates alone. It was more fair, more broad in its scope, more statesmanlike than anything that had previously emanated from the camp of free traders. But he had invited no Republican member of the committee to its preparation, and excluded all who would advise or instruct him. He might have welcomed them in safety, for he had the votes at his back to defeat every recommendation they might make, and adopt every paragraph that commended itself to him. But he saw fit to refuse audience to representatives of industrial concerns who knew far more of the subject than did Mr. Mills or his advisers, and an opposition suddenly sprung up which could not be overcome. Mr. McKinley made his most telling point against the Mills bill, in these burning words:

"The industries of the country, located in every section of the Union, representing vast interests closely related to the prosperity of the country, touching practically every home and fireside in the land, which were to be affected by the bill, were denied a hearing; the majority shut the doors of the committee against all examinations of producers, consumers and experts, whose testimony might have enlightened the committee. The farmers, whose investments and products were to be disastrously dealt with, were denied an opportunity to address the committee. The workingmen of the country, whose wages were at stake, were denied audience. The Representatives on the floor of the House were not permitted to voice the wants of their constituents. Proposing a grave measure, which would affect all of the people in their employments, their labor and their incomes, the majority persistently refused the people the right of hearing and discussion; denied them the simple privilege of presenting reasons and arguments against their proposed action."

The report of the minority of the Ways and Means Committee was prepared and presented by Mr. McKinley. He had come to be recognized as the best equipped and most formidable protectionist in Congress, and the report he submitted fully sustained that opinion. From that report the following extract will still be read with profound interest:

"The bill is a radical reversal of the tariff policy of the country which for the most part has prevailed since the foundation of the Government, and under which we have made industrial and agricultural progress without a parallel in the world's history. If enacted into law, it will disturb every branch of business, retard manufacturing and agricultural prosperity, and seriously impair our industrial independence. It undertakes to revise our entire revenue system; substantially all of the tariff schedules are affected; both classification and rates are changed. Specific duties are in many cases changed to ad valorem, which all experience has shown is productive of frauds and undervaluations. It does not correct the irregularities of the present tariff; it only aggravates them. It introduces uncertainties in interpretation, which will embarrass its administration, promote contention and litigation, and give to the customs officers a latitude of construction which will produce endless controversy and confusion. It is marked with a sectionalism which every patriotic citizen must deplore. Its construction takes no account of the element of labor which enters into production, and in a number of instances makes the finished or advanced product free, or dutiable at a less rate than the material from which it is made. 'The poor man's blanket,' which the majority has made a burning issue for so many years, is made to bear the same rate of duty as the rich man's. More than one-third of the free list is made up from the products of the farm, the forest and the mine; from products which are now dutiable at the minimum rates, ranging from seven to twenty-five per cent. and even this slight protection, so essential, is to be taken from the farmers, the lumbermen and the quarry-men."

But it was not until the bill was put upon its passage that he rose to his greatest height as a debater and as a statesman. Men old in public life concede that the speech he made, May 18, 1888, was the greatest ever delivered on a purely economic question in the halls of the American Congress. It did more to fix the policy of protectionism unalterably upon the country than any other one influence. It did more to justify the protectionists of the past, and to pave the way for whatever great policy might come after when new occasions brought new duties, when a subsequent era should arise, than all the campaigning and all the labors in or out of Congress that the nation had known. Here are some extracts from that notable address:

"What is a protective tariff? It is a tariff upon foreign imports so adjusted as to secure the necessary revenue, and judiciously imposed upon those foreign products the like of which are produced at home, or the like of which we are capable of producing at home. It imposes the duty upon the competing foreign product; it makes it bear the burden or duty, and, as far as possible, luxuries only excepted, permits the noncompeting foreign product to come in free of duty. Articles of common use, comfort and necessity, which we cannot produce here, it sends to the people untaxed and free from custom-house exactions. Tea, coffee, spices and drugs are such articles, and under our system are upon the free list. It says to our foreign competitor: If you want to bring your merchandise here, your farm products here, your coal and iron ore, your wool, your salt, your pottery, your glass, your cottons and woolens, and sell alongside of our producers in our markets, we will make your product bear a duty; in effect, pay for the privilege of doing it. Our kind of tariff makes the competing foreign article carry the burden, draw the load, supply the revenue; and in performing this essential office it encourages at the same time our own industries and protects our own people in their chosen employments. That is the mission and purpose of a protective tariff. That is what we mean to maintain, and any measure which will destroy it we shall firmly resist; and if beaten on this floor, we will appeal from your decision to the people, before whom parties and policies must at last be tried. We have free trade among ourselves throughout thirty-eight States and the Territories, and among sixty millions of people. Absolute freedom of exchange within our own borders and among our own citizens, is the law of the Republic. Reasonable taxation and restraint upon those without is the dictate of enlightened patriotism and the doctrine of the Republican party.

"Free trade in the United States is founded upon a community of equalities and reciprocities. It is like the unrestrained freedom and reciprocal relations and obligations of a family. Here we are one country, one language, one allegiance, one standard of citizenship, one flag, one Constitution, one Nation, one destiny. It is otherwise with foreign nations, each a separate organism, a distinct and independent political society, organized for its own, to protect its own, and work out its own destiny. We deny to those foreign nations free trade with us upon equal terms with our own producers. The foreign producer has no right or claim to equality with our own. He is not amenable to our laws. There are resting upon him none of the obligations of citizenship. He pays no taxes. He performs no civil duties; he is subject to no demands for military service. He is exempt from State, county and municipal obligations. He contributes nothing to the support, the progress and glory of the Nation. Why should he enjoy unrestrained equal privileges and profits in our markets with our producers, our labor and our taxpayers? Let the gentleman who follows me answer. We put a burden upon his productions, we discriminate against his merchandise, because he is alien to us and our interests, and we do it to protect our own, defend our own, preserve our own, who are always with us in adversity and prosperity, in sympathy and purpose, and, if necessary, in sacrifice. That is the principle which governs us. I submit it is a patriotic and righteous one. In our country each citizen competes with the other in free and unresentful rivalry, while with the rest of the world all are united and together in resisting outside competition as we would foreign interference.

"Free foreign trade admits the foreigner to equal privileges with our own citizens. It invites the product of foreign cheap labor to this market in competition with the domestic product, representing higher and better paid labor. It results in giving our money, our manufactures and our markets to other nations, to the injury of our labors, our trades people and our farmers. Protection keeps money, markets and manufactures at home for the benefit of our own people. It is scarcely worth while to more than state the proposition that taxation upon a foreign competing product is more easily paid and less burdensome than taxationn upon the noncompeting product. In the latter it is always added to the foreign cost, and therefore paid by the consumer, while in the former, where the duty is upon the competing product, it is largely paid in the form of diminished profits to the foreign producer. It would be burdensome beyond endurance to collect our taxes from the products, professions and labor of our own people.

"There is no conflict of interests and should be none between the several classes of producers and the consumers in the United States. Their interests are one, interrelated and interdependent. That which benefits one benefits all; one man's work has relation to every other man's work in the same community; each is an essential part of the grand result to be attained, and that statesmanship which would seek to array the one against the other for any purpose, is narrow, unworthy and unpatriotic. The President's message is unhappily in that direction. The discussion had on this floor takes that turn. Both have been calculated to create antagonisms where none existed. The farmer, the manufacturer, the laborer, the tradesman, the producer and the consumer all have a common interest in the maintenance of a protective tariff. All are alike and equally favored by the system which you seek to overthrow. It is a National system, broad and universal in its application; if otherwise, it should be abandoned. It çannot be invoked for one section or one interest, to the exclusion of others. It must be general in its application within the contemplation of the principle upon which the system is founded. We have been living under it for twenty-seven continuous years, and it can be asserted with confidence that no country in the world has achieved such industrial advancement, and such marvelous progress in art, science and civilization, as ours. Tested by its results, it has surpassed all other revenue systems.

"From 1789 to 1888, a period of ninety-nine years, there has been forty-seven years when a Democratic revenue-tariff policy has prevailed, and fifty-two years under the protective policy, and it is a noteworthy fact that the most progressive and prosperous periods of our history in every department of human effort and material development were during the fifty-two years when the protective party was in control and protective tariffs were maintained; and the most disastrous years—years of want and wretchedness, ruin and retrogression, eventuating in insufficient revenues and shattered credits, individual and National—were during the free-trade or revenue-tariff eras of our history. No man lives who passed through any of the latter periods but would dread their return and would flee from them as he would escape from fire and pestilence; and I believe the party which promotes their return will merit and receive popular condemnation. What is the trouble with our present condition? No country can point to greater prosperity or more enduring evidences of substantial progress among all the people. Too much money is being collected, it is said. We say, stop it; not by indiscriminate and vicious legislation, but by simple business methods. Do it on simple, practical lines, and we will help you. Buy up the bonds, objectionable as it may be, and pay the Nation's debt, if you cannot reduce taxation. You could have done this long ago. Nobody is chargeable for the failure and delay but your own administration.

"Who is objecting to our protective system? From what quarter does the complaint come? Not from the enterprising American citizen; not from the manufacturer; not from the laborer, whose wages it improves; not from the consumer, for he is fully satisfied, because under it he buys a cheaper and better product than he did under the other system; not from the farmer, for he finds among the employes of the protected industries his best and most reliable customers; not from the merchant or the tradesman, for every hive of industry increases the number of his customers and enlarges the volume of his trade. Few, indeed, have been the petitions presented to this House asking for any reduction of duties upon imports. None, that I have ever seen or heard of, and I have watched with the deepest interest the number and character of these petitions, that I might gather from them the drift of public sentiment. I say I have seen none asking for the passage of this bill, or for any such departure from the fiscal policy of the Government so long recognized and followed, while against this legislation there has been no limit to petitions, memorials, prayers and protests, from the producer and consumer alike. This measure is not called for by the people; it is not an American measure; it is inspired by importers and foreign producers, most of them aliens, who want to diminish our trade and increase their own; who want to decrease our prosperity and augment theirs, and who have no interest in this country except what they can make out of it. To this is added the influence of the professors in some of our institutions of learning, who teach the science contained in books, and not that of practical business. I would rather have my political economy founded upon the every-day experiences of the puddler or the potter, than the learning of the professor, or the farmer and factory hand than the college faculty. Then there is another class who want protective tariffs overthrown. They are the men of independent wealth, with settled and steady incomes, who want everything cheap but currency; the value of everything clipped but coin—cheap labor but dear money. These are the elements which are arrayed against us.

"Men whose capital is invested in productive enterprises, who take the risks of business, men who expend their capital and energy in the development of our resources, are in favor of the maintenance of the protective system. The farmer, the rice-grower, the miner, the vast army of wage-earners from one end of the country to the other, the chief producers of wealth, men whose capital is their brain and muscle, who aspire to better their condition and elevate themselves and their fellows; the young man whose future is yet before him, and which he must carve out with his hand and head, who is without the aid of fortune or of a long ancestral line—these are our steadfast allies in this great contest for the preservation of the American system. Experience and results in our own country are the best advisers, and they vindicate beyond the possibilities of dispute the worth and wisdom of the system."

But the bill passed the House.

There were members enough on the Democratic side of carry it through, though by a perilously small majority.

The senate, however, could not be brought to an approval, and the Mills bill failed there.

That, however, was but the beginning of William McKinley's victory. So strong a case had he made for protection that in 1888 his party leaders had been roused to appreciate the stupendous interests involved in the issue. They ceased to temporize, to avoid, to "trim." They had been on the defensive for twenty years. They took in 1888 the aggressive, made protection the issue, named General Harrison as their candidate, and echoing William McKinley's arguments in every school district of the nation, achieved a splendid victory.

But it was wholly due to the wisdom and foresight, the ability and eloquence of Major William McKinley, of Ohio.

Then came his crowning work. That was the measure which has taken its place in the history of the nation as "the McKinley Tariff Law." It was adopted in May, 1890, and took effect October 6 of the same year.

There is no royal road to success, no short cut-off to eminence. What-

ever is of great worth must cost great labor. William McKinley had put
into his preparation for that work all the years of his adult life. He knew
the subject as no other man in the nation knew it. And when, as chairman
of the Ways and Means Committee at last he was commissioned to write a
tariff bill, he gave himself wholly and utterly to the task. No laborer in the
mills which his policy safeguarded put in so many hours daily as did William
McKinley in the preparation of that great measure. He worked all day in
Committee or on the floor of the House, consuming nervous force in a manner which would have utterly broken down a less magnificent physique than
his own. And then every night he received representatives of various industries from all over the nation—from the farms, from the mines, from the
mills, from the stores, from the offices of transportation companies. And
they testified a thousand times that he knew their case far better than did
they. Yet he heard them patiently, respectfully, discussed the schedules
with them, and out of all the information he could gather produced that bill
which stands for the highest expression of statesmanship any republic has
ever known.

It was characteristic of the man that he should in the very van of his
argument place a statement that would challenge the general attention of
the public, regardless of party. No reader who recognizes the significance
of effective work in debate can fail to catch the value of these calm, deliberate
sentences:

"If any one thing was settled by the election of 1888, it was that the protective policy, as promulgated in the Republican platform, and heretofore
inaugurated and maintained by the Republican party, should be secured in
any fiscal legislation to be had by the Congress chosen in that great contest
and upon that mastering issue. I have interpreted that victory to mean, and
the majority in this House and in the Senate to mean, that a revision of the
tariff is not only demanded by the votes of the people, but that such revision
should be on the line and in full recognition of the principle and purpose of
protection. The people have spoken; they want their will registered and
their decree embodied in public legislation. The bill which the Committee
on Ways and Means have presented is their answer and interpretation of
that victory, and in accordance with its spirit and letter and purpose. We
have not been compelled to abolish the internal-revenue system that we
might preserve the protective system, which we were pledged to do in the
event that the abolition of the one was essential to the preservation of the
other. That was unnecessary.

"The bill does not amend or modify any part of the internal-revenue taxes applicable to spirits or fermented liquors. It abolishes all the special taxes and licenses, so called, imposed upon the manufacture of tobacco, cigars and snuff, and dealers thereof, reduces the tax upon manufactured tobacco from eight to four cents per pound, and removes all restrictions now imposed upon the growers of tobacco. With these exceptions, the internal-revenue laws are left undisturbed. From this source we reduce taxation over $70,000,000, and leave with the people this direct tax which has been paid by them upon their own products through a long series of years.

"The tariff part of the bill contemplates and proposes a complete revision. It not only changes the rates of duty, but modifies the general provisions of the law relating to the collection of duties. These modifications have received the approval of the Treasury Department, and are set forth in detail in the report of the committee, and I will not weary you by restating them.

"We propose this advanced duty to protect our manufacturers and consumers against the British monopoly, in the belief that it will defend our capital and labor in the production of tin plate until they shall establish an industry which the English shall recognize has come to stay, and then competition will insure regular and reasonable prices to consumers. It may add a little, temporarily, to the cost of tin plate to the consumer, but will eventuate in steadier and more satisfactory prices. At the present prices for foreign tin plate, the proposed duty would not add any thing to the cost of the heavier grades of tin to the consumer. If the entire duty was added to the cost of the can, it would not advance it more than one-third, or one-half of one cent, for on a dozen fruit cans the addition would properly only be about three cents.

"We have now enjoyed twenty-nine years continuously of protective tariff laws—the longest uninterrupted period in which that policy has prevailed since the formation of the Federal government—and we find ourselves at the end of that period in a condition of independence and prosperity the like of which has never been witnessed at any other period in the history of our country, and the like of which had no parallel in the recorded history of the world. In all that goes to make a nation great and strong and independent, we have made extraordinary strides. In arts, in science, in literature, in manufactures, in invention, in scientific principles applied to manufacture and agriculture, in wealth and credit and National honor we are at the very front, abreast with the best, and behind none.

"In 1860, after fourteen years of a revenue tariff, just the kind of a tariff that our political adversaries are advocating to-day, the business of the country was prostrated, agriculture was deplorably depressed, manufacturing was on the decline, and the poverty of the government, itself, made this Nation a by-word in the financial centers of the world. We neither had money nor credit. Both are essential; a nation can get on if it has abundant revenues, but if it has none it must have credit. We had neither as the legacy of the Democratic revenue tariff. We have both now. We have a surplus revenue and a spotless credit. I need not state what is so fresh in our minds, so recent in our history, as to be known to every gentleman who hears me, that from the inauguration of the protective tariff laws of 1861, the old Morrill tariff—which has brought to that veteran statesman the highest honor and will give to him his proudest monument—this condition changed. Confidence was restored, courage was inspired, the government started upon a progressive era under a system thoroughly American.

"With a great war on our hands, with an army to enlist and prepare for service, with untold millions of money to supply, the protective tariff never failed us in a single emergency, and while money was flowing into our treasury to save the government, industries were springing up all over the land—the foundation and cornerstone of our prosperity and glory. With a debt of over $2,750,000,000 when the war terminated, holding on to our protective laws, against Democratic opposition, we have reduced that debt at an average rate of more than $62,000,000 each year, $174,000 every twenty-four hours for the last twenty-five years, and what looked like a burden almost impossible to bear has been removed under the Republican fiscal system, until now it is less than $1,000,000,000, and with the payment of this vast sum of money the Nation has not been impoverished, the individual citizen has not been burdened or bankrupted, National and individual prosperity have gone steadily on, until our wealth is so great as to be almost incomprehensible when put into figures.

"The accumulations of the laborers of the country have increased, and the working classes of no nation in the world have such splendid deposits in savings banks as the working classes of the United States. Listen to their story: The deposits of all the savings banks of New England in 1886 equaled $554,532,434. The deposits in the savings banks of New York in 1886 were $482,686,730. The deposits in the savings banks of Massachusetts for the year 1887 were $302,948,624, and the number of depositors was 944,778, or $320.67 for each depositor. The savings banks of nine States have in nineteen years increased their deposits $628,000,000. The

PRESIDENT McKINLEY WITH HIS G. A. R. POST.

From a photograph taken for and used by courtesy of the Chicago Inter Ocean.

GEORGE FOSTER, SECRET SERVICE DETECTIVE, TALKING WITH PRESIDENT

English savings banks have in thirty-four years increased theirs $350,000,-000. Our operative deposits $7 to the English operative's $1. These vast sums represent the savings of the men whose labor has been employed under the protective policy which gives, as experience has shown, the largest possible reward to labor.

"Free trade, or as you are pleased to call it, 'revenue tariff,' means the opening up of this market, which is admitted to be the best in the world, to the free entry of the products of the world. It means more—it means that the labor of this country is to be remitted to its earlier condition, and that the condition of our people is to be leveled down to the condition of rival countries, because under it every element of cost, every item of production, including wages, must be brought down to the level of the lowest paid labor of the world. No other result can follow, and no other result is anticipated or expected by those who intelligently advocate a revenue tariff. We cannot maintain ourselves against unequal conditions without the tariff, and no man of affairs believes we can. Under the system of unrestricted trade which you gentlemen recommend, we will have to reduce every element of cost down to or below that of our commercial rivals, or surrender to them our own market. No one will dispute that statement; and to go into the domestic market of our rivals would mean that production here must be so reduced that with transportation added we could undersell them in their own market; and to meet them in neutral markets and divide the trade with them would mean that we could profitably sell side by side with them at their minimum price.

"First, then, to retain our own market under the Democratic system of raising revenue, by removing all protection, would require our producers to sell at as low a price and upon as favorable terms as our foreign competitors. How could that be done? In one way only—by producing as cheaply as those who would seek our markets. What would that entail? An entire revolution in the methods and conduct of business here, a leveling down through every channel to the lowest line of our competitors, our habits of living would have to be changed, our wages cut down fifty per cent. or more, our comfortable homes exchanged for hovels, our independence yielded up, our citizenship demoralized. These are conditions inseparable to free trade; these would be necessary, if we would command our own market among our own people; and if we would invade the world's markets, harsher conditions and greater sacrifices would be demanded of the masses. Talk about depression—we would then have it in its fulness. We would revel in unrestrained trade. Everything would indeed be cheap, but how costly when measured by the degradation which would ensue! When merchandise is the cheapest, men are the poorest; and the most distressing experiences in the history of our country—aye, in all human history—have been when everything was the lowest and cheapest measured by gold, for everything was the highest and the dearest measured by labor. We have no wish to adopt the conditions of other nations. Experience has demonstrated that for us and ours, and for the present and the future, the protective system meets our wants, our conditions, promotes the national design, and will work out our destiny better than any other.

"With me, this position is a deep conviction, not a theory. I believe in it and thus warmly advocate it, because enveloped in it are my country's highest development and greatest prosperity; out of it come the greatest gains to the people, the greatest comforts to the masses, the widest encouragement for manly aspirations, with the largest rewards, dignifying and elevating our citizenship, upon which the safety and purity and permanency of our political system depend."

But the year of his supreme success was also the year of his enemies' seeming triumph. His congressional district in Ohio, three times vainly gerrymandered with the aim of throwing him out, had finally been so arranged as to make his re-election impossible. It was the end of his career in the House. Yet it was only the vestibule of a greater eminence. The people of Ohio made him their Governor. And when the lighter duties of four years in the state executive mansion had recuperated his powers, the nation made him its candidate for President, and elected him on an issue that meant bravery, progress and wise statesmanship.

This closes the chapter of his life which was concerned in legislation. It is the end of his congressional career. If any man shall ask what was the greatest achievement of those fourteen years, the answer must be: "William McKinley's triumph for Protection!" He was the champion of that doctrine, the first man to advocate it as a principle to be preserved until the need should pass, the first to put a conscience in the discussions of a tariff. And he was, without exception, the ablest man that ever defended it, the bravest man that ever advocated it, the most successful man that ever supported it. Protection was by no means his one accomplishment. He was active in all legislation, neglectful of none. But his position on the Ways and Means Committee, so long held, made this master issue his chief concern.

CHAPTER XIII.

McKINLEY'S LIFE WAS PROTECTION'S ERA.

It is a curious fact that the public service of William McKinley began with the rise of the protective era, and ended with the passing of that system as a dominant and paramount policy in the history of the American republic.

His life embraces the era of protection to American industry. As he was its most sagacious and successful champion, as he in his labors expressed that thought as the controlling motive in governmental policy, so his death falls in the year when a protective tariff is recognized on all hands as having accomplished its great and useful mission. And the passing of McKinley is the retiring-time of that issue which has, more than anything else, made a mighty nation on the western continent.

It may be fairly said that there was no protective tariff, as such, until the close of the war. Such efforts in that direction as had been made under the leadership of Henry Clay and the earlier theorists among statesmen never rose to the magnitude of impressing a national policy, for the reason that the country was not ripe for them. In that formative period which preceded the election of Lincoln, men might speculate and debate and prophesy about free trade and protection, but the Union as a nation was growing; and it needed the great issue no more than a boy of fifteen needs the book called "Every Man His Own Lawyer." The nation was growing. It wanted farmers to broaden the plowland area, to lay the wide and deep foundation of agriculture, which must be the first step toward the construction of a great and permanent country.

Of course the Morrill tariff bill was not a measure of protection. It was a war measure. The question of economics was by no means necessary, and by no means invoked in that debate which preceded the enactment of the great tariff measure of 1861, or the supplementary bills which succeeded it in the process of raising revenue for the struggling nation. But when the war was over men of all parties and of every section were face to face with the greatest problem that has ever affected civil government.

The time had come when a burdened people demanded a reduction of taxes. It was no wonder. They had suffered grievously and with a splendid patriotic patience through four years of war; had paid the mighty demands of a government which needed the sacrifices of its people if it were to escape sacrifice itself, and now, in the relaxation which followed a disbandment of the armies, the public expected a lightening of their burdens.

The tendency of thoughtless men was to return to the free trade schedules of that formative period when the God of Destinies helped the farmer and bade the manufacturer "Wait!" There were few men wise enough to see the peril in that transition. Lot Morrill had said the tariff was a war measure, and it was. But free trade would have been a peace measure more disastrous than war. And Major William McKinley, returning from four years' service for a nation worth saving, knew that protection was none the less the policy demanded by all the best interests of the nation, now no less than when the national expenses were millions a day.

It required a brave man to face the storm of protest against a policy of protection, and an able man to prove arguments for the fortifying of that position. But William McKinley was both brave and capable, and he was hardly home from the army when he was entangled in a debate with a free-trade resident of Poland. It was a public occasion, and the speakers were allowed half an hour each, with a board of judges to decide as to who had won the debate. No election or other observable political significance hung on the issue, but none the less it was a notable night, a stupendous incident in the life of William McKinley. He knew the nation needed a policy of protective tariff for the building up of an industrial empire on the broad and deep foundation of agriculture which three quarters of a century had laid. He knew that the time had come when the mills were important if the nation would grow strong—and that the mills could be summoned into existence only by the adoption of a policy of encouragement and fostering care.

So far as the decision of the judges was concerned, William McKinley lost the debate. Two of the three held to the untaught sentiment that free trade was holy and the tariff a curse. The third saw and apprehended the logic and the argument of Major McKinley; but he was outvoted, and the public decision was that a protective tariff was impolitic and unjust, and should be abandoned.

Probably no event in the life of this advancing young man is more important than that. Probably no night of his life is so crowded with national interest as was this when he gave his mature thought and the rare powers of his young manhood to the discussion of this great question. He could easily smile at the verdict in that little room, in that little Ohio town by two little men who are now dead and forgotten. For he knew that a greater verdict in a greater arena, by a nation that shall never die and be forgotten, would abundantly and triumphantly and gloriously sustain him.

And he worked harder after that, finding support for the position which he recognized as essentially right and wise. He had enjoyed debates in the old days of his boyhood, of his school and college experience; and now he felt the impulse of a national summons to service as sacred as that which led him into the career of a soldier. In the confusion which followed war, men of all parties and from every part of the nation, and of every degree of influence, were either openly declaring or tacitly confessing that the protective tariff must and would be repealed. There was an element wise as McKinley, which recognized the error of the doctrine, but there were very few as brave. And the result was that in the first ten years after the war a public sentiment was formed which led inevitably toward absolute free trade. And even twenty years after the war the courage of this strong young son of Ohio was so largely wanting in the public men of his party that they dodged the issue; that they continued to promise a reduction or a repeal; that they appointed by presidential act, authorized by congressional action a tariff commission which should devise ways and means for the reduction or obliteration of the protective tariff. It is small credit to those men to add that the general motive was delay—temporizing; that they felt the wisdom of retaining the protective feature, and hoped "something would happen" to convince the country without sacrificing the growing industries. Braver men would have faced the truth as William McKinley faced it, and have fought for a high protective policy as a matter of principle.

Meantime, he went to the Albany Law School; for he had resisted the temptation to adopt a military life, and had declined with thanks the offer of a commission in the regular army. And at the Albany Law School he studied with diligence, and fitted himself for the successful career at the bar, and for that wider career as an advocate in the court of the nation, toward which he had been unwaveringly moving from his earliest boyhood.

He came back from the institution which had developed the talents of some of America's ablest jurists, and looked about him for a good location. He chose Canton, the seat of Stark County, as offering the best opportunities for a young lawyer. And because he had been a soldier, because he was as modest as able, and as industrious as orderly, he received recognition at the hands of that portion of the public which finds litigation necessary.

He had all his life kept up his connection with the Methodist Church, and the denomination at Canton was in a flourishing condition. He was possessed of a pleasing address, and easily made and retained friendships. He was a Republican, and while never fanatical, regarded the success of that party as best for the prosperity of the nation. And as he was in all ways deserving, he won favor in the eyes of Stark County Republicans. The county was Democratic by more than a thousand majority. But when the county convention was held at Canton in 1868, William McKinley, "as a mark of recognition," was placed upon the ticket as a candidate for prose-cuting attorney.

And he was elected. He had a genius for politics, and became a cam-paigner whom his political opponents recognized as embodying danger to him. So, when he had completed his first term, and was honored by his party with a renomination, the opposing forces perfected their lines, and he was defeated at the polls. That year of 1870 was not a Republican year in Ohio, anyway. It certainly was not a favorable time for a young man of ability, who sturdily held that the policy of a protective tariff was theoreti-cally right and practically a national necessity. So he continued his private practice after the expiration of his term.

In 1871 William McKinley was married. His wife was the young and beautiful daughter of J. A. Saxton, editor of the Canton Repository, a weekly newspaper, who had made enough money out of his business, and out of his talent for trading and real estate speculation, to establish a bank in the thriving and growing town. The daughter, Miss Ida Saxton, had received a good education, had enjoyed all the advantages that a prosperous and generous father could provide, and had traveled abroad, which was an unu-sual privilege even for wealthy women in the middle west. Two children, both daughters, were born of this union, but the privilege of bringing them up was denied the man who in all else realized the accomplishment of all his purposes. For the children died.

But it was a natural outgrowth of this period of his life that William Mc-Kinley should follow with a still more assiduous energy the path opening before him. And in 1876 he had won a place of sufficient prominence in the party to be nominated for congress. It was the old Eighteenth district, and was represented by L. D. Woodsworth, of Mahoning, a strong Demo-crat and an able man. But his young rival had won a host of friends in Stark County. He could "carry his own party" to the last man. And there were hundreds of Democrats who, on personal grounds, gave him their support. Added to that, Poland was in the second county of his district, and Poland people without regard to politics, had a pride in William Mc-Kinley. He had been one of them. He had gone to the war from their town. He had come back there on his furloughs through the four busy years. And he had lived among them after laying down the sword and uniform of a soldier, preparing himself for that wider field to which they knew they must resign him. And so Poland people were for William McKinley; and the Democratic majority of 1872 was more than erased. For William McKinley was elected congressman by a majority of 1,300. And his career as a states-man had begun.

'Probably no one thing contributed so much to his success in this instance as the rise and development of manufacturing interests in and about his home. Because of the encouragement afforded by the protective tariff, the mills there had started; and already the impetus of a wise economic policy was felt in his native state. And he had but to point to the smoke from multiplied chimneys, to summon the laboring men who were busy and well paid, to remind the farmers of their better market and higher prices—he had but to present these, his credentials, and his fight was won. He was a young man—a congressman at thirty-three. But he was recognized from the first as one of the best informed and least timid of the advocates of the Republican policies. James A. Garfield was the member of the Ways and Means committee from Ohio, and the younger man was at first assigned to positions of less importance. But there never was an hour from William McKinley's appearance on the floor of the House at Washington when his counsel was not sought. Fresh from the people, rooted and grounded in the soundest policy, able to express himself in a forcible, convincing and yet pleasing manner, he occupied from the start a position of importance in congressional circles.

So that it was with a sense of genuine loss that his confreres learned he had failed of re-election in 1878. But the Ohio legislature was Democratic at the time, and it redistricted the state, so that Stark County was placed in a district hopelessly opposed in politics; and he could but make a losing fight.

Yet the hope that this rising prophet of protection for protection's sake was removed from the field of political activity was destined to disappoint-ment. In 1880 he accomplished the impossible, and was returned to Con-gress, where he resumed his labors, and renewed his march to the very leadership of the greatest legislative body in the world. In 1882 he was re-elected, but by only eight votes. And it will be remembered that 1882 was not a Republican year. The Republicans, on the one great national policy which should have inspired them, were apologetic, defensive, full of excuses and promises. They could not catch the bravery of William Mc-Kinley's policy, nor adopt the frank straightforwardness which seemed to him not only the best policy but the most creditable statesmanship. And in 1882 the Democrats, rising to a courage and vigor hardly to be expected and rarely found in that organization, with a unity of purpose in its assaults on the tariff, had carried the country by storm. Cleveland was made Governor of New York State by the astounding majority of 192,000 against Folger, a consistent Republican of the most unexceptional character. Factional quarrels between the "Stalwart" and "Mugwump" branches of the party had given the opposition its opportunity. Congress was Democratic, and McKinley's opponent in the campaign of 1882 brought a contest into the house, for the elimination of those eight votes. And toward the end of the session the Canton man was unseated, and his place was given to the Democrat.

But it was the destiny of this man to do a great national work, to correct the national conscience, to fix a national policy of economic truth. And when his party in the Eighteenth district met in congressional convention in 1884 no name but that of "Major McKinley" was thought of. He was elected by the greatest majority ever accorded to a candidate there. He remained in the House through the Forty-ninth, Fiftieth and Fifty-first Congresses. In 1890 his district had again been gerrymandered with a view to his overthrow, and he was defeated at the polls for the Fifty-second.

But his work in the Lower House was done, and nothing could undo it. He had made a record as the champion of the protective tariff, had called back the leaders of his party to their duty, and had reinspired them with a courage which has never since faltered nor diminished. In his second term he made a national reputation as a tariff debater, and when James A. Garfield was advanced from the House, William McKinley succeeded him on the Ways and Means Committee, the most valuable man on the most important group of men in the nation.

In 1882 he began a systematic movement for the enactment of a tariff law which should be the expression of "the American idea," and four years later that idea took form and effectiveness in the McKinley tariff bill which went into effect Oct. 6, 1886.

His enemies tried to see the rejection of his policy when he was defeated for re-election, after his bill became a law; but his return to Congress two years later was sufficient answer to that. And the law which he imprinted on the statute books of the nation was the crystallization of his people's sober judgment as to a national policy, as to the wisest course in an economic system.

Remember that no tariff before that of the bill of 1890 had been openly and frankly advocated and adopted as an expression of the policy of protection to American industries. Every other bill of like nature had been devised with a view to raising revenue simply. Protection, the encouragement of industries, was a mere incident.

But this man stood for the policy which, he was confident, would bring the greatest good to the greatest number; would, both for the present and the future, be of most benefit to the nation.

The two systems are essentially different, though the purpose in each case, both by protectionists and free traders, was, of course, the good of the country. The aim of all men contending in that twenty-year debate was to achieve the best results for the people of the United States. But the forces for which William McKinley spoke held that the era of agriculture had passed, and that, while the farming interests might in no wise be neglected, the period of the factory had arrived. This man recognized the fact that a nation has definite eras in its life, as there are distinctive periods in the life of a man. St. Paul said: "When I was a child, I thought as a child. But now I am a man, and have put away childish things." The childish things are none the less needful and important IN THAT PERIOD; but when another period comes a different treatment will appeal. And as the ante-bellum era was the era of opening the new land, of reducing the forests and reclaiming the prairies, so now had arrived the era of manufacturing the raw material produced. And for this era of the mills, a protective tariff was an absolute essential.

That bill increased the tariff rate on most articles of foreign manufacture, with a view to discourage their importation and insure a market for the goods of American making. It was prophesied by his opponents that the result of that bill, which went into effect in 1890, would be the instant paralysis of all the industries of the nation, the crushing of labor and the impoverishment of trade. But an exactly opposite effect resulted. Though the McKinley bill was permitted to remain in its entirety through but four years of life, the industrial interests of the nation went forward with an amazing advance, and the material wealth of the country—farming, manufacturing, labor, both skilled and unskilled, together with commerce by both land and sea—was vastly increased. It was the master work of William McKinley's life. It was the crowning achievement of his labors. It was the expression of his best statesmanship. It stands to-day and it will stand to the end of time as the wisest revenue measure within the possible power of the country's securing. He had fixed upon the world a recognition of "the American policy." And the commerce of the world demonstrates to-day the wisdom of that schedule.

It was said at the beginning of this chapter that William McKinley's public life embraced the whole era of protection. It began with his first election to Congress. It closed with the sudden and lamentable closing of his career by the bullet of an assassin at Buffalo. The existence of the era of protection was co-extensive with his civil service to the nation. It is identified with him, and will so remain forever. When the passing years evolved new issues—when "new occasions brought new duties"—William McKinley was ready for them. He had finished his earlier work, and was ready for the newer demands.

No one who witnessed that session of the House in 1890, when William McKinley was at the height of his congressional career, and no one who followed the published accounts of it can ever forget the great occasion. The sentiment in favor of protection was clearly the dominant sentiment of the nation. But there were conflicting interests. And the man's masterly leadership was never more signally shown than when he won over all opposition within his party by summoning representatives of each industry, and skillfully guiding them into agreement upon a series of schedules which should be fair to all interests, and just to the people of the country. That essential unity of support having been secured, the McKinley bill became a law. Men said no agreement could be arrived at—that the rival interests were too strong and insistent to be adjusted. But the man who saw in 1866 the justness and wisdom of tariff protection as a national policy, won in 1890 the victory toward which his best abilities had been guiding him for twenty-four years.

Ten years more, and the policy he had supported, defended and glorified with his genius had accomplished its work. And with the transition into another era, this great man laid down his life.

There is something approaching the sacred in that view of the case which marks him as the alpha and omega, the beginning and the end, the prophet and the champion of "the American system."

CHAPTER XIV.

McKINLEY AS GOVERNOR OF OHIO.

Major McKinley's defeat for Congress in 1890 resulted in his nomination and triumphant election as governor of the State of Ohio. The passage of the "McKinley Bill" made the major the target for the vilest abuse from the free traders of the country, and from those whose mental range would never qualify them to judge of statecraft. But at the same time it stimulated his friends in his own State, and they determined not to lose his valuable services. The Republican press of the State clamored for his election as governor, and the Republican papers of other States agreed that no more fitting reward could be bestowed on Major McKinley than to make him chief executive of his State.

When the matter was broached to Major McKinley he expressed his willingness to accept the nomination for the office if it came spontaneously, but declared he would not enter into a contest for the honor. Though Ohio had numerous distinguished sons, many of whom were deserving of reward at the hands of the electors, there was really only one candidate for governor before the Republican convention, which was held in June, 1891. Major McKinley was nominated by acclamation, and he began a campaign that was typical of the man. He proposed that everybody should be informed on the economic questions of the day, and that every argument in opposition to the expediency and justice of the McKinley bill should be fairly met. With this object in view he started on a campaign of education, and during the canvass spoke in 86 out of 88 counties in the State. He made 130 speeches and won the admiration of Democrats as well as the heartiest support of his party-followers.

In one of his speeches, while discussing the McKinley bill, he said:

"The law of 1890 was enacted for the American people and the American home. Whatever mistakes were made in it were all made in favor of the occupations and the firesides of the American people. It didn't take away a single day's work from a solitary American workingman. It gave work and wages to all such as they had never had before. It did it by establishing new and great industries in this country, which increased the demand for the skill and handiwork of our laborers everywhere. It had no friends in Europe. It gave their industries no stimulus. It gave no employment to their labor at the expense of our own.

"During more than two years of the administration of President Harrison, and down to its end, it raised all the revenue necessary to pay the vast expenditures of the government, including the interest on the public debt and the pensions. It never encroached upon the gold reserve, which in the past had always been sacredly preserved for the redemption of outstanding paper obligations of the government.

"During all its operations down to the change and reversal of its policy by the election of 1892, no man can assert that in the industries affected by it wages were too high, although they were higher than ever before in this or any other country. If any such can be found, I beg that they be named. I challenge the enemies of the law of 1890 to name a single industry of that kind. Further, I assert that on the industries affected by that law, which that law fostered, no American consumer suffered by the increased cost of any home products that he bought. He never bought them so low before, nor did he ever enjoy the benefit of so much open, free, home competition. Neither producer nor consumer, employer or employe suffered by that law."

As governor of the State, Major McKinley was animated by the broadest and most patriotic motives. His long legislative experience had equipped him admirably to meet the responsibilities of his office, and to its duties he gave the same painstaking care that marked his career as Congressman. When his first term as governor was drawing to a close, the Republicans re-nominated him, and after a vigorous and exciting campaign he was re-elected by a majority of 80,000 votes.

During his incumbency as chief executive of Ohio, Major McKinley endeavored to improve in every way the institutions of the State, to accelerate industry, and to conserve in every way the interests of the people. The canal interests of the State were improved; tax reforms agitated, and brought to the attention of the legislature; labor questions received his earnest attention, and through his initiative the State Board of Arbitration was established in Ohio. Laws providing for the better protection of the lives and limbs of those engaged in industrial pursuits were passed during his rule.

His sympathy with the just complaints of the workingmen was further exemplified by his use of the State troops in turbulent periods. Many times during his term of office it became necessary to call out the militia to quell disturbances and to maintain order, but never was any abuse of power permitted. During the great railroad strike, sometimes called the "Debs Rebellion," which occurred in 1894, the State troops were on duty for three weeks guarding property and protecting citizens. There was at no time on the part of the soldiers any undue display of authority, nor any oppression of the strikers. The governor had long before given evidence of his honest regard for the welfare of the workingman. As early as 1886, when the O'Neill bill for the adjustment of controversies between inter-State common carriers and their employes by arbitration was before the House of Representatives, he said, speaking on the subject:

"I believe in the principle and tendency of the bill. It confers no rights or privileges touching arbitration which are not now enjoyed by common carriers and those engaged in their service. It leaves them where it finds them, with the right of voluntary arbitration to settle their differences through a peaceful, orderly tribunal of their own selection. It only follows the principle recognized in many States of the Union, notably in Ohio and Massachusetts, and gives national sanction and encouragement to a mode of settlement of grievances between employer and employe which is approved by the best judgment of the country and the enlightened sentiment of all civilized people. While the bill does not compel arbitration, its passage here will not be without influence as a legislative suggestion in commending the principle to both capital and labor as the best and most economic way of composing differences and settling disagreements, which experience has uniformly shown, in the absence of an amicable adjustment, results in loss to all classes of the community, and to none more than to the workingmen themselves. If by the passage of this simple measure arbitration as a system shall be aided to the slightest extent or advanced in private and public favor, or if it shall serve to attract the thoughtful attention of the people to the subject, much will have been accomplished for the good order of our communities and for the welfare and prosperity of the people."

He declared that the bill placed both parties on an equality, in pursuing an investigation, and permitted the humblest and poorest to send for persons and papers "without incurring an expense which very often they can illy bear." He closed his speech as follows:

"I believe, Mr. Chairman, in arbitration as a principle. I believe it should prevail in the settlement of international differences. It represents a higher civilization than the arbitrament of war. I believe it is in close accord with the best thought and sentiment of mankind; I believe it is the true way of settling the differences between labor and capital; I believe it will bring both to a better understanding, uniting them closer in interests, and promoting better relations, avoiding force, avoiding unjust exactions and oppression, avoiding loss of earnings to labor, avoiding disturbances to trade and transportation; and if this House can contribute in the smallest measure, by legislative expression or otherwise, to these ends, it will deserve and receive the gratitude of all men who love peace, good order, justice and fair play."

The bill was passed with amendments which made it conform more fully than it did originally to the views of Major McKinley.

It was logical to assume therefore that as governor he would give to workingmen in all their acts the largest license which the security of society would permit. During the trying days of the summer of 1894 it is related that a man who employed a large number of men went to the governor and inquired what he would do about ordering out the militia in case certain contingencies arose. Governor McKinley promptly answered:

"It is needless to ask what a public officer in Ohio will do. He does his duty. The practical question is, what can you do, and what will your employes do, what can we all do properly, to divert the necessity of using force? That is the question for immediate solution, at which I have been engaged for some days."

The same day, July 17, 1894, there was a meeting, called at his instance, in the governor's office, between the employer, the State Board of Arbitration and citizens and business men concerned. Before midnight that same day the governor received a dispatch from Nelsonville, the headquarters of the strikers, announcing the end of the great American Railway Union strike on the Hocking Valley Railway.

In 1895 he gave another evidence of his deep concern for the welfare of the workingmen. January 7 of that year the Trades and Labor Union of the Hocking Valley mining district held a meeting at Nelsonville for the purpose of effecting an organization and formulating plans for the relief of the distress and destitution existing among the miners and their families. For months the miners had been at war with their employers, and the continued loss of income had reduced them to a state of great wretchedness. A memorial was adopted at the meeting and a committee appointed to present it to the governor. They performed the duty imposed on them, and the governor, after hearing what they had to say, requested them to return to Nelsonville and ask the mayor to call a meeting of citizens to consider the question of relief. He promised that when advised of the result of that meeting he would take immediate action looking to the carrying out of their wishes. The meeting was called, and the action of the miners at their previous meeting approved. At 11:45 p. m., January 9, the governor received a message from the chairman of the Rel'ef Committee, saying: "Immediate relief needed." He at once sent messengers to the proprietor of a wholesale grocery, a dealer in vegetables, flour, etc., a transfer company and the officials of the Hocking Valley Railroad Company to meet him immediately at his rooms. The object of the meeting was for the purchase of a carload of provisions and to arrange for the shipment early in the morning. The supplies were purchased and loaded in the car before 5 o'clock a. m., and within nine hours after the receipt of the message the carload of provisions was in Nelsonville ready to be distributed to the hungry.

McKinley not only purchased the supplies, but also assumed the payment of the same. It was not his purpose to ask the people to provide for the payment of this car of provisions, amounting to nearly $1,000, but some of his friends learned that he had assumed the obligation and they at once took the matter in hand and secured from State officers and heads of departments the larger proportion of the amount, which they turned over to him, this being added to his own liberal subscription, thus meeting the obligation assumed by him.

Several times afterwards he was called upon for assistance, and he responded in every instance with alacrity. He was called away from the capital on several occasions during the progress of the relief work, but each time before leaving he gave positive instructions that in the event of appeals being made for help, to see that every demand was met and not allow any one to go hungry. These instructions were adhered to, and the chairman of the General Committee reported at the close of the work that the promptness with which McKinley acted, and the liberal contributions made, prevented hunger and suffering. The result of his efforts, as shown by the report of the chairman of the Relief Committee, was that 2,723 miners and their families had been made comfortable at an expenditure of $32,796.95.

Another marked characteristic of Governor McKinley was his respect for law. He never wavered in his belief in the institutions of his country, and desired always that the law be upheld, and that every man, no matter how humble, or for what, or by whom accused, should have the benefit of all the safeguards that civilized society had erected. This was shown in October, 1894, during a lawless outbreak at Washington Court House. A man accused of a heinous crime had been apprehended, tried and sentenced to undergo the full penalty of the law. He was in jail when a mob gathered for the purpose of lynching him. The militia was sent to the scene under command of Colonel Coit for the protection of the prisoner, and the preservation of order. A conflict ensued between the troops and the populace, and three people were killed.

At once a great cry arose against Colonel Coit, the claim being set up that he should not have allowed his men to fire. A court was ordered to inquire into his action, and he was exonerated. The governor sustained him throughout, and said concerning the occurrence:

"The law was upheld as it should have been, and, as I believe, it always will be in Ohio—but in this case at fearful cost. Much as the destruction of life which took place is deplored by all good citizens, and much as we sympathize with those who suffered in this most unfortunate affair, surely no friend of law and order can justly condemn the National Guard, under command of Colonel Coit, for having performed its duty fearlessly and faithfully, and in the face of great danger, for the peace and dignity and honor of the State.

"Lynching cannot be tolerated in Ohio. The law of the State must be supreme over all, and the agents of the law, acting within the law, must be sustained.

"The proceedings and findings of the court of inquiry have been carefully considered by me. I hereby announce my approval of the conclusions of said court, which find that Colonel Coit and his officers and enlisted men of the Fourteenth Infantry, O. N. G., acted with prudence and judgment and within the law, supporting the civil authority of Fayette county, and in the aid of it, and acting in pursuance of lawful orders, and that they performed their duty with singular fidelity, and that through them the majesty of the law and government by law was vindicated and sustained."

Other mobs were met in like manner by the governor, and it became known that under his administration, at least, there could be no recurrence of such scenes as had been witnessed in Cincinnati ten years before, when an unrestrained mob burned the court house, destroyed much other property, and caused the sacrifice of many lives before order was restored.

WILLIAM McKINLEY AS GOVERNOR OF OHIO.

THE MILBURN RESIDENCE IN BUFFALO WHERE PRESIDENT McKINLEY DIED.

CHAPTER XV.

McKINLEY AS A CAMPAIGNER.

It does not appear that William McKinley, at the beginning of his career as a politician, or at any other time in his life, endeavored to project himself into any sort of leadership. His forcefulness was innate, it is true, but the motive power, always, that surcharged his work was the demand of occasion. When he became a candidate for Congress for the first time, it was because he was needed from his district to do something. That he did earnestly, energetically and thoroughly for his immediate constituents. But, in Congress, the environment of national affairs brought to him national work. It presented itself to him as being the man for that, and he took it up with the same earnestness of purpose and the same commendable self-reliance that possessed his nature in all things. He went at it thinking only of what was needed, his duty in the premises being a matter of course, just as he quietly became a private soldier when the country needed every able bodied and faithful man that it could get to do the work of war.

In the harness McKinley did, simply, always that which was for the best, as he saw it, and always in the strongest and best manner possible to him, and his career has exhibited the fact that what he thought was best, and what he was able to do, was ever valuable to those interests, including himself. In this he exemplified the principle that to do right is to do that which is for the best.

Being in politics on the most commendable plane McKinley was a politician of shrewdness without cunning and he campaigned in the strongest way without descending to questionable methods. His power as a campaigner was of the kind that does its work steadily, unfalteringly and irresistibly, straightforwardly and fairly.

Thus, in 1876, when McKinley was first set forth as a candidate for Congress, he had three rivals from his own county for the nomination, but the choice fell upon him at the first ballot, over all other candidates. Being elected, he was rechosen at each recurring convention and election for fourteen years, and always representing the district in which his county was, though it was not always the same district otherwise, for his opponents, not relishing the prominent and important place that he had taken in Congress, gerrymandered the district three times in that fourteen years hoping thus to defeat him, but in that they failed signally until the last time that game was played, but the defeat was only of a temporary character and was pitifully unsuccessful in keeping McKinley out of politics.

The first attempt to change the McKinley district resulted in the formation of a district that would have naturally presented a majority for the opposition of 1,800. But this McKinley overcame with a majority of 1,300.

In 1882, when McKinley's party suffered everywhere and especially in his state, this resourceful man managed nevertheless to hold his own quite safely.

In 1884 the opposition gerrymandered the district again, but McKinley was not to be downed, and came to the front with a majority of 1,500.

In 1890, the very year in which the McKinley bill became a law, the district being again gerrymandered, and Stark County—that in which McKinley lived—having been districted with other counties that gave a majority for the opposition of 2,000, and McKinley's opponent being ex-Lieutenant Warwick, a prominent and exceedingly popular man, in the fierce battle that ensued McKinley was defeated by 363 votes. The figures showed, however, that the vote was the fullest ever cast in the counties that now composed the district, and that McKinley received 2,500 more votes than had been cast for President Harrison in 1888, when Harrison was elected.

This defeat took McKinley out of Congress, but not out of public life. McKinley was thirty-four years old when he entered Congress. At that time Samuel J. Randall was the Democratic leader and Speaker and James A. Garfield at the head of the Republicans. The new Congressman from Ohio soon attracted attention, and when he left the House fourteen years afterwards he was the Republican leader by virtue of his position as chairman of the Ways and Means Committee. The McKinley bill, which in the latter capacity he urged through Congress, at first met with disapproval by the people and was practically rejected at the next Presidential election when Cleveland was successful. Four years afterward, however, the voters saw their mistake and William McKinley was elected President on the identical issue which it was supposed had ended his political fortunes in 1892.

With fair intent, youthful ardor, a large and valuable fund of information on economic problems, painstaking industry, fidelity to political convictions, commanding address, parliamentary and diplomatic tact, dignified demeanor and philosophic turn, Congress was a wide and fertile field for the work of William McKinley. Being always at his best, because of healthfulness of mind, body and motive, he grew rapidly in strength, popularity and respect among the members of that body, and especially among his party associates. The appreciation of his ability and industry was quickly and continuously illustrated by the assignments that came to him of places upon various and important committees. On the floor of the House of Representatives he took rank early in his membership among the ablest debaters, by reason of his sincere interest in public questions, remarkable facility and power in the marshalling of facts, his forceful logic, fascinating rhetoric, fairness to opposition, freedom from excitement and bitterness, readiness and keenness in repartee and a palpable evidence at all times of cool reserve strength. In it all, however, he never spoke without occasion nor without full knowledge of his subject. He ornamented and exhausted the subject matter with which he happened to be occupied. Depth and honesty of conviction were apparent in his earnestness and his expression, lucidity of thought and easy clearness of detail gave delight when he spoke to friend and foes alike.

It was particularly fortunate to Mr. McKinley and the country that upon entering Congress as a young man he was placed upon the Ways and Means Committee that proved congenial as well as specially adaptable to him. Here, under the tutelage of such chairmen as Kelley and Garfield, it was natural that with his bent he should reach the chairmanship of that great committee himself. It was thus that the opportunity came to him for the exercise of his special genius in tariff matters. His first speech in Congress was on the tariff and his last discussed the same theme.

From the beginning of his public career McKinley was the unfaltering, sturdy, consistent and intelligent advocate of the principle of protection to American industries by tariff duties imposed with the purpose of keeping the cheap labor products of European and Asiatic countries out of our vast and desirable American markets. He was not, as was Garfield, for such protection as would lead to ultimate free trade. He believed that free trade is a dream of theorists, which would bring industrial ruin and poverty to the United States if it were put into practice, benefiting no class but the importing merchants of the seaboard cities. He had no patience with tariffs formed to "afford incidental protection."

Tariff bills, he thought, should aim primarily at protection, and tariff legislation should be scientific and permanent, with a view to the continuous prosperity of the industrial classes. This was the chief aim of the McKinley bill, passed when he was chairman of the Ways and Means Committee. No doubt other minds in both House and Senate helped to frame that measure, but McKinley's thought and work were on every page of it. When the Republican party was defeated in 1892, largely through public misapprehension of that measure and before it had received a fair trial, McKinley was one of the few Republican leaders who continued to breast the adverse current and who never faltered a moment in the faith that the tide would set back to protection.

Others wanted to change front and abandon the high protection principle. He refused, and proceeded to realign his party on the old line of battle. He set out to educate public sentiment anew, and during his memorable stumping tour of 1894 he made 367 speeches and spoke in the States of Indiana, Illinois, Missouri, Kansas, Nebraska, Iowa, Minnesota, Wisconsin, Michigan, Kentucky, Tennessee, Alabama, Mississippi, Louisiana, West Virginia, Pennsylvania, New York, and Ohio. For eight weeks he averaged seven speeches a day, ranging in length from ten minutes to an hour.

In these speeches McKinley addressed himself to the country upon the demerits of the Wilson tariff bill, then on its passage, which had been denounced by President Cleveland, who belonged to the same political party as did its author, and who was of the opposite political party to that of McKinley, as "a product of perfidy and dishonor," but who permitted it to become a law without his signature. At the same time McKinley spoke in favor of the underlying principle of the act of 1880.

This latter bill, of which McKinley was the father and which bore his name, occupied the entire time of the first session of the Fifty-first Congress, and in all that terrific debate McKinley stood as the special champion of the measure. Its passage was a monument to his ability, patience and endurance, and to his great power as a debater.

By 1884 he had won the title of "Champion of American Protection," and in 1888 his committee report was delivered, which headed the "Mills Tariff Bill," and that, with the speech delivered by McKinley at the time, became potent factors in the campaign that followed and in which Harrison was elected President and the political complexion of Congress was changed to one of harmony with the administration.

After his defeat for Congress McKinley remained quietly at his home, where he was again called from its privacy to consider the question of his nomination for the Governorship of Ohio. Governor Campbell had frequently boasted that he had made Ohio a permanent Democratic State, but

McKinley dispelled his illusion. The Republican State convention was held at Columbus in June, 1891, and at it William McKinley was nominated Republican candidate for the Governorship, and the following November was elected Governor by 21,000 majority.

It was a typical "campaign of education" that McKinley made at this time and in it he visited eighty-six counties and delivered one hundred and thirty addresses. In all of that arduous campaign, as well as the many others that he made during his political life, McKinley's speeches were always models of unaffected art. There was never anything that even so much as gave a hint or suggestion of "playing to the gallery." There were no funny declamations, no pandering to anything or anybody. He stood strong, self-reliant, comfortably poised, well at ease; he spoke with an evenly-modulated and clear voice; his enunciation was distinct and his words short and simple. There was truth in sentences and sincerity in his declarations. Everybody who heard him believed what he said. He had the happy faculty of talking to all manner of persons in a way that commanded respect with awe. He was easily approached—made those who spoke to him feel "at home." He gave comradeship naturally and commanded perfect respect in such a way that the visitor, the highest or humblest, never felt. Beside his magnetism as a politician and an orator, there was a personal charm about the man that made him as attractive to the many as he was admirable as a leader among his partisans. He won distinction for his uniform courtesy to men and deference to women. He had the same power to win men to him that Napoleon had in making himself the idol of his soldiers. Simple in his tastes, quiet in his manner, firm in his stand for a principle he believed to be right, he was ever the most courteous of men in public life. He made few enemies and held all of his friends. His patience was equal to his physical endurance and he could travel, speak, shake hands all day and yet sit down in the evening and explain to an associate the mysteries or intricacies of a tariff schedule or be a charming companion in a social circle. But in all his sociability there was a purity of speech and thought that made it impossible for even a thoughtless man of rough habits to introduce a suggestion of coarseness, profanity or vulgarity into the conversation.

In all of the trials of his political and official life no moment came when he was not plainly devoted to his invalid wife. All the world loves a noble, true lover, and such McKinley was, tender and gallant to his sweetheart wife, as he ever was before they were married a quarter of a century ago.

Illustrative of this, and exhibiting another phase of his campaigning, was an incident of June 18, 1896.

Major McKinley believed, as did nearly every other person in the United States at all interested and informed, that he would be nominated for President by the National Republican convention, then in session at St. Louis, and he was in close communication with his friends there while seated in his comfortable cottage home at Canton, Ohio. Here were assembled a few close friends, some newspaper reporters, a telegraph operator, with Major McKinley, his wife and mother. The day had passed pleasantly and in happy expectancy. At last came one telegram that brought a sparkle of delight to the eyes of the great man who was most interested, personally. It told of the nomination by an enthusiastic and overwhelming vote of McKinley.

Without a word McKinley took the telegram across the room to where his wife sat, bent lovingly over her and kissed her flushed and fevered cheek, giving her at the same time the pleasant message. She did not speak. Her heart was too full. She who had watched him through so many years in his ever upward course, she who was proud of him as her husband and hero, and whom she had seen cast aside honors, riches and glory, when to accept them would have been to compromise his moral honor and to stain his conscience; she looked all her gratefulness and love, and then found words to say, affectionately, "Thank you, dear!"

The wisdom that had marked McKinley's entire course in politics was destined to break the way for him to the White House, and now it had already made him the central figure of one of the most brilliant and yet unostentatious campaigns that the republic has ever known.

When his prominent rival announced that he would travel over the country making his campaign of speeches from the rear platform of a railway coach, Major McKinley did not become alarmed, but chose the opposite and more potent course. Although urged to do so, he refused to enter joint debates, not fearing his ability to cope with his opponents, but believing that the best interests of his party would not be subserved thereby. He remained at home and his popularity became so great that large delegations from every walk in life visited him daily, making speeches which evinced their faith in this wise leader and their loyalty to him.

McKinley was, of course, called upon to reply, and then the wisdom of his manner of campaign became palpably evident. The press of the country reported all the speeches of McKinley and his visitors, and Canton became the political center of the United States.

Trainloads of people, delegations from cities and clubs, from organizations of old soldiers, labor organizations, social circles, and all manner of industrial combinations, employers and employed, came day in and day out, through all of the long campaign. These proceeded at once to the McKinley cottage, and all were cordially received by the future President. Such unique scenes have never been witnessed in a political campaign, and have only been suggested by the "Log Cabin Campaign," of 1840, when "Tippecanoe and Tyler Too" was the rallying cry of the elder Harrison's confident and enthusiastic partisans. Nothing could have more eloquently and earnestly emphasized the faith of the great body of the people in their loyalty and trust in McKinley and the hopeful expectations of the country, than did the Canton campaign, which was carried to a common center rather than scattered abroad, and which was conducted by the voters rather than the candidate.

Many of the speeches delivered on the lawn at the McKinley home have properly taken a place in the records of the nation's history, because they not only show the earnest trust of the people in McKinley, but from those delivered by him have given him the stamp of the patriot, statesman and orator, and they will be always valuable as edifying and instructive in their dealing with American policies, and brilliantly illustrative of the economics involved.

Three great questions—tariff, currency and pensions—were specially involved as being uppermost in the minds of the people, and McKinley's exact position, with relation to these important propositions, was a matter of deep concern. No doubt seemed to exist, however, as to his views, because all through his past life the record had shown his loyalty to the cardinal principles of which these questions were phases, shades and details, and his faithfulness now was accepted, his reindorsement of it all was simply a pleasant campaign ceremony and a reiteration for the benefit of misinformed. The whole affair was another and a greater "campaign of education."

On the three questions that were special issues McKinley gave forth no uncertain sound. Equivocation was foreign to him under any circumstances, and in these he was at all times earnestly the advocate of a protective tariff, sound money and liberal pensions to the Union soldiers who had responded so nobly to their country's call when its life and weal were endangered. Upon all questions of national policy McKinley was clear and emphatic, and never in the history of politics has there been a candidate for the exalted place of President who has been accepted with such cordiality and unanimity by his party.

The campaign progressed satisfactorily to the managers of the McKinley interest and the great candidate deeply endeared himself to the public by expressing unbounded faith and unwavering hope in the judgment and good will of the common people. The campaign, however, presented many new and confusing phases and there were obstructing conditions that had never before arisen. Populism had grown formidable and party alignments had become much confused. A feeling of extreme anxiety had grown out of the uncertainties of the business situation. The wheels of industry stood still, and all business was inert, alarmed and awaiting the results of the election and the developments that would follow.

The world was interested, for "Hard Times" was walking with it, arm in arm, and holding it back. Europe preserved an anxious silence, Asia felt the unusual depression of uncertainty, South America was eagerly listening for the result. Election day came and the vast mass of voters in the United States arose early, impressed by the words of William McKinley as to what should be done. Patriotic duty was the thought of the hour. Upon that day a vast majority of the sovereign voters, throwing off all trammels, cast their ballots in favor of industry and against calamity. The day was bright throughout the land, the friends of industrious prosperity took the color of the day, and the noiseless fall of ballots established and stamped the people's will. The result was quickly known—McKinley and prosperity were elected. The largest popular majority ever given was that by the people for the people, and William McKinley's power as a campaigner had wrought wondrous good to the republic and the world.

CHAPTER XVI.

GOVERNOR McKINLEY'S FINANCIAL TROUBLES.

One of the sad events in the career of President McKinley was the loss of his fortune in the year 1893. It was during his first term as Governor of Ohio, and was a period of humiliation and anguish to the Governor and his wife, but they met the crisis with that quiet fortitude that ever characterized them, and found friends in abundance to aid them in their distress. This money trouble was not brought about by any wild speculation on the part of the Governor. He had never evinced any desire to seek riches through such agencies, and so faithfully had he applied himself to the people's interests that, notwithstanding his years of hard work, he was worth not to exceed $20,000, which was invested in securities and real estate.

The difficulty which swallowed up the Governor's fortune, and that of his wife, resulted from his endorsing notes for a friend. This friend was Robert L. Walker, a capitalist banker and manufacturer, of Youngstown. Mr. Walker was president of the Farmers' National Bank of Youngstown, the Girard Savings Bank, a stamping mill company, a stove and range company, and was interested in several coal mines in Western Ohio and Eastern Pennsylvania. He was one of the strongest men in the community, was supposed to be worth more than $250,000, and enjoyed the confidence of everybody who knew him.

When Major McKinley returned from the war and was ambitious to become a lawyer, he found the struggle a hard one. His service as a soldier had not enabled him to save anything of consequence, and when poverty pressed him he turned to Mr. Walker for aid. He was not disappointed. Mr. Walker proved a friend in need, and the Major was not the man to forget a kindness. After he entered political life, he again had need of financial assistance. In his first congressional campaign his expenses were heavy, and it became necessary for him to raise $2,000 with which to cancel a mortgage on his wife's property. Mr. Walker loaned him the money, and it is probable that at subsequent periods other loans were made to the Major. He was constantly under heavy expense, owing to the illness of his wife, and had no regular income save his salary of $5,000 as Congressman.

The first loan was repaid by Major McKinley out of his salary within two years, and it is certain that all of his subsequent financial obligations were promptly met up to the time of the crash.

Under such circumstances it was not strange that Major McKinley, having become Governor, and having become possessed of some money of his own, should be called upon to help out his old friend when he needed a little accommodation. Mr. Walker applied to the Governor to indorse his paper from time to time and the Governor willingly accommodated him, never questioning the amount, nor the circumstances for which the money was required.

These accommodations were spread over a considerable period of time, and it is probable that in the course of his business Mr. Walker took up many of the notes endorsed by the Governor. But his affairs became more and more involved, and early in 1893 Mr. Walker informed the Governor that he was in great need of money and asked the Governor to endorse his notes, which he desired to have discounted. The Governor did not hesitate an instant. The man who had befriended him needed aid, and so far as the Governor could render it he did so. Governor McKinley understood at the time that the notes signed by him aggregated about $15,000. They were good at any bank in Ohio, and no trouble was experienced by Mr. Walker in discounting them.

The Governor gave no further thought to the matter until February 17, 1893, when Youngstown, as well as the commercial circles of Ohio, were startled by the announcement of the assignment of Robert L. Walker. A judgment for $12,000 had been entered against the Youngstown Stamping Company, and inability to meet it caused Mr. Walker to assign. As soon as the fact became known Mr. Walker's other enterprises began to topple, and the next day all were swallowed up in the crash.

Governor McKinley was on his way to attend a banquet given by the Ohio Society in New York when he was informed of the disaster which had overtaken his friend. He cancelled his engagement in New York by telegraph and immediately started for Youngstown. In the meantime those interested had been figuring, and it was estimated that the liabilities of Mr. Walker aggregated about $200,000. His available assets were figured at about one-half that amount.

At Youngstown the Governor began to receive telegrams from banks all over the state, announcing that they held some of his paper. He had been led to believe that the notes had been discounted at only three banks, and was at a loss to understand the situation, until it transpired that instead of a liability of $15,000, his name was on paper amounting to nearly $100,-000! The Governor was under the impression that many of the notes he had signed were executed for the purpose of taking up notes previously given and which had fallen due. It was soon found that the old notes had not been paid, and that the Governor's obligations amounted to far more than he was able to pay.

The Governor had not a particle of interest in any of Mr. Walker's properties, and all that he had done for that unfortunate gentleman was done out of pure gratitude. After a conference with his Youngstown friends, in which the true state of affairs was disclosed, the Governor said:

"I can hardly believe this, but it appears to be true. I don't know what my liabilities are, but whatever I owe shall be paid dollar for dollar."

At this time Mrs. McKinley owned property valued at $75,000, which had been left her by her father. As there seemed no other way of meeting the crisis, the Governor and his wife, on February 22, made an absolute assignment of all their property to a board of trustees, to be used, without preference, for the equal payment of the creditors. The trustees were: H. H. Kohlsaat, Chicago; Myron T. Herrick, Cleveland; and Judge Day, of Canton, Ohio. Friends urged Mrs. McKinley, at this time, to retain an interest in her property, but she refused to do so, transferring all her fortune to M. A. Hanna, of Cleveland.

This calamity weighed heavily upon the Governor, and he thought of giving up public life and returning to the practice of his profession. To friends with whom he talked, he said:

"I did what I could to help a friend who had befriended me. The result is known. I had no interest in any of the enterprises Mr. Walker was carrying. The amount of my endorsements is in excess of anything I dreamed. There is but one thing for me to do—one thing I would do—meet this un-looked for burden as best I can. I have this day placed all my property in the hands of trustees, to be used to pay my debts. It will be insufficient, but I will execute notes and pay them as fast as I can. I shall retire from politics, take up the practice of law, and begin all over again."

It was at this time that the Governor's friends throughout the country began to bestir themselves for the purpose of aiding him financially. The Chicago Inter-Ocean started a popular fund for the purpose, and money began to roll in. Governor McKinley refused to accept a dollar of this money, and it was by his direction returned to the donors, with his thanks for their disinterested friendship. His friends were not to be denied, however, and a number of them decided to subscribe privately to a fund to take up the Walker notes. Among these gentlemen were M. A. Hanna and Myron T. Herrick, Cleveland; P. D. Armour, Marshall Field and H. H. Kohlsaat, Chicago; and Bellamy Storer and Thomas McDougall, Cincinnati. The management of the fund was placed in the hands of Mr. Kohlsaat, who afterwards said of the matter:

"One of the chief reasons why the subscription plan was adopted was because a number of subscriptions were received anonymously and could not be returned. There were over 4,000 subscriptions sent in, and when the last piece of paper was taken up bearing Major McKinley's name, no more subscriptions were received, and some were returned. No list of the subscribers was kept, and Governor McKinley does not know to this day, with the possible exception of four or five names, who contributed the money.

"When Governor McKinley saw the publication of the subscription scheme he wrote me absolutely declining to receive a dollar. Mr. Hanna and his other friends told him to leave the matter alone, for if his friends wished to assist him they should have the privilege."

The indebtedness having been satisfied in full, Mrs. McKinley's property was deeded back to her, and she and the Governor were left in the same position financially they were before the crash occasioned by Mr. Walker's failure.

It was a graceful and fitting act for the people thus to have relieved the Governor of the burden resting upon him. He had given practically all his life to the public service, and was comparatively a poor man. If he had given to his own interests the same fidelity which he devoted to the interests of the public his financial reward would have been such that he would have had no need of assistance in carrying such an indebtedness. As it was, he did the only manly thing possible. He acknowledged the debt, and made such preparations to pay it as were within his power. He did not consider the hardship he must endure in "beginning all over." People had paid out their money on their faith in his endorsement, and he did not intend they should lose a penny. It was no stain on the Governor's honor that he had endeavored to help a friend and been financially ruined in the effort; and he was in no wise to be criticised when he permitted his friends, for whose interests he had so long labored, to bear the burden his generosity had put upon him.

CHAPTER XVII.

McKINLEY'S LOYALTY TO SHERMAN, BLAINE AND HARRISON.

Governor McKinley's splendid record as a public servant made him a presidential quantity long before he was put forward for the nomination as the "favorite son" of Ohio; but he was ever loyal to his party's interest, and his party associates, and at no time allowed ambition to blind him to duty. This was clearly evidenced in the Republican National conventions held in 1884 and 1888. It was in these gatherings that Major McKinley's claims to leadership—or at least to be considered as one of the prominent men of the nation in the councils of his party—came to be recognized. He was a "Blaine" man at this convention. In supporting Mr. Blaine he but represented the overwhelming sentiment of the Mahoning valley; and yet, while he favored Mr. Blaine, he had the kindliest feeling for the illustrious Senator from Ohio, John Sherman, who at that convention was also a candidate for the Presidency. Major McKinley was a strong advocate of the sentiment that all legitimate means should be sought to nominate Mr. Blaine, but if that was impossible, Ohio should cast a solid vote for Mr. Sherman.

The Ohio Republican state convention was held at Cleveland in April, 1884. McKinley went to Cleveland fresh from a tariff debate in Congress, and was made permanent chairman of the convention. The Blaine following manifestly was in the majority at the convention, but the Sherman men had the best organization, and most of the "old-time" politicians of the state were pronouncedly in favor of the Ohio Senator. The great struggle at the convention was on the election of four delegates-at-large. Although it was well understood that Foraker's first choice was Sherman, the Blaine men generously acquiesced in his election by acclamation as a delegate-at-large. A number of names were then presented for the remaining three places, and a sensation was created when one delegate mounted a chair and nominated Major McKinley.

Major McKinley from his place as presiding officer thanked the convention, but said that he could not allow his name to go before it at that time, as he had promised that he would not allow his name to be used while the names of certain candidates were before the convention. The uproar became

tumultuous. A majority of the delegates were plainly in favor of the election of Major McKinley by acclamation, although there was some objection.
One of the delegates, assuming the prerogatives of the chair, put the motion,
and declared it carried. Major McKinley ruled that the motion had not
prevailed. General Grosvenor mounted the platform and the second time
put the motion and declared it carried.

Again Major McKinley ruled that the motion had not prevailed and
insisted on the vote being taken on the names already submitted, excluding
his own. Once more General Grosvenor arose—this time to a point of
order. He insisted that Major McKinley had been elected by acclamation,
and that the convention had now to elect two more delegates-at-large. The
chair overruled the point of order, and amid tumultuous confusion ordered
the balloting to go on. A delegate arose and asked the convention to consider Major McKinley as having been put in nomination, despite his declina-
tion. At this there were thunders of cheers. From early in the balloting
it was evident that Major McKinley was bound to be elected. Counties
that had favored other candidates abandoned them and voted solidly for
the Major. After between 300 and 400 votes had been cast for Major
McKinley and it was recognized by everybody that he had already been
elected, a motion was made that he be elected by acclamation. Further
contest was stopped, and Major McKinley was elected a delegate-at-large
by acclamation.

In the National Convention at Chicago Major McKinley bore himself
modestly, but his great quality of leadership came to the front by force of
circumstances. He only spoke two or three times from the floor of the
convention, but every time he arose he attracted attention, and the influence
he exerted was remarkable. At the critical time during the convention his
was the voice that rallied the Blaine forces. Three ballots had been taken.
Blaine gained on each ballot. The final and desperate effort was made by
the other candidates under the lead of the dashing Foraker, in Sherman's
behalf, for an adjournment. There was pandemonium, and there threatened
to be a panic.

In the midst of the storm Major McKinley arose. He waved his hand and
the tumult ceased. Calm and like granite he stood the master spirit of the
convention. His short speech was carried in clarion tones all over the
immense hall. As a friend of Blaine, he said, he recognized and respected
the rights of the friends of other candidates to secure an adjournment, and
concluded:

"Let the motion be put and let everybody favorable to the nomination of Blaine vote against it."

That settled it. Under Major McKinley's leadership, assumed spontaneously and boldly, the Blaine men accepted the challenge, the motion for an adjournment was voted down, and the victory was won. It was not defeat that Major McKinley turned aside—the situation was not so serious as that—but in a crisis, when the Blaine men were getting demoralized and the convention was turning itself into a mob, the Major, leaping to the front, by one command marshaled the Blaine men into line and pressed them forward to their already sighted victory. Major McKinley was chairman of the committee on resolutions at that convention, and when he appeared to read the platform he received an ovation that was one of the features of that great event.

Major McKinley's next appearance at a Republican national convention was in 1888, and this time he came at the head of the Ohio delegation, and in John Sherman's behalf. At this convention Mr. McKinley conspicuously illustrated his character for loyalty to his friends and his word. No candidate had been able to secure a majority. Sherman, Alger, Allison, Harrison, Gresham, and Depew, all had a strong following, but none was near a nomination. Major McKinley, at the head of the Ohio delegation, instructed to vote his delegation solidly for Sherman, was one of the heroes of the convention. His entrance at each session was greeted with the wildest enthusiasm. Day and night he was at work among the various state delegations, laboring to secure votes for Ohio's great financier. On the sixth ballot a delegate voted for William McKinley, and was greeted by cheers which swelled again and again before silence could be restored. The next state that was called cast seventeen votes for Major McKinley, and again the cheers broke forth. The drift was unmistakably setting toward McKinley like an ocean tide.

Everyone expected to see the Garfield nomination of 1880 repeated. But they were disappointed. The roll call was interrupted by the Major, who, leaping upon a chair at the end of the middle aisle, pale, but calm and determined, uttered a speech which, unpremeditated as it was, has seldom been surpassed for eloquence, candor and unselfish loyalty. In it he declared his inability to be a candidate with honor to himself, and proclaimed his unswerving loyalty to the Ohio chieftain. The tide was turned. On the seventh ballot Benjamin Harrison was named, but McKinley went home to Ohio stronger than ever in the hearts of his fellow men.

Some time before the Republican National Convention of 1892, held in Minneapolis, Minn., June 7, Governor McKinley had privately and publicly expressed himself as in favor of the renomination of President Harrison. Having committed himself, the Governor stood by his declaration. He was elected a delegate-at-large as a Harrison man, and the understanding was that Ohio would vote solidly for the President's nomination.

The convention elected Governor McKinley its permanent chairman. R. M. Nevin of Dayton was his alternate. Before he took the chair as presiding officer the Governor specifically charged Mr. Nevin to vote for Harrison. Only one vote was taken on the nomination for President. When Ohio was called ex-Governor Foraker said Ohio asked time for a consultation, and after a pause the vote of the state was announced as: Harrison, 2 votes; William McKinley, 44. Chairman McKinley immediately sprang from his seat and shouted:

"I challenge the vote of Ohio!"

A brief and animated debate then ensued between ex-Governor Foraker and Governor McKinley, in which Foraker told the chairman that he had ceased to be a member of the Ohio delegation on assuming the post of presiding officer, and could not be recognized. Finally a roll call of the Ohio delegation was ordered, and this resulted, McKinley, 45; Harrison, 1. The only vote for Harrison cast by the Ohio delegation was that cast by Governor McKinley's alternate. President Harrison was renominated on the first and only ballot, but the Governor had 182 votes cast for him despite the fact that he was not a candidate. At the conclusion of the balloting Governor McKinley took the floor and moved that the President's nomination be made unanimous, and the motion carried. The Governor was chosen chairman of the commission that officially notified the President of his nomination.

The result of the campaign of 1892 was a surprise to both the leading political parties. Grover Cleveland, the Democratic candidate for president, was elected, and both the house and senate had large Democratic majorities. The political revolution was remarkable, and was largely due to the Populist movement, and to fusion between the Populists and Democrats in the South and West. The clamor for the free coinage of silver, at the ratio of 16 to 1, and the industrial depression which set in in 1893, brought Governor McKinley into the public eye as the man calculated to restore prosperity to the country. Meanwhile he adhered strictly to his duties as governor of Ohio.

From a photograph taken for and used by courtesy of the Chicago Inter Ocean.

DR. P. M. RIXEY, PRESIDENT McKINLEY'S FAMILY PHYSICIAN.

GOVERNOR McKINLEY IN HIS LIBRARY GIVING INSTRUCTIONS
TO HIS POLITICAL MANAGERS. (1896.)

CHAPTER XVIII.

FIRST NOMINATION FOR PRESIDENT.

At no time in the history of the Republican party has there been such an array of brilliant and worthy men before the country named for the honor of Presidential candidates as at that period when the National Republican Convention of 1896 was to make a choice from the shining list. That convention was remarkable and unique, more so than any other convention of this organization, whose first President, a pioneer of universal freedom, a pathfinder across the western wilderness that is now an empire, Colonel John Charles Fremont, who was presented for the suffrage of the people forty years before. That pioneer candidate was defeated because the day of broad thought had not arisen. The rising storm of civil strife swept the next candidate of the party, immortal Lincoln, to the highest place in the nation, from whence he guided the Republic and its destinies through the raging tempest until an assassin's missile laid him low, and that at the moment when the country could least have spared him, and when it seemed that fate to be just might have been more kindly to both him and his people, for he deserved to enjoy the fruit of his work, and the people would have had pleasure and profit in his presence.

Of no other such conventions is there a more interesting story than that which might be given of the convention at St. Louis in June, 1896, which made William McKinley its candidate, and who is another martyr of the Republic, slain by organized assassination, because the nation had placed him in conspicuous exaltation.

Of the great ones whose personal partisans and whose high places among the people had made them prominent in the premises, Thomas B. Reed of Maine was among the foremost. He was without a superior among that many for intelligence, wit and general ability, and there can be no question that, had he been nominated and elected as Chief Magistrate, he would have given the country a worthy and thoroughly, even distinctly, American administration.

William B. Allison of Iowa, who was a delegate to the Chicago convention of 1860, that nominated Abraham Lincoln, and a Senator, who had made a national and well-deserved fame for patriotic statesmanship, was another, now demanded by a large following, and he had already been a prominent candidate for President before preceding conventions.

Levi P. Morton, ex-Vice-President of the United States and governor of the mighty State of New York, a man of glorious record and accepted ability, who was honored and respected by friends and foes, was also of the array of eligible men whose friends asked for him the nomination.

Quay of Pennsylvania, Alger of Michigan, Sherman of Ohio, Thurston of Nebraska, all of the best kind of "Presidential timber," and numerous others of more or less distinction, capacity and merit, were warmly and enthusiastically urged by their partisans.

Governor Morton quickly announced that he would not allow himself to be made a candidate before the convention unless a real one, meaning that he must not be placed in such a position as a compliment to himself and his following, or with the idea of using him as the means for securing the nomination of some one else. Hon. Thomas Platt, the shrewd and powerful manipulator of politics and politicians, had secured the pledge of the New York delegation for Morton, and with such an array of 34 electoral votes from such a State, Morton seemed to be a formidable man in the situation, with an endorsement to be proud of and one that would command the deference of that great body.

New England was strong in her pride and confidence in her brilliant son, and had won many promises for Reed, but small revolts here and there made his hold precarious, and the defection of Congressman Manley of Maine at the very moment when his influence and assistance was most necessary seriously and dangerously affected Reed's chances. Appalled by the mighty array that favored McKinley, the Maine Congressman deserted the New England favorite and dismay and disorganization took possession of their camp.

Much there was of this preliminary skirmishing among the partisans of all the available ones, but in it all a potent fact was staring at the fight, and became so apparent that it was at last candidly acknowledged.

The feeling for Governor William McKinley of Ohio was constantly gathering strength. The pressure from outside was too strong to withstand. For weeks before the convention the Republican public had been shouting McKinley, and in a tone that could not be ignored. The voice and the force of the people pressed hard upon the convention. The newspapers teemed with his praise; his face and record were constantly being presented; buttons bearing his portrait and mottoes that epitomized his principles were seen everywhere, in city, town and country, and thousands who had been, theretofore, but little interested in politics became enthusiastic champions of the man from Ohio.

William McKinley had been before the people, not as a candidate for President, but as the ardent advocate of measures that intelligent persons thought more of national prosperity than of partisan politics. The quick-seeing people had heard and read of his plans for redeeming the country and casting off its burden of distress, "Hard Times," and this had brought the tide of public favor and endorsement.

With this and all the excellent qualities of the man, in which the people had been instructed, wise, sagacious, far-seeing and powerful friends, adepts in the science of politics, who made no mistakes, took the matter in hand, before the convention had assembled, and then into it, at the proper time, and they kept the front of the fight well aligned and unbroken to victory.

The movement for McKinley was skillfully presented as that of "the masses against the bosses." In some respects that was what it was. The bosses fought for others in the convention, but the will of the people carried. The pressure of the masses was for McKinley, and though the people stood on the outside the avalanche of popular opinion swept over all. The politicians opposed the "Ohio idea" and fought desperately. Platt, the most adroit of them all, threatened, cajoled, combined and bluffed. Reed's managers tried tact, diplomacy, compromise and all else available, the opponents of McKinley of all elements held all sorts of "star chamber" sessions time and time again, and on the night before the convention planned together until daylight endeavoring to fix some combination to defeat McKinley, but Mark Hanna, the manager of the McKinley campaign, kept in the even tenor of his way, doing his work as past master of political strategy, smiled and feared not. Certain safety gave him ease, and masterly he held his way with coolness and calculation.

It was evident from the first that there was only one dangerous rock upon which the great convention might split. There were those in the convention from the far West, whose local interests in silver would overcome party fealty and the question of a gold standard of currency or unlimited silver coinage was one that required strong, unfailing nerve to face it. As strong a factor as the tariff always was and always will be, it was temporarily relegated to the background, as there was not a possibility of serious dissension upon the question of protection, for which the party of the convention naturally stood, under any circumstances.

But unquestionably there was a wide variance in many quarters between the "gold" and "silver" men. While the East and the older sections of our country were uncompromising in their demand for gold as the single standard, some of the Republicans beyond the Mississippi insisted upon a plank acknowledging silver, and open threats were made that in case of refusal they would bolt the convention and affiliate with the party representing their views. The question was as to how far this disaffection extended. The pages immediately following will answer that question.

Meanwhile Governor McKinley at his home in Canton, Ohio, gave no sign. The lessons of former candidates who had undone themselves by tongue or pen were not lost upon him, and he remained resolutely mute. He was referred to as the "wabbling candidate," and some of his earlier expressions were quoted against him; but nothing sufficed to draw him out. He quietly bided his time, and who shall say he was not wise?

It was about half an hour past noon, on Tuesday, June 16, 1896, that the eleventh national convention of the Republican party was called to order by the Hon. Thomas Henry Carter, chairman of the Republican National Committee. The tremendous structure, known as the Auditorium or Convention Hall, is capable of accommodating an immense assemblage, and it is estimated that more than 40,000 visitors had flocked to St. Louis. Fortunately the torrid weather for which the Mound City is noted and dreaded held off, though it gave a taste of its terrible power to smite before final adjournment came.

For the first time in the history of national conventions, the opening prayer was made by an Israelite, in the person of Rabbi Samuel Sale, pastor of the Shaare Emeth congregation. His invocation was devout, and, at its close, the secretary read the call issued by the National Committee for the convention. He was not heard fifty feet away, not so much because of his weakness of voice, as on account of the wretched acoustic qualities of the building. Chairman Carter then presented the name of Hon. Charles W. Fairbanks of Indiana as temporary chairman. No voice was raised in opposition, and the tall, slender man, with close-cropped beard and mustache, came forward and delivered an address that was frequently interrupted by applause. It was an arraignment of the Democratic administration for its many shortcomings, and an argument that the prosperity of the country at large could be secured only by the adoption of the principles of the Republican party. Sound currency, protection, sympathy for Cuba, and the certainty that the candidates about to be named would be the next President and Vice-President of the United States, were the principal features of Chairman Fairbanks' speech, which was received with many expressions of approval. At its conclusion the necessary officials of the convention were appointed, the members of the various committees announced, and, after a session of less than two hours, an adjournment was had to 10 o'clock Wednesday.

Between the adjournment and the coming together on the morrow, much effective work was done. While the sentiment of the delegates was overwhelmingly in favor of "sound currency," or the single gold standard, there was a diversity of opinion in many quarters as to whether the word "gold" should be used in the platform. A considerable number thought the latter was sufficiently explicit without the word, but the insistence of others compelled a yielding of the point: it was decided that the all-potent word should appear. Since adjournment Mr. Hanna has asserted that the gold plank was agreed upon by him or his associates before the arrival of the delegates from the East, who were popularly credited with the formulation of the clause in question.

The convention reassembled at a quarter to eleven on Wednesday, and was opened with prayer by Rev. Dr. W. G. Williams, after which the real work began. The report of the Committee on Permanent Organization presented the name of Senator J. N. Thurston of Nebraska as chairman, made the secretaries, sergeant-at-arms and other temporary officers permanent officers of the convention, and gave a list of vice-presidents, consisting of one from each State. It was accepted and Senator Thurston was loudly applauded as he took his seat.

The address of Mr. Thurston pleased all by its terseness and brevity.

Awaiting the report of the Committee on Credentials the convention adjourned until 2 o'clock, and at 3 that afternoon Chairman Thurston called the body to order. Bishop Arnett of Ohio offered the opening prayer and Mr. Madden of Chicago presented to the chairman a gavel made from timber of a house in which Abraham Lincoln once lived. Another gavel was also presented, carved from the homestead of Henry Clay, "The Father of Protection."

The Committee on Credentials then presented majority and minority reports, the former of which favored the seating of the Higgins delegates and those at large from Delaware as against the Addicks delegates, and the seating of the list of Texas delegates, which was headed by John Grant. After a warm discussion the majority report was adopted by the vote of $545\frac{1}{2}$ to $359\frac{1}{2}$. This vote was considered a test one between McKinley and his opponents and removed all doubts of the invincibility of the Ohio man.

The full Committee on Resolutions met at the Lindell Hotel in the evening and went into secret session. The proposed platform was read by paragraphs, the agreement being that each paragraph should be voted on separately. There was unanimous accord upon the tariff plank and the sugar plank was accepted. A strong declaration was formulated for a protective duty on wools and woolens and a demand made for the protection of American shipbuilding and the development of American commerce.

When the financial plank was reached Senator Teller of Colorado presented a minority report which declared in favor of the free and unlimited coinage of silver at the ratio of 16 to 1. Mr. Teller, with deep emotion, declared that the time had come when, if the single gold standard was adopted, he should be compelled to leave the party with which he had been associated for thirty-five years.   There was much sympathy felt for this able leader, whose association with the Republican party had earned for him the respect of political foes as well as friends.   Mr. Cannon of Utah was hardly less agitated when he announced a decision similar to that of Teller, and Mr. Dubois of Idaho declared that, much as he regretted the step, he would follow Messrs. Teller and Cannon.   Then, after earnest argument, Mr. Hartman of Montana said that he never would support a candidate upon the proposed platform.

The substitute of Senator Teller received 10 votes, which included the delegates from Colorado, California, Utah, Montana, Idaho, Wyoming, Arizona, Nevada, North Carolina and New Mexico.   The substitute was defeated by 41 votes.   After further discussion, the gold plank, as it appears in the platform, was adopted by a vote of yeas 40, nays 11, the member from Oklahoma having joined the silver men.

The convention came together on Thursday morning, only five minutes late, with all of the delegates in their seats, and the galleries packed to suffocation, many ladies being among the spectators.   Rev. John R. Scott of Florida, a negro, opened with a brief and appropriate prayer.

The first order of business was the reception of the report of the Committee on Resolutions.   Senator-elect Foraker of Ohio was cheered as he advanced to the platform and said: "As chairman of the Committee on Resolutions, I have the honor to report as follows:"

He then read the platform, as printed elsewhere, in a clear, ringing voice and with distinct enunciation.   He emphasized the endorsement of President Harrison, and was applauded, and when, in a loud voice and with impressive manner, he declared: "The Republican party is unreservedly for sound money," the applause was greater than ever, it rising to a still more enthusiastic pitch when the pledge to promote international agreement for free coinage of silver was read.   Mr. Foraker was compelled to stop reading and the applause continued so long that the chairman rapped repeatedly for order.

The demand for American control of the Hawaiian Islands was warmly approved, but the convention remained mum over the proposed building of the

Nicaragua Canal by the United States and the purchase of the Danish Islands for a naval station. If any enthusiasm was felt in that direction it did not manifest itself. But the sympathy of the people found ardent expression when the Cuban paragraph was read, dropping again to zero over the civil service plank. The negro delegates applauded noisily the demand for a free ballot and the condemnation of lynching.

It took twenty-five minutes for the reading of the platform, during which the convention gave close attention, breaking out again into cheers at the close. When the tumult had subsided, Mr. Foraker moved the adoption of the report as the National platform for 1896.

As Mr. Foraker reached the closing paragraph of the report, Senator Teller left his place with the Colorado delegation and took his seat on the platform. He was recognized by the chairman and sent to the secretary's desk and had read the following minority report: "We, the undersigned members of the Committee on Resolutions, being unable to agree with that part of the majority report which treats of the subjects of coinage and finance, respectfully submit the following paragraph as a substitute therefor:

"The Republican party favors the use of both gold and silver as equal standard money, and pledges its power to secure the free, unrestricted and independent coinage of gold and silver at our mints at the ratio of 16 parts of silver to 1 of gold."

Mr. Teller then advanced to the front of the platform to utter his "farewell." The universal respect felt for him was shown by the cordial greeting of the twelve thousand people, who saw that the distinguished gentleman was almost overcome with emotion. It may be doubted whether there was one in that immense assemblage who did not feel a sincere sympathy for the man who was taking the most painful step of his public career.

Mr. Teller asserted that we might as well have two flags in the Nation, if the present money system is to be maintained, for the reason that two flags are not more important than this all-absorbing question of gold and silver money. He declared that he was not actuated by the fact that Colorado is a silver-producing State, but he had come to the earnest conclusion, after twenty years of study, that bimetallism is the only safe money doctrine for the United States and all other countries.

Mr. Teller insisted that a protective tariff cannot be maintained on a gold standard. Then, with uplifted hands, he declared: "When God Almighty made these two metals, He intended them for use as money."

Senator Teller said that the years of study which he had devoted to this question had brought convictions to him which were binding upon his conscience, and it was because he was an honest man that he could not support the gold money plank. The declaration was received with cheers and hisses, and moisture gathered in the eyes of the speaker as he looked out over the sea of faces and felt that he had at last reached the parting of the ways. Then the tears coursed down his cheeks and his handkerchief went to his eyes. The sight caused a respectful hush to fall over the convention, while more than one friend wept in silent sympathy.

Recovering himself, Senator Teller declared that the best thoughts of the world favored bimetallism, and it was advocated by the greatest teachers of political economy in Europe.

"Do you suppose," he asked, "that we can take this step and leave the party without distress? Take any methods you please to nominate your man, but put him upon the right platform, and I will support him. I was for free men, free speech, and a free Government. I was with the Republican party when it was born. I have become accustomed to abuse, but I have voted for every Republican candidate since the foundation of the party, and I have been in close communication with its distinguished men for forty years."

At this point, Senator Teller broke down again. The tears streamed over his face and he was greatly distressed. In a broken voice he added:

"But if I am to leave the Republican party, I do not leave it in anger. I believe that my doctrine is for the good of the people. I believe that the Republican party will see the error of its way, and, although I may never be permitted again to address a Republican National Convention, I shall live in the hope that before I die this great party will come to a thorough understanding of the silver question and treat it solemnly and with the keenest interest in support of all the people."

The vote to lay Senator Teller's motion on the table disclosed an interesting state of facts. It was supported by seven friends in Alabama, fifteen in California, his eight delegates of Colorado, two from Florida, three from Georgia, the six from Idaho, and one from Illinois. In addition, his plank received the following support: Kansas, four votes, Michigan, one; Missouri, one; Montana, six; Nevada, six; South Carolina, fourteen and one-half; South Dakota, two; Tennessee, one; Utah, six; Virginia, five; Wyoming, six; and in the Territories: Arizona, six; New Mexico, three, and Oklahoma, one, making one hundred and five and one-half votes in all. The vote for the majority report was eight hundred and eighteen and one-half.

Senator Teller, who was still on the platform, asked permission from the chairman to introduce Senator Cannon of Utah, who desired to read a statement from the silver men. The manner of Senator Cannon was defiant and quickly stirred up impatience. He declared he would bow to the majority in the matter of votes, but would never bow when a question of principle was at stake. He said they would withdraw from the convention, and he predicted trouble in the future for the Republican party. This was greeted with hisses and urgent requests for him to sit down. In the midst of the storm, the chairman turned to Senator Cannon and shouted: "The Republican party do not fear any declaration."

This threw the convention into a tumult of enthusiasm. Men sprang to their feet, swung flags and shouted at the top of their voices. Senator Cannon calmly awaited the subsidence of the storm, when he continued with his generalities, and read the list of free silver men who would leave the convention. The names of the signers were greeted with hisses, and someone in the rear called out, "Good-by, my lover, good-by," as Senator Teller and his associates filed out of the hall, marching down the main aisle. The whole convention was again on its feet yelling, waving flags, hats and fans, while the band played patriotic airs and the assemblage sang the chorus, "Three Cheers for the Red, White and Blue."

The silver delegates who withdrew were Congressman Hartman of Montana; Senator Cannon, Congressman Allen and Delegate Thomas Kearns, of Utah; Senator Pettigrew, of South Dakota; Delegates Cleveland and Strother, of Nevada; the entire Idaho delegation of six, headed by Senator Dubois; the whole Colorado delegation of eight; including Senator Teller, the total number of bolters being twenty-one, including four senators and two representatives.

Waiting until the excitement had subsided, the chairman announced in deliberate fashion: "Gentlemen of the Convention, there seem to be enough delegates left to do business. (Great cheering.) The chair now asks that a gentleman from Montana who did not go out"—Cheers drowned the rest of the sentence, and cries were made for Lee Mantle, who was asked to come to the platform, but declined.

On the call of states for nominations for the Presidency, the first response was from Iowa. R. M. Baldwin, of Council Bluffs, nominated Senator W. B. Allison, in a glowing tribute to Senator Allison's worth and services.

Senator Lodge, of Massachusetts, in a speech of characteristic eloquence, nominated Hon. Thomas B. Reed.

Hon. Chauncey M. Depew received a warm welcome as he made his way to the platform to nominate Governor Levi P. Morton, of New York State, which he did in his usual felicitous style of speech.

Then came the call of Ohio.   Amid intense interest and expectation Governor Foraker went to the platform, and when silence had been obtained he said:

"Mr. President and Gentlemen of the Convention: It would be exceedingly difficult, if not entirely impossible, to exaggerate the disagreeable situation of the last four years.   The grand aggregate of the multitudinous bad results of a Democratic National Administration may be summed up as one stupendous disaster.   It has been a disaster, however, not without, at least, this one redeeming feature—that it has been fair; nobody has escaped. (Loud laughter.)

"It has fallen equally and alike on all sections of the country and on all classes of our people; the just and the unjust, the Republican and the Democrat, the rich and the poor, the high and the low, have suffered in common. Poverty and distress have overtaken business: shrunken values have dissipated fortunes; deficiencies of revenue law have impoverished the Government, while bond issues and bond syndicates have discredited and scandalized the country.

"Over against that fearful penalty is, however, to be set down one great, blessed compensatory result—is has destroyed the Democratic party.   (Cheers and laughter.)   The proud columns which swept the country in triumph in 1892 are broken and hopeless in 1896. Their boasted principles when put to the test have proved to be delusive fallacies, and their great leaders have degenerated into warring chieftains of petty and irreconcilable factions. Their approaching National Convention is but an approaching National nightmare. No man pretends to be able to predict any good result to come from it.   And no man is seeking the nomination of that Convention except only the limited few who have advertised their unfitness for any kind of a public trust by proclaiming their willingness to stand on any sort of a platform that may be adopted.   (Laughter.)

"The truth is, the party which would stand up under the odium of human slavery, opposed to the war for the preservation of the Union, to emancipation, to enfranchisement, to reconstruction and to specie resumption, is at last to be overmatched and undone by itself.   It is writhing in the throes and agonies of final dissolution.   No human agency can prevent its absolute overthrow at the next election, except only this Convention.   If we make no mistake here, the Democratic party will go out of power on the 4th day of

March, 1897 (applause), to remain out of power until God, in His infinite wisdom and mercy and goodness, shall see fit once more to chastise His people. (Loud laughter and applause.)

"So far we have not made any mistake. We have adopted a platform which, notwithstanding the scene witnessed in this hall this morning, meets the demands and expectations of the American people.

"It remains for us now, as the last crowning act of our work, to meet again that same expectation in the nomination of our candidates. What is that expectation? What is it that the people want? They want as their candidate something more than 'a good business man' (an allusion to Mr. Depew's characterization of Governor Morton). They want something more than a popular leader. They want something more than a wise and patriotic statesman. They want a man who embodies in himself not only all these essential qualifications, but those, in addition, which, in the highest possible degree, typify in name, in character, in record, in ambition, in purpose, the exact opposite of all that is signified and represented by that free-trade, deficit-making, bond-issuing, labor-assassinating, Democratic Administration. (Cheers.) I stand here to present to this Convention such a man. His name is William McKinley."

At this point pandemonium was let loose, and the Convention gave up to unrestrained yelling, cheering, horn-blowing, whistling, cat-calling and all the other devices common to such occasions. A number of red, white and blue plumes, which (carefully wrapped up) had been brought into the Convention earlier in the proceedings, were uncovered and waved, while almost every delegate seemed to be wildly gesticulating with either a fan or a flag in the air. The band tried in vain to compete with the ear-splitting clamor, but at last the strains of "Marching Through Georgia" caught the ears of the crowd, and they joined in the chorus and gradually quieted down.

Then a portrait of McKinley was hoisted on a line with the United States flag on the gallery facing the platform, and the cheering began over again, to which the band responded by playing "Rally Round the Flag," the Convention joining in the chorus.

After at least twelve minutes of this kind of proceeding the chair began to rap for a restoration of order, but without avail.

Senator-elect Foraker stood during all this wild scene smiling his approval. Mr. Hepburn, of Iowa, had in the meantime been called to the chair by Senator Thurston, but just when he had nearly restored order, Mrs. H. W. R. Strong, of California, who had presented the plumes in honor of

Ohio's choice, made her appearance on the floor, waving one of them, and another uncontrollable outbreak of wholesale temporary insanity occurred. During the interval of confusion, a three-quarter face, life-size sculptured bust of McKinley was presented to Mr. Foraker by the Republican Club of the University of Chicago. The portrait was in a mahogany frame, decorated with red, white and blue ribbons, and with a bow of maroon-colored ribbons forming the colors of the university. The portrait was the work of Harris Hirsch, and was presented by Dr. Lisston H. Montgomery, of Chicago, with a letter signed by H. L. Ickes, president of the club. It was accepted by Senator-elect Foraker in dumb show.

After twenty-five minutes of incessant turmoil Mr. Foraker was allowed to resume his speech.

He spoke of the great champions of Republicanism in the past, eulogizing Mr. Blaine particularly, and continued:

"But, greatest of all, measured by present requirements, is the leader of the House of Representatives, the author of the McKinley Bill, which gave to labor its richest awards. No other name so completely meets the requirements of the occasion, and no other name so absolutely commands all hearts. The shafts of envy and malice and slander and libel and detraction that have been aimed at him lie broken and harmless at his feet. The quiver is empty, and he is untouched. That is because the people know him, trust him, believe him, and will not permit any human power to disparage him unjustly in their estimation.

"They know that he is an American of Americans. They know that he is just and able and brave, and they want him for President of the United States. (Applause.) They have already shown it—not in this or that State, nor in this or that section, but in all the States and in all the sections from ocean to ocean, and from the Gulf to the Lakes. They expect of you to give them a chance to vote for him. It is our duty to do it. If we discharge that duty we will give joy to their hearts, enthusiasm to their souls and triumphant victory to our cause. (Applause.) And he, in turn, will give us an administration under which the country will enter on a new era of prosperity at home and of glory and honor abroad, by all these tokens of the present and all these promises of the future. In the name of the forty-six delegates of Ohio, I submit his claim to your consideration." (More applause.)

The high-water mark of enthusiasm was reached when Senator Thurston rose to second the nomination of McKinley, which he did in eloquent and forceful words.

In the midst of cries of "vote," Governor Hastings placed in nomination Matthew Stanley Quay, at the conclusion of which, amid a profound hush, the Convention began balloting for a nominee for President of the United States.

Alabama led off with 1 for Morton and 19 for McKinley, Arkansas and California following with a solid vote for McKinley. Connecticut gave 5 for Reed and 7 for McKinley; Delaware, its full vote for McKinley; Florida, 8 for McKinley; Georgia, 2 for Reed, 2 for Quay, and 22 for McKinley.

When all of the States had been called, the chairman stated, before the announcement of the result, that application had been made to him for recognition by delegates of the defeated candidates to make a certain motion. He thought it the fairest way to recognize them in the order in which the nominations had been made. He then announced that William McKinley had received $661\frac{1}{2}$ votes.

Before the chairman could get any further, the enthusiasm of the Convention broke all bounds. Every man was on his feet, shouting, hurrahing, cheering, swinging hats and canes in the air, waving flags and banners and the pampas plumes of California, while through the Niagara-like rush and roar were caught the notes of "My Country, 'Tis of Thee," as the band played with might and main in its attempt to gain the mastery of the cyclone. The women, if possible, were more frantic than the men. Parasols, fans, opera-glasses, gloves—anything, everything—were compelled to help in the magnificent burst of enthusiasm which swept over and submerged all alike, until it looked as if order could never again be evolved from the swirling pandemonium.

One fancy caught on with wonderful effect. A young man on the platform waved on the point of the national banner a laced cocked hat, such as appears in most of popular representations of the mighty Napoleon. This symbol of enthusiasm was greeted with rapturous applause, to which the booming of artillery on the outside contributed.

Finally, after a long, long time, the chairman gained a chance to complete the announcement of the vote. It was: Thomas B. Reed, $84\frac{1}{2}$; Senator Quay, $61\frac{1}{2}$; Levi P. Morton, 58; Senator Allison, $35\frac{1}{2}$, and Don Cameron 1.

The vote by States was as follows:

	McKinley.	Morton.	Quay.	Reed.	Allison.
Maine	..	..	..	12	..
Maryland...............	15	..	..	1	..
Massachusetts.........	1	..	..	29	..
Michigan...............	28	..	..	..	..
Minnesota.............	18	..	..	..	..
Mississippi.............	17	..	1	..	..
Missouri...............	34	..	..	..	..
*Montana..............	1	..	..	..	..
Nebraska..............	16	..	..	..	..
Nevada................	3	..	..	..	..
New Hampshire........	..	..	..	8	..
New Jersey............	19	..	..	1	..
New York.............	17	55	..	..	..
North Carolina........	19½	..	..	2½	..
North Dakota..........	6	..	..	..	..
Ohio..................	46	..	..	..	..
Oregon...............	8	..	..	..	..
Pennsylvania..........	6	..	58	..	..
Rhode Island..........	..	..	..	8	..
South Carolina........	18	..	..	..	..
South Dakota..........	8	..	..	..	..
Tennessee.............	24	..	..	..	..
Texas.................	21	..	..	5	3
Utah..................	3	..	..	..	3
Vermont..............	8	..	..	..	..
Virginia...............	23	..	..	1	..
Washington...........	8	..	..	..	..
West Virginia.........	12	..	..	..	..
Wisconsin.............	24	..	..	..	..
Wyoming..............	6	..	..	..	..
Arizona...............	6	..	..	..	..
New Mexico...........	5	..	..	..	1
Oklahoma.............	4	..	..	1	1
Indian Territory.......	6	..	..	..	..
District of Columbia.....	..	..	..	1	1
Alaska................	4	..	..	..	..
Totals............	661½	58	61½	84½	35½

*Blank, 4, and one vote for Cameron from Montana.
Necessary for choice, 454. Total number of delegates present, 906.

Senator Lodge, rising in his delegation, in a forceful speech moved to make the nomnation of Mr. McKinley unanimous. Mr. Hastings, of Pennsylvania, who had nominated Quay, seconded the motion, as did Thomas C. Platt on behalf of New York, Mr. Henderson, of Iowa, and J. Madison Vance, of Louisiana. In answer to loud calls Mr. Depew mounted his chair in the back of the room, where the rays of the sun beamed on his countenance, which itself was beaming with good humor, and delivered a short and characteristically humorous speech.

The chair then put the question, "Shall the nomination be made unanimous?" and by a rising vote it was so ordered, and the chair announced that Mr. William McKinley of Ohio was the candidate of the Republican party for President of the United States.

This great step having been taken, Senator Lodge moved to proceed to the nomination of a candidate for Vice-President; and, although the Convention had been in continuous session for eight and a half hours, the motion was carried, and at twenty minutes past six the roll of the States was called for such nominations.

Mr. Fessenden nominated the Hon. Morgan G. Bulkeley of Connecticut, while Judge Franklin Fort of New Jersey placed the Hon. Garret A. Hobart in nomination. Judge Fort concluded one of the most telling speeches with the following tribute to his nominee:

"His capabilities are such as would grace any position of honor in the Nation. Not for himself, but for our State; not for his ambition, but to give to the Nation the highest type of public official, do we come to this convention by the command of our State and in the name of the Republican party of New Jersey unconquered and unconquerable, undivided and indivisible— with one united voice speaking for all that counts for good citizenship in our State, and nominate to you for the office of Vice-President of this Republic, Garret A. Hobart of New Jersey."

Mr. Humphrey seconded the nomination of Mr. Hobart in the name of the State of Illinois. Delegate Randolph of Tennessee nominated Henry Clay Evans of that State, the nomination being seconded by colored Delegate Smith of Kentucky, who declared the Republican party "the grandest organization this side of eternity." Mr. I. C. Walker (colored) of Virginia, put his fellow-delegate in nomination.

By the time the balloting reached South Dakota it was so evident that Hobart was to be the fortunate one that many of the delegates began leaving the hall. The result of the ballot as announced by the chair was: Hobart, 535½; Evans, 277½; Bulkeley, 39; Lippitt, 8; Walker, 24; Reed, 3; Thurston, 2; Frederick Grant, 2; Depew, 3; Morton, 1; absent, 23.

Then at ten minutes to eight o'clock, the eleventh National Republican Convention adjourned *sine die*.

Six hundred miles away, in the State of Ohio, is the pleasant town of Canton, the home of the nominee of the Republican party for the Presidency of the United States. What an impressive illustration of the wonderful studies in discovery it was, that William McKinley, during the tempestuous scenes we have attempted to describe, sat in his library and heard the cheering, the shouts, the speeches and the whirlwind which accompanied his nomination and kept as close track of the proceedings as if he were sitting on the platform and looking into the sea of upturned faces! Such was the amazing fact, for the telephone to which his ear was turned reported everything almost as faithfully as his own eyes and ears could have done, and he, more than half a thousand miles distant, knew the result as soon as did the excited delegates themselves.

During the stormy week of the Convention that is described in the preceding pages, Governor McKinley was sitting on the porch of his cottage talking to a group of friends, when an old lady was seen approaching the gate.

"That's my mother!" he exclaimed, springing to his feet and hurrying down the walk to meet her. He gave her his arm and, bringing her to the porch, introduced her to each in turn, saw that she was provided with the most comfortable chair, and to none gave more loving attention than to her.

FUNERAL DECORATIONS IN THE EAST ROOM OF THE WHITE HOUSE.

PRESIDENT AND MRS. McKINLEY, SENATOR HANNA, GENERAL
ALGER AND THEIR FAMILIES AT DINNER.

CHAPTER XIX.

THE GREAT CAMPAIGN OF 1896.

Long before the National Convention of 1896 was held, the issues which were to be paramount in the campaign had begun to crystallize. Throughout the country there was a wail of distress growing out of the depression of 1893, and the people were thinking, thinking, as to the cause of the trouble which oppressed them. No nation was ever better equipped to intelligently discuss matters pertaining to its welfare than the United States at that period. Theorists had conceived numerous remedies for the economic depression, and right or wrong, had found many adherents.

The Republican National Convention had declared for the first time in the history of the party in favor of establishing the financial system of the country on a gold basis. Protection to American interests, which had long been a cherished principle of the party, also had its place in the platform. The Democrats, on the other hand, adopted a platform demanding the free coinage of silver at the ratio of 16 to 1, and a tariff for revenue only.

As before stated, however, the issues had already been firmly fixed in the public mind. The advocates of the free coinage of silver had been preaching their doctrines for months, and as their arguments were easily comprehended, the masses took to them with avidity. The cry was that the Republicans intended to destroy silver except as a subsidiary coin, and make gold the basic money of the country. It was asserted that there was not gold enough in the world to provide a currency for the wants of trade, hence the volume of money would be contracted, if the policy of the Republicans prevailed. Prices of commodities, already extremely low, would fall lower, because there would be less money for the people to purchase them with, hence the distress would grow apace.

These arguments had been disseminated in a small book the writer of which pretended to hold a "financial school," and to expound for the benefit of the people, and for the benefit of capitalists especially, the true gospel of finance. Millions of copies of this book had been sold, and people throughout the length and breadth of the land were familiar with its arguments. Those of opposite beliefs had not been asleep during this period. They had formulated arguments in contradiction, and four or five books had been written and printed to offset the influence of the silver campaign document.

The Democrats nominated William Jennings Bryan, of Nebraska, as their standard bearer. Mr. Bryan was an ex-member of Congress, and prior to the Convention had not been regarded as a prominent candidate for the Presidency. He was young, and there were wheel-horses in the party to be rewarded. "Silver Dick," as the Hon. Richard P. Bland, of Missouri, was called, because of his long defence of silver in the House of Representatives as a money metal, was one of the most formidable candidates, and Governor Horace Boies, who had succeeded in winning the Republican State of Iowa for the Democrats, also had a large following. Mr. Bryan came to the Convention as a delegate, a pronounced champion of the silver theory, and a representative of the producing classes of the country. He had already achieved fame as an orator, and during the Convention he took the platform and made a most brilliant speech in favor of the free coinage of silver. The address so electrified the Convention that delegation after delegation voted for Mr. Bryan when the balloting began, and before the roll call was finished it was seen that he was nominated.

Neither the Republican nor the Democratic party committed itself to the money question without a serious fight within its own ranks. When the Republicans declared against silver, an influential section of the delegates, led by United States Senator Henry M. Teller, of Colorado, bolted the Convention, and were, perforce, compelled to support Mr. Bryan as a Presidential candidate. A faction of the Democratic party, led by Senator Hill, of New York, refused absolutely to subscribe to the silver doctrine enumerated by their party, and as a result the Gold Democrats nominated a ticket for President, headed by United States Senator Palmer, of Illinois, and S. B. Buckner, of Kentucky. Mr. Bryan was also the candidate of the Populistic party.

Following the nomination of Mr. Bryan began a campaign the like of which has perhaps never been seen in any country. It was full of spectacular features, and there was more eloquence to the square inch than had ever been known before. Everybody turned speech-maker, and few places were regarded as too sacred, and few moments as improper, in which to discuss the momentous questions. On the streets, in railway cars, on steamboats, in hotels, stores, factories, and at the family board the great question was threshed out. The excitement was intense. On both sides the people believed a crisis had arrived. The Republicans declared the election of Mr. Bryan meant repudiation of obligations, ruin and national dishonor. The

Democrats retorted that there could be no repudiation in sticking to the money of the Constitution and the argument was so apparently conclusive that the Republicans became alarmed. It was found that the silver belief was fully grounded—the people of the great West seemed impressed with the idea that more money would make times better, and more money could easily be coined. The Government had practically ceased under the Cleveland Administration to purchase silver bullion. The mines of Colorado, Utah, Arizona, New Mexico, Montana, and other sections, could produce the metal in abundance, and for the Government to coin it into money would produce the supply of money necessary to relieve the stringency.

Such arguments appealed to those who felt the pinch of poverty, and the Republicans found it necessary to send their best and most eloquent speakers into the field, in order to counteract the influence of the silver advocates. Printing presses throughout the land were set to work to print pamphlets and tracts exploded the Democratic doctrine, and great discs of base metal were cast to show how much silver at the prevailing price would have to go into a dollar, to make it the equivalent of a gold dollar. The bullion value of the silver in a dollar was at that time about 50 cents, and the object lesson had its effect upon certain minds.

As indicative of the arguments used by the leading orators during the campaign, the following examples are given:

Congressman Joseph C. Sibley, of Pennsylvania, one of the prominent Eastern men who supported the doctrine of free coinage of silver, said in one of his speeches:

"Silver is the only stable standard of values maintaining at all times its parity with every article of production except gold. The ounce of silver, degraded by infamous legislation from its normal mintage value of 1.2929 an ounce to about 60 cents, has kept its parity with the ton of pig iron, the pound of nails, and all the products of our iron mills. The ounce of silver has maintained its parity with the barrel of petroleum, with granite blocks, with kiln-burnt bricks. With lumber growing scarcer year by year it still keeps its parity. It is at parity with the ton of coal; with the mower, reaper, thresher, the grain drill, the hoe, and the spade. Silver at 1.2929 and beef at 7 cents per pound in the farmer's field has kept its parity, and the ounce of silver at 60 cents buys to-day beef at 2 cents per pound on foot. The pound of cotton and the ounce of silver have never lost their level. No surer has the sun indicated on the dial the hour of the day than has the ounce of silver shown the value of the pound of cotton. As surely as the moon has given high tide or low tide, just so surely has the ounce of silver given the high and low tide prices of wheat. The ounce of silver has maintained its parity with your railway dividends, with the earnings in your shops and factories, in all departments of effort.

"If parity with gold is demanded, and the Secretary of the Treasury construes the law to mean whenever demanded to pay gold, then let us maintain the parity by reducing the number of grains in the gold dollar from 23.22 grains pure gold to 15 grains, or to such number of grains as will keep it at parity. While we may wrong by so doing the creditor class, through the increased value of the products of human industry, we much remember that for every one creditor there are a thousand debtors; and we should remember that the aim of the Government is the greatest good to the greatest number, and also the minimum amount of evil. But no such drastic measure is necessary. Parity may be maintained and every declaration of governmental policy fully met by accepting for all dues, public and private, including duties upon imports, silver and paper issues of the Nation of every description whatsoever.

"In all the gold-standard nations destitution and misery prevail. With great standing armies in Europe outbreaks are not of frequent occurrence, and yet one rarely peruses his paper without reading of these outbreaks. In Nebraska and Kansas, the land of wheat and corn, we read of starving households; even in Ohio appeals are sent out for the relief of thousands of starving miners, and yet men have the temerity to tell us that the evils arise from overproduction.

"Men tell us that there is an overproduction of silver, and that its price had diminished in comparison with gold because of its great relative increase. Such statements are not only misleading, but absolutely false. Figures show that in 1600 we produced 27 tons of silver to 1 ton of gold; in 1700, 34 tons of silver to 1 ton of gold; in 1800, 32 tons of silver to 1 ton of gold; in 1848, 31 tons of silver to 1 ton of gold; while in 1880 the production of silver had declined until we produced 18 tons of silver to 1 ton of gold; and in 1890 but 18 tons of silver to 1 ton of gold; and that, instead of the ratio of coinage being increased above 16 to 1, if relative production of the two metals is to determine the ratio, then the ratio should have been diminished rather than increased, and confirms the fact that merely the denial of mintage upon terms of equality with gold is responsible for all depreciation in the value of silver bullion.

"All the silver in the world to-day can be put in a room 66 feet in each dimension, and all the gold can be melted into a cube of 18 or 20 feet. There are to-day less than twenty-five millions of bar silver in all Europe. Mr. St. John, the eminent banker of New York, had stated that there was not over five millions of silver that could be made available to send to our mints. Begin to coin silver to the full capacity of our mints, and we would have to coin it for twenty years before giving to each inhabitant a per capita circulation that France, the most prosperous nation in the world to-day, possesses.

"The struggle to-day is between the debtor and creditor classes. With one-half the world's money of final account destroyed, the creditor can demand twice as much of the products of your field, your shop, and your enterprise and labor for his dues. In this struggle between debtor and creditor the latter has taken undue advantage and by legislation doubled and trebled the volume of the debt. For example, suppose you had given a note to your neighbor promising to pay, one year after date, 1,500 bushels of wheat. You thresh the grain, measure it into the bin, and notify your creditor that the wheat is at his disposal. He goes to the granary, sacks the wheat, and then brings up your note and states, 'I have taken 500 bushels, which I have endorsed on your note. I will call on you for the balance when next year's crop is harvested.' You say, 'Why did you not take all the wheat and let me make full payment?' The note-holder answers, 'I did take all the wheat, and there were only 500 bushels in the bin instead of 1,500.'

You fail to understand how that can be possible. You know that you threshed out and measured into that bin 1,500 bushels of wheat. You go to the granary and find that it is true. No wheat is there, but there appears to be an enormous lot of wheat upon those wagons for 500 bushels, and you ask the note-holder, 'Who measured this wheat? and let me see how you measured it.' You see something in the form of a measure about as large as a washtub, and you ask him what that is. He tells you that is the half-bushel measure which he measured your wheat; but you reply, 'My dear sir, that holds more than half a bushel; that measure will hold 6 pecks.' He answers, 'Correct, it does hold six pecks, but it now takes 12 pecks to make a bushel, instead of four pecks. Together with other friends who had wheat coming to us we went before the Committee on Coinage, Weights, and Measures and secured the passage of a legislative enactment, that it should require 12 pecks instead of 4 pecks to make a bushel. We have secured this legislation for the proper protection of the holders of wheat obligations, for our own security, and for fear that we should become timid and lose confidence in your ability to pay unless we changed the standard of measure.' But you reply, 'Sir, we who have obligations maturing, contracts long standing, have never asked or consented to the enactment of such legislation. Our representatives in Congress never permitted us to understand that any such legislation was pending.' He replies, 'Sir, you might have known it had you desired to do so, or had you kept yourself as well posted in legislative affairs as do the holders of obligations calling for products of the soil for payment. We have our representatives in Congress. We reward them for their fidelity to our interests; we punish them for fidelity to yours.'

"This, in my judgment, is not a far-fetched illustration, but depicts the exact condition against which production to-day protests. The debtor's obligation, true, does not call for wheat in specific terms. It calls for dollars, but by legislation we have made the dollar three times as large in purchasing power or in measuring values as it was before. We talk about gold being the only money of intrinsic value, and attempt to befog and mystify the masses by telling them that it has intrinsic value, when its value is merely the artificial product of legislation.

"Enact a law, to be rigidly enforced, providing that no meat of any kind, whether 'fish, flesh or fowl,' except mutton, shall be used for food. What will be the intrinsic value of your beef cattle, of your swine, your poultry, and your fish to-morrow? The mutton-headed monometallists would tell you that the great increase in the value of mutton was because of its intrinsic worth. Let this Nation and the commercial nations of the globe enact a law to-morrow, that neither cotton, nor silk, nor fabric should be used for clothing or covering, forbid the factories of the world to spin or weave aught but wool, and what will be the intrinsic value of cotton or silk thereafter? Wool will be king; its value will be enhanced, but cotton, hemp, and silk will be as valueless as weeds or as gossamer webs.

"With the mints open to free and unlimited coinage of both gold and silver there has never been a moment when silver has not maintained its parity with gold, and a ratio of 16 to 1 commanded a premium of more than 3 per cent over gold. And if, by some fortunate discoveries to-morrow, gold should be found in great quantities sufficient to lessen the income of the annuitant, the bondholding, or the fixed-income class, there would arise a demand for the demonetization of gold and the establishment of the pearl, ruby, or diamond standard of values. Whatever standard can bring to grasping hands and greedy hearts the most of the toil, the sweat, and unrequited efforts of his fellowman, this standard will be demanded by the representatives of greed, and must be resisted by those who represent humanity and Christianity."

United States Senator Julius C. Burrows, of Michigan, in replying to free coinage argument, said :

"Coin silver dollars at the ratio of 16 to 1 or 20 to 1 and you have a dollar intrinsically worth less than the gold dollar, and coin such a dollar as that— permit the owners of silver bullion to bring to the mints of the United States, and have manufactured into dollars, a certain number of grains, worth in bullion much less than after they are coined, is a proposition to which I cannot give my assent.

"But it has been stated and repeatedly asserted that the present silver dollar is the 'dollar of the fathers.' That statement is not true. It is not the 'dollars of the fathers,' and the fathers if living would repudiate such an assumption as a reflection upon their integrity and sagacity. The silver dollar of the fathers was intended to be and was in fact practically equal to the gold dollar in intrinsic value.

"This contest for the free coinage of silver began in 1874, and it has been prosecuted with unceasing vigor ever since. Why? Up to that time the silver dollar was worth more, intrinsically, than the gold dollar, being worth in 1873 $1.03 as compared with gold.

"Up to that time the coinage of silver dollars in this country had been very limited. One would think from the tenor of this discussion that all at once a great outrage had been perpetrated upon silver, that it had been stricken from our monetary system at a blow, by the force of law, when the fact is that from 1793 to 1805, a period of twelve years, we coined but 1,439,517 silver dollars. From 1806 to 1836, a period of thirty years, we did not coin a single silver dollar. From 1836 to 1873, a period of thirty-seven years, we coined only 6,606,321 silver dollars. In eighty years we only coined a total of 8,045,838 silver dollars. So long as silver remained more valuable than gold there was no clamor for the free coinage of silver, but in 1878, when resumption was an assured fact, and the people had decreed that they would keep faith with their creditors and pay their unredeemed promises, then the champions of cheap money turned their attention to silver finding it had declined in value from $1.03 in 1873 to $0.89 in 1878.

"The battle is now renewed under the plea of bimetallism, and the advocates of the free coinage of silver seek to delude the people by asserting that they are in favor of bimetallism while its opponents are not. We have bimetallism to-day.

"The free and unlimited coinage of silver at any of the ratios named will destroy bimetallism and will reduce this country to a single standard, that of silver, and that depreciated, and I am suspicious that for this very reason some gentlemen are anxious for its triumph. The opening of the mints of the United States to the unrestricted minting for individuals of silver into legal dollars at any ratio to gold less than the commercial value of both metals, under the pretense of aiding the cause of bimetallism or for the purpose of establishing or maintaining bimetallism in the United States, is simply playing upon the sentiment and credulity of the American people.

Mr. Bryan toured the country during the campaign, and spoke in all sections of the country. He went into the eastern States, where the opponents of the free silver doctrine were strongest and made numerous speeches, but did the most of his work in the South and West. His fame as an orator drew thousands to hear him, and under the spell of his eloquence millions were brought to believe with him. When the campaign was well under way, and the Republican leaders had in a measure checked the spread of the free silver doctrine, they put forward again the doctrine of a protective tariff, and declared it to be the real issue before the people, and its maintenance necessary to the renewed prosperity of the nation.

During this stirring period the calm equipoise and splendid intellectuality of Governor McKinley stood him in good stead. He kept to his modest home in Canton, Ohio, and there received millions of people who called upon him. They came from all walks in life—manufacturers, business men, professional men, teachers, mechanics and laborers—and to each delegation he made an apt address, always broad-minded, always touching the peculiar concerns of his hearers, and always breathing a high note of patriotism and fidelity to principle. The speeches made by Governor McKinley on the lawn at Canton during the memorable summer of 1896 rank him as one of the most thoroughly informed men of his generation, and as possessing all the elements of highest statecraft.

When election day came, McKinley was triumphant, receiving 7,061,142 votes, against 6,460,677 for Bryan. In the electoral college, Mr. McKinley had 271 votes, and Mr. Bryan, 176.

CHAPTER XX.

THE SPANISH WAR CLOUD.

There were but very few Americans whose warmest sympathies did not go out to the gallant Cuban patriots who for decades struggled to throw off the galling yoke of one of the most tyrannical governments that ever held despotic sway over a people or devastated their country. The several attempts at revolution were pathetic beyond words and the war for independence that eventuated in American assistance that made Cuba free resembled in many respects the sufferings, hardships and sacrifices of our own forefathers in the dark days of the Revolution.

The atrocious rule of Spain in America, when she once overshadowed all the other nations, caused her colonies, one by one, to writhe from her grasp, until Cuba, "The Queen of the Antilles," and Porto Rico were the only ones of importance left.

Cuba is a very large island, being 720 miles long with an average width of 60 miles and an area equal to more than one-half of all the other West India Islands together. Being so near to the United States geographically and of such close importance commercially and socially, a wide-spread feeling had long existed in this Republic, and especially in the Gulf States that the "Ever Faithful Isle" should be associated with this government as a part of the Republic, but as there would have been no excuse for such annexation under international law, without the consent of Spain, of course the matter had never been officially considered.

Nevertheless Cuba became a favorite field for American filibusters, and from 1849 to 1852 three such expeditions were made from this country, incited by Narcisso Lopez, a South American adventurer, who led Governor Dintman of Mississippi and other Southerners to believe that Cuba was ready for revolt and annexation to the United States. All these expeditions failed and Lopez was captured and executed by the Spanish authorities in Cuba.

Many pathetic and dramatic incidents marked these spasmodic attempts at revolution, the death of W. L. Crittenden, son of the Attorney-General of the United States, being one of the most striking of them. Crittenden was a graduate of West Point and resigned a colonelcy in the army in 1851 that he might aid the Cubans in their struggle for liberty. He succeeded in landing on the island and was left with one hundred and fifty men to guard the baggage and ammunition, while Lopez with a larger body of men marched into the interior. Lopez was attacked before he had proceeded further than a few miles, and, being compelled to surrender, his execution followed quickly. An overwhelming assault was then made upon Crittenden and his little force, but after offering the most desperate resistance Crittenden was taken prisoner with all of the survivors of his band. They were taken to Havana, and condemned to death, without trial.

August 16, 1851, an immense crowd gathered to witness the execution. The prisoners were ordered to kneel, facing a stone wall, and with their backs toward the soldiers a few paces away. When the command was given to Crittenden he wheeled about, and, standing in an attitude of defiance, said:

"A Kentuckian never turns his back on an enemy, and kneels only to his God!"

Thus refusing to obey the order, he was shot dead where he stood.

Other filibustering expeditions have since been made to Cuba, and several times the people revolted against Spain, but in every instance she crushed the rebellion with a bloody and merciless hand.

The insurrection of 1895 broke out in February, and the situation became so critical that the home government authorized the Governor-General to proclaim martial law. At the same time Jose Marti and General Maximo Gomez arrived in the island. The former had been nominated by the revolutionary junta to be head of the provisional government, while Gomez was to take chief command of the insurgent forces. There were two rallying points for the insurgents, one in the province of Matanzas in the western end, and the other in the province of Santiago in the eastern end.

At the beginning there was little organization among the rebels, but as time passed, discipline came and the object of the patriots was clearly defined. They had among them a number of skilled officers, who, like many of the privates, had been active in former revolts, and were full of ardor for the liberty of their native land.

One plan of the patriots was to establish free communication among themselves, through every part of the island, and to press as near Havana, the headquarters of the loyalists, as possible. The outlook for success was more promising than ever before, and never was the enthusiasm among the Cubans and their friends at so high a point. Money was liberally gathered in New York, and from many of the leading cities of the United States.

arms, ammunition, supplies, and brave men were shipped to Cuba, most of them managing to elude the vigilance of the Spanish cruisers and to join the insurgents, who, in early autumn, had an army numbering fully 30,000 in the field. This was in two divisions, the eastern commanded by General Maceo, while the western, occupying the province of Puerto Principe, was under General Gomez. The Spanish army was more than double in numbers, though the force available was about equal to that of the insurgents.

The Spanish troops were under the command of Marshal Martinez de Campos, probably the ablest general in Spain. His plan was to march eastward from Havana, clearing out the rebels as far as the province of Santiago de Cuba; but insurmountable difficulties interfered with his purpose. The insurgents were familiar with the ground, were skilled in the use of arms, thoroughly acclimated and abounding with patriotic ardor. The Spanish soldiers were neither inured to the trying climate, nor familiar with the rough country through which they had to fight their way.

Meanwhile, Spain was in financial straits, but after a time secured a large loan and announced its determination to crush the rebellion at whatever cost of life and treasure. Reinforcements were sent to Cuba, and it was plain that the home government would never loosen her grip upon the throat of her last American possession until her hand was pried loose.

The Cubans appointed a permanent government in October and adopted a constitution. The President was Salvador Cisnero, Vice-President, Bartolome Masso, with Carlos Roloff secretary of war, Maximo Gomez general in-chief, and Antonio Maceo his lieutenant-general. In this new government five of the six provinces were represented.

General Campos, being recalled by the home government, was succeeded by General Weyler, characterized as "The Butcher," because of his cruelty to prisoners.

Spain in 1896 took great offence at the pronounced friendship of the American Congress to Cuba, which was indeed only a reflex of the feelings of the nation. Many members of Congress, indeed, and millions of the people of the country strongly favored interference on behalf of Cuba, with the certainty of war with Spain, but the more conservative only favored the granting of belligerent rights to the insurgents.

The increase of Spanish cruelties in the island and Spain's arrogant demands upon the United States, became so offensive that in his message to Congress December 6, 1897, President McKinley reviewed in detail the Cuban situation and showed how he had on repeated occasions entered protests against Spain's uncivilized methods of warfare against the Cuban insurgents. Of the different lines of action open to the United States he rejected recognition of the insurgents as belligerents, and recognition of Cuban independence, and advocated that of intervention on the ground of humanity.

On February 15, 1898, the United States Battleship Maine that had been sent to Havana on a friendly mission, and at all events as a visitor from a neutral power, was blown up in Havana harbor. Instantly the country was ablaze and a just and true course for the administration became difficult. House and Senate both proved impetuous and indulged in heated debates, whose prevailing sentiment was speedy war with Spain, without waiting the results of investigation by either the Navy Department or other commissions.

President McKinley remained calm and retained hope of a peaceful settlement. He was chided by the hot-headed of both parties. It became plain that Congress was bent upon some radical step, and the President took occasion again, April 11, to review the entire Spanish and Cuban situation in a special and deliberate message, and to state that he had now exhausted every obligation imposed on him by the constitution to relieve an intolerable condition of affairs. He therefore left the issue with Congress, with the request that it authorize him to intervene for the purpose of stopping the war in Cuba and securing a stable government for the island by the use of the military and naval forces of the United States.

On April 19 Congress, after exciting debates, passed a joint resolution demanding that Spain relinquish at once her authority in Cuba and withdraw her land and naval forces, and that the President of the United States be empowered to use the entire land and naval forces of the United States, and to call on the militia of the several states to carry the resolution into effect.

On the next day the Spanish minister at Washington demanded his passports, and Spain declared diplomatic relations with the United States ended. A state of war existed, and Sampson's fleet was ordered to blockade Cuban ports.

President McKinley threw into the war all his personal experience as a soldier, all his energy as a statesman, and all the power and influence of his administration, which last he had so deliberately and happily conducted as to leave it and the country free from the charge of seeking war in a hasty spirit and through selfish aims. It was an unsought war, one rendered necessary only after every honorable means to avert it had been exhausted one whose existence was justified by every humanitarian principle. But it was nevertheless one to be fought in earnest and to the nation's glory. So it was fought. The country and Congress reposed the utmost confidence in the President. He had acted wisely in every preliminary step. He had disarmed fear of intervention by foreign powers. Congress voted him fifty millions of dollars to meet preliminary and extraordinary expenses, and on April 23 he called for 125,000 volunteers. The complement was quickly filled, and on May 25 he called for 75,000 additional men. The response was immediate. Transports were provided for the invasion of Cuba, the navy was strengthened by additional ships and Commodore Dewey, in command of the naval squadron at Hongkong was ordered to strike the Spaniards at Manila, and on May 1 occurred the great battle there, which resulted in the destruction of the Spanish fleet, and the events that followed to give to the United States the group of islands, known as the Philippines that are so opulent in resource as to be of great commercial value, as well as strategic. These events are matters of history familiar to all readers, or readily available in the records of the war.

Thus from April 19, when a state of war was recognized, to August 12, when the protocol was signed, within a period of 115 days, the United States had swept from Spain her island possessions in both the West and East Indies, destroyed her effective fleets and humbled her in the eyes of nations. Victory was as complete as the war had been brief and brilliant. Congress and the country had stood by the administration as it had stood by them.

As executive of the nation and Commander-in-Chief of its forces, President McKinley had achieved for his country a new place among the powers, and his directing hand was more than ever needed to guide her through the intricate paths of responsibility entailed by signal victory. And, let it be remembered in this connection, that the multitudinous problems of conquest were of a kind wholly within his keeping until Congress could act upon them. As head of the military he alone was responsible for that provisional rule of ceded territory which its holding, its peace, or its disposition under treaty terms required.

In all that affair of the Spanish war President McKinley stood a watch tower and bulwark, a light and a safeguard. His sense of right and justice prevented heedless and harmful complications. His wisdom and patriotism placed the Republic in equity before the nations. His sagacious statesmanship attained the proper war footing when war was inevitable; his soldier experience and general knowledge of war made of him a successful commander-in-chief. His humanity and fairness, the honor and manhood that were his, gave him breadth and the country credit in the clearing up of the situation.

Never until that hour when President McKinley, commissioned by his country and blest by his God, issued the Republic's mandate to a king, had the United States of America for one hour ventured to take part in the affairs of nations. Singularly strong, admittedly brave and progressive, confessedly full of the vigor drawn from the best blood in all nations, it had never asked for place beside them, nor joined in their age-old contendings for spoil. And never in the century and a quarter of our national life had the kings and emperors of Europe given more than a good-humored credence to the theory that the American Republic was a nation. It was no small matter to so wisely choose the time, so judiciously select the occasion as that America's entrance into the affairs of the world should meet no united opposition in the conservative courts of the continent. A day too soon or a day too late, a warrant less adequate or a reason more impelling, would have arrayed the world against the Republic, and launched a nation of peace upon a limitless era of war.

But the master hand of this Chief Executive saw the instant under the shadow of the Spanish war-cloud when advance might be sounded; and that moment, well employed, lifted the Republic to the crest of the world, widened her borders and enriched her people, and made substantial peace a certainty.

He proved himself a prophet and statesman in peace, a soldier and leader in war, equally strong in all situations.

Able, fair, fearless, successful was his record in this—as in all things.

CHAPTER XXI.

McKINLEY'S OWN STORY OF THE SPANISH WAR.

In all that has been written of the Spanish war and the way in which it was conducted by President McKinley's administration, no history can give such a clear and complete account of it as was written by the President himself. President McKinley's own history of the Spanish war is contained in an official message to Congress sent by him after the war had been brought to such a successful close. It is as follows:

For a righteous cause and under a common flag military service has strengthened the national spirit and served to cement more closely than ever the fraternal bonds between every section of the country.

In my annual message very full consideration was given to the question of the duty of the Government of the United States toward Spain and the Cuban insurrection as being by far the most important problem with which we were then called upon to deal. The considerations then advanced, and the exposition of the views then expressed, disclosed my sense of the extreme gravity of the situation.

Setting aside, as logically unfounded or practically inadmissible, the recognition of the Cuban insurgents as belligerents, the recognition of the independence of Cuba, neutral intervention to end the war by imposing a rational compromise between the contestants, intervention in favor of one or the other party, and forcible annexation of the islands, I concluded it was honestly due to our friendly relations with Spain that she should be given a reasonable chance to realize her expectations of reform, to which she had become irrevocably committed. Within a few weeks previously she had announced comprehensive plans, which it was confidently asserted would be efficacious to remedy the evils so deeply affecting our own country, so injurious to the true interests of the mother country as well as to those of Cuba, and so repugnant to the universal sentiment of humanity.

The ensuing month brought little sign of real progress toward the pacification of Cuba. The autonomous administration set up in the capital and some of the principal cities appeared not to gain the favor of the inhabitants nor to be able to extend their influence to the large extent of territory held by the insurgents, while the military arm, obviously unable to cope with the still active rebellion, continued many of the most objectionable and offensive policies of the government that had preceded it.

No tangible relief was afforded the vast numbers of unhappy reconcentrados, despite the reiterated professions made in that regard and the amount appropriated by Spain to that end. The proffered expedient of zones of cultivation proved illusory. Indeed, no less practical nor more delusive promises of succor could well have been tendered to the exhausted and destitute people, stripped of all that made life and home dear and herded in a strange region among unsympathetic strangers hardly less necessitous than themselves.

By the end of December the mortality among them had frightfully increased. Conservative estimates from Spanish sources placed the deaths among these distressed people at over 40 per cent. from the time General Weyler's decree of reconcentration was enforced. With the acquiescence of the Spanish authorities a scheme was adopted for relief by charitable contributions raised in this country and distributed, under the direction of the Consul General and the several Consuls, by noble and earnest individual effort through the organized agencies of the American Red Cross. Thousands of lives were thus saved, but many thousands more were inaccessible to such forms of aid.

The war continued on the old footing, without comprehensive plan, developing only the same spasmodic encounters, barren of strategic result, that had marked the course of the earlier Ten Years' rebellion as well as the present insurrection from its start. No alternative save physical exhaustion of either combatant, and therewithal the practical ruin of the island, lay in sight, but how far distant no one could venture to conjecture.

DESTRUCTION OF THE MAINE.

At this juncture, on the 15th of February last, occurred the destruction of the battleship Maine, while rightfully lying in the Harbor of Havana on a mission of international courtesy and good will—a catastrophe the suspicious nature and horror of which stirred the nation's heart profoundly.

It is a striking evidence of the poise and sturdy good sense distinguishing our national character that this shocking blow, falling upon a generous people, already deeply touched by preceding events in Cuba, did not move them to an instant, desperate resolve to tolerate no longer the existence of a condition of danger and disorder at our doors that made possible such

POLICE STATION NO. 1, BUFFALO, WHERE THE ASSASSIN WAS TAKEN.

REMOVING THE CASKET FROM THE HEARSE AT THE CITY HALL, BUFFALO.

a deed by whomsoever wrought. Yet the instinct of justice prevailed and the nation anxiously awaited the result of the searching investigation at once set on foot.

The finding of the naval board of inquiry established that the origin of the explosion was external by a submarine mine, and only halted through lack of positive testimony to fix the responsibility of its authorship.

All these things carried conviction to the most thoughtful, even before the finding of the naval court, that a crisis in our relations with Spain and toward Cuba was at hand. So strong was this belief that it needed but a brief executive suggestion to the Congress to receive immediate answer to the duty of making instant provision for the possible and perhaps speedy probable emergency of war, and the remarkable, almost unique, spectacle was presented of a unanimous vote of both houses on the 9th of March, appropriating $50,000,000 for the national defense and for each and every purpose connected therewith, to be expended at the direction of the President.

That this act of provision came none too soon was disclosed when the application of the fund was undertaken. Our forts were practically undefended. Our navy needed large provision for increased ammunition and supplies and even numbers to cope with any sudden attack from the navy of Spain, which comprised vessels of the highest type of continental perfection. Our army also required enlargement of men and munitions.

The details of the hurried preparation for the dreaded contingency are told in the reports of the Secretaries of War and of the Navy, and need not be repeated here. It is sufficient to say that the outbreak of war, when it did come, found our nation not unprepared to meet the conflict.

Nor was the apprehension of coming strife confined to our own country. It was felt by the Continental powers, which, on April 6, through their Ambassadors and Envoys, addressed to the Executive an expression of hope that humanity and moderation might mark the course of this government and people, and that further negotiations would lead to an agreement which, while securing the maintenance of peace, would affirm all necessary guarantees for the re-establishment of order in Cuba.

In responding to that representation I also shared the hope that the Envoys had expressed that peace might be preserved in a manner to terminate the chronic condition of disturbance in Cuba so injurious and menacing to our interests and tranquillity, as well as shocking to our sentiments of humanity; and, while appreciating the humanitarian and disinterested character of the communication they had made on behalf of the powers, I stated the confidence of this government, for its part, that equal appreciation would be shown for its own earnest and unselfish endeavors to fulfill a duty to humanity by ending a situation the indefinite prolongation of which had become insufferable.

VAIN EFFORTS TO AVERT WAR.

Still animated by the hope of a peaceful solution and obeying the dictates of duty, no effort was relaxed to bring about a speedy ending of the Cuban struggle. Negotiations to this object continued actively with the Government of Spain, looking to the immediate conclusion of a six months' armistice in Cuba with a view to effecting the recognition of her people's rights to independence. Besides this, the instant revocation of the order of reconcentration was asked, so that the sufferers, returning to their homes and aided by united American and Spanish effort, might be put in a way to support themselves and, by orderly resumption of the well-nigh destroyed productive energies of the island, contribute to the restoration of its tranquillity and well being.

Negotiations continued for some little time at Madrid, resulting in offers by the Spanish Government which could not but be regarded as inadequate. It was proposed to confide the preparation of peace to the insular parliament, yet to be convened under the autonomous decrees of November, 1897, but without impairment in any wise to the constitutional powers of the Madrid government, which, to that end, would grant an armistice, if solicited by the insurgents, for such time as the General-in-Chief might see fit to fix.

How and with what scope of discretionary powers the insular parliament was expected to set about the "preparation" of peace did not appear. If it were to be by negotiation with the insurgents, the issue seemed to rest on the one side with a body chosen by a fraction of the electors in the districts under Spanish control and on the other with the insurgent population holding the interior country, unrepresented in the so-called parliament, and defiant at the suggestion of suing for peace.

Grieved and disappointed at this barren outcome of my sincere endeavors to reach a practicable solution, I felt it my duty to remit the whole question to the Congress. In the message of April 1, 1898, I announced that with this last overture in the direction of immediate peace in Cuba, and its disappointing reception by Spain, the effort of the Executive was brought to an end.

I again reviewed the alternative course of action which I had proposed, concluding that the only one consonant with international policy and compatible with our firm-set historical traditions was intervention as a neutral to stop the war and check the hopeless sacrifice of life, even though that resort involved "hostile constraint upon both the parties to the contest, as well to enforce a truce as to guide the eventual settlement."

The grounds justifying that step were: The interests of humanity, the duty to protect life and property of our citizens in Cuba, the right to check injury to our commerce and people through the devastation of the island, and, most important, the need of removing at once and forever the constant menace and the burdens entailed upon our government by the uncertainties and perils of the situation caused by the unendurable disturbance in Cuba. I said:

"The long trial has proved that the object for which Spain has waged the war cannot be attained. The fire of insurrection may flame or may smoulder with varying seasons, but it has not been, and it is plain that it cannot be, extinguished by present methods. The only hope of relief and repose from a condition which can no longer be endured is the enforced pacification of Cuba. In the name of humanity, in the name of civilization, in behalf of endangered American interests, which give us the right and the duty to speak, the existing war in Cuba must stop."

In view of all this the Congress was asked to authorize and empower the President to take measures to secure a full and final termination of hostilities between Spain and the people of Cuba and to secure in the island the establishment of a stable government, capable of maintaining order and observing its international obligations, insuring peace and tranquillity, and the security of its citizens as well as our own, and for the accomplishment of those ends to use the military and naval forces of the United States as might be necessary, with added authority to continue generous relief to the starving people of Cuba.

DECISIVE ACTION BY CONGRESS.

The response of the Congress, after nine days of earnest deliberation, during which the almost unanimous sentiment of that body was developed on every point save as to the expediency of coupling the proposed action with a formal recognition of the republic of Cuba as the true and lawful government of that island—a proposition which failed of adoption—the Congress, after conference, on the 19th of April, by a vote of 42 to 35 in the Senate and 311 to 6 in the House of Representatives, passed the memorable joint resolution, declaring:

"1.   That the people of the Island of Cuba are, and of right ought to be, free and independent.

"2.   That it is the duty of the United States to demand, and the Government of the United States does hereby demand, that the Government of Spain at once relinquish its authority and government in the Island of Cuba, and withdraw its land and naval forces from Cuba and Cuban waters.

"3.   That the President of the United States be and he hereby is directed and empowered to use the entire land and naval forces of the United States, and to call into the actual service of the United States the militia of the several States to such extent as may be necessary, to carry these resolutions into effect.

"4.   That the United States hereby disclaims any disposition or intention to exercise sovereignty, jurisdiction or control over said island, except for the pacification thereof, and asserts its determination, when that is accomplished, to leave the government and control of the island to its people."

This resolution was approved by the Executive on the next day, April 20. A copy was at once communicated to the Spanish Minister at this capital, who forthwith announced that his continuance in Washington had thereby become impossible, and asked for his passports, which were given him. He thereupon withdrew from Washington, leaving the protection of Spanish interests in the United States to the French Ambassador and the Austro-Hungarian Minister.

Simultaneously with its communication to the Spanish Minister, General Woodford, the American Minister at Madrid, was telegraphed confirmation of the text of the joint resolution, and directed to communicate it to the Government of Spain, with the formal demand that it at once relinquish its authority and government in the Island of Cuba, and withdraw its forces therefrom, coupling this demand with announcements of the intentions of this government as to the future of the island, in conformity with the fourth clause of the resolution, and giving Spain until noon of April 23d to reply.

The demand, although, as above shown, officially made known to the Spanish Envoy here, was not delivered at Madrid. After the instruction reached General Woodford on the morning of April 21st, but before he could present it, the Spanish Minister of State notified him that upon the President's approval of the joint resolution the Madrid Government, regarding the act as "equivalent to an evident declaration of war," had ordered its Minister in Washington to withdraw, thereby breaking off diplomatic relations between the two countries, and ceasing all official communication between their respective representatives. General Woodford thereupon demanded his passports and quitted Madrid the same day.

FORMAL DECLARATION OF WAR.

Spain having thus denied the demand of the United States and initiated that complete form of rupture of relations which attends a state of war, the executive powers authorized by the resolution were at once used by me to meet the enlarged contingency of actual war between Spain and the United States.

On April 22d I proclaimed a blockade of the northern coast of Cuba, including ports on said coast between Cardenas and Bahia Honda, and the port of Cienfuegos on the south coast of Cuba, and on the 23d I called for volunteers to execute the purpose of the resolution.

By my message of April 25th the Congress was informed of the situation, and I recommended formal declaration of the existence of a state of war between the United States and Spain. The Congress accordingly voted on the same day the act approved April 25, 1898, declaring the existence of such war, from and including the 21st day of April, and re-enacted the provisions of the resolution of April 20th, directing the President to use all the armed forces of the nation to carry that act into effect.

Due notification of the existence of war as aforesaid was given April 25th by telegraph to all the governments with which the United States maintain relations, in order that their neutrality might be assured during the war.

The various governments responded with proclamations of neutrality, each after its own methods. It is not among the least gratifying incidents of the struggle that the obligations of neutrality were impartially discharged by all, often under delicate and difficult circumstances.

In further fulfillment of international duty, I issued, April 26th, a proclamation announcing the treatment proposed to be accorded to vessels and their cargoes as to blockades, contraband, the exercise of the right of subjects and the immunity of neutral flags and neutral goods under the enemy's flag. A similar proclamation was made by the Spanish government. In the conduct of hostilities the rules of the declaration of Paris, including abstention from resort to privateering, have accordingly been observed by both belligerents, although neither was a party to that declaration.

RECRUITING OF ARMY AND NAVY.

Our country thus, after an interval of half a century of peace with all nations, found itself engaged in deadly conflict with a foreign enemy. Every nerve was strained to meet the emergency.

The response to the initial call for 125,000 volunteers was instant and complete, as was also the result of the second call of May 25th for 75,000 additional volunteers. The ranks of the regular army were increased to the limits provided by the act of April 26th.

The enlisted force of the navy on the 15th of August, when it reached its maximum, numbered 24,123 men and apprentices. One hundred and three vessels were added to the navy by purchase, one was presented to the government, one leased and the four vessels of the International Navigation Company—the St. Paul, St. Louis, New York and Paris—were chartered. In addition to these the revenue cutters and lighthouse tenders were turned over to the Navy Department and became temporarily a part of the auxiliary navy.

The maximum effective fighting force of the navy during the war, separated into classes, was as follows:

Regular—Four battleships of the first class, one battleship of the second class, two armored cruisers, six coast defense monitors, one armored ram, twelve protected cruisers, three unprotected cruisers, eighteen gunboats, one dynamite cruiser, eleven torpedo boats, fourteen old vessels of the old navy, including monitors.

Auxiliary Navy—Sixteen auxiliary cruisers, twenty-eight converted yachts, twenty-seven converted tugs, nineteen converted colliers, fifteen revenue cutters, four lighthouse tenders and nineteen miscellaneous vessels.

Much alarm was felt along our entire Atlantic seaboard lest some attack might be made by the enemy. Every precaution was taken to prevent possible injury to our great cities lying along the coast. Temporary garrisons were provided, drawn from the State militia. Infantry and light batteries were drawn from the volunteer force. About 12,000 troops were thus employed.   The coast signal service was established for observing the approach of an enemy's ships to the coast of the United States, and the life-saving and lighthouse services co-operated, which enabled the Navy Department to have all portions of the Atlantic coast, from Maine to Texas, under observation.

The auxiliary navy was created under the authority of Congress and was officered and manned by the naval militia of the several States.   This organization patrolled the coast and performed the duty of a second arm of defense.

Under the direction of the chief of engineers submarine mines were placed at the most exposed points. Before the outbreak of the war permanent mining casements and cable galleries had been constructed at all important harbors.   Most of the torpedo material was not to be found in the market and had to be specially manufactured.   Under date of April 19th district officers were directed to take all preliminary measures, short of the actual attaching of the loaded mines to the cables, and on April 22d telegraphic orders were issued to place the loaded mines in position.

The aggregate number of mines placed was 1,535 at the principal harbors from Maine to California.   Preparations were also made for the planting of mines at certain other harbors, but owing to the early destruction of the Spanish fleet these mines were not placed.

The signal corps was promptly organized and performed service of most difficult and important character.   Its operations during the war covered the electrical connection of all coast fortifications and the establishment of telephonic and telegraphic facilities for the camps at Manila, Santiago and in Porto Rico.

There were constructed 300 miles of line at ten great camps, thus facilitating military movements from those points in a manner heretofore unknown in military administration.   Field telegraph lines were established and maintained under the enemy's fire at Manila, and later the Manila-Hongkong cable was reopened.   In Porto Rico cable communications were opened over a discontinued route, and on land the headquarters of the commanding officer were kept in telegraphic or telephonic communication with the division commanders of four different lines of operation.

There was placed in Cuban waters a completely outfitted cable ship, with war cables and cable gear suitable both for the destruction of communications belonging to the enemy and the establishment of our own.   Two ocean cables were destroyed under the enemy's batteries at Santiago.   The day previous to the landing of General Shafter's corps at Caimanera, within twenty miles of the landing place, cable communications were established and cable stations opened, giving direct communication with the Government at Washington. This service was invaluable to the Executive in directing the operations of the army and navy.

With a total force of over 1,300 the loss was by disease and field, officers and men included, only five.

PATRIOTISM IN BOND BIDS.

The national defense under the $50,000,000 fund was expended in large part by the army and navy, and the objects for which it was used are fully shown in the reports of the several Secretaries. It was a most timely appropriation, enabling the government to strengthen its defense and making preparations greatly needed in case of war.

This fund being inadequate to the requirements of equipment and for the conduct of the war, the patriotism of the Congress provided the means in the war revenue act of June 13th, by authorizing a 3 per cent popular loan, not to exceed $400,000,000, and by levying additional imposts and taxes. Of the authorized loan, $200,000,000 were offered and promptly taken, the subscriptions so far exceeding the call as to cover it many times over, while, preference being given to the smaller bids, no single allotment exceeded $5,000.

This was a most encouraging and significant result, showing the vast resources of the nation and the determination of the people to uphold their country's honor.

DEWEY'S HISTORIC VICTORY.

The first encounter of the war in point of date took place April 27th, when a detachment of the blockading squadron made a reconnaissance in force at Matanzas, shelled the harbor forts and demolished several new works in construction.

The next engagement was destined to mark a memorable epoch in maritime warfare. The Pacific fleet, under Commodore Dewey, had lain for some weeks at Hongkong. Upon the colonial proclamation of neutrality being issued and the customary twenty-four hours' notice being given, it repaired to Mirs Bay, near Hongkong, whence it proceeded to the Philippine Islands under telegraphed orders to capture or destroy the formidable Spanish fleet then assembled at Manila.

At daybreak on the 1st of May the American force entered Manila Bay, and after a few hours' engagement effected the total destruction of the Spanish fleet, consisting of ten warships and a transport, besides capturing the naval station and forts at Cavite, thus annihilating the Spanish naval power in the Pacific Ocean and completely controlling the Bay of Manila, with the ability to take the city at will. Not a life was lost on our ships, the wounded only numbering seven, while not a vessel was materially injured.

For this gallant achievement the Congress, upon my recommendation, fitly bestowed upon the actors preferment and substantial reward.

The effect of this remarkable victory upon the spirit of our people and upon the fortunes of the war was instant. A prestige of invincibility thereby attached to our arms, which continued throughout the struggle. Re-enforcements were hurried to Manila under the command of Major-General Merritt and firmly established within sight of the capital, which lay helpless before our guns.

On the 7th day of May the government was advised officially of the victory at Manila, and at once inquired of the commander of our fleet what troops would be required. The information was received on the 15th day of May, and the first army expedition sailed May 25th and arrived off Manila June 30. Other expeditions soon followed, the total force consisting of 641 officers and 15,058 men.

Only reluctance to cause needless loss of life and property prevented the early storming and capture of the city, and therewith the absolute military occupancy of the whole group. The insurgents meanwhile had resumed the active hostilities suspended by the uncompleted truce of December, 1897. Their forces invested Manila from the northern and eastern side, but were constrained by Admiral Dewey and General Merritt from attempting an assault.

It was fitting that whatever was to be done in the way of decisive operations in that quarter should be accomplished by the strong arm of the United States alone. Obeying the stern precept of war, which enjoins the overcoming of the adversary and the extinction of his power wherever assailable as the speedy and sure means to win a peace, divided victory was not permissible, for no partition of the rights and responsibilities attending the enforcement of a just and advantageous peace could be thought of.

CAMPAIGN IN CUBA REVIEWED.

Following the comprehensive scheme of general attack, powerful forces were assembled at various points on our coast to invade Cuba and Porto

Rico. Meanwhile naval demonstrations were made at several exposed points. On May 11th the cruiser Wilmington and torpedo boat Winslow were unsuccessful in an attempt to silence the batteries at Cardenas, against Matanzas, Worth Bagley and four seamen falling.

These grievous fatalities were, strangely enough, among the very few which occurred during our naval operations in this extraordinary conflict.

Meanwhile the Spanish naval preparations had been pushed with great vigor. A powerful squadron under Admiral Cervera, which had assembled at the Cape Verde Islands before the outbreak of hostilities, had crossed the ocean, and by its erratic movements in the Caribbean Sea delayed our military operations while baffling the pursuit of our fleets. For a time fears were felt lest the Oregon and Marietta, then nearing home after their long voyage from San Francisco of over 15,000 miles, might be surprised by Admiral Cervera's fleet, but their fortunate arrival dispelled these apprehensions and lent much needed re-enforcement.

Not until Admiral Cervera took refuge in the Harbor of Santiago de Cuba about May 9th was it practicable to plan a systematic military attack upon the Antillean possessions of Spain. Several demonstrations occurred on the coasts of Cuba and Porto Rico in preparation for the larger event. On May 13th the North Atlantic squadron shelled San Juan de Porto Rico. On May 30th Commodore Schley's squadron bombarded the forts guarding the mouth of Santiago Harbor. Neither attack had any material result. It was evident that well-ordered land operations were indispensable to achieve a decisive advantage.

The next act in the war thrilled not alone the hearts of our countrymen but the world by its exceptional heroism.

On the night of June 3d Lieutenant Hobson, aided by seven devoted volunteers, blocked the narrow outlet from Santiago Harbor by sinking the collier Merrimac in the channel, under a fierce fire from the shore batteries, escaping with their lives as by a miracle, but falling into the hands of the Spaniards.

It is a most gratifying incident of the war that the bravery of this little band of heroes was cordially appreciated by the Spaniards, who sent a flag of truce to notify Admiral Sampson of their safety and to compliment them upon their daring act. They were subsequently exchanged July 7th.

By June 7th the cutting of the last Cuban cable isolated the island. Thereafter the invasion was vigorously prosecuted. On June 10th, under a heavy protecting fire, a landing of 600 marines from the Oregon, Marble-

head and Yankee was effected in Guantanamo Bay, where it had been determined to establish a naval station.   This important and essential port was
taken from the enemy after severe fighting by the marines, who were the
first organized force of the United States to land in Cuba.   The position
so won was held despite desperate attempts to dislodge our forces.

By June 16th additional forces were landed and strongly intrenched.
On June 22d the advance of the invading army under Major-General Shafter
landed at Baiquiri, about fifteen miles east of Santiago.   This was accomplished under great difficulties, but with marvelous dispatch.   On June 23d
the movement against Santiago was begun.

On the 24th the first serious engagement took place, in which the First
and Tenth Cavalry and the First United States Volunteer Cavalry, General
Young's brigade of General Wheeler's division, participated, losing heavily.
By nightfall, however, ground within five miles of Santiago was won.

The advantage was steadily increased.   On July 1st a severe battle took
place, our forces gaining the outworks of Santiago.   On the 2d El Caney
and San Juan were taken after a desperate charge, and the investment of
the city was completed.   The navy co-operated by shelling the town and
the coast forts.

DESTRUCTION OF THE ARMADA.

On the day following this brilliant achievement of our land forces, July
3d, occurred the decisive naval combat of the war.   The Spanish fleet,
attempting to leave the harbor, was met by the American squadron under
command of Commodore Sampson.   In less than three hours all the Spanish ships were destroyed, the two torpedo boats being sunk, and the Maria
Teresa, Almirante Oquendo, Vizcaya and Cristobal Colon driven ashore.
The Spanish Admiral and over 1,300 men were taken prisoners, while the
enemy's loss of life was deplorably large, some 600 perishing.

On our side but one man was killed, on the Brooklyn, and one man
seriously wounded.   Although our ships were repeatedly struck, not one
was seriously injured.

Where all so conspicuously distinguished themselves, from the commanders to the gunners and the unnamed heroes in the boiler-rooms, each
and all contributing toward the achievement of this astounding victory, for
which neither ancient nor modern history affords a parallel in the completeness of the event and the marvelous disproportion of casualties it
would be invidious to single out any for especial honor.

Deserved promotion has rewarded the more conspicuous actors—the nation's profoundest gratitude is due to all of those brave men who by their skill and devotion in a few short hours crushed the sea power of Spain and wrought a triumph whose decisiveness and far-reaching consequences can scarcely be measured. Nor can we be unmindful of the achievements of our builders, mechanics and artisans for their skill in the construction of our warships.

With the catastrophe of Santiago Spain's effort upon the ocean virtually ceased. A spasmodic effort toward the end of June to send her Mediterranean fleet under Admiral Camara to relieve Manila was abandoned, the expedition being recalled after it had passed through the Suez Canal.

The capitulation of Santiago followed. The city was closely besieged by land, while the entrance of our ships into the harbor cut off all relief on that side. After a truce to allow of the removal of non-combatants protracted negotiations continued from July 3d to July 15th, when, under menace of immediate assault, the preliminaries of surrender were agreed upon. On the 17th General Shafter occupied the city.

The capitulation embraced the entire eastern end of Cuba. The number of Spanish soldiers surrendered was 22,000, all of whom were subsequently conveyed to Spain at the charge of the United States.

The story of this successful campaign is told in the report of the Secretary of War, which will be laid before you. The individual valor of officers and soldiers was never more strikingly shown than in the several engagements leading to the surrender of Santiago, while the prompt movements and successive victories won instant and universal applause.

To those who gained this complete triumph, which established the ascendancy of the United States upon land as the fight off Santiago had fixed our supremacy on the seas, the earnest and lasting gratitude of the nation is unsparingly due.

Nor should we alone remember the gallantry of the living; the dead claim our tears, and our losses by battle and disease must cloud any exultation at the result and teach us to weigh the awful cost of war, however rightful the cause or signal the victory.

OCCUPATION OF PORTO RICO.

With the fall of Santiago, the occupation of Porto Rico became the next strategic necessity. General Miles had previously been assigned to organize an expedition for that purpose. Fortunately he was already at Santiago, where he had arrived on the 11th of July, with re-enforcements for General Shafter's army.

With these troops, consisting of 3,415 infantry and artillery, two companies of engineers, and one company of the signal corps, General Miles left Guantanamo on July 21st, having nine transports convoyed by the fleet under Captain Higginson, with the Massachusetts (flagship), Dixie, Gloucester, Columbia and Yale, the two latter carrying troops. The expedition landed at Guanica July 25th, which port was entered with little opposition. Here the fleet was joined by the Annapolis and the Wasp, while the Puritan and Amphitrite went to San Juan and joined the New Orleans, which was engaged in blockading that port.

The major-general commanding was subsequently re-enforced by General Schwann's brigade of the Third Army Corps, by General Wilson, with a part of his division, and also by General Brooke, with a part of his corps, numbering in all 16,973 officers and men. On July 27 he entered Ponce, one of the most important ports in the island, from which he thereafter directed operations for the capture of the island.

With the exception of encounters with the enemy at Guayama, Hormigueres, Coamo and Yauco, and an attack on a force landed at Cape San Juan, there was no serious resistance. The campaign was prosecuted with great vigor, and by the 12th of August much of the island was in our possession, and the acquisition of the remainder was only a matter of a short time.

At most of the points in the island our troops were enthusiastically welcomed. Protestations of loyalty to the flag and gratitude for delivery from Spanish rule met our commanders at every stage.

As a potent influence toward peace, the outcome of the Porto Rican expedition was of great consequence, and generous commendation is due to those who participated in it.

WAR'S LAST SCENE AT MANILA.

The last scene of the war was enacted at Manila, its starting place. On August 15th, after a brief assault upon the works by the land forces, in which the squadron assisted, the capital surrendered unconditionally. The casualties were comparatively few.

By this the conquest of the Philippine Islands, virtually accomplished when the Spanish capacity for resistance was destroyed by Admiral Dewey's victory of the 1st of May, was formally sealed.

To General Merritt, his officers and men, for their uncomplaining and devoted services, for their gallantry in action, the nation is sincerely grateful. Their long voyage was made with singular success, and the soldierly conduct of the men, most of whom were without previous experience in the military service, deserves unmeasured praise.

LOSSES OF ARMY AND NAVY.

The total casualties in killed and wounded during the war were as follows:

ARMY.

Officers killed	23
Enlisted men killed	257
Total	280
Officers wounded	113
Enlisted men wounded	1,464
Total	1,577

NAVY.

Killed	17
Wounded	67
Died as result of wounds	1
Invalided from service	6
Total	91

It will be observed that while our navy was engaged in two great battles and in numerous perilous undertakings in the blockades and bombardment, and more than fifty thousand of our troops were transported to distant lands and engaged in assault and siege and battle and many skirmishes in unfamiliar territory, we lost in both arms of the service a total of 1,948 killed and wounded; and in the entire campaign by land and sea we did not lose a gun or a flag or a transport or a ship, and with the exception of the crew of the Merrimac not a soldier or sailor was taken prisoner.

On August 7th, forty-six days from the date of the landing of General Shafter's army in Cuba and twenty-one days from the surrender of Santiago, the United States troops commenced embarkation for home, and our entire force was returned to the United States as early as August 24th. They were absent from the United States only two months.

It is fitting that I should bear testimony to the patriotism and devotion of that large portion of our army which, although eager to be ordered to the post of greatest exposure, fortunately was not required outside of the United States. They did their whole duty, and, like their comrades at the front, have earned the gratitude of the nation.

In like manner, the officers and men of the army and of the navy who remained in their departments and stations of the navy, performing most important duties connected with the war, and whose requests for assignments in the field and at sea I was compelled to refuse because their services were indispensable here, are entitled to the highest commendation. It is my regret that there seems to be no provision for their suitable recognition.

In this connection it is a pleasure for me to mention in terms of cordial appreciation the timely and useful work of the American National Red Cross, both in relief measures preparatory to the campaign, in sanitary assistance at several of the camps and assemblage, and later, under the able and experienced leadership of the president of the society, Miss Clara Barton, on the fields of battle and in the hospitals at the front in Cuba. Working in conjunction with the governmental authorities and under their sanction and approval and with the enthusiastic co-operation of many patriotic women and societies in the various States, the Red Cross has fully maintained its already high reputation for intense earnestness and ability to exercise the noble purposes of its international organization, thus justifying the confidence and support which it has received at the hands of the American people.

To the members and officers of this society and all who aided them in their philanthropic work, the sincere and lasting gratitude of the soldiers and the public is due and is freely accorded.

In tracing these events we are constantly reminded of our obligations to the Divine Master for His watchful care over us and His safe guidance, for which the nation makes reverent acknowledgment and offers humble prayer for the continuance of His favor.

SIGNING OF THE PROTOCOL.

The annihilation of Admiral Cervera's fleet, followed by the capitulation of Santiago, having brought to the Spanish Government a realizing sense of the hopelessness of continuing a struggle now becoming wholly unequal, it made overtures of peace through the French Ambassador, who, with the assent of his government, had acted as the friendly representative of Spanish interests during the war.

On the 26th of July M. Cambon presented a communication signed by the Duke of Almodovar, the Spanish Minister of State, inviting the United States to state the terms upon which it would be willing to make peace.

On July 30th, by a communication addressed to the Duke of Almodovar and handed to M. Cambon, the terms of this government were announced, substantially as in the protocol afterward signed.

On August 10th the Spanish reply, dated August 7th, was handed by M. Cambon to the Secretary of State. It accepted unconditionally the terms imposed as to Cuba, Porto Rico and an island of the Ladrones group, but appeared to seek to introduce inadmissible reservations in regard to our demand as to the Philippines.

Conceiving that discussion on this point could neither be practicable or profitable, I directed that in order to avoid misunderstanding the matter should be forthwith closed by proposing the embodiment in a formal protocol of the terms on which the negotiations for peace were to be undertaken.

The vague and inexplicit suggestions of the Spanish note could not be accepted, the only reply being to present as a virtual ultimatum a draft of a protocol embodying the precise terms tendered to Spain in our note of July 30th, with added stipulations of detail as to the appointment of commissioners to arrange for the evacuation of the Spanish Antilles.

On August 12th M. Cambon announced his receipt of full power to sign the protocol so submitted. Accordingly, on the afternoon of August 12th, M. Cambon, as the plenipotentiary of Spain, and the Secretary of State, as the plenipotentiary of the United States, signed the protocol, providing:

"Article 1. Spain will relinquish all claim of sovereignty over and title to Cuba.

"Article 2. Spain will cede to the United States the Island of Porto Rico and other islands now under Spanish sovereignty in the West Indies, and also an island in the Ladrones to be selected by the United States.

"Article 3. The United States will occupy and hold the city, bay and harbor of Manila pending the conclusion of a treaty of peace which shall determine the control, disposition and government of the Philippines."

The fourth article provided for the appointment of joint commissions on the part of the United States and Spain, to meet in Havana and San Juan, respectively, for the purpose of arranging and carrying out the details of the

From a photograph taken for and used by courtesy of the Chicago Inter Ocean.

CARRYING PRESIDENT McKINLEY'S CASKET INTO THE CITY HALL, BUFFALO.

From a photograph taken for and used by courtesy of the Chicago Inter Ocean.

HEARSE PASSING ST. PAUL'S EPISCOPAL CHURCH EN ROUTE TO THE FUNERAL TRAIN

stipulated evacuation of Cuba, Porto Rico and other Spanish islands in the West Indies.

The fifth article provided for the appointment of not more than five commissioners on each side to meet at Paris not later than October 1st and to proceed to the negotiation and conclusion of a treaty of peace, subject to ratification according to the respective constitutional forms of the two countries.

The sixth and last article provided that upon the signature of the protocol, hostilities between the two countries should be suspended, and that notice to that effect should be given as soon as possible by each government to the commanders of its military and naval forces.

CESSATION OF STRIFE.

Immediately upon the conclusion of the protocol I issued a proclamation on August 12th, suspending hostilities on the part of the United States. The necessary orders to that end were at once given by telegraph. The blockade of the ports of Cuba and San Juan de Porto Rico were in like manner raised.

On August 18th the muster out of 100,000 volunteers, or as near that number as was found to be practicable, was ordered. On December 1st, 101,165 officers and men had been mustered out and discharged from the service; 9,002 more will be mustered out by the 10th of the month. Also a corresponding number of Generals and general staff officers have been honorably discharged from the service.

The military committees to superintend the evacuation of Cuba, Porto Rico and the adjacent islands were forthwith appointed—for Cuba, Major-General James F. Wade, Rear Admiral William T. Sampson and Major-General Matthew C. Butler; for Porto Rico, Major-General John C. Brooke, Rear Admiral Winfield S. Schley and Brigadier-General W. W. Gordon, who soon afterward met the Spanish commissioners at Havana and San Juan respectively.

WORK OF EVACUATION.

The Porto Rican joint commissions speedily accomplished its task, and by October 18th the evacuation of the island was completed. The United States flag was raised over the island at noon on that day.

As soon as we are in possession of Cuba and have pacified the island it will be necessary to give aid and direction to its people to form a government for themselves. This should be undertaken at the earliest moment consistent with safety and assured success.

It is important that our relations with these people shall be of the most friendly character and our commercial relations close and reciprocal. It should be our duty to assist in every proper way to build up the waste places of the island, encourage the industry of the people and assist them to form a government which shall be free and independent, thus realizing the best aspirations of the Cuban people.

Spanish rule must be replaced by a just, benevolent and humane government, created by the people of Cuba, capable of performing all international obligations, and which shall encourage thrift, industry and prosperity, and promote peace and good will among all of the inhabitants, whatever may have been their relations in the past. Neither revenge nor passion should have a place in the new government.

WM. McKINLEY,
President of the United States.

CHAPTER XXII.

McKINLEY AND EXPANSION.

When the thirteen original states won freedom from England and independence before the world, the new republic possessed an area of 827,844 square miles.

That expansion, or an extending of the borders of the republic, has been the fixed policy of the nation it is necessary only to say that there have since been added 2,895,380 square miles. The territory now embraced within the confines of the United States of America is almost five times as great as the original area, vast as was the extent of that great region which America won for Americans—native and naturalized. The territory acquired by expansion since the Revolutionary War is three-and-a-half times greater than the original thirteen states.

With such a record it is pretty clear expansion is an American policy, and in keeping with the traditions of the republic.

In the one hundred and fifteen years following the peace with Great Britain, 2,771,040 square miles had been added by conquest or purchase—usually by conquest first, and later by a sort of consolatory payment of what the property would have been worth if the enemy had ceded it without the trouble or expense of a war.

In the three last years of McKinley's administration the area of the nation was extended 124,340 square miles. In truth, however, this extension of territory was all accomplished in a single year. It may be interesting to add, however, that the total annexation preceding the war with Spain averaged 24,696 square miles annually; while the expansion accomplished by President McKinley's administration from the moment he secured the first treaty of addition down to the present time averages 41,446 square miles annually.

He secured almost double the average annual increase of territory credited to any or all previous administrations.

Briefly stated, the several former annexations were as follows:

ANNEXATION FROM 1783 TO 1893:

	Amount Paid.	Square Miles.
Louisiana	$15,000,000	1,171,931
Florida	5,000,000	52,268
Texas	28,500,000	376,133
California		545,783
Gadsden Purchase	10,500,000	45,535
Alaska	7,200,000	577,390
	$66,200,000	2,769,040

ANNEXATION FROM 1893 TO 1901:

	Amount Paid.	Square Miles.
Hawaii		6,740
Philippine Islands	$20,000,000	114,000
Porto Rico		3,600
	$20,000,000	124,340

	Square Miles.
Original territory	827,844
Annexed first 110 years	2,769,040
Annexed last three years	124,340
	3,721,224

But the territory acquired in the McKinley administration has been for the purpose of safeguarding that matchless possession secured in all the preceding century, and of insuring to the millions who inhabit this land the certainty that they shall continue in the enjoyment of that prosperity their past labors and the sacrifices of their fathers have placed in their possession.

For example, the annexation of the Hawaiian Islands was a war measure. At the moment of Admiral Dewey's victory in Manila Bay, the United States became an active power in the Pacific, and every consideration, naval and commercial, made it desirable that the American flag should float over this fertile group. Figuratively speaking, Hawaii was sitting on Uncle Sam's doorstep waiting to come in. The islands had offered themselves to the United States Government. It was not necessary to wage a war of conquest or open peaceful negotiations. All that was necessary was to pass a resolution of annexation.

Accordingly, on June 15, the Newlands annexation resolution was passed by the House of Representatives by a vote of 209 to 91. The Senate passed the same resolution by a vote of 42 to 21, and President McKinley approved it July 7, 1898.

The Hawaiian Islands, formerly known as the Sandwich Islands, are situated in the North Pacific Ocean, and lie between longitude 154 degrees 40 minutes and 160 degrees 30 minutes west from Greenwich, and latitude 22 degrees 16 minutes and 18 degrees 55 minutes north. They are thus on the very edge of the tropics, but their position in mid-ocean and the prevalence of the northeast trade winds give them a climate of perpetual summer without enervating heat. The group occupies a central position in the North Pacific, 2,089 nautical miles southwest of San Francisco; 4,640 from Panama; 3,800 from Auckland, New Zealand; 4,950 from Hongkong, and 3,440 from Yokohama. Its location gives it great importance from a military as well as from a commercial point of view.

Broadly speaking, Hawaii may be said to lie about one-third of the distance on the accustomed routes from San Francisco to Japanese and Chinese ports; from San Francisco to Australia; from ports of British Columbia to Australia and British India, and about halfway from the Isthmus of Panama to Yokohama and Hongkong. The construction of a ship canal across the isthmus would extend this geographical relation to the ports of the Gulf of Mexico and of the Atlantic Seaboard of North and South America. No other point in the North Pacific has such a dominating relation to the trade between America and Asia, as a place of call and depot of supplies for vessels.

From a naval standpoint, Hawaii is the great strategic base of the Pacific. Under the present conditions of naval warfare, created by the use of steam as a motive power, Hawaii secures to the maritime nation possessing it an immense advantage as a depot for the supply of coal. Modern battleships, depending absolutely upon coal, are enabled to avail themselves of their full capacity of speed and energy only by having some halfway station in the Pacific where they can replenish their stores of fuel and refit. A battleship or cruiser starting from an Asiatic or Australian port, with the view of operating along the coast of either North America or South America, is unable to act effectively for any length of time at the end of so long a voyage unless she is able to refill her bunkers at some point on the way. On the other hand, the United States, possessing Hawaii, is able to advance its line of defense 2,000 miles from the Pacific coast, and, with a fortified harbor and a strong fleet at Honolulu, is in a position to conduct either defensive or offensive operations in the North Pacific to greater advantage than any other power.

For practical purposes, there are eight islands in the Hawaiian group. The others are mere rocks, of no value at present. These eight islands, beginning from the northwest, are named Niihau, Kauai, Oahu, Molokai, Lanai, Kahoolawe, Maui and Hawaii. The areas of the islands are:

	Square Miles.
Niihau	97
Kauai	590
Oahu	600
Molokai	270
Maui	760
Lanai	150
Kahoolawe	63
Hawaii	4,210
Total	6,740

On Oahu is the capital, Honolulu. It is a city numbering 30,000 inhabitants, and is pleasantly situated on the south side of the Island. The city extends a considerable distance up Nuuanu Valley, and has wings extending northwest and southeast. Except in the business blocks, every house stands in its own garden, and some of the houses are very handsome.

The city is lighted with electric light, there is a complete telephone system, and tramcars run at short intervals along the principal streets and continue out to a sea-bathing resort and public park, four miles from the city. There are numerous stores where all kinds of goods can be obtained. The public buildings are attractive and commodious. There are numerous churches, schools, a public library of over 10,000 volumes, Y. M. C. A. Hall, Masonic Temple, Odd Fellows' Hall, and theater. There is frequent steam communication with San Francisco, once a month with Victoria (British Columbia), and twice a month with New Zealand and the Australian colonies. Steamers also connect Honolulu with Japan. There are three evening daily papers published in English, one daily morning paper and two weeklies. Besides these, there are papers published in the Hawaiian, Portuguese, Japanese and Chinese languages, and also monthly magazines in various tongues.

United States Consul-General Mills, of Honolulu, under date of February 8, 1897, transmitted to the Department of State the official figures showing the result of the census of the Hawaiian Islands, which had just been completed. The Hawaiians head the list with a total of 31,019. The Japanese colonization comes next, with the Chinese a close third. The official table, as prepared at the census office, in 1890, is:

Nationality.	Males.	Females.	Total.
Hawaiian	16,399	14,620	31,019
Part Hawaiian	4,249	4,236	8,485
American	1,975	1,111	3,086
British	1,406	844	2,250
German	866	566	1,432
French	56	45	101
Norwegian	216	162	378
Portuguese	8,202	6,989	15,191
Japanese	19,212	5,195	24,407
Chinese	19,167	2,449	21,616
South Sea Islanders.......	321	134	455
Other nationalities	448	152	600
Total..............	72,517	36,503	109,020

The acquiring of Porto Rico, with its 3,600 square miles and nearly a million inhabitants, did not require the firing of a gun so far as the natives were concerned. The slight resistance offered by the Spaniards who had for so many years held the island, was not serious enough to earn the name of warfare, though so good a judge and careful an observer as Richard Harding Davis declares this was due more to the masterly management of General Miles, who commanded there in person, than to any other cause— a conclusion which he reaches by comparing the Porto Rican campaign with General Shafter's invasion of Cuba. The conditions, however, do not present a parallel case. The Cubans wanted the Spaniards expelled, to be sure; but they wanted to govern that island themselves. And they had grown so strong, had fought so long and stubbornly, and had consequently compelled the Spaniards to maintain so great a strength that the Americans found "the Gem of the Antilles" held with a force that could offer quite a stubborn dispute. The Porto Ricans, on the contrary, while wanting the Spaniards expelled, had never made much effort at self government, and the Spaniards there were by no means equipped to defend their possessions. Indeed, their defense was the merest formality. And once they ceased opposition to the forces of General Miles, the native and resident people rushed to welcome the Americans.

So that these richest and most valuable objects of McKinley expansion came to the possession of the great republic at practically no cost at all—of either "blood or treasure."

Of course the military occupation of Porto Rico did not formally invest title to the island in the United States. The case with Hawaii was different, because no power but the resident people made any claim to that rich prize.

Porto Rico, the most beautiful island of the Antilles, which was ceded to the United States by the Spanish-American treaty at Paris, 1898, is situated at the entrance to the Gulf of Mexico, east of Haiti, from which it is separated by the Mona Passage. Haiti lies between it and Cuba. Porto Rico is 95 miles long and 35 broad, with an area of about 3,600 square miles, or nearly three-fourths the size of the State of Connecticut (4,990 square miles), and considerably larger than that of the States of Delaware and Rhode Island, which aggregate 3,300 square miles. The island has always been noted for its mineral and agricultural wealth; hence the Spanish name, which, in English, means "rich harbor."

Porto Rico, or Puerto Rico (the Spanish name), was discovered by Columbus on his second voyage, November 16, 1493. The discoverer first sighted land near Cape San Juan and for three days sailed along the northern coast, landing at Aguadilla. The richness and fertility of the island caused him to name it Puerto Rico or "rich port." He saw little or nothing of the natives, who fled at his approach, believing that they were about to be attacked.

The actual conquest of the island was made in 1510, two years after his first visit, by Juan Ponce De Leon, Governor of the Island of Haiti, then known as Hispaniola. He won the confidence of the natives and landed an expedition to subjugate them. The Spanish conquest of Porto Rico was marked by the bloodshed and cruelty that has characterized Spanish conquest in all parts of the Western world. Natives were slaughtered, or condemned to slavery. The colonization of Porto Rico by Spaniards then followed, and to-day there is scarcely a trace of aboriginal blood in the islands.

The aboriginal population numbered about 600,000; they were copper-colored, though somewhat darker than the Indians of the North American continent. The aborigines called the island Boringuen and themselves Boringuenans.

Physically, Porto Rico is a continuation of the emerged lands of Haiti.

It is very mountainous, the altitudes ranging from 1,500 to 3,600 feet, and among the rocks coralligenous limestones predominate. All lands exposed to the northeast trade winds have abundant rains. The mean temperature at the city of San Juan is 80.7 degrees F. In January and February it is 76.5 degrees, and in July and August, 83.2 degrees. The island is known as the most healthful of the Antilles. There are no reptiles and no wild animals, except rats, which are numerous. The hills are covered with tropical forests and the lands are very productive. The streams are numerous and some of them are navigable to the foothills.

The most flourishing plantations of Porto Rico are situated on the littoral plains and in the valleys of rivers, which are diligently cultivated. The principal products are sugar, molasses, coffee, tobacco; then maize, rice, cotton, tobacco, hides, dyewoods, timber, and rice. Coffee is produced to the extent of over 16,000 tons per annum, and the annual sugar production averages 67,000 tons.

The forests abound in mahogany, cedar, ebony, dyewoods, and a great variety of medicinal and industrial plants. All kinds of tropical fruits are found. An average of 190,000,000 bananas, 6,500,000 oranges, 2,500,000 cocoanuts, and 7,000,000 pounds of tobacco is produced annually.

Sugar cane is cultivated on 61,000 acres, and the production of sugar is the most important industry. Coffee is another staple product; and the tobacco, which ranks second to that of the famous Cebu variety, may be produced in almost limitless quantities. The mineral resources are not extensive. Gold has been found, but by no means in paying quantities. Lead, copper and iron are present, and may be profitably mined.

The government of the people of Porto Rico is by a governor-general, who acts wholly under the direction of the President and Congress of the United States, and all the subordinate officers of the islands are appointees of the home government.

The most important of the lands embraced in the McKinley expansion is the group of islands known as the Philippine archipelago, the westernmost of the four great tropical groups of the Pacific. To be exact, the Philippines are situated between 4 and 20 degrees north latitude and 161 and 127 degrees east longitude, in front of China and Cochin China. The archipelago is composed of some 2,000 islands, with an approximate area of 114,000 square miles.

The principal islands are Luzon (Batanes, Babuyanes, Polillo, Calanduanes, Mindoro, Marinduque, Burias, Masbate, etc., lying adjacent) on the north; the Visayas (Tablas, Panay, Negros, Cebu, Bohol, Leyte, Samar, etc.), prolonged southwest by the Calamaines, Palawan, and Balabac; Mindanao and the adjacent islands Dinagat, Surigao, Basilan, etc., and on the extreme south, the Sulu archipelago. The Island of Luzon, on which the capital is situated, is larger than New York and Massachusetts, and Mindanao is nearly as large. An idea of the extent of the Philippines may be formed when it is stated that the six New England States and New York, New Jersey, Maryland and Delaware have 10 per cent less area.

The approximate area of the larger islands is as follows: Luzon, 41,000; Mindanao, 37,500; Samar, 5,300; Panay, 4,600; Palawan, 4,150; Mindoro, 4,050; Leyte, 3,090; Negros, 2,300; Cebu, 1,650; Masbate, 1,315; Bohol, 925.

The population has been estimated at from 8,000,000 to 10,000,000, of which number about 25,000 are Europeans, about half of the latter residing in the city of Manila. The present American population is not included in these figures.

Manila, the capital of the entire archipelago, is situated in the Island of Luzon, at the mouth of the River Pasig, which empties into the Bay of Manila. The city has 300,000 inhabitants, of whom 15,000 are Europeans and 100,000 Chinese, who are largely engaged in industry. It is the seat of a yearly increasing commerce. The houses are built with reference to earthquakes, and although large, possess few pretensions to architectural beauty. The city proper within the walls is small, little more than two miles in circumference. Here are grouped the government buildings and religious institutions. The suburbs, of which Binondo ranks first in order of importance, are the centers of trade. The police of the city were under military discipline and composed of natives. A force of watchmen, paid by the tradesmen, patrolled the more populous part of the city from 10 o'clock at night until 5 in the morning. A very low average of crime is said to exist, though the native classes are much addicted to gambling, cock-fighting, etc. At the time of American occupation there were six daily papers: "El Diario de Manila," "La Oceania Española," published in the morning, and "El Comercio," "La Voz Española," "El Español," and "El Noticero," which appear in the evening.

Manila has a cathedral of the seventeenth century, an Archbishop's palace, a university school of art, an observatory, a large government cigar factory, and many educational and charitable institutions

There are some 4,000 horses in the city, used for carriages and street cars. Buffaloes are employed for dray and other heavy work.

On February 6, 1898, Manila suffered from a severe fire, and it is interesting to note that the city would have been lost had it not been for the excellent service of a fire engine which had been imported from the United States.

Iloilo, the chief town of the populous province of the same name, in the Island of Panay, is situated in latitude 10 degrees 48 minutes W., near the southeastern extremity of the island, and 250 miles from Manila. The harbor is well protected and the anchorage good. At spring tides, the whole town is covered with water, but notwithstanding this it is a very healthy place, there being always a breeze. It is much cooler in Iloilo than in Manila. The means of communication with the interior are very inadequate, and retard the development of the port. The principal manufacture is pineapple cloth. The country around Iloilo is very fertile and is extensively cultivated, sugar, tobacco, and rice being grown, and there are many towns in the vicinity that are larger than the port.

Cebu, the capital of the island of this name, was at one time the seat of the administration of revenue for the whole of the Visayas. It is well-built and possesses fine roads. The trade is principally in hemp and sugar.

Other towns are Laog, with a population (1887) of 30,642; Banang, 35,598; Batangas, 35,587, and Lipa, 43,408.

The principal mineral productions are gold, galena, copper, iron, mercury and coal. Extensive auriferous ore deposits have been opened up, and they are known to exist in many of the islands, chiefly in Luzon, Bengues, Vicols and Mindanao. Very little exploration or systematic mining has been attempted, but it is said that there is no brook that empties into the Pacific Ocean, whose sand and gravel does not at least pan the color of gold. Heavy nuggets are sometimes brought down from the sierras.

Galena (50 per cent of pure metal) is found in veins in Luzon and Cebu. Copper has been discovered in many parts of the Philippines. Iron—from 75 to 80 per cent. pure metal—is known to exist in Luzon. The coal found up to the present time is not true coal, but lignite; but it is probable true coal will be found, as the mountains of Japan abound in that mineral, and the geological formation in both groups seems to be the same.

Hemp (abaca), the most important product of the archipelago, is the fiber of a species of banana, and is produced by scraping the leaves with a peculiar knife, which requires expert handling. Improved machinery will vastly increase the profit of this product. Thread is spun from the fiber, and cloth is woven that excels in fineness the best Tussore silk.

The production of sugar is being rapidly developed, the principal sugar provinces being those of the north, or most progressive part of the island. But at present the means of reducing the cane to sugar are crude. It is quite certain the business will become immensely profitable as soon as modern methods can be introduced.

Tobacco would be an important resource of the Philippines with proper management. But the timber wealth of the islands is incalculable. There are many varieties of trees, the forests yielding resins, gums, dye products, fine-grained ornamental wood, and also heavy timber suitable for building purposes. Teak, ebony, and sandalwood are found; also ilang-ilang, camphor, pepper, cinnamon, tea and all tropical fruits.

But the securing of the Philippines has differed in many essential respects from the methods obtaining in the other cases. The expansion in that direction has cost the $20,000,000 paid to Spain for a relinquishment of her rights there, besides the cost of the war with Spain, and the succeeding war with the natives. Just what these two items may in the end appear cannot at present be definitely stated, any more than the value of the islands so acquired can be declared at once.

But if there were nothing beside Admiral Dewey's victory at Manila Bay, May 1, 1898, to place on the credit side of the ledger, and all the expense for military, naval and civil operations since accrued to charge against it on the debit side, the balance would be still vastly in favor of the United States. All the losses of every description that have fallen in any way upon the republic since May 1, 1898, are more than compensated by the value of that one day.

Before the Manila Bay fight the United States was an unconsidered nation. It was not regarded as a power at all. The world treated the American Republic with a good natured contempt, or refrained altogether from considering it. The nations across the seas made all their arrangements of peace or war, of commerce and of crowns, without even remotely considering "the States." So far as the large questions affecting world interests were concerned, the United States provoked no more calculation than did Uruguay.

Of course it was understood that the Republic was big, and abounding full of material resources—a sort of undeveloped and untrained giant. It was conceded that the Republic kept a sort of curmudgeon watch over the whole hemisphere—barring Canada; and that no "Power" could make war on Mexico or Latin America without the certainty of getting into a fight which might be extremely distressing. And so no one made war there.

But the Republic was a hermit nation before Dewey received McKinley's order to fire, and, obeying, won his marvelous victory.

From that time forward the United States of America has been a world power. It has actually dominated every European nation in the China affair. It has in a day leaped to a place where it towers above the Powers of older lands, and commands them. And they must obey. A nation with such a navy as Dewey exhibited, with such power as the fleet under Schley demonstrated at Santiago, is a nation to make terms with. A nation which could in a month fling an army of 97,000 men across twelve thousand miles of ocean, and never miss them at home, is a nation to respect. A nation with such a navy and army and such boundless resources, which had also possessed itself of Hawaii, the half-way house in the wide Pacific; which also held the Philippines, garrisoned and guarded at the very doors of Asia, and which had made the islands of the Atlantic its outposts against an advance from Europe—that nation is Master of the World. They all recognized it. And every day that has passed since the Olympia led that line of boats past Corregidor has increased the estimate which the nations of the earth have of the United States of America.

The recent purchase of the Danish West India Islands is but another link in the chain which secures to the Republic the vast possessions the years have brought. When that transaction is completed, which can not be until the Senate shall ratify the act, this young world power will be girdled with guardians against any enemy who may advance.

It is a curious commentary on the scornful estimate of the Republic entertained by the old world powers, and a definite proof of its existence, that they never confessed America had captured their markets until they discovered it had captured the means of holding the markets, and extending them. They never rallied to combine against "the encroachments of American trade" until the time had passed when their combining might be effective. They can not stop either the commercial or the military advance of the Republic. And the crown of the world's control rests to-day on the head of the nation which William McKinley roused from lethargy; which he summoned from a fat and comfortable repose, and charged with the duty of taking its rightful place among the nations of the earth. And that crown, so wisely secured, can never be taken away.

A longer life would have given President McKinley opportunity to develop the field into which he had led the Republic; but it is proof of the man's quality that he did his work so well it cannot be undone. He stood like a rock against declaring war with Spain not only until he knew what was the will of the people, but until they knew it. He did not go forward until, out of the mighty passions of April, 1898, the millions of Americans had come to know themselves. When the vital purpose of the nation was so fixed it never could turn back, then the hand of the President made the signal which flung wide the gates of the great Republic, and commanded his legions to possess the earth.

That was a mighty trial a supreme test of a marvelous man. He knew the vital consequences bound up in action then. Things could never again be as they were before war was declared. It was not simply a fight with Spain, and a victory over her; it was an advance upon the world. It was not simply measuring lances with Leon and Castile; it was measuring the might of brain and brawn, of courage and skill, of America's splendid manhood, against all the forces of all the world, and for all time! He could not let his people make a mistake. If he had yielded at the first hot demand for war, the recall would have sounded from millions before the first day's march was done. But he waited till the pressure of his people proved that they were all of one mind; that they had heard the assembly call of a world duty, and had all "fallen in." And then he gave the command: "Forward!"

McKinley and expansion!

Has it ever occurred to the reader how small a part of the McKinley expansion is expressed in these figures: "124,340 square miles annexed?"

That is only the land, the rock and soil, the food and drink, the most material and least expressive of all the elements in this material advance. Even in square miles, imagine what the annexation of Hawaii means. Compute the vastness of that realm acquired in the Philippines. Why, it is the breadth of the whole Pacific Ocean, and a path so wide that no nation can send a ship around the world without trespassing on the boundless domain of the young Republic. William McKinley has advanced the borders of his nation to include the seas. He has set the boundaries of the United States of America so far that they embrace one-half the earth. From the sentinel, St. Thomas, eastern outpost in the Atlantic's waves, across the continent, and out to the farthest verge of the mighty Pacific, to the gates of ancient Asia, he has fixed the frontiers of his country.

That is expansion under McKinley!

CHAPTER XXIII.

SECOND PRESIDENTIAL NOMINATION AND ELECTION OF McKINLEY.

That McKinley would receive a second nomination at the hands of his party was settled long before the convention of 1900 was called. The fact that under his administration prosperity had been restored, at once gave him a prestige that only the most egregious blundering could overcome. To blunder was not a characteristic of the President, and he made no false step. His hand was steadily on the helm of the ship of state, and while he never sought for troubled waters, he never turned aside if it was necessary for the public good that they should be encountered.

His splendid handling of all the delicate questions that grew out of the Spanish war, as well as the firmness with which he met that great emergency in our national life, made it appear that to him, and him alone, must be entrusted the task of shaping the policy of the government in its new and suddenly acquired position of a world power.

No Republican throughout the land gave thought for an instant to succeeding the President. His leadership was as pronounced as that of Lincoln, in 1864, or Grant in 1872. Nor was there any question as to party policy. To define the relations of the government as a world power; to tranquillize the new possessions; give them stable government, and ultimately to work out whatever destiny had in store for them and the United States—these were the pressing questions.

To be sure, there were the cries against trusts, a clamor against "government by injunction," a recrudescence of the silver question, and other matters, but who so well qualified to meet them all safely and creditably to his country as the man who had for so many years, in different spheres of activity, proved his fitness for the work, and his loyalty to the people?

It was in some such frame of mind as to the head of the ticket that the delegates to the Republican national convention gathered in the convention hall at Philadelphia, June 19, 1900.

While President McKinley's renomination was a foregone conclusion, there was a lively fight in progress over the nomination of Vice President. The death of Garret A. Hobart, Vice President, had brought forward a host of aspirants for that position. Favorite sons from various states were brought out, and the contest was keen. Lieutenant-Governor Timothy Woodruff of New York was one of the persistent seekers after the honor, and he had a considerable following. Cornelius N. Bliss of the same state was also put forward, and the name of Governor Roosevelt was often mentioned. Illinois had in the forefront Private Joe Fifer and Congressman Hitt; Iowa presented Congressman Dolliver; Senator C. K. Davis of Minnesota was also mentioned, and Secretary Long of the Navy was considered a possibility.

Senator Platt, of New York, was credited with a desire to force the nomination of Governor Roosevelt, for the purpose of taking that energetic young man out of New York state politics, and the administration was said to be opposed to such a proceeding. There was no doubt concerning the attitude of the Governor. He declared openly and frequently that he did not want the nomination, and finally went so far as to assert he would not accept the place if tendered.

The convention was called to order by Senator M. A. Hanna, chairman of the National Committee, amidst the greatest enthusiasm. There were 906 delegates, and they roared with an exuberance rarely heard apart from such a gathering. In his opening remarks, Chairman Hanna said: "We are now forming our battalions under the leadership of our general, William McKinley," and a roar arose that continued for several minutes. The chairman then introduced Senator Wolcott, of Colorado, as temporary chairman of the convention. In his address to the convention, Senator Wolcott said:

"The spirit of justice and liberty that animated our fathers found voice three-quarters of a century later in this same City of Brotherly Love, when Fremont led the forlorn hope of united patriots who laid here the foundations of our party, and put human freedom as its corner-stone. It compelled our ears to listen to the cry of suffering across the shallow waters of the gulf two years ago. While we observe the law of nations and maintain that neutrality which we owe to a great and friendly government, the same spirit lives today in the genuine sympathy we cherish for the brave men now fighting for their homes in the veldts of South Africa. It prompts us in our determination to give the dusky races of the Philippines the blessings of good government and republican institutions, and finds voice in our indignant protest against the violent suppression of the rights of the colored men in the South. That spirit will survive in the breasts of patriotic men as long

CROWDS IN LINE AT THE CITY HALL, BUFFALO, WAITING TO VIEW THE
PRESIDENT'S REMAINS.

From a photograph taken for and used by courtesy of the Chicago Inter Ocean.

FUNERAL TRAIN LEAVING BUFFALO.

as the nation endures, and the events of the past have taught us that it can find its fair and free and full expression only in the principles and policy of the Republican party.

"The first and pleasant duty of this great convention, as well as its instinctive impulse, is to send a message of affectionate greeting to our leader and our country's President, William McKinley. In all that pertains to our welfare in times of peace his genius has directed us. He has shown an unerring mastery of the economic problems which confront us, and has guided us out of the slough of financial disaster, impaired credit, and commercial stagnation, up to the high and safe ground of national prosperity and financial stability. Through the delicate and trying events of the late war he stood firm, courageous and conservative, and under his leadership we emerged triumphant, our national honor untarnished, our credit unassailed, and the equal devotion of every section of our common country to the welfare of the republic, cemented forever. Never in the memory of this generation has there stood at the head of the government a truer patriot, a wiser or more courageous leader, or a better example of the highest type of American manhood. The victories of peace and the victories of war are alike inscribed upon his banner."

The second day's proceedings of the convention introduced Senator H. C. Lodge, of Massachusetts, as the permanent chairman of the body. Twenty thousand people attended the session, in the expectation that President McKinley would be renominated, but for the time being they were disappointed. In his opening speech Chairman Lodge said:

"Dominant among the issues of four years ago was that of our monetary and financial system. The Republican party promised to uphold our credit, to protect our currency from revolution and to maintain the gold standard. We have done so. Failing to secure, after honest effort, any encouragement for international bimetallism, we have passed a law strengthening the gold standard and planting it more firmly than ever in our financial system, improving our banking laws, buttressing our credit, and refunding the public debt at 2 per cent interest, the lowest rate in the world. It was a great work well done."

Concerning the war with Spain he said:

"Here they are, these great feats: A war of a hundred days, with many victories and no defeats, with no prisoners taken from us, and no advance stayed; with a triumphant outcome startling in its completeness and in its world-wide meaning. Was ever a war more justly entered upon, more quickly fought, more fully won, more thorough in its results? Cuba is free. Spain has been driven from the Western hemisphere. Fresh glory has come to our arms and crowned our flag. It was the work of the American people, but the Republican party was their instrument.

"So much for the past. We are proud of it, but we do not expect to live upon it, for the Republican party is pre-eminently the party of action, and its march is ever forward. The deeds of yesterday are in their turn a pledge and proof that what we promise we perform, and that the people who put faith in our declarations in 1896 were not deceived, and may place the same trust in us in 1900. But our pathway has never lain among dead issues, nor have we won our victories and made history by delving in political graveyards.

"We are the party of today, with cheerful yesterdays and confident tomorrows. The living present is ours; the present of prosperity and activity in business, of good wages and quick payments, of labor employed and capital invested; of sunshine in the market-place and the stir of abounding life in the workshop and on the farm. It is with this that we have replaced the depression, the doubts, the dull business, the low wages, the idle labor, the frightened capital, the dark clouds which overhung industry and agriculture in 1896. This is what we would preserve, so far as sound government and wise legislation can do it. This is what we offer now."

In such an atmosphere of optimism the convention proceeded to adopt the platform on which the candidates should ask the suffrages of the American electorate. That document set forth that four years before—

"When the people assembled at the polls after a term of Democratic legislation and administration, business was dead, industry was paraylzed, and the national credit disastrously impaired. The country's capital was hidden away and its labor distressed and unemployed.

"The Democrats had no other plan with which to improve the ruinous conditions, which they had themselves produced, than to coin silver at the ratio of 16 to 1. The Republican party, denouncing this plan as sure to produce conditions even worse than those from which relief was sought, promised to restore prosperity by means of two legislative measures—a protective tariff and a law making gold the standard of value.

"The people, by great majorities, issued to the Republican party a commission to enact these laws. This commission has been executed, and the Republican promise is redeemed. Prosperity, more general and more abundant than we have ever known, has followed these enactments. There is no longer controversy as to the value of any government obligations. Every American dollar is a gold dollar, or its assured equivalent, and American credit stands higher than that of any other nation. Capital is fully employed and everywhere labor is profitably occupied.

"We endorse the administration of William McKinley. Its acts have been established in wisdom and in patriotism, and at home and abroad it has distinctly elevated and extended the influence of the American nation. Walking untried paths and facing unforeseen responsibilities, President McKinley has been in every situation the true American patriot, and the upright statesman, clear in vision, strong in judgment, firm in action, always inspiring, and deserving the confidence of his countrymen."

The platform further declared in favor of a renewal of "allegiance to the principle of the gold standard"; of a law to effectually restrain and prevent all conspiracies and combinations intended to restrict business, to create monopolies, to limit production or to control prices; the protection policy was endorsed, and legislation in favor of the interests of workingmen advocated; help to American shipping, pensions for soldiers, maintenance of the civil service system, construction of an isthmian canal, and endorsement of the treaty of Paris were also favored.

This brought the convention to its third and last day's session, and it was a veritable love feast. Factional fights and all friction as to policy had been swept away. All that was now necessary was the naming of the ticket. Twenty thousand people again crowded the convention hall, and the great building was shaken again and again by the enthusiastic applause of the multitude.

Alabama yielded to Ohio when the call of States began, and Senator Foraker, to whom had been accorded the honor of nominating the President, arose and said:

"Mr. Chairman and Gentlemen of the Convention: Alabama yields to Ohio, and I thank Alabama for that accommodation. Alabama has so yielded, however, by reason of a fact that would seem in an important sense to make the duty that has been assigned to me a superfluous duty, for Alabama has yielded because of the fact that our candidate for the Presidency has in fact been already nominated. He was nominated by the distinguished Senator from Colorado when he assumed the duties of temporary chairman. He was nominated again yesterday by the distinguished Senator from Massachusetts, when he took the office of permanent chairman, and he was nominated for a third time when the Senator from Indiana yesterday read us the platform.

"And not only has he been nominated by this convention, but he was also nominated by the whole American people. From one end of this land to the other, in every mind, only one and the same man is thought of for the honor which we are now about to confer, and that man is the first choice of every other man who wishes Republican success next November. Upon this account, it is indeed not necessary for me or anyone else to speak for him here or elsewhere. He has already spoken for himself, and to all the world.

"He has a record replete with brilliant achievements; a record that speaks at once both his performances and his highest energy. It comprehends both peace and war, and constitutes the most striking illustration possible of triumphant and inspiring fidelity and success in the discharge of public duty."

The nomination was seconded by Governor Roosevelt, Senator Thurston, John W. Yerkes, of Kentucky, George Knight, of California, and Governor Mount, of Indiana. When Senator Foraker pronounced the name of the President, there was a great demonstration on the part of the convention. Someone threw into the delegate's division a great bundle of red, white and blue plumes, made of pampas grass. The delegates caught them up, and with flags, handkerchiefs and State banners waving, shouted themselves hoarse. The whole convention, 926 delegates, voted for President McKinley.

Then came the nomination for Vice-President. The wisdom of the convention had decided on Governor Roosevelt, and all other candidates had withdrawn from the contest. Though strongly against his inclination, the Governor had agreed to accept the position. Colonel Lafayette Young, of Iowa, nominated the Governor, and Butler Murray, of Massachusetts, Gen. J. M. Ashton, of Wisconsin, and Senator Depew, of New York, seconded the nomination. Senator Depew said, in closing:

"We have the best ticket ever presented. We have at the head of it a Western man with Eastern notions, and we have at the other end, an Eastern man with Western character—the statesman and the cowboy, the accomplished man of affairs, and the heroic fighter. The man who has proved great as President, and the fighter who has proved great as Governor. We leave this old town simply to keep on shouting and working to make it unanimous for McKinley and for Roosevelt."

CHAPTER XXIV.

PRESIDENT McKINLEY AND THE CHINESE CRISIS.

When, in 1899 and 1900 all the civilized world was filled with indignation over the atrocities of the "Boxers," a vast element in China, and when it became necessary for the United States to send its contingent of soldiers to the scene, for the protection of United States interests there, and of its diplomatic corps, this government's hand in the matter was guided by President McKinley.

The result was like that of all other affairs in which the comity of nations has been involved, during President McKinley's incumbency of the executive place, so far as the United States were concerned. It was creditable to this country, and was ramified by the judicious and commendably conservative character of the man.

The conduct of our country in it all was devoid of elements of greed and spoliation, or revenge, or any sort of unnecessary violence, and there was an utter and entire absence of outrage.

The great uprising of a large part of the Chinese population against the presence of foreigners in the empire, which began in the latter part of 1899 and resulted in the loss of untold thousands of lives, was one of the strangest occurrences in the history of the world. At its inception little was thought of it by the other nations, for China has been the home of disorders, insurrections, uprisings and rebellions for many centuries, but when the revolt spread from one province to another; when Christian missionaries were ruthlessly slaughtered on every hand; when natives who had been converted to Christianity were subjected to the most horrible tortures; when foreign ministers in Peking were assassinated and legations burned; when the guards of other countries whose duty it was to protect the foreign representatives and members of legations were attacked by the imperial Chinese troops and forced to shoot down the soldiers of the empire as well as the rioters by the thousand in order to save themselves; when millions of dollars' worth of property belonging to missionaries and citizens of other countries had been burned; when the fleets of foreign nations were fired upon by the Chinese, as was the case at Taku on the morning of June 17th, 1900, resulting in the taking of the forts by the foreign fleets after a brisk bombardment; and, finally, when the American, British, German, Russian, French, Italian and Japanese soldiers, sailors and marines sent to the relief of the imprisoned ambassadors and ministers of the great powers of the world were beaten back by the Chinese troops with heavy loss, then, and then only, did the other nations fully realize the great danger that confronted them. The awful Yellow Terror was wild for blood, and determined to drive every one of the "white devils," as the Celestials call all foreigners, out of the Empire.

When the outside countries demanded that their ambassadors and ministers, as well as their citizens in China, be protected, the Chinese government replied that the uprising was too widespread to be controlled, and then the powers took the matter in hand themselves and sent troops by the thousand —the aggregate by the end of July, 1900, being nearly 100,000, with fully that many on their way or ready to start. Meanwhile the Chinese imperial troops, most of them having joined the insurgents, showed their fighting qualities in several engagements, and the tried and trained warriors of the United States, England, France, Russia, Germany, and other countries soon found they were opposed by no mean foe. The Chinese have a contempt for death, and are stoical when undergoing the most frightful punishment; they fell in ranks and rows and heaps before the steady fire of the invaders, but yet they came on. The one thing they did not like, however, was the use of the bayonet against them, and when the foreign troops resorted to the cold steel and rushed upon them with it the Chinese invariably gave way.

The uprising which began in 1899 was the most extensive China had ever known, and the national government soon found itself helpless. It was incited by the secret society Ye-Ho-Chuan, or "Boxers," the literal meaning or translation of the name of the society being "Righteousness, Harmony and Fists." It had about 4,000,000 members in the Empire, and while the society was formed for the purpose of overthrowing the Manchu dynasty, which represented not more than 12,000,000 of the 450,000,000 people of China, its hatred of all foreigners was the predominating spirit. The "Boxers" first began by attacking the outlying foreign mission settlements and then worked their way to the capital of the Empire, leaving a bloody trail behind them.

China had always hated the people of outside countries, and never had much to do with them until about the first quarter of the nineteenth century. China traded as little as she could with the outside world. Indeed, there was formerly a law punishing with death any Chinaman who ever visited any other country. "China for the Chinese," was the watchword, and the lives of foreigners have never been safe in the Flowery Kingdom.

China is thousands of years old, and was known to the ancients—the oldest nations of which history makes record. It was mentioned in ancient Sanskrit literature, but little was known of it. It was called by the earliest civilizations as Seres; two thousand or more years ago it was known as Chin, possibly because of the Thsin dynasty, which occupied the throne some two hundred years before Christ. In the Middle Ages it was called Cathay. The probabilities are that the name China comes from the race called Chinas, who lived in the mountains near the Indies, and was a branch of the Dard races. This name probably reached Europe through the Arabs.

In 1840 China had her first experience with a civilized power. She had been fighting barbarian nations like herself for many centuries, but had never become embroiled with any of the western countries. England had been doing a large trade with China in opium, to which the mandarins of the Empire, who really ruled the country, objected, and finally they stopped all foreign trade whatever. England declared war and captured Canton, Shanghai and other important cities, after subjecting them to bombardment, and China, to gain peace, being defenseless, paid England an indemnity of $21,000,000 and opened the ports of Amoy, Fuh-Chow-Foo, Ningpo and Shanghai to foreign trade.

Troubles then began to visit poor China in hordes. A rebellion broke out in consequence of the failure of the Emperor Heenfung to carry out promised reforms, and taking advantage of this, one Hung Sew-tseuen, who had been converted to Christianity, and who knew the longing of his countrymen for a native Chinese dynasty, proclaimed the inauguration of the Taiping dynasty with himself as the first Emperor. This was in 1852. He overran several provinces and captured Nanking, which he made his capital, and was further aided in his schemes by England, which declared war against the Tartar or Manchu dynasty in 1857 and gained further trade advantages. France also joined in this campaign and the allies marched to the very gates of Peking. A war indemnity of 8,000,000 taels was also paid by the imperial government to the victors.

China quarreled with Japan over Corea, the Hermit Kingdom, in 1894, and was badly whipped both on sea and land. The Japanese fleet and army captured and occupied Port Arthur and Wei-Hai-Wei, the two strongest harbors on the northern China coast. Japan proposed to keep Port Arthur. Russia, with the assistance of Germany and France, compelled Japan to restore Port Arthur to China.   Afterwards Russia took Port Arthur herself, and proceeded to make it the strongest military and naval base in the Pacific.

From 1895 until 1899 the outrages in China on foreign missions, schools, and hospitals were of monthly occurrence.   At the same time foreign aggression on Chinese territory became more marked.   Russia, Germany, France and England acquired large areas of territory, either by lease or by force, and began fortifications, railroads, factories, etc.   This foreign aggression only intensified the popular discontent among the Chinese masses, and the secret societies flourished as never before.

The "Boxers" had been ravaging, pillaging and murdering for some months before the European powers became awakened to the seriousness of the situation.   During the latter part of May, 1900, the Washington government addressed a note of warning to Peking to the effect that the United States could not stand idly by and see its citizens slaughtered and their property destroyed, as the Chinese government was bound by treaty to protect the persons and property of citizens of friendly nations.   No reply was made to this, for it soon became apparent that the Dowager Empress was friendly to the "Boxers."   Small bodies of imperial troops were sent against the "Boxers," but the latter easily overcame the soldiers, who at once joined them.

The "Boxers" society was organized in the province of Shan-Tung, and it grew so rapidly that the great provinces of Shan-Tung, Honan and Pechili were completely under its control.   Soon it had branches in every province of the Empire, and entirely dominated Pechili, the province in which Peking lies.   Its leaders were energetic and resourceful, and by the end of May, 1900, all China was aflame.

The 4,000,000 membership of the "Boxers" society was made up of coolies, river men, idlers, pirates, bandits, and criminals of all classes.   But their leaders, although unknown to the European authorities in the far East in the latter part of 1899 when the great uprising was inaugurated, were men of ability and shrewdness.

The "Boxers" might reasonably be considered as simply a part and parcel of the revolutionary propaganda in China.   The society differed little from other societies known at different times as the "Society of Heaven," the "Heaven and Earth Society," the "Triads," the "Black Flags," the "Teente Brotherhood," the "Tea Society," the "Water Lilies," the "Floods," or the "Vegetarians."

These societies and others with different names but similar purposes, waged constant war against the foreigners. They always resented the presence of Christian missions and commercial enterprises alike. To them the engineer who surveyed a railroad, the physician who came to end an epidemic, and the missionary were equally the objects of aversion, and the secret society murdered the one as cheerfully as the other.

Previous to the "Boxer" outbreak there were three or four rebellions which tended to put the Celestials in the humor to fight anything and anybody, particularly the foreigners.

China is yet honeycombed, and has been for centuries, as no other country in the world with secret societies, embracing all classes, having an existence dating from the second century of the Christian era—an existence not of tradition but vouched for by record.

Up to 1898 these secret societies had for their main object the overthrow of the Manchu or Tartar dynasty, but after that they devoted their attention to the expulsion of the foreigner from the land. It has always been a mistake to believe that John Chinaman was a stranger to patriotism. Indeed, so passionately devoted is he to his native country that he makes arrangements for the return of his bones to the Flowery Kingdom in the event of his dying in foreign lands. This fiber of patriotism was utilized in 1900 by that extraordinarily clever woman, the Dowager Empress, to rally the entire nation into the presentation of a virtually united front to the foreigner, to convert the secret societies from anti-dynastic into anti-foreign movements, and to achieve that which the Triad sought in vain to bring about at the time of the Taiping rebellion—namely: coöperation of all the secret societies, one with another, against the common foe, which this time was not the Manchu conqueror but the white foreigner.

It can hardly be denied that from about 1840 to 1900 China was subjected to a degree of indignity, insult, extortion, and bullying on the part of some of the foreign powers no Christian power would have tolerated. Treaties were imposed upon her by force, her finest harbors seized, and vast stretches of her littoral successively placed under foreign rule. She was compelled to consent to agreements providing for the transfer of her immense river trade to foreign flags, and for the gridironing of the entire land by means of foreign built and foreign controlled railroads, while for every concession made by her a dozen new ones were presented by the foreign powers.

In December, 1899, the Empress issued a secret edict, addressed to the Viceroys of the various provinces.

"The various foreign powers cast upon us looks of tigerlike voracity, hustling each other in their endeavors to be the first to seize upon our innermost territories," she declared.

"They fail to understand that there are certain things which this Empire can never consent to do, and that if hard pressed we have no alternative but to rely upon the justice of our cause."

Four weeks later another edict was dispatched to the same officials by the Dowager Empress, who had, it was said, English or American blood in her veins, her mother having been a Eurasian, or child of a white father and Manchu mother. In this second edict the Viceroys were warned to exercise a prudent discrimination towards the disturbers of public peace.

"The reckless fellows who band together and create riot on the pretext of securing the inauguration of reforms," were to be punished, while those "loyal subjects who learn gymnastic drill for the protection of their families and their country," that was to say, the members of the "Righteous Harmony Fists ('Boxers') association," were to be favored. The "Boxers" association was openly a society for the cultivation of gymnastics, but secretly an anti-foreign political movement, something like those "Turnverein" or gymnastic societies which played so important a political rôle in Germany at the beginning of the nineteenth century, becoming one of the most important factors in the liberation of the fatherland from the presence of the French invader. From the time the "Boxers" were openly encouraged by the Empress, they became a means of union among all the various secret societies, and the fact that these societies in all parts of the immense Chinese Empire simultaneously took to arms to drive out the foreigner was due to the adroitness of the old Empress, who thus, at the close of the nineteenth century, emulated in a way the rôle played by Queen Louise of Prussia when she roused her countrymen to rid Germany from the thraldom of Napoleon.

However, the Chinese went about it in the most horrible fashion, subjecting the objects of their hatred to the most agonizing tortures and inflicting upon them every conceivable atrocity the barbarian mind could invent.

The fact that Hon. Edwin H. Conger, United States Minister to China, his wife and daughter, were among the foreign ambassadors and ministers shut up in Peking, and sometimes reported massacred, was sufficient reason that the United States should join with the allied armies in the war against "The Yellow Terror," and there were other good reasons. Thus came about the part that the United States naval and military forces took in that war, in which occurred the battle of Tien-Tsin and the relief of Peking, together with the development of the fact that Minister Conger and his family were safe. All of which are matters of recent history, and for which there is no reason that it should be repeated here.

In the entire war, however, the exemplary conduct of the American soldiers was apparent to the world, and it has been shown that the kindness of President McKinley and the humane nature that characterized him in all things was the spirit that pervaded the American camp.

The brutality and savagery of the Russian troops composing a part of the allied forces which captured the City of Tien-Tsin July 14, 1900, were almost beyond belief. In view of the frightful excesses of the soldiers of the Czar, it was not at all strange that the Chinese should have regarded the people of the so-called civilized nations with distrust. It should be said in this connection, and in justice to the other troops of the international column, that the Russians were the only ones who committed excesses of any sort, while the United States troops did what they could to prevent looting and murder. The Americans commanded the admiration of all by their conduct, but the Russians were condemned on every side.

Further testimony of the great respect and admiration manifested for the United States troops is shown in the story of the march to Peking:

A correspondent, in describing the men as they appeared when sweeping through a town not far from Tien-Tsin, said the Americans impressed the spectators more than any other troops because they looked and acted so business-like. It was most gratifying to the people of the United States that the reports from China were invariably favorable to their soldiers, who compelled the respect and admiration of the allies and Chinese alike. It was demonstrated as never before that the American soldier was the most effective fighter on earth. It was not claimed that he led all others in bravery, but certainly no one ranked higher than he in that respect. All had courage and daring, but no other soldier shot so accurately. The Chinese gave testimony to that effect, and they had the best kind of an opportunity to learn the facts.

"When we see so many falling around us that we are forced to run," said a captured Chinaman, "then we know we are fighting Americans."

This superiority in marksmanship was conceded by the allies, too. They had seen it demonstrated often, and the brave man is quick to give credit where credit is due. "When firing at the top of a wall," said one correspondent, "the American bullets chip the masonry." The Japanese gave especially convincing evidence of the opinion in which the American soldier was held in China. They are enthusiastic little fellows, and are ever anxious to learn all that friend or foe can teach them, and they gave particular attention to the methods and work of the Americans.

"We do not shoot as well as you," said a Japanese officer, "but we have seen the importance of learning it. Look out for us; in a few years more we shall shoot even as well as the Americans."

If imitation is the sincerest flattery, Uncle Sam's enlisted men have reason to feel proud, for no one is so quick as the Jap to see what is worth imitating. His judgment and perceptive power in this line are what brought him so rapidly to the front.

All in all, the people of the United States had ample excuse for pride in the men who were representing them on the battlefield in China. The record made was splendid.

After describing the appearance of the troops of other nationalities on the march, the correspondent said:

"Then came the Americans, looking so hardy and determined, marching like veterans, although so many of them were very young, and carrying their rifles like men who know how to use them. They do know how to use them, as the Chinese are well aware. When there is any hot work to do—where fine marksmanship is needed—they always have the United States troops attend to it, and the job is always well done.

"Captain Reilly's Battery—only about 200 horses and six guns—closed the United States column. Poor Reilly! He fell while directing his men before the walls of the Sacred City at Peking, and died like the hero he was. There was no attempt at show when Reilly's battery passed the spot where we were standing—none of the 'pomp and circumstance of glorious war'— and Reilly himself, a little bald, gray man, a sort of Joe Wheeler. But Reilly is the fashion here today and everybody wants to see him."

Thoroughly illustrative of President McKinley's attitude in that war, and characteristic of him and his administration, is the following correspondence between him and the Emperor of China:

On July 19th the Emperor of China appealed to President McKinley to intercede with the powers to bring about peace. It reached Washington July 23rd. The following is the Emperor's appeal:

"The Emperor of China. To his Excellency the President of the United States, Greeting:—China has long maintained friendly relations with the

United States, and is deeply conscious that the object of the United States is international commerce. Neither country entertains the least suspicion or distrust toward the other. Recent outbreaks of mutual antipathy between the people and Christian missions caused the foreign powers to view with suspicion the position of the imperial government as favorable to the people and prejudicial to the missions, with the result that the Taku forts were attacked and captured. Consequently, there has been clashing of forces with calamitous consequences. The situation has become more and more serious and critical.

"We have just received a telegraphic memorial from our envoy, Wu Ting Fang, and it is highly gratifying to us to learn that the United States government, having in view the friendly relations between the two countries, has taken a deep interest in the present situation. Now China, driven by the irresistible course of events, has unfortunately incurred well-nigh universal indignation. For settling the present difficulty, China places special reliance in the United States. We address this message to your excellency in all sincerity and candidness with the hope that your excellency will devise measures and take the initiative in bringing about a concert of the powers for the restoration of order and peace. The favor of a kind reply is earnestly requested, and awaited with the greatest anxiety.

"KWANG-HSU, 26th year, 6th Moon, 23rd day (July 19)."

President McKinley at once replied as follows:

"The President of the United States, to the Emperor of China, Greeting:—I have received your majesty's message of the 19th of July, and am glad to know that your majesty recognizes the fact that the government and people of the United States desire of China nothing but what is just and equitable. The purpose for which we landed troops in China was the rescue of our legation from grave danger and the protection of the lives and property of Americans who were sojourning in China in the enjoyment of rights guaranteed them by treaty and by international law. The same purposes are publicly declared by all the powers which have landed military forces in your majesty's empire.

"I am to infer from your majesty's letter that the malefactors who have disturbed the peace of China, who have murdered the Minister of Germany and a member of the Japanese legation, and who now hold besieged in Peking those foreign diplomatists who still survive, have not only not received any favor or encouragement from your majesty, but are actually in rebellion against the imperial authority. If this be the case, I most solemnly urge upon your majesty's government to give public assurance whether the foreign Ministers are alive, and, if so, in what condition.

"2. To put the diplomatic representatives of the powers in immediate and free communication with their respective governments and to remove all danger to their lives and liberty.

"3. To place the imperial authorities of China in communication with the relief expedition so that coöperation may be secured between them for the liberation of the legationers, the protection of foreigners and the restoration of order.

"If these objects are accomplished, it is the belief of this government that no obstacles will be found to exist on the part of the powers to an amicable settlement of all the questions arising out of the recent troubles, and the friendly good offices of this government will, with the assent of the other powers, be cheerfully placed at your majesty's disposition for that purpose.

"WILLIAM McKINLEY.

"By the President: JOHN HAY, Secretary of State.

"July 23, 1900."

By reason of the good offices of President McKinley, a settlement of the Chinese troubles was had that was equitable to all parties concerned. It is doubtful if such a result could have been reached otherwise.

As it was, instead of attempted dismemberment of the Chinese Empire, and a program of wholesale looting, spoliation and consequent disturbances between the powers interested, the matter was settled with honor to all the world.

McKinley's kindly heart and hand was of the leaven that leavened it all.

CHAPTER XXV.

McKINLEY: BUILDER OF A WORLD POWER.

The traveller standing close at the foot of a mountain can form no idea of its altitude nor of its bulk. He can have no conception of its grandeur, of its majesty, of the myriad beauties which embellish its sides and crown its summit, nor of the limitless riches concealed in its bosom. It is only when time and distance and reflection; when frequent returns and thoughtful visits have set the scene in fair perspective that he appreciates the marvels of the mountain.

The American citizen to-day cannot easily appreciate the full value of William McKinley's life work. It was not his career as a soldier, his record as a lawyer, his achievements in the halls of Congress; it was not as Governor nor as President that posterity will recognize him at his very greatest, and it was not in either of these capacities that he made his mightiest impress upon the American Republic.

His master work was in giving his country its proper place in the family of the world.

Extravagant eulogy would say he reconstructed the Republic; that he conjured a new nation into life; that he lifted the millions of his countrymen from darkness into light; that he bestowed the grandeur of imperial sunshine upon the humble inhabitants of a neglected land. The extravagant eulogy would not be wholly inaccurate in essence, nor necessarily offensive in terms. And yet the more modest statement more nearly comprehends the essential truth.

He did not recreate the Republic. Practically all the elements here at the end of his life were here at the beginning. He did not conjure up a new nation. The mighty people who followed his bidding in 1898 and so on to the end could never have been conjured from its elements by any force less potential than Omnipotence!

And yet the true American can get a better conception of the dignity of his citizenship; a better estimate of the majesty of national life, a prouder view of world-wide actions upon the theater of the world if he will but patiently and justly consider the steps in the transition which certainly has occurred, and trace the credit through each crisis to the influence most potent in producing that result.

It is believed the work and influence of William McKinley was that most potent force; that, more than any other one man he has led his people from the halls of an heritage of which they were justly proud up to the threshold of an estate immeasurably more magnificent.

Let us begin at the beginning. When he came back from the army he deliberately studied the whole situation. He saw the national condition then existing, judged with astonishing accuracy what would be the salient successive features in its future development, calculated with rare discrimination what treatment would be best in each era, and devoted all his energies to aiding in that progress to the very limit of his ability. He had never a doubt from the first what the end would be. But he did have a more sure foresight of what the future held than had most other Americans then living. One cannot say that he foresaw the time when the Republic should issue its mandate to a monarch of the old world, when it should serve notice of ejectment upon a king; when it should lay the restraining hand upon a mob of emperors and potentates struggling in disgraceful melee for the spoliation of an ancient nation. And yet, standing in the shadow of his funeral flags, with the echoes of knelling bells in the ears, and the memory of that mighty work so late accomplished, one can but see abundant reason for the belief that HE KNEW! How else shall one account for that conduct which admits of explanation on no other ground than that the guiding spirit understood? How else shall one justify the actions which committed him to criticism, which could reflect honor upon him only in the event of this marvelous accomplishment?

It was clear to him that for twenty years after the war the nation would be busy in construction; that the general aim would be to establish productive industries—North and South—that men would be building homes, advancing into new country, opening new mines, reaching farther into the wilderness, reclaiming more and more of the waste land, building more railroads, launching more steamships; and that there would come a period of erecting new homes, of beautifying, of adornment, of polish; and that then would come an era of study toward the conservation of forces, the learning of less expensive ways of doing what had been effectively done before—the era of economizing—to be swiftly followed by the era of stupendous wealth. And let that man who contends the essentials of this picture were not foreseen by William McKinley account on any other basis, if he can, for that

THE CATAFALQUE IN THE ROTUNDA OF THE CAPITOL AT WASHINGTON.

From a photograph taken for and used by courtesy of the Chicago Inter Ocean.

SCENE AS THE PRESIDENT'S BODY WAS BORNE UP THE STEPS OF THE CAPITOL.

statesman's steadfast progress toward the one result which they alone could produce. Let that man who denies, reflect for a moment that these stages of development—from first to last—were foretold by William McKinley in a thousand speeches. It is not contended that in 1876 he "revealed" to his fellows that war with Spain would come in 1898; nor that he declared in 1880 that "the flag of the free" would wave over lands in the shadows of Asia at the sunrise of a new century. But no man who knows the history of his country and follows well this true story of William McKinley's life can contend that he did not in 1876 see the imminence of that tariff struggle which culminated in 1880; nor that he failed in 1892 to see the need of a financial reform which 1896 should usher in; or that he underrated in 1898 the mighty consequences of that step which launched his people into a foreign war.

It has been said that he, almost alone of Americans, stood for a protective tariff at the very close of the Civil War. Foreseeing that period of industrial development, he looked at the rolling oceans, and knew each billow would bear on its foamy back a load of goods for American markets; and that each departing ship would heap in its hold the dollars that Americans had paid for those goods. And he knew that, with such a policy, American development could never go beyond the bondman stage; that "the land of the free and the home of the brave" would indefinitely remain mortgaged to the lords of cheaper labor, the host of shrewder men.

So from the first he struggled for a tariff rate which seemed small lessening of the burden that the war had left. Against the superficial charge of injustice he offered the defense of ultimate benefit, and if some of his countrymen were slow to see, let it be said to the credit of a majority that they followed him—not always seeing, but ever trusting until the crisis had passed.

Surely it is no exaggeration to say that William McKinley did more than any other man in America to fix and maintain the policy of protection. It can scarcely be too much to say that, without him, the protective policy would have been overthrown.

If these are conceded, it must follow that the preparation for the newer era, developed from that in which he labored, may be chiefly credited to him.

It was necessary to foster the industries of the United States. Maybe in the following of that policy some selfish persons took a mean and unpatriotic advantage of their countrymen, and claimed a concession they neither needed nor deserved. But in the main the effort was to build up such a wealth as no nation on earth ever before acquired in a similar lapse of time, by peaceful pursuits or the conquests of a victorious war. And if the day came when all that wealth was needed, it may be triumphantly rejoined that the money was here.

Over and over again Mr. McKinley had been assailed with the contention that, while protection would infallibly enrich a certain favored class—the manufacturers—it would as certainly impoverish and keep in poverty the people who must buy their goods. But the issue confounded them. Every class in America shared in the stupendous prosperity which protection insured. Never was labor so largely employed, never had it been so munificently rewarded. Never was the farmer so fortunately situated. Wide as were his fields, he added to them. Bountiful as were his harvests, he found markets for them. Never was the mechanic so much in demand. Never was the artisan so much sought after. And—as the flight of time brought the inevitable desire for refinement—never was there such a compensation for the artist, or the writer, the singer or the sculptor. The overflowing coffers of the country enriched all the countrymen who deserved.

Then came the pause when a nation, rising to the stature of maturity, looked over the mountain boundary, looked over the ocean wall, and felt the unformed impulse to share in the affairs of the world. It was so natural, as inevitable, as that the youth of health and strength should feel the stirring of desire to mingle with his kind. It is not scorn of home. It is not contempt for the precious past. But it is obedience to a law which Abram heard away there in Ur, of the Chaldees, and obeyed in his western pilgrimage. It is the process of growth which the Creator meant all mankind should feel.

At the doors of the continent lay the island of Cuba. From time before the Republic was founded, that island had been the spoil of the Spaniards. There was not a day since Ovando landed that did not see the Cubans cruelly treated by the Don. How they ever throve under a domination so severe is one of the mysteries. The Ruler of all the Earth must have raised up that people and preserved it through awful adversity for a purpose neither its leaders nor their task masters could foresee.

But the tax collector was there. The Castilian despoiler was there. The hand of the oppressor was laid heavily upon the Cubans, and they died at the edge of the sword through two hundred years of tyranny.

And in that day when the American Republic had attained its growth, had reached its manhood, there was a protest against a continuance of cruelty. The Republic demanded that the Don cease from troubling; that the Cubans be rescued.

President McKinley waited until the united voice of his countrymen convinced him that they had surely arrived at years of national discretion, and that their challenge was not the utterance of a passionate mood but the expression of an unalterable determination. And then he issued his order to Spain:

"Leave the West Indies forever!"

There was reason in the demand. Cuba lay so close to our shores that her continual suffering, the outrages perpetrated upon her people, became a scandal in the eyes of the Republic. It was like a strong man standing unmoved while a child is being beaten by a bully.

Besides, one consequence of such rule as the Spaniards maintained was a perilous sanitary condition in the cities that traded continually with the ports of the States. American cities had learned the rules of health, and had banished yellow fever and the cholera. But what profit in that provision if a ship sailed across the narrow sea and spread the plague upon our shores? There was reason in self defense for the notice to quit.

That fundamental principle of the nation called the "Monroe doctrine" forbade any power in the old world from extending its rule in the new. It is but a logical sequence of that system that an old world power which cannot in two hundred years complete its subjugation of a new world people has never had a right it could maintain here; that no king from Europe had title to soil in the Western hemisphere if he could not perfect that title in that lapse of time. And as a policy of the nation and the interest of the nation joined in dictating the action, the Spaniards were commanded to retire. The time had come when President McKinley could make his case good even in the courts of old-world kings. And there was not a murmur of protest from a palace abroad when Madrid received that portentous command.

But there was another reason—another consideration which men too often overlook, yet which was of the most stupendous value to the Republic. War with a foreign power would reunite a country divided by civil strife, and stubbornly, ill-temperedly refusing to perfect its peace.

It was probably admitted that the passions following the rebellion and particularly provoked by the assassination of President Lincoln, served as warrant for a severity in dealing with the Southern States which was far beyond the boundaries of justice. There was a Draconian rigidity about the laws which the losers were compelled to obey; a perhaps needless austerity in impressing the fact of conquest. Sectional passions were aroused, sectional jealousies and animosities were inflamed until unthinking men both North and South had achieved the bad success of creating a religion of hate. In the years when Major McKinley was acting the citizen-soldier part—putting away his sword and devoting himself to the activities of peace—many less patriotic and wise than he were teaching their children to hate the South. As the Swiss youth imbibed hatred of Austria with their mother's milk, so these children in the North were filled with a bitter rage against the children who sat in the Southland, under the shadow of the stars and stripes. And the generation grew up in that enmity for brothers in the Republic, and many men profited by making the propagation of strife their one profession—the division of their country their one occupation. The poets say that love begets love. It is certainly as true that hatred begets hate. And if the youth of the North approached public questions always with the poison of sectional prejudice rankling in their hearts and warping their judgments, be sure the people of the South most cordially reciprocated. To thousands above the Ohio river, the states below that stream were still "rebel." To thousands below the people of the North were brutal and murderous invaders.

Through all the period when the nation was gathering material strength the effort of wise men was to heal that hurt, to reunite the nation, to erase forever that bitter dividing sectional line. But they could not succeed. Throughout Major McKinley's public speeches, dating from that first debate, when he was scarcely out of uniform, clear to the end of his career, one finds to-day no word of anger against the South; one finds unnumbered expressions of fraternal love and good will.

Others followed his example, and swelled the rising chorus of a newer Union. But it was from 1865 to 1898, a mere mockery. The fabric of fraternity was but a gossamer web. The bridge that spanned the chasm was a network of fancy, and men knew they could not cross. The very brotherhood in which men from the two sections met in public and private life was the sheerest superficiality, and each was ready to fly to arms at a moment's notice.

What, above all things, was needed as an absolute condition precedent to national advance? Why, national unity! And no man had been able to effect it. But when William McKinley heard that rising demand for stern measures with Spain, he heard as well the pledge of a new and everlasting bond of union.

So that the war with Spain was not merely the checking of a bully, the act of a humane power, the safeguarding of cities from the descent of the plague, the assuring of security to Americans resident in Cuba and the protection to American trade with that island. It was, as well, the master magic which could banish strife at home; it was the building of a Vulcan forge to weld beyond the power of breaking the one bond "from the lakes to the gulf." For the first stroke at Americans by Spaniards was a challenge that was answered by indignant manhood in every state from the everglades of Florida to the snow-crowned heights of Mount Tacoma. And OUR NATION sprang to arms!

Sometimes there is internal strife in your family, in your circle of friends, in your party. That is a wise father who can deftly devise a situation which compels his household to make common cause. That is a shrewd citizen who can rally his friends by a stroke which menaces all of them. That politician is skillful who can swiftly sweep away dissension by a turn which menaces the whole organization. And that was a wise President who saw behind the rising war cloud the rainbow of a hope which nothing else could reveal.

There was no need for them to blow up the Maine. Without that dastardly act, there would inevitably have come a change. Spanish oppression in Cuba would have ceased. The reforms demanded by the Republic would have been accomplished—every one. But, it would have been by the action of Spain, and without inflicting upon that nation the expense, the humiliation and the disaster of a war. Possibly, too, had those reforms been made, had the conscience and humanity of Americans been satisfied without striking a blow, the abolishing of the sectional line would not have occurred.

But it is needless to speculate on what might have occurred. What did occur is known. It was definite. At the moment when Spain, had she rightly appreciated the situation, should have borne herself with all dignity and honor, the blow which hurled down her house was struck. In the middle of the night the darkness was rifted with a lance of flame, the world was rocked with the shock of explosion, and a battleship, on an errand of peace and courtesy, was crushed in the grip of a submarine mine—and all over the still surface of the starlit bay floated the mangled corpses of the slain. The darkest deed since St. Bartholomew night, the most savage act since Calcutta's Black Hole had stained the page of history, and Christian civilization had seen a Christian nation sound the deepest deep of infamy.

That bursting mine jolted the molecules of mankind into a new combination, and the Republic became a Union indeed. After all, blood is thicker than water; and he who uttered that—

> "—bubbling cry
> Of some strong swimmer in his agony—"

was an American. Of course America was roused.

The story of the War with Spain has been well told. But it fails to impress its moral if you miss the master hand of President McKinley in fixing forever the unity of the Union. He appointed to the command of American soldiers those who had commanded with ability, either North or South, in the Civil War. And they proved his sagacity, for—without exception—they quit them like men. They were strong. The flag of Washington at Valley Forge, of Gates at Yorktown, of Jackson at New Orleans, of Perry on Lake Erie, of Lawrence, and Fremont, and Grant was the one banner about which they rallied. They won the war. And they brought no honor to either North or South—but brought it all HOME.

This cannot well be overestimated. The time had come when the Republic must advance from the formative stage to the stature of a power of the world. It could not do so divided. Through the skillful use of possibilities placed in his hands by the war, President McKinley at a stroke, and within a week from that night in February when Havana harbor heaved with the heaving of a treacherous stroke, made his people one.

Then they were ready!

Swiftly came the knocking of Hawaii for admission to the national fold. It needed no war. No cannon, no circling sword or plunging bayonet was in demand. The thousands of lives sought citizenship in the Republic, and the material millions offered themselves for the nation's enrichment. And in a day the United States of America held half the ocean as its own.

No need of recapitulating. The Ladrones, Porto Rico, and the Philippines, an empire wider than Ferdinand knew, a region richer in wealth and more pregnant with possibility than Carthage conquered, was added to the Republic in a year. The nation which had insisted on a home market, had taken command of the markets of the world. The nation which had only insisted that no foreign power interfere on this side the Atlantic, stretched the arm of might and the word of command into the camps of kings—and secured obedience.

Nothing that occurred in the United States could in any way have produced the events which took place in China. The Boxer rebellion was a local event, due solely to conditions existing there. American interests—of merchant and missionary, of embassador and traveller, of scientist and scholar—were all affected by those massacres which amazed the world. Imagine, if you will, what would have been the result had the Republic been in 1900 what it was in 1890. Then we had no army in the Philippines. The nations of Europe, hurrying in response to that cry for help from the hundreds in the legation, had small thought of America. Well, American merchants had been massacred, American property destroyed, American missions burned and American consuls assailed. But to the European of 1890 there would not have been a suggestion of America appearing on the scene with force of arms.

But the America of 1900 providentially had a force at hand. The fact had already been established that the Republic was a world power, and must be considered as such. And when General Chaffee marched from Tien Tsin to Pekin, he was not regarded as an intruder. He was not looked upon with cold superciliousness. The king's men knew there was no place on the face of the earth where the Republic might not appear. They knew it had the right to appear at any point where its interests were menaced, or where honor called. And they knew it had the power to go, to do, and to return with laurels.

Perhaps the Republic's influence over the king's men at Pekin was the greatest evidence of President McKinley's masterly administration. That influence checked the looting. It preserved native rights. It assisted in a just retribution, and then stayed the mailed fist of unchristian vengeance. It prevented the partition of China, and insured the integrity of that ancient empire. And it loomed before the world as a nation strong enough to take care of itself at home or abroad, and wise enough to be just. It was an exhibition that did more for the good fame of the Republic than any other act imaginable.

And not a detail of it could have happened had not the army been in Luzon. Not a detail could have happened in 1890!

It is not easy for a little man to change his mind. The small man must be "consistent," because he can see nothing but small things; because he can not appreciate the changes which inevitably come in the world. But the world does change; and he who tries to make the clothes of yesterday fit the occasion of to-day makes utter failure. Not many men who followed Major McKinley, the protectionist, could easily grasp the purpose of President McKinley, the supporter of the gold standard. Not all who indorsed

him in his financial policy could appreciate the swift changes which succeeded each other in the world policies from 1898 to 1901. Yet each was
necessary in its place, and if the President had failed to grasp the situation,
if he had failed to take at its flood that tide in the affairs of nations, the Republic that mourns him to-day would be but a hermit Union, refusing to
employ its majestic powers and of no more consideration in the assembly of
nations than is the navy of Switzerland in a marine exhibition.

No year ever brought swifter development to a people than did 1898 to
the United States of America. Questions of military policy and questions
of statesmanship, matters of immediate expediency and matters that looked
to the future—all these crowded the hurrying hours of that most immemorial
year. It is not curious that even the President was outrun by the speeding
conditions. When Porto Rico became a part of the United States it was
asked: "Shall her products come in free at the ports of the mainland?" And
President McKinley, pressed upon by a multitude of duties, occupied with a
myriad cares, filling his days and his nights with most careful watching of
details that had multiplied in a twelvemonth, said: "It is our plain duty to
give free trade to Porto Rico." And the word was heralded to the ends of
the earth. Then came the practical. If that sound theory should be enforced in actual commerce, a disturbance would arise which would prove
lamentable. It were better to preserve the forms of a tariff until such time
as revenues of the island would support the government of the island, giving
back, meanwhile, every dollar derived from the Porto Ricans by that tariff.
The changing conditions had made that the wiser plan.

President McKinley led his fellow countrymen through the changes of
the passing years, guiding them always in the way most wise for that peculiar
time, and turning to new methods when the new occasion demanded. And
in the end we see the magnificent structure which his planning and his
labors have perfected. We see the very greatest nation on earth, made
great by protection; we see the richest nation, made rich with a sound
money; we see the strongest nation, made strong by an actual union; and we
see the most potent and influential nation on earth, made so by the foreign
policy of William McKinley. Remember—

> "For I doubt not through the ages
>   One increasing purpose runs;
> And the thoughts of men are widening
>   With the process of the suns."

CHAPTER XXVI.

PRIVATE LIFE OF WILLIAM McKINLEY.

"Mother McKinley" often expressed the keynote of the case when she said: "He was a good boy."

She by no means meant that young William lacked virile and manly qualities. On the contrary, she used to delight in telling of the mischievous pranks which had made a part of his boyhood existence. But there was a judgment and good sense about his escapades which absolutely prevented them from partaking of the nature of cruelty and saved him at all times from acts which might bring shame in their train of consequences. He was a "good" boy, in the sense that he was not a "mean" boy. And so, while he was always certain to command the respect of his companions—of all that was best in boyhood—he was a loving and a dutiful son. He was never afflicted with the silly theory that a boy need not obey nor respect his parents. For this those parents doubtless deserve a large measure of credit. Besides so measuring their lives as to deserve his respect, they so ordered his life as to insure his obedience. And in his whole life it is said that he never wounded either father or mother with an insolent word.

He was kind to his brother and his sisters. The money he earned he was always willing to share with them, and paid out many a dollar of his hard-earned wages for their education or for little presents which could add to their happiness.

Toward his mother he was always lovingly deferential. To the day of her death he was solicitous about her, tenderly caring for her, unwaveringly thoughtful. A very beautiful relation was that which existed between them. And no mother was ever more proud of her son, or with more reason declared that he had grown up to be precisely the sort of man she knew from the beginning he would be. Toward his father there was always a gentle deference, a filial respect and the fellowship which wise men can cultivate in their sons. His father lived to see him honored by his countrymen, and in the enjoyment of a happy home and a competence. And the stern old man who had chosen his location with a view of his children's good always a little relaxed the grim lines of mouth and brow when this son of his honest manhood was in his presence.

293

And so it was that when he grew to maturity and established a home temple of his own, the habit of a lifetime was guaranty that he would bring happiness and not sorrow with him.

There is a pretty story current in Canton to the effect that young Major McKinley first met Ida Saxton shortly after locating in the little city, and that he admired her greatly. But she was scarcely more than a school girl at the time, the daughter of a banker, the granddaughter of an editor, and a girl of such beauty that the young man, with nothing but his profession and his hopes, with little practice and no property, might well regard her hopeless. Besides, there was small opportunity for them to be thrown together. The Saxtons were not attendants at the Methodist church, and were rarely seen at its social functions. They were persons of wealth and established position and much sought after.

Yet it could not escape him that the charmingly beautiful girl was his ideal, the divinity about whom the dreams of an honorable young man may be woven. She completed her studies at school, and went for a trip to Europe in company with her mother. They were gone a year. When they returned young Major McKinley had evidently advanced somewhat in worldly estate. He had secured a number of fees, and was saving money. As he lived at all times within his means, he had arrived at the honorable distinction of a bank account. It is probable he selected the Saxton bank solely because it was convenient of location, being near the stairway which led to his modest office, and directly on his way as he passed to and from the court-house. And yet it must have been a matter of agreeable surprise to him when he entered the bank one morning and found Miss Ida Saxton occupying a place at the cashier's window.

Of course they had met. It would scarcely have been possible for them to escape that. But there had been small acquaintance between them. And this new relation, which touched on the borders of both the business and the social life, was a means of developing an attachment which it is doubtful if any other course could have afforded.

Miss Saxton had taken a place in the bank because of an impulse, as common as it is honorable, that she must "do something." There was, of course, no necessity for her to struggle to become self-supporting. But there was, on the other hand, no purpose in her mind to be weakly dependent.

There was the place of their better acquaintance. There he learned to admire more and more the bright, happy young woman, as fair as the morning, and as careful as the American daughter should be. And there she learned to respect the strong, steady young lawyer, the masterful man, the prudent and sagacious citizen.   The fact was, he was fair to look upon, strong, healthful of body, and that he still possessed somewhat of the glow which military glory sheds upon those who had honorable part in the great struggle.

Of their courtship it were both bold and unpardonable to speak.   Whatever detail of that interesting period might, with propriety, have been said while both were living, is hushed in the shadow of the death chamber now and becomes too sacred for discussion.

They were married January 25, 1871.   William McKinley was at that time twenty-eight years old and his bride was five years younger.   It is a significant fact in the life of this good woman that she almost immediately united with the Methodist church, and joined her husband in attendance upon its forms of worship.

In 1873 a girl baby was born to them, and the fond mother bestowed upon it the name of Kate.   It is said to have been a beautiful child, and was adored by its parents, and by the grandparents on either side.   For by this time the father and mother of William McKinley had removed from Poland and taken up their residence in Canton.   The strong son had drawn them from the place which had been home so long and established them in the city that had given him so cordial a welcome.

When little Kate was nearly four years old Mrs. Saxton, mother of Mrs. McKinley, died. The blow was a peculiarly severe one, for within a month her second child, also a girl, was born—but to close her eyes on the earth almost as soon as she had opened them.   They named her Ida, the father hoping in the brief days of the delicate little life that the child would bring back vigor and interest in existence to the depressed wife, whose grief at the death of her own mother was scarcely assuaged.

But in this gentle hope he was doomed to disappointment, for little Ida faded from among them.   And then the third great blow fell, for a few weeks after the baby's death little Kate sickened and died.

Ida Saxton had been a strong, healthy girl.   She was not delicate of physique; and while she was in no sense buxom or amazonian, she was far from frail.   Yet the accumulated shocks and sorrows of those sad days completely unstrung her.   And the woman who deserved and might have had a world of happiness, a heaven of domestic joy on earth, never again was blest with health.

No more children came to them, but their home has always catered to the rippling laughter and the joyous songs of young life.   Even to the end, even on that last day at Buffalo, when horror leaped from the heart of happiness, there were young people with them. But in that hour of his wife's great trial, when he could not share her suffering, nor take an iota from the black pall of grief which enveloped her, William McKinley began a life of devotion a thousand times more gentle and kind than the intensest courtship of a lover. And through all the long years that have followed—for twenty-four long years—he has never wavered night nor day in the most assiduous care a husband can possibly bestow. No time has been so hurried, no demand of politics so exacting, no weariness so heavy that he has failed to remember her. If near her, he has gone to her, and expressed by his presence the thoughtful love which he felt. If she were absent he has always sent her a message. And, however brief, however little he might have to say that would interest her, he has kept strong and true that faith in her wifely heart that he would "love, cherish and protect" her in an infinitely more tender way then any vow could bind him.

For a while after the death of the little girls Mrs. McKinley concluded she wanted to live near "Mother McKinley," and they two took a couple of rooms in the house of the elders. Her own mother was dead, and the grief-stricken woman sorely needed the strong, steadfast hand and hearty comfort of that fine old matron who had done so much in building the character of a grand American.

But presently Major McKinley found a new interest with which he hoped to distract his wife's mind from the cloud of sorrows that would not lift. He was building a house. He was establishing a home of their very own. And in the occupation of watching the workmen her spirits came back again. She could not regain her physical health, and never has. But the clouds were dispelled, and the old cheerful, happy look came back to the blue eyes, and the fair face again resumed its wonted roundness of outline and sweetness of expression. And these have never again departed.

Of course no man deserves praise or credit for kindness to his wife; and when her illness renders attention the more necessary, there is still less reason for indulging in adulatory phrases. But in the case of William McKinley there is, even with the most undemonstrative, warrant for expressing the admiration which every good man and true woman must certainly feel.

In spite of a physical weakness which stubbornly clung to the little woman, the home life of Major and Mrs. McKinley has always been singularly happy. She loved children, as has been said, and always had them around her. She loved music; and there has always been singing and the best of instrumentalists at her home. She loved roses; and the house has always been a bower of floral beauty and of perfume.

In time a larger house was builded, and into it the family removed. It was really but an extending of the dwelling which had been their home in the old days. And it is the house to which unnumbered thousands made pilgrimages in 1896. It will be understood that Mrs. McKinley possessed a fortune in her own right. Her father died late in the seventies, following his wife's demise; and the Saxton estate was divided between three heirs— a sister, a brother, and Mrs. McKinley. But the man who could attend her with all the solicitude of a mother was not the man to use a dollar he had not earned. When financial disaster came upon him, in 1893, his wife—for once opposing his will—turned over all her property for the benefit of those creditors whom a security debt had created. The good home went too. And the man who had done so much for his country, who was so nearly a model of American manhood, began paying rent as at the beginning. The debts were all wiped out, absolutely, and Mrs. McKinley's estate was released to her, and the old home became again the property of the man who had earned it, and who so richly deserved it. But even in that hour of a new tribulation, he never faltered in his loving care for his wife, or the filial considerateness he had always paid his mother.

When that mother fell ill and died, her son had reached the highest honor the greatest nation can bestow. But he hurried from the presidential mansion to her bedside at Canton, and sorrowfully followed her to the grave.

It may seem by a reading of the domestic side of President McKinley's life that it is more sad and somber than is the lot of most men to suffer. But this, a thousand friends will testify, is clearly an error. The home life of the President has been uniformly happy. Never an unkind word, never a frown, never a sorrow inflicted within the portals, and always the music of song and laughter, the perfume of roses and the blessing of loving words— there is no sadness in such a picture.

CHAPTER XXVII.

McKINLEY'S EULOGY OF LINCOLN.

In self-sacrifice and patriotism, President McKinley reflected many qualities of Abraham Lincoln. How closely he had studied the character of the great Lincoln is shown in an address delivered by Mr. McKinley on Lincoln's Birthday anniversary, February 12, 1895, before the Unconditional Republican Club of Albany, N. Y. Mr. McKinley said:

"A noble manhood, nobly consecrated to man, never dies. The martyr of liberty, the emancipator of a race, the savior of the only free government among men may be buried from human sight, but his deeds will live in human gratitude forever.

"The story of his simple life is the story of the plain, honest, manly citizen, true patriot and profound statesman who, believing with all the strength of his mighty soul in the institutions of his country, won, because of them, the highest place in its government—then fell a sacrifice to the Union he held so dear, and which Providence spared his life long enough to save. We meet to-night to do honor to one whose achievements have heightened human aspirations and broadened the field of opportunity to the races of men. While the party with which we stand, and for which he stood, can justly claim him, and without dispute can boast the distinction of being the first to honor and trust him, his fame has leaped the bounds of party and country, and now belongs to mankind and the ages.

"Lincoln had sublime faith in the people. He walked with and among them. He recognized the importance and power of an enlightened public sentiment and was guided by it. Even amid the vicissitudes of war he concealed little from public review and inspection. In all he did he invited rather than evaded examination and criticism. He submitted his plans and purposes, as far as practicable, to public consideration with perfect frankness and sincerity. There was such homely simplicity in his character that it could not be hedged in by the pomp of place, nor the ceremonials of high official station. He was so accessible to the public that he seemed to take the people into his confidence. Here, perhaps, was one secret of his power. The people never lost their confidence in him, however much they unconsciously added to his personal discomfort and trials. His patience was almost superhuman. And who will say that he was mistaken in his treatment of the thousands who thronged continually about him? More than once when reproached for permitting visitors to crowd upon him, he asked, in pained surprise, 'Why, what harm does this confidence in men do me?'

"In all the long years of slavery agitation, Lincoln always carried the people with him. In 1854 Illinois cast loose from her old Democratic moorings and followed his leadership in a most emphatic protest against the repeal of the Missouri Compromise. In 1858 the people of Illinois indorsed his opposition to the aggression of slavery, in a State usually Democratic, even against so popular a leader as the Little Giant. In 1860, the whole country indorsed his position on slavery, even when the people were continually harangued that his election meant the dissolution of the Union. During the war the people advanced with him step by step to its final overthrow. Indeed, in the election of 1864, the people not only indorsed emancipation, but went far toward recognizing the political equality of the negro. They heartily justified the President in having enlisted colored soldiers to fight side by side with the white man in the noble cause of union and liberty. Aye, they did more; they indorsed his position on another and vastly more important phase of the race problem. They approved his course as President in re-organizing the government of Louisiana, and a hostile press did not fail to call attention to the fact that this meant eventually negro suffrage in that State.

"The greatest names in American history are Washington and Lincoln. One is forever associated with the independence of the States and formation of the Federal Union; the other with universal freedom and the preservation of the Union. Washington enforced the Declaration of Independence as against England; Lincoln proclaimed its fulfillment not only to a downtrodden race in America, but to all people for all time who may seek the protection of our flag. These illustrious men achieved grander results for mankind within a single century, from 1775 to 1865, than any other men ever accomplished in all the years since first the flight of time began. Washington engaged in no ordinary revolution; with him it was not who should rule, but what should rule. He drew his sword not for a change of rulers upon an established throne, but to establish a new government which should acknowledge no throne but the tribute of the people. Lincoln accepted war to save the Union, the safeguard of our liberties, and re-establish it on 'indestructible foundations' as forever 'one and indivisible.' To quote his own grand words: Now we are contending 'that this Nation under God shall have a new birth of freedom, and that government of the people, by the people, for the people, shall not perish from the earth.'

"Each lived to accomplish his appointed task. Each received the unbounded gratitude of the people of his time and each is held in great and ever-increasing reverence by posterity. The fame of each will never die; it will grow with the ages, because it is based upon imperishable service to humanity; not to the people of a single generation or country, but to the whole human family, wherever scattered, forever.

"The present generation knows Washington only from history, and by that alone can judge him. Lincoln we know by history also, but thousands are still living who participated in the great events in which he was leader and master. Many of his contemporaries survived him; some are here yet in almost every locality. So Lincoln is not far removed from us; he may be said to be still known to the millions—not surrounded by the mist of antiquity, nor a halo of idolatry that is impenetrable. He never was inaccessible to the people; thousands carry with them yet the words which he spoke in their hearing; thousands remember the pressure of his hand; and thousands have not forgotten that indescribably sad, thoughtful, far-seeing expression which impressed everybody. Nobody could keep the people away from him, and when they came he would suffer no one to drive them back. So it is that an unusually large number of the American people came to know this great man and that he is still so well remembered by them. It cannot be said that they were all mistaken about him or that they misinterpreted his greatness. Men are still connected with the Government who served during his administration. There are at least two senators, and perhaps twice as many representatives, who participated in his first inauguration—men who stood side by side with him in the trying duties of his administration and who have been, without interruption, in one branch or another of the public service ever since. The Supreme Court of the United States still has among its members one whom Lincoln appointed, and so of other branches of the Federal judiciary. His faithful private secretaries are still alive and have rendered posterity a great service in their history of Lincoln and his times. They have told the story of his life and public services with such entire frankness and fidelity as to exhibit to the world 'the very inner courts of his soul.'

"This host of witnesses, without exception, agree as to the true nobility and intellectual greatness of Lincoln. All proudly claim for Lincoln the highest abilities and the most distinguished and self-sacrificing patriotism.

ARRIVAL OF THE FUNERAL   PROCESSION AT THE EAST   FRONT OF THE CAPITOL,
WASHINGTON.

SAILORS FROM THE BATTLESHIP ILLINOIS IN THE FUNERAL PROCESSION, WASHINGTON.

Lincoln taught them, and has taught us, that no party or partisan can escape responsibility to the people; that no party advantage, or presumed party advantage, should ever swerve us from the plain path of duty, which is ever the path of honor and distinction. He emphasized his words by his daily life and deeds. He showed to the world by his lofty example, as well as by precept and maxim, that there are times when the voice of partisanship should be hushed and that of patriotism only be heeded. He taught that a good service done for the country, even in aid of an unfriendly administration, brings to the men and the party, who rise above the temptation of temporary partisan advantage, a lasting gain in the respect and confidence of the people. He showed that such patriotic devotion is usually rewarded, not only with retention in power and the consciousness of duty well and bravely done, but with the gratification of beholding the blessings of relief and prosperity, not of a party or section, but of the whole country. This he held should be the first and great consideration with all public servants.

"Lincoln was a man of moderation. He was neither an autocrat nor a tyrant. If he moved slowly sometimes, it was because it was better to move slowly and he was only waiting for his reserves to come up. Possessing almost unlimited power, he yet carried himself like one of the humblest of men. He weighed every subject. He considered and reflected upon every phase of public duty. He got the average judgment of the plain people. He had a high sense of justice, a clear understanding of the rights of others, and never needlessly inflicted an injury upon any man. He always taught and enforced the doctrine of mercy and charity on every occasion. Even in the excess of rejoicing, he said to a party who came to serenade him a few nights after the Presidential election in November, 1864: 'Now that the election is over, may not all having a common interest reunite in a common effort to save our common country? So long as I have been here I have not willingly planted a thorn in any man's bosom. While I am deeply sensible to the high compliment of a re-election, and duly grateful, as I trust, to Almighty God for having directed my countrymen to a right conclusion, as I think, for their own good, it adds nothing to my satisfaction that any other man may be disappointed or pained by the result.'"

CHAPTER XXVIII.

PRESIDENT ROOSEVELT TAKES THE OATH OF OFFICE.

Theodore Roosevelt became President of the United States at 3:32 o'clock Saturday afternoon, September 14, 1901. The oath of office was administered by Judge John R. Hazel, of the United States District Court, in the library of the residence of Mr. Ansley Wilcox, at Buffalo. Mr. Wilcox was an old friend of the Vice-President, and the latter had made Mr. Wilcox's house his home during his stay in Buffalo, after the shooting of the President.

The delay in taking the oath after the death of the President was the result of the sanguine feeling among the people that President McKinley would recover from his wounds. No one shared this feeling in a higher degree than the Vice-President. When the news that the President had been shot became public Vice-President Roosevelt was in the East. He started immediately for Buffalo, and was at the President's bedside as soon as possible. He remained in Buffalo until the physicians announced that there was no fear of the President's death, and then left for the Adirondacks.

When the President began to sink Thursday night messages were sent to the Vice-President and those members of the Cabinet who, like himself, had left Buffalo, deluded into the belief that the President would soon be able to return to the Capital. The Vice-President, with his usual promptitude, started on the return trip to Buffalo, greatly saddened by the news which made such a step necessary. He made a hard night ride from the North Woods to Albany, and by the use of a special train reached Buffalo at 1:35 o'clock Saturday afternoon.

To avoid the crowd which had gathered at the Union Station to see him the Vice-President alighted at the Terrace Station of the New York Central, where a police and military escort awaited him. He insisted first of all on visiting Mrs. McKinley and offering condolences to her in her hour of anguish. This step he desired to take simply as a private citizen, and when it was accomplished the Vice-President announced himself as ready to take the oath as President. A strong escort of military and police had assembled at the Milburn house to escort him to Mr. Wilcox's, but its presence annoyed the Vice-President, and he halted the guards with a quick, imperative military command, saying he would have only two policemen to go along with him. Later he announced that he did not want to establish the precedent of going about guarded.

The place selected for the administration of the oath was the library of Mr. Wilcox's house, a rather small room, but picturesque, the heavy oak trimmings and the massive bookcases giving it somewhat the appearance of a legal den. A pretty bay window with stained glass and heavy hangings formed a background, and against this Colonel Roosevelt took his position.

Judge Hazel stood near him in the bay window, and Colonel Roosevelt showed his almost extreme nervousness by plucking at the lapel of his long frock coat and nervously tapping the hardwood floor with his heel.

He stepped over once to Secretary Root and for about five minutes they conversed earnestly. The question at issue was whether the President should first sign an oath of office and then swear in or whether he should swear in first and sign the document in the case after.

Secretary Root ceased his conversation with Colonel Roosevelt, and, stepping back, while an absolute hush fell upon every one in the room, said, in an almost inaudible voice:

"Mr. Vice-President, I——" Then his voice faltered, and for fully two minutes the tears came down his face and his lips quivered so that he could not continue his utterances. There were sympathetic tears from those about him, and two great drops ran down either cheek of the successor of William McKinley.

Mr. Root's chin was on his breast. Suddenly throwing back his head as if with an effort, he continued in broken voice:

"I have been requested, on behalf of the Cabinet of the late President, at least those who are present in Buffalo, all except two, to request that for reasons of weight affecting the affairs of government, you should proceed to take the constitutional oath of President of the United States."

Colonel Roosevelt stepped farther into the bay window, and Judge Hazel, taking up the constitutional oath of office, which had been prepared on parchment, asked him to raise his right hand and repeat it after him. There was a hush like death in the room as the Judge read a few words at a time, and Colonel Roosevelt, in a strong voice and without a tremor, and with his raised hand steady, repeated it after him.

"And thus I swear," he ended it. The hand dropped by the side, the chin for an instant rested on the breast, and the silence remained unbroken for a couple of minutes as though the new President of the United States were offering silent prayer. Judge Hazel broke it, saying:

"Mr. President, please attach your signature," and the President, turning to a small table near by, wrote "Theodore Roosevelt" at the bottom of the document in a firm hand.

The new President was visibly shaken, but he controlled himself admirably, and with the deep solemnity of the occasion full upon him, he announced to those present that his aim would be to be William McKinley's successor in deed as well as in name.   Deliberately he proclaimed it in these words:

"In this hour of deep and terrible bereavement, I wish to state that it shall be my aim to continue absolutely unbroken the policy of President McKinley for the peace and prosperity and honor of our beloved country."

The great, far-reaching significance of this pledge to continue the policy of the dead President, announced at the very threshold of a new governmental regime, profoundly impressed his hearers, and President Roosevelt's first step after taking the oath was in line with its redemption.   His first act was to ask the members of the Cabinet to retain their portfolios in order to aid him to conduct the government on lines laid down by him whose policy he had declared he would uphold.   Such an appeal was not to be resisted, and every member of the Cabinet, including Secretary of State Hay and Secretary of the Treasury Gage, who were communicated with in Washington, have agreed for the present, at least, to retain their several portfolios.

President Roosevelt remained in Buffalo until the funeral cortege started for Washington, when he accompanied it.

Theodore Roosevelt was born October 20, 1858, at No. 28 East Twentieth street, New York City.   His father, also Theodore Roosevelt, was a member of an old New York Dutch family, and Mr. Roosevelt is of the eighth generation of the stock in the United States.   Mingled with the Dutch in Theodore Roosevelt's veins are strains of English, Celtic, and French.   His mother was Miss Martha Bulloch, and came of a distinguished Georgia family, which had given to that state a Governor, Archibald Bulloch, in revolutionary times.   In a later generation a member of the family built the Confederate privateer Alabama.

The father of Theodore Roosevelt was a merchant and importer of glassware.   During the Civil War he was a noted figure in New York.   He had great strength of character and liking for practical benevolence, which made him foremost in many such charities.   Newsboys' lodging-houses, the allotment system, which permitted soldiers during the war to have portions of their pay sent to their families, and other forms of direct help to the poorer classes found in him a champion.   His ancestors had been aldermen, judges of the supreme court of the city, and representatives in the National Congress. In revolutionary times New York chose a Roosevelt to act with Alexander Hamilton in the United States Constitutional Convention. Roosevelt street was once a cowpath on the Roosevelt farm, and the Roosevelt hospital is the gift of a wealthy member of a recent generation of the family.

As a child Theodore Roosevelt was puny and backward. He could not keep up with his fellows either in study or play, and on this account was taught by a private tutor at home. The country residence of the Roosevelts was at Oyster Bay, Long Island, and here the children were brought up. They were compelled by their father to take plenty of outdoor exercise, and young Theodore, soon realizing that he must have strength of body if he was to do anything in life, entered into the scheme for the improvement of his physical condition with the same enthusiasm and determination which has characterized every act of his life. He grew up an athlete, strong and active, and when he entered Harvard in 1875 he soon became prominent in field sports. He became noted as a boxer and wrestler, and was for a time captain of the college polo team. He did not neglect his studies, and when he was graduated, in 1880, he took high honors. During his stay in the university he had been editor of the Advocate, a college paper, and gave particular attention to the study of history and natural history. He became a member of the Phi Beta Kappa Greek letter fraternity.

At the conclusion of his college course he went abroad for a year, spending part of the time in study in Dresden. His love for athletics led him to successfully attempt the ascent of the Jung-Frau and the Matterhorn, and won for him a membership in the Alpine Club of London. He returned to New York in 1881, and in the same year married Miss Alice Lee of Boston. Two years later he had the misfortune to lose his wife and his mother within a week.

Theodore Roosevelt has been an ardent student of history from his college days, and before he was twenty-three years old had entered the field himself as a writer. He is an enthusiastic admirer of Washington, Lincoln, and Grant. On his return from Europe, and while engaged on his historical work, he entered the law office of his uncle, Robert B. Roosevelt, with the design of fitting himself for the bar. He was of too restless a disposition to find content in such a sober calling, and the whole bent of his mind, as shown by his reading, his writing, and the effort to do something extraordinary, something that would mark him above his fellows, which had made him a bidder for college championships and prompted him to tempt the dangers of the Swiss mountain peaks, sent him hurrying into politics before he had settled down to anything like deep study of the law.

He attended his first primary in 1881, in the Twenty-first assembly district of New York. It was a gathering with little to charm the ordinary young man of aristocratic lineage and wealth, but Theodore Roosevelt had studied history with a purpose. He knew that through the primary led the way to political preferment, and he at once entered into the battle of politics, in which he was to prove a gladiator of astonishing prowess, routing and terrifying his enemies, but often startling his allies by the originality and recklessness of his methods.

The natural enthusiasm of young Roosevelt, his undeniable personal charm, and the swirl of interest with which he descended into the arena of local politics, made him friends on every side in a community where leaders are at a high premium, and within a few months the young college man was elected to the Assembly of the state from his home district.

His ability and his methods were in strong evidence at the following session of the Legislature. He proved a rallying power for the Republican minority, and actually succeeded in passing legislation which the majority submitted to only through fear and which his own party in the state would never have fathered had it been in power. Mr. Roosevelt was the undisputed leader of the Republicans in the Assembly within two months after his election, and he immediately turned his attention to the purification of New York City. This would have appalled a man less determined or more experienced. But the young aspirant for a place in history reckoned neither with conditions nor precedents. His success, considering the strength of the combination against which he was arrayed, was extraordinary. He succeeded in securing the passage of the bill which deprived the city council of New York of the power to veto the appointments of the mayor, a prerogative which had nullified every previous attempt at reform and had made the spoliation of the city's coffers an easy matter in the time of Tweed and other bosses.

Mr. Roosevelt's methods, it was cheerfully predicted by his political opponents, would certainly result in his retirement from participation in the state councils of New York, but this proved far from the case. Wherever Theodore Roosevelt has been thrown with any class of people, wherever they have come to know him personally, he has attracted to himself enthusiastic friendship and confidence. Theatrical though many of his acts have appeared, his honesty, his personal fearlessness, and the purity of his motives have not been questioned.

He became so popular that not only was he returned to three sessions of the Assembly, but his party in the state soon realized that he was one of its strongest men, and he was sent to the Republican National Convention of 1884 as chairman of the New York delegation.

Meanwhile he had been hammering away at corruption in New York, and had secured the passage of the act making the offices of the county clerk, sheriff, and register salaried ones. He had been chairman of the committee to investigate the work of county officials, and, as a result of that investigation, offered the bill which cut off from the clerk of the county of New York an income in fees which approximated $82,000 per annum; from the sheriff, $100,000, and from the register also a very high return in fees. From the county offices to the police was·not far and Roosevelt was agitating an investigation and reform in the guardianship of the city when he left the Legislature. After the convention, to which he went uninstructed, but in favor of the nomination of Mr. Edmunds against James G. Blaine, his health failed. The deaths of his wife and mother had been a severe shock, for Mr. Roosevelt is a man of the strongest personal attachments. He turned aside from public life for a time and went West.

He had been a lover of hunting from boyhood, and when he decided to spend some time in the wilds of Montana, he took up the life as he found it there. On the banks of the Little Missouri he built a log house, working on it himself, and there turned ranchman, cowboy and hunter. He engaged in one of the last of the big buffalo hunts, and saturated himself with the life of the West. His trips in this and later years were not alone confined to this section of the West, and his courage, intelligence, and companionable nature made him a name which in later years drew to his standard thousands of cowboys, among whom his name had come to mean all that they admire, and all that appeals to their natures. The love and admiration was not one-sided, for Mr. Roosevelt came to regard these hardy, open-hearted, plain-spoken guardians of the wilderness as the finest types of manhood.

In these years and between 1886 and 1888 Mr. Roosevelt was also busy on much of his literary work. The most important of his works—"The Winning of the West," a history in four volumes of the acquisition of the territory west of the Alleghenies—required an enormous amount of research. On its publication it leaped at once into popularity, and soon acquired a reputation as a most reliable text-book.

His hunting trips and his months of life among the men and the game of the West have supplied the material for a number of Mr. Roosevelt's books, among them "The Wilderness Hunter," "Hunting Trips of a Ranchman," and "Ranch Life and the Hunting Trail." His most noted work of recent years is "The Rough Riders," being a history of the formation, the battles, career, and disbandment of the remarkable body of soldiers comprising the regiment which Mr. Roosevelt recruited largely himself, and of which he was lieutenant-colonel and colonel in the brief campaign in Cuba. His style is interesting and clear, and while the story is told in the first person, there is a simplicity of narrative and a cordiality of praise to all who seem to deserve.

Mr. Roosevelt's more important works have been historical, but his writings have not been confined to this subject. He has contributed many articles to scientific magazines, particularly on discrimination of species and sub-species of the larger animals of the West. A species of elk is named after him, and he made known the enlarged Western species of a little insectivora called the shrew.

This period of writing and hunting was broken by two important events. He was defeated as candidate for mayor of New York and he married again. The second wife of the Vice President elect was Miss Edith Kermit Carow, daughter of an old New York family. They have five children—three sons and two daughters. The marriage took place in 1886, and in the same year Theodore Roosevelt was the Republican nominee for mayor of his native city. Opposed to him were Abram S. Hewitt, the Democratic candidate, and Henry George, the apostle of single tax. So great an enthusiasm had been created by Mr. George's book, "Progress and Poverty," and so quickly did he attach to himself all the floating element dissatisfied with the regime of both the old parties and without the vested wealth threatened by the theories of their leader that both of the old parties were alarmed. It was said that fear that George would be elected sent thousands of Republican votes to Hewitt, whose chances of success seemed greatly better than those of his young Republican opponent. Hewitt was elected, but Mr. Roosevelt received a larger proportion of the votes cast than had any other Republican candidate for mayor up to that time.

For years after this Mr. Roosevelt was not prominent in politics. He spent his time in writing and hunting trips to the West. Never an idle man, he accomplished an immense amount of research in the preparation of his historical works.

President Harrison appointed Theodore Roosevelt a member of the United States Civil Service Commission May 13, 1889. While in the New York Legislature much of his efforts had been directed to the improvement of the public service. He was one of the most noted advocates in the country of the merit system, and his enmity to the spoilsman had won him objurgations of press and party on numberless occasions. To his new duties he brought enthusiastic faith in the righteousness and the expediency of a civil-service system, and he at once embarked on a campaign for establishing its permanency and for its extension, which again made him the butt of almost daily attacks. In Congress and in the ranks of the leaders of his party hundreds of opponents sprang up to attack him, but he held to his way and eventually won to his own way of thinking many public men. Though always determined and aggressive, Mr. Roosevelt is a man of great tact, and to this no less than to the resolute assurance of his methods was due the success of his efforts for the extension of the civil service in the national service.

He served for six years, two of them under President Harrison's successor, Mr. Cleveland. In that time the number of persons who were made subject to the civil-service law was increased from 12,000 to nearly 40,000, and the still further great increase made by the orders of President Cleveland in the late years of his first administration was largely due to Mr. Roosevelt's efforts. He was not a member of the commission when they were promulgated, but they had been considered by the commission and were favorably regarded by the President almost a year before they were made law by the President's order.

In the years he then spent in Washington Mr. Roosevelt made many strong friends. In the commission he was loved and respected by every one, from his fellow commissioners to the laborers. He declined to be president of the commission, though the place was offered him more than once, but he was the acknowledged force and head of its work. When the great extensions afterward made by the President were first proposed to Mr. Cleveland he suggested that it would be better to codify the rules of the commission before taking such action. This was done, though it took some time, and shortly after it had been accomplished the chief examiner of the commission, Mr. Webster, died, which again put affairs in such shape that it was regarded as inexpedient to add greatly to the duties of the commission at that time.

As a result, the order for the large extension of the operation of the civil-service law, which had been in contemplation by the President and the commission for more than a year, and with which Mr. Roosevelt had much to do, was not promulgated until after he had resigned from the commission to accept the appointment as police commissioner of the city of New York under Mayor Strong. President Cleveland, who had reappointed Mr. Roosevelt as civil-service commissioner, though he had been originally named for the place as a Republican by President Harrison, strongly advised Mr. Roosevelt not to leave the commission and not to take the New York place. The President's letter to Mr. Roosevelt on his resignation is full of expressions of the highest esteem and appreciation of his services.

In the wave of reform which swept over New York in 1894-95 the men, including Mayor Strong, who were borne into power were something of the same stamp as the civil-service commissioner. They were of the class which fought political rings, and they turned to Mr. Roosevelt to take a hand in purifying the police force of New York City, which was alleged to be a sink of political rottenness and studied inefficiency. Mr. Roosevelt resigned as civil-service commissioner May 5, 1895, and was appointed police commissioner of New York City May 24 following.

The uproar that followed the introduction of Roosevelt methods in the conduct of the New York police force has never been equaled as a police sensation in that city. Within a month after his appointment the whole force was in a state of fright. The new commissioner made night rounds himself, and, being unknown to the men, he caught scores of them in dereliction of duty. He dismissed and promoted and punished entirely on a plane of his own. Politics ceased to save or help the men, and the bosses were up in arms. In this emergency an attempt was made to have Roosevelt's appointment by Mayor Strong vetoed by the city council, and it was discovered that an act of the Legislature, passed some twelve years prior, had taken the power of veto from the city council. Theodore Roosevelt was the author of this act, and its passage had been secured after one of the strongest fights he had made when a member of the State Legislature.

Commissioner Roosevelt announced that he would enforce the laws as he found them. He gave special attention to the operations of the excise law on Sunday, and after severe measures had been used on some of the more hardy saloon-keepers, New York at last had, in June, 1895, for the first time within the memory of living man, a "dry" Sunday. A great deal of good was done by Commissioner Roosevelt in breaking up much of the blackmail which had been levied by policemen; in transferring and degrading officers who were notoriously responsible for the bad name the force had, and in making promotions for merit, fidelity, and courage, Mr. Roosevelt's career as a police commissioner made him extremely unpopular with the class at which his crusade was aimed.

The fierce crusade against the saloon-keepers was brief, and its effect lasted but a few weeks. The new commissioner gave his attention to more important matters, and really made the force cleaner than it had been before. He undoubtedly gained the hearty devotion of the better class of policemen. He was most careful of their comfort, and quick to see and reward merit. He was also quick to punish, and this kept the worse half of the men on their good behavior.

One important result Mr. Roosevelt obtained in this position was the dissipation of much of the antagonism which had theretofore been apparent on every occasion between labor unions and the force. Men on strike had been accustomed to regard the policeman as a natural enemy, but all this was changed. On one occasion, when a large number of operatives were out of work, Mr. Roosevelt sent for their leaders, and, after a discussion on the situation, suggested that the strikers should organize pickets to keep their own men in order. He promised that the police should support and respect the rights of these pickets and the result was most satisfactory. The threat of a cordon of police was removed from the strikers, and no collision such as had occurred on so many similar occasions, took place with the guardians of the law.

The attacks of the enemies which Mr. Roosevelt's methods raised up against him were not confined to verbal denunciation nor expressions through the press. Dynamite bombs were left in his office, a part of his associates on the police board fought his every move, and all the skill of New York politicians with whom he interfered was exercised to trap him into a situation where he would become discredited in his work. In this they were unsuccessful and the stormy career of the police force continued. In the end the new commissioner conquered. He had the necessary power and the personal courage and tenacity of purpose to carry out his plans. He fought blackmail until he had practically stopped it and he promoted and removed men without regard to color, creed, or politics. He resigned in April, 1897, to become Assistant Secretary of the Navy.

Theodore Roosevelt was appointed Assistant Secretary of the Navy April 19, 1897. The troubles of the Cubans with Spain, the long history of oppression and outrage to which they had been subjected, and the years of warfare they had known with the armies of Weyler and Campos, had excited American sympathy, and many public men realized that interference by the United States was almost assured. In this connection it was realized by President McKinley and his advisers that the navy was not in condition to make it an effective war instrument in the impending conflict. In casting about for a man to fill the position of Assistant Secretary of the Navy, which place carried with it much of the executive work which would be required in putting fighting ships into shape, the President and Secretary Long were favorably disposed toward Mr. Roosevelt, who was one of the many candidates for the place. His work on the naval war of 1812 had acquired fame for its accuracy and its exhibition of wide knowledge of naval matters on the part of the author and Mr. Roosevelt was asked to accept the appointment.

He brought to the duties of the office a great interest in the work, as well as the tremendous energy and talent for closely studying and mastering his work which had characterized him in other fields. He also brought to the position some of his startling methods, and again proved himself "a storm center," a name he had already been given, and to which he has earned better title in each succeeding year. In the fall of 1897 he was detailed to inspect the fleet gathered at Hampton Roads, and he kept the commanders and their jackies in a ferment for a week. Whenever he thought of a drill he would like to see, he ordered it. The crews were called to night quarters and all sorts of emergency orders were given at all sorts of hours. When the Assistant Secretary came back to Washington to report, he had mastered some of the important details of the situation, at least.

During his rather brief connection with the department Mr. Roosevelt was a strong advocate of the naval personnel bill. He was also in charge of the purchase of auxiliary vessels after war was actually declared.

He had brought about the purchase of many guns, much ammunition, and large stores of provisions for the navy. He had secured a great increase in the amount of gunnery practice. He had hurried the work on the new ships and had the old ones repaired. He had caused every vessel to be supplied with coal to her full capacity, and had the crew of every ship recruited to its full strength. His services were fully recognized by Secretary Long, who thanked him in a letter full of appreciation when he left his place in the Navy Department. Mr. Roosevelt was urged to remain in his place by many of the most prominent newspapers of the country, who believed that his services there would be of great value in the approaching struggle.

Mr. Roosevelt had determined to resign his position in order to take active service in the field. His adventurous nature would not allow him to remain in an office when there was a prospect of fighting for the flag. He had determined to organize a regiment of Western men, whom, he rightly believed, would strike terror to the hearts of the Spaniards. Mr. Roosevelt's resignation as Assistant Secretary of the Navy bears date of May 6, 1898. His appointment as lieutenant-colonel, First Regiment, United States Volunteer Cavalry, is dated May 5, 1898.

The First United States Volunteer Cavalry was one of the most remarkable fighting aggregations ever enlisted in any country. It was chosen from some 3,500 applicants and numbered about 900. The plains gave it its largest membership, and the name under which it soon came to be known was "Roosevelt's Rough Riders."

Dr. Leonard Wood, a United States Army officer, and a close friend of Colonel Roosevelt, was made colonel of the regiment. Colonel Roosevelt believed he was not sufficiently well informed concerning military matters to handle the regiment during the preliminary work, and he readily acquiesced in the appointment of his friend. The regiment rendezvoused at San Antonio, Texas, and there was kept at work learning the discipline of soldier life, until it was finally called to the front. Among the recruits were hundreds of cowboys who were perfect horsemen as well as dead shots. But such an outburst of popular interest attended the recruiting of this regiment that Colonel Wood and Lieutenant-Colonel Roosevelt were soon overwhelmed with applications for enlistment from the college men, athletes, clubmen, sons of millionaire parents, who loved the idea of adventure and battle in such company. As a result several companies were recruited from the pick of the young men of the country. Nearly every noted club of the country had its quota, and scores of Wall street stockbrokers wore khaki in the ranks. When finally the regiment was gathered at Tampa, Florida, it constituted a body of men than whom it would be hard to find any more perfectly fitted for such war as the conflict with Spain in the jungles of Cuba assured. Old Indian fighters were there by the score, and there were even six full-blooded Indians among the enlisted men.

The Rough Riders, it was originally intended, should be mounted, and as cavalry they went to the rendezvous at Tampa. But when the time came to go to Cuba there was no room on the transports for horses, and these cavalrymen, like the rest of the men who had enlisted in all the regiments assembled at the Florida port, were mad to get to the front. Rather than not see some of the fighting, the commander of the Rough Riders secured a place for his men among the troops sent to participate in the siege of Santiago, and they went as dismounted cavalry. As such they went to Cuba and fought through the brief but bloody campaign before the besieged city. They never had an opportunity to display their skill as horsemen after they left the training camps at San Antonio and Tampa, but they won a reputation for courage and cheerful patience under hardship, battle, and disease which is not surpassed in history.

This was not the first military service of Roosevelt. Soon after his graduation from Harvard he had joined the Eighth Regiment, New York National Guard, and had been in time promoted to the captaincy of a company. He remained a militiaman for four years, leaving his command only when he took up his permanent residence in Washington as a member of the civil-service commission.

The transports carrying the army of invasion to Cuba sailed from Port Tampa June 13, 1898. Thirty large vessels carried the troops and took six days to reach Daiquiri, the little port to the east of the harbor of Santiago, where the army was disembarked. The Rough Riders were in the brigade commanded by General S. B. M. Young, together with the First (white) and Tenth (colored) Regular Cavalry Regiments, and was a part of the division commanded by General Joseph Wheeler.

The first fight of the Rough Riders took place in the advance from Daiquiri toward Santiago. They were sent out on a hill trail to attack the position of the Spaniards, who blocked the road to the town. The Spanish occupied ridges opposite to those along which the trail used by the Rough Riders led, and a fierce fight took place in the jungle. The Spanish had smokeless powder, and it was almost impossible to locate them in the underbrush. The Rough Riders behaved with great gallantry, and took the position occupied by the enemy, but not without considerable loss. For distinguished gallantry in this action, Lieutenant-Colonel Roosevelt was promoted to be Colonel July 11, 1898. The place of this engagement is called Las Guasimas, "the thorns," from the large number of trees of that species found there. The Rough Riders in this action acted in concert with other attacking forces composing the vanguard of the army. Several days after this General Young was taken with fever, and Colonel Wood, taking command of the brigade, Colonel Roosevelt became commanding officer of the regiment.

In this capacity he commanded the Rough Riders in the battle of San

Juan, where they withstood a heavy fire for a long time, and finally, when ordered to advance, made a gallant charge, capturing two of the hills occupied by the enemy. The fall of Santiago followed the American success, and a period of inactivity began for the American troops. Insufficient transportation had entailed improper and insufficient food, and, together with the effects of the climate, began to have serious effects on the troops. Fever decimated their ranks, and those who were still able to attend to their duties were weakened by disease.

It soon became apparent to the officers in command of the Americans that the only salvation for their men was removal to the North. It had been reported that yellow fever was epidemic among the soldiers in camp about Santiago, and while this was not at all true, most of the men were suffering from malarial fever, and there was some fear of the introduction of the tropic scourge into the United States if the troops were brought home suffering from it.

Colonel Roosevelt was in command of the brigade at this time, owing to General Wood having been made Governor-General of Santiago, and as such the commander of the Rough Riders discussed with the other Generals an appeal to the authorities to remove the troops back to the United States. There was disinclination on the part of the regular officers to take the initiative, as much correspondence had taken place between General Shafter and the War Department, the latter stating the reasons why it seemed inexpedient to cause the removal at that time. In this emergency Colonel Roosevelt prepared a presentation of the situation, and, after reading over the rough draft to the other commanders, submitted it to General Shafter.

Directly afterward a circular letter was prepared and signed by all the Generals and commanding officers and presented to General Shafter. This came to be known as "the round robin," and its result was instantaneous. Both letters, Colonel Roosevelt's and the round robin, were published throughout the United States and created a profound sensation. Within three days after they had been delivered to General Shafter the order for the return of the army was issued.

The Rough Riders, with their Colonel, returned to Camp Wikoff, at the northern extremity of Long Island, in late August, and on September 15, 1898, were mustered out of service with Colonel Roosevelt.

The campaign for the control of New York State in the approaching election of a Governor had already begun when the Rough Riders returned from Cuba. Colonel Roosevelt's name had often been mentioned for the

Republican nomination and the popular enthusiasm for this selection was supported by the leaders of the party in the state. Governor Frank S. Black had been elected by an enormous plurality two years previously, and according to all traditions should have been renominated. He was set aside, however, for the new hero, and the convention at Saratoga nominated Colonel Roosevelt with a hurrah. The friends of Governor Black had fought bitterly so long as there seemed a chance of success, and they started the rumor that Colonel Roosevelt was ineligible for the nomination, as he had relinquished his residence in New York when he went to Washington to enter the Navy Department.

The actual campaign was a most picturesque one. B. B. Odell, chairman of the state committee and now Governor of New York, was opposed to Colonel Roosevelt stumping the state in his own behalf, but it soon became apparent that general apathy existed, and consent was reluctantly given to the candidate to do so. There followed a series of speeches that woke up the voters. Colonel Roosevelt, by nature forceful, direct, and theatrical in his manner and method, went back and forward, up and down New York, accompanied by a few of his Rough Riders in their uniforms. These cowboys made speeches, telling, usually, how much they thought of their Colonel, and the tour met with success. Colonel Roosevelt was elected Governor over Augustus Van Wyck, the Democratic candidate, by a plurality of about 17,000 votes.

Among the achievements of Governor Roosevelt as chief executive of the Empire State were the enforcement of the law to tax corporations, which had been passed at a special session of the Legislature called by the Governor for that purpose; making the Erie Canal Commission non-partisan; his aid to the tenement commission in their work for the betterment of the poor in New York, and in breaking up the sweatshops through rigid enforcement of the factory law.

As a writer Mr. Roosevelt has been a contributor to magazines of innumerable articles on historical, political, and scientific subjects. A list of his more extended and important works includes "The Winning of the West," "Life of Governor Morris," "Life of Thomas Hart Benton," "Naval War of 1812," "History of New York," "American Ideals and Other Essays," "The Wilderness Hunter," "Hunting Trips of a Ranchman," "Ranch Life and the Hunting Trail," "The Strenuous Life," and "The Rough Riders."

SCENE ON MARKET STREET, CANTON.

RECEIVING VAULT, WESTLAWN CEMETERY, CANTON, OHIO.

CHAPTER XXIX.

GREAT EVENTS OF THE WORLD DURING PRESIDENT McKINLEY'S ADMINISTRATIONS.

William McKinley was inaugurated as the twenty-fifth President of the United States March 4, 1897, succeeding Grover Cleveland, who was serving his second term. Garret A. Hobart was sworn in as Vice-President on the same day. The campaign between Bryan and McKinley had been one of the most vigorously-fought in the history of the nation. The Democratic party made the money question paramount, and the Republican victory on that issue induced McKinley to call an extra session of Congress eleven days after his inauguration. The gold standard was adopted, after which Congress adjourned.

During April, May and June Turkey and Greece were 't war. Greece was the aggressor, but the outcome of the short campaign wa, disastrous for King George's troops, which were defeated in every battle by the Turks, who displayed a knowledge of warfare that struck surprise throughout Europe. Greece was made to pay a heavy indemnity and to cede Thessaly to Turkey at the treaty of peace, signed September 18.

The first heavy shipments of gold from the Klondike region began to arrive at San Francisco and Puget Sound ports. The output reached over $20,000,000 a year.

The boundary treaty between Venezuela and Great Britain was ratified at Washington June 14. It was regarding this boundary that President Cleveland in the previous December threatened Great Britain with war unless justice was done the South American republic.

July 24 the Dingley tariff bill became a law, the President having signed it. This bill was practically a substitution of the old McKinley tariff for the Wilson bill.

The first general knowledge of automobiles was spread by long newspaper reports of a race between horseless carriages in France. The machines were driven by electricity and gasoline.

August 25 is Independence day in Uruguay. While engaged in celebrating the event President Borda was shot and killed by an assassin.

Star Pointer, the famous pacing stallion, on August 28 lowered the world's record for a mile at Readville, Mass., to 1:59¼.

Charles A. Dana, for years famous as the editor of the New York Sun, died at Glen Cove, Long Island, October 17.

An attempt to assassinate President Diaz of Mexico September 15 failed. During Diaz's term in office—more than twenty years—no less than eight attempts to kill him were made. Twice he was slightly injured.

Dr. Frithof Nansen, the Norwegian arctic explorer, whose expedition came nearer reaching the North Pole than any previous attempt, reached America in October on a lecture tour. He was paid $65,000 for fifty lectures, probably the largest sum every paid for such work.

A conspiracy against the President of Brazil resulted in a concerted attack on him November 5. He was not injured, but his brother was fatally wounded and the minister of war was killed in his efforts to save the life of the President.

Mrs. Nancy A. McKinley, the aged mother of President McKinley, died at Canton December 12. She was buried in the President's family plot at Canton, where McKinle·'s two daughters lie buried.

1898 was an eve tful year in McKinley's administration owing to the outbreak of the Spanish war. In Europe it will be best remembered because of deaths of Gladstone and Bismarck.

The insurrection in Cuba had reached a stage when humanitarian efforts on the part of this country seemed necessary owing to the reconcentrado methods introduced by Weyler. The battleship Maine was sent to Havana, arriving there January 25. No demonstration was made, but it was hoped the moral effect of the presence of a warship would lead to good results.

The Maine was blown up by a submarine mine February 15. The events of the Spanish war will follow chronologically.

February 8—Letter was published written by Minister De Lome disparaging President McKinley. After publication of the letter De Lome asked the Spanish government to accept his resignation.

February 15—Battleship Maine blown up.

February 17—United States government appointed a naval court to inquire into the cause of the destruction of the Maine.

March 5—General Fitzhugh Lee's recall requested by the Spanish government and promptly refused by the United States.

March 7—Bill introduced in the House appropriating $50,000,000 for national defense. Passed the House March 7 and the Senate March 8, and was signed by the President.

March 12—Battleship Oregon sailed from San Francisco to meet the Atlantic squadron.

March 12—Spain offered armistice to the Cuban insurgents.

March 25—Report of the Maine Court of Inquiry delivered to the President and transmitted to Congress, reaching there March 28.

April 5—United States consuls in Cuba recalled.

April 11—President McKinley sends message to Congress on the Cuban situation, in which he advises intervention without recognition of the Cuban government.

April 19—Congress recognizes independence of Cuba and authorizes the use of United States forces in intervention.

April 20—President issues ultimatum to Spain.

April 21—An infernal machine was sent President McKinley, but the White House detectives grew suspicious of the peculiar package and it was investigated. It was filled with a powerful explosive.

April 22—Proclamation announcing war issued by President McKinley.

April 23—President McKinley issued a call for 125,000 volunteers.

April 24—War against the United States formally declared by Spain.

May 1—Spanish fleet at Manila entirely destroyed by Dewey's fleet.

May 8—Miss Helen Gould sent the government a check for $100,000 to add to the war fund.

May 19—William Ewart Gladstone died at Hawarden. He was England's greatest parliamentarian and a leader for many years. He was acknowledged throughout the world as one of the ablest men of modern times. He was born in 1809.

May 19—Arrival of Admiral Cervera's fleet in the harbor of Santiago, Cuba.

May 25—Second call for 75,000 volunteers issued by the President.

June 3—Merrimac sunk in the harbor of Santiago by Lieutenant Hobson.

June 20—United States Army of Invasion landed in Cuba under General Shafter.

July 1 and 2—El Caney and San Juan, Cuba, captured by United States troops with heavy loss.

July 3—Admiral Cervera's fleet attempted to escape and was entirely destroyed by United States fleet under command of Commodore Schley.

July 3-6—No newspapers were published in Chicago in these days of great events on sea and land, owing to a strike of the stereotypers. New men were secured July 6 and publication resumed. The newspaper owners formed a trust to fight the workers. Bulletin boards throughout the city were used to convey the latest news to the citizens.

July 4—The French line steamer La Bourgoyne collided with the British ship

Cromartyshire sixty miles south of Sable Island, near Newfoundland, and sunk. Five hundred and sixty of the 725 persons on board were drowned.

July —Agitation of the Dreyfus case in France followed by anti-Semitic riots.

July 26—Spanish government, through French Ambassador Cambon, asked for terms of peace.

July 30—Prince Otto Leopold von Bismarck died at Friedrichsruh. He had been chancellor of the German Empire and for thirty years was the greatest figure in European politics. He was born in 1815.

August 12—Peace protocol signed and armistice proclaimed. Cuban blockade raised.

September 18—Miss Winnie Davis, daughter of Jefferson Davis and known as the "Daughter of the Confederacy," died at Narragansett Pier, R. I. She was born in Richmond, Va., in 1864. Her efforts to cement the union between the North and the South in recent years received high praise.

October 17—University of Chicago conferred the degree of LL. D. on President McKinley.

October 18—United States takes formal possession of Porto Rico.

December 10—Peace treaty signed at Paris.

The year 1899 witnessed the closing acts of the Spanish war proper, but in the meantime the troops left in the Philippine Islands came in conflict with Aguinaldo's forces, and the friction soon lead to the Filipino outbreak. Hostilities were opened February 4, when the American lines just without Manila were attacked by 20,000 insurgents. The attack was repulsed with great loss, and the American troops under General Otis then took the aggressive. Several fierce engagements resulted, in which the Americans were invariably victorious.

In Europe the Dreyfus trial attracted great attention during July and August. Later the South African trouble came up and overshadowed all other subjects. The war was the final outcome of the Jameson raid of 1895, by which a party of Englishmen hoped to overthrow the Transvaal Republic under President Kruger, and establish a province under the protection of England.

Kruger's reply to England's demands for a new franchise law was given September 17. It repudiated England's claim, and both sides knew war to be inevitable. Preparations for the conflict at once began.

October 12 the Boers invaded British territory and on the 20th of that month the first battle, at Glencoe, resulted.   Both commanders were killed. The battle did not give either side the advantage.   Mafeking was besieged October 26 and Ladysmith October 28.   Kimberley, where Cecil Rhodes was at the time, next found a cordon of Boer soldiers and batteries surrounding it.   The Boers were successful in the engagements at Modder River and Colenso, although both sides sustained heavy loss.   The year closed with the three towns under siege and the British disheartened.

President McKinley signed the peace treaty with Spain February 10, and the Queen Regent of Spain signed the document March 17, ending the war formally.   Already there had been severe engagements in the Philippines and many of the volunteers who served in Cuba were sent to the new possessions in the Pacific.

General Lawton and General McArthur were the most prominent in the campaigns in the interior of Luzon. They drove the enemy from town to town, capturing many prisoners.   On April 27 Colonel Funston of the Twentieth Kansas Regiment, with two volunteers as companions, swam the Rio Grande River in the face of a murderous fire from the concealed enemy. A rope was carried across and by this means the soldiers were enabled to follow on rafts.   The exploit ranks next to Dewey's victory in Philippine war annals.

The "embalmed beef" investigation ended at Washington February 6. On the following day the President suspended General Eagan from duty for six years for his attack on General Miles during the hearing of the beef scandal.

Dewey was made a full admiral by Congress March 3.

Charles M. Murphy rode a mile on a bicycle in 57 4-5 seconds, behind an engine with a wind shield.

Captain Alfred Dreyfus returned to France from Devil's Island July 1. His trial began July 7.   He was again found guilty, but the sentence of ten years' imprisonment was not enforced, which was a practical vindication of the artillery officer.

Secretary of War Alger resigned July 15, and Elihu Root was appointed to succeed him July 22.

Cornelius Vanderbilt, born 1843, died at New York September 12.

Admiral Dewey arrived at New York from the Philippines via the Suez Canal September 26.   A great naval demonstration in the harbor and an immense parade followed.

The American Cup defender, Columbia, defeated Sir Thomas Lipton's

Shamrock I. off New York harbor in the international yacht races October 20.

Vice-President Hobart died at Paterson, N. J., November 21. He was born in 1844.

World interest at the opening of the year 1900 was centered in the heroic struggle of the Boers, who in the rapid campaigns of November and December, 1899, had won several notable victories over the British forces and had Mafeking, Ladysmith and Kimberley beleaguered. The tide of war swept the soldiers of the Transvaal and the Orange Free State irresistibly along. It was in the dark days of England's plight, that orders were issued from London to recall General Buller, and Lord Roberts was selected to take charge of the South African armies.

Roberts arrived at Cape Town, January 10. In a few weeks all was in readiness for the advance and the tide had turned. General French's dash relieved Kimberley February 15, and Cronje was driven back at Modder drift the same day. The intrepid Boer leader with his 4,000 men intrenched himself at Paardeberg on the Modder River, but was forced to capitulate on February 27. This was a severe blow to the republican forces.

The onward march of Roberts continued, Bloemfontein, the capital of the Orange Free State, being entered March 13. On March 28, the siege of Ladysmith was raised. June 5, Pretoria was entered and then began the guerrilla warfare which continued throughout the year. In October Kruger fled from South Africa, landing in France November 22.

Next in importance to the Boer war was the Boxer uprising in China, which horrified the entire civilized world by its atrocities. Beginning in March and April reports began to come from China telling of hordes of fanatics, who were threatening the lives and property of missionaries. The real state of affairs was not realized until in May, when the Boxers grew so strong they overawed the government, and on May 28, they seized Peking, the capital. Then the world stood aghast, but it was too late to save the lives of thousands of Christian Chinese.

Threats from Europe failed to accomplish the all-important object and when, on June 16, Baron von Ketteler, the German minister to China, was murdered, armed forces were rushed to China. After weeks of desultory fighting, in which several hundred of the allied forces were killed, the international relief column entered Peking, August 15. Minister Conger was alive, he along with many other whites having fortified the British legation, where the attacks of the armed rabble and Boxers were repulsed.

The European powers took possession of the Chinese government and each demanded a heavy indemnity for the losses sustained. It was through the intervention of President McKinley and Secretary Hay, that the Chinese were enabled to make satisfactory terms with the other nations which had troops in China. The "open door" policy, by which commercial rights were accorded all nations at the ports of China, was a victory for the United States. At the end of the year the allies were in possession of Peking, while the Emperor and Dowager Empress were in the interior. There was no fighting of any consequence after August.

In the Philippines, the insurgents were gradually falling back before the advance of the American forces. Aguinaldo retreated to the mountains and his followers were in great part dispersed. Here and there would be found a small armed band, but the skirmishes invariably resulted in American victories.

The result of the gubernatorial election in Kentucky, in 1899, was long in doubt and both Democrats and Republicans attempted to seize the State government. Excitement was intense when, on January 30, William Goebel, the Democratic aspirant, was shot and fatally wounded. He died February 3. Governor Taylor, the Republican incumbent, was indicted as an accessory to the crime. For a time serious trouble was feared, but the courts were allowed to settle the claim and civil war was averted.

February 5, the Hay-Pauncefote treaty was signed, amending the Clayton-Bulwer treaty. The chief feature of the old treaty was the agreement that any canal joining the Atlantic and Pacific would be jointly controlled. America is now free to build and control an isthmian canal.

A fire at Ottawa, Canada, swept several square miles of area April 26, rendering 1,500 persons homeless and destroying $15,000,000 worth of property.

May 28, a total eclipse of the sun was visible in most of the Southern States, and several good photographs of the heavenly bodies obtained.

McKinley and Roosevelt were nominated at Philadelphia, June 21.

Three hundred lives were lost and $10,000,000 worth of property destroyed in a fire which started in the North German Lloyd piers at New York and communicated to the ocean liners Saale, Bremen and Main.

July 5, Bryan and Stevenson were nominated at the Kansas City convention.

King Humbert of Italy was assassinated by an anarchist from Paterson, N. J., named Bresci, July 30.

A hurricane swept the gulf states on the night of September 8, reaching the proportions of a tidal wave at Galveston. A large portion of the city was wrecked, 6,000 lives lost, and property worth $12,000,000 destroyed. The havoc created by the waters has no parallel in American annals, with the possible exception of the Johnstown disaster.

John Sherman, of Ohio, Senator, Secretary of Treasury, and Secretary of State, died at Washington, October 21. He was one of the Republican leaders for many years.

November 6, the national election resulted in the re-election of President McKinley by a large majority.

Conditions in South Africa remained practically unchanged during the fall of 1900, and the spring of 1901. The Boers refused to surrender and harassed the British whenever possible. England formally annexed both the Transvaal and the Orange Free State, but the encouragement of the continental powers of Europe induced the Boers to continue the struggle. President Kruger made his home in Holland. Mrs. Kruger died at Pretoria, where she remained when her husband left for Europe.

England's gloom was intensified when, in January, it was announced that the health of the aged Queen Victoria was rapidly failing. She died January 22, and the Prince of Wales was proclaimed King Edward VII. The coronation will take place in 1902.

McKinley and Roosevelt were inaugurated March 4.

Former President Benjamin Harrison died at his Indianapolis home, March 13. After his term as President, he resumed the practice of law and appeared in some of the most important international cases of recent years.

The rebellion in the Philippines, which had lost its effectiveness in 1900, received another blow when, on March 23, General Funston, with a few companions, captured Aguinaldo. The Americans were accompanied by a band of Filipinos. The natives announced that they had taken the Americans prisoners, and were taking them to Aguinaldo. By this ruse his hiding place was discovered. Aguinaldo took the oath of allegiance to the United States and was given a residence in Manila, where he is under surveillance.

In industrial circles, the most momentous event of the year was the incorporation of the billion dollar steel trust, by J. Pierpont Morgan, Andrew Carnegie, and others, April 1. The consolidation of the various interests lead to a strike by the Amalgamated Association of Steel, Iron and Tin Workers, June 30, under the leadership of Theodore Shaffer, of Pittsburg.

The strike was not well organized and many of the men refused to obey the orders to walk out.

President and Mrs. McKinley left Washington on an extended tour, April 29. They travelled through the South, along the Mexican border and through Southern California, reaching San Francisco May 12. Here Mrs. McKinley was taken seriously ill. The tour was announced at an end. After a week of rest Mrs. McKinley was able to return to Washington by easy stages.

May 28, Cuba voted to accept the Platt amendment to the Constitution.

During the first few days of July an oppressively hot wave swept over the country, hundreds dying from the heat. In New York the suffering was pathetic. Following this wave came a period of drouth, which extended over the entire country doing inestimable damage to crops. In some districts rain did not fall for two months, and vegetation all perished. Prices of produce rose rapidly, but copious rains in August and September saved many of the late crops.

Dowager Empress Frederick, mother of Emperor Wilhelm of Germany, died at Berlin in August. She had been living in practical retirement since the death of her husband, Emperor Frederick, in 1888. She was the oldest child of Queen Victoria.

After years of negotiations, the United States and Denmark arranged satisfactory terms, September 2, and the Danish West Indies, three small islands near Porto Rico, will be transferred to this country. The chief object in acquiring these islands was to get possession of the port of St. Thomas, one of the best in the West Indies. The islands are St. Thomas, St. John and St. Croix. The price paid is a little over $4,000,000.

September 2, President and Mrs. McKinley started for the Pan-American Exposition, where the President had arranged to deliver an address on President's Day, September 5. The address was a notable one, as it outlined McKinley's national policy for the coming years. Within 24 hours cf the deliverance of the famous speech, the President was shot down by the assassin.

CHAPTER XXX.

THE FUNERAL SERVICE AT BUFFALO.

The first funeral service over the remains of President McKinley was held at the Milburn house in Buffalo, Sunday, September 15, at 11 o'clock.

At the house only the President's wife, his relatives, his personal friends, and his official family were gathered for their last farewell. It was simply the funeral of William McKinley, the man.

Grief is too weak a word for what Mrs. McKinley suffered. It was not merely the loss of one dear to her. It was the loss of all there was in the world, the one strong arm on which for years she has leaned for support, almost as a child leans upon its mother.

There is a story of unwavering patience and devotion in that part of the late President's life which only has been touched upon, much as has been said about it, and which even those who knew most of its details can hardly grasp, in the all but unparalleled depth of love that it involves.

Even in their own sorrow the thoughts of all who were gathered about the dead President's bier in the room below were going out in pity to her whose desolation was so utter, so far beyond all hope.

The extremity of pathos was reached when, before the ceremony, Mrs. McKinley, the poor, grief-crushed widow, had been led into the chamber by her physician, Dr. Rixey, and had sat awhile alone with him who had supported and comforted her through all their years of wedded life.

Her support was gone, but she had not broken down. Dry-eyed, she gazed upon him. She fondled his face. She did not seem to realize he was dead.

Then she was led away to the head of the stairs, where she could hear the services.

The extremity of impressiveness followed when the new President stood beside the casket steeling himself for a look into the face of the dead.

The tension in the room was great. Every one seemed to be waiting. The minister of the gospel stood with the holy book in his hand ready to begin.

Perhaps it might have been sixty seconds. It seemed longer. Then the President turned and advanced one step. He bowed his head and looked. Long he gazed, standing immovable, save for a twitching of the muscles of the chin. At last he stepped back. Tears were in President Roosevelt's eyes as he went to the chair reserved for him.

Another dramatic scene came when the service was over and the Rev. Mr. Locke had pronounced the benediction. Before any one had moved, and while there was the same perfect stillness, Senator Hanna, who had not before found courage to look upon the dead face of his friend, stepped out from where he had been standing behind Governor Odell. It was his last chance to see the features of President McKinley. There was a look on his face that told more than sobs would have done. It was the look of a man whose grief was pent up within him.

The Senator had quite a few steps to take to get to the head of the casket. When he got to the head of the bier, by President Roosevelt, he stood with his head resting on his breast and his hands clasped behind his back, looking down on the face of his friend. He stood there possibly a minute, but to every one it seemed more like five. No one stirred while he stood. The scene was beyond expression.

As the Senator turned his head around those in the room saw his face, and there were tears trickling down it. One of the Cabinet members put out his arm and the Senator instinctively seemed to follow it. He went between Senator Long and Attorney-General Knox and sat down in a chair near the wall; then he bowed his head.

To most of those present at the services at the Milburn house, the dead President had been friend and comrade, a relationship beside which that of President seemed for the moment to sink into insignificance. It was as his friends that they heard the two hymns sung and the passage from the Bible read.

It was so impressive that the people who were there stood silent, with something tugging at their throats and making sobs impossible. There were no sobs heard, and yet there were those there who had known the dead President all his life. Many eyes were filled with tears, but they were shed softly. While the services proceeded there was no audible sound of grief.

But in the faces of every one, from President and the Cabinet Ministers down to soldier and servant, grief of the deepest kind was written too plainly to be mistaken, and the tears stole silently down the furrows in the faces of gray-haired friends who had known intimately the man whose funeral it was.

The service at the Milburn house began a few minutes after 11 o'clock and it was over in about fifteen minutes.

The entire military and naval force formed in company front near the house and there awaited the time for the services to begin.

Meantime the members of the Cabinet, officials high in the government service, and near friends of the martyred President began to fill the walks leading up to the entrance of the Milburn residence. They came separately and in groups, some walking, while those in carriages were admitted within the roped enclosure up to the curb.

Two and two, a long line of men of dignified bearing marched up to see the house—the foreign commissioners sent to the exposition, and after them the State commissioners. With the foreigners was a colonel of the Mexican army in his full uniform of black with scarlet stripes and peaked gold braided cap. The other members of the Cabinet in the city, Secretary Long, Attorney-General Knox, Postmaster General Smith, the close confidants and friends of the late chief, Senator Hanna, Judge Day, Governors Odell, Yates, and Gregory, Representatives Alexander and Ryan, Major-General Brooke, E. H. Butler, H. H. Kohlsaat, and many others were present.

It was just eight minutes before the opening of the service when a covered barouche drove up to the house, bringing President Roosevelt and Mr. and Mrs. Wilcox, at whose home he is a guest. The President looked grave as he alighted and turned to assist Mrs. Wilcox from the carriage. His face did not relax into a smile to the salutation of those nearest the carriage, but he acknowledged the greetings silently and with an inclination of the head. Word passed up the well filled walk that the President had arrived, and those waiting to gain entrance fell back, making a narrow lane, through which Mr. Roosevelt passed along to the house.

Outside the house there was a half hour of silence and waiting. Within the house of death was woe unspeakable.

In the drawing-room, to the right of the hall, as President Roosevelt entered, the dead chieftain was stretched upon his bier. His head was to the rising sun. On his face was written the story of the Christian forbearance with which he had met his martyrdom. Only the thinness of his face bore mute testimony to the patient suffering he had endured.

The dead President was dressed as he always was in life. The black frock coat was buttoned across the breast where the first bullet of the assassin had struck. The black string tie below the standing collar showed the little triangle of white shirt front. The right hand lay at his side. The left was across his body. He looked as millions of his countrymen have seen him.

The body lay in a black casket on a black bearskin rug. Over the lower limbs was hung the starry banner he had loved so well. The flowers were few, as befitted the simple nature of the man. A spray of white chrysanthemums, a flaming bunch of blood red American Beauty roses, and a magnificent bunch of violets were on the casket. That was all. Behind the head, against a pier mirror, between the two curtained windows, rested two superb wreaths of white asters and roses. These were the only flowers in the room.

Two sentries, one from the sea and one from the land, guarded the remains. They stood in the window embrasures behind the head of the casket. The one on the north was a sergeant of infantry. In the other window was the sailor, garbed in the loose blue blouse of the navy.

The family had taken leave of their loved one before the others arrived. Mrs. Hobart, widow of the Vice-President during Mr. McKinley's first term; Mrs. Lafayette McWilliams of Chicago, Miss Barber, Miss Mary Barber, and Dr. Rixey remained with Mrs. McKinley during the services.

The other members of the family—Mr. and Mrs. Abner McKinley, Miss Helen McKinley, Mrs. Duncan, Miss Duncan, Mr. and Mrs. Barber, and Dr. and Mrs. Baer—had withdrawn into the library to the north of the drawing-room, in which the casket lay, and here also gathered other friends when the service was held.

The friends and public associates of the dead President all had opportunity to view the remains before the service began. The members of the Cabinet had taken their leave before the others arrived. They remained seated beside their dead chief while the sad procession viewed the body. They were on the north side of it. A place directly at the head had been reserved for President Roosevelt. Secretary Root sat alongside this empty chair. Then came Attorney-General Knox, Secretary Long, Secretary Hitchcock, Secretary Wilson, and Postmaster-General Smith, in the order named.

Senator Hanna entered the room at this time, but did not approach the casket. His face was set like an iron-willed man who would not let down the barriers of his grief. The Senator spoke to no one. His eyes were vacant. He passed through the throng and seated himself behind Governor

Odell, sinking far down into his chair and resting his head upon his hand. During all the service that followed he did not stir.

Just before 11 o'clock President Roosevelt entered, coming into the room from the rear through the library. After passing into the hall he had made his way around through the sitting-room behind into the library. There was an instantaneous movement in the room as the President appeared. The procession was still passing from the south side, around the head of the casket and back between it and the members of the Cabinet seated at its side.

Every one rose and all eyes were turned toward the President. He moved forward again with the tide of the procession to his place at the head of the line of Cabinet officers. He held himself erect, his left hand carrying his silk hat. Those who were coming toward him fell back on either side to let him pass. He paused once or twice to shake hands silently, but there was no smile to accompany his greetings. He, too, like the man deep down in his seat against the wall, who had forgotten to rise when the President of the United States entered, seemed to be restraining a great grief.

When President Roosevelt reached the head of the line of Cabinet officers he kept his face away from the casket. The infantryman guarding the dead stood before him rigid as a statue. Although the Commander-in-Chief approached until he could have touched him, the soldier did not salute. The President spoke to Secretary Root, or perhaps it would be more precise to say that the latter spoke to him.

Colonel Bingham, the aid to the President, standing ten feet below the foot of the casket at the side of the loyal Cortelyou, glanced in the direction of the Rev. Charles Edward Locke of the Delaware Avenue Methodist Episcopal Church, who was to conduct the service.

The pastor was at the door leading into the hall, a station whence his words could be heard at the head of the stairs. The signal was given and there welled out from the hall the beautiful words of "Lead, Kindly Light," sung by a quartet. It was one of President McKinley's favorite hymns. Every one within sound of the music knew it and half of those in the room put their faces in their hands to hide their tears. Controller Dawes leaned against a bookcase and wept. President Roosevelt seemed to be swaying to and fro as if his footing were insecure.

When the singing ended the clergyman read from the fifteenth chapter of the First Corinthians. All had risen as he began and remained standing through the remainder of the service. Again the voices rose with the words of "Nearer, My God, to Thee," the words President McKinley had repeated at intervals of consciousness during the day of agony before he died. As the music died away the pastor spoke again.

"Let us pray," he said, and every head fell upon its breast. He began his invocation with a stanza from a hymn sung in the Methodist Church. His prayer was as follows:

"O, God, our help in ages past,
Our hope for years to come,
Our shelter from the stormy blast
And our eternal home.

"We, thy servants, humbly beseech thee for manifestations of thy favor as we come into thy presence. We laud and magnify thy holy name and praise thee for all thy goodness. Be merciful unto us and bless us, as, stricken with overwhelming sorrow, we come to thee. Forgive us for our doubts and fears and faltering faith; pardon all our sins and shortcomings and help us to say, 'Thy will be done.'

"In this dark night of grief abide with us till the dawning. Speak to our troubled souls, O God, and give to us in this hour of unutterable grief the peace and quiet which thy presence only can afford. We thank thee that thou answerest the sobbing sigh of the heart, and dost assure us that if a man die he shall live again. We praise thee for Jesus Christ, thy Son, our Savior and elder brother; that he came 'to bring life and immortality to light,' and because he lives we shall live also. We thank thee that death is victory, that 'to die is gain.'

"Have mercy upon us in this dispensation of thy providence. We believe in thee, we trust thee, our God of love—'the same yesterday, to-day, and forever.' We thank thee for the unsullied life of thy servant, our martyred President, whom thou hast taken to his coronation, and we pray for the final triumph of all the divine principles of pure character and free government for which he stood while he lived and which were baptized by his blood in his death.

"Hear our prayer for blessings of consolation upon all those who were associated with him in the administration of the affairs of the government; especially vouchsafe thy presence to thy servant who has been suddenly called to assume the holy responsibility of our Chief Magistrate.

"O God, bless our dear nation, and guide the ship of State through stormy seas; help thy people to be brave to fight the battles of the Lord and wise to solve all the problems of freedom.

"Graciously hear us for comforting blessings to rest upon the family circle of our departed friend. Tenderly sustain thine handmaiden upon whom the blow of this sorrow most heavily falls. Accompany her, O God, as thou hast promised, through this dark valley and shadow, and may she fear no evil because thou art with her.

"All these things we ask in the name of Jesus Christ, our Lord, who has taught us when we pray to say, 'Our Father, who art in Heaven, hallowed be thy name. Thy kingdom come; thy will be done on earth as it is in Heaven. Give us this day our daily bread, and forgive us our trespasses as we forgive those who trespass against us; and lead us not into temptation, but deliver us from evil, for thine is the kingdom and the power and the glory forever. Amen.'

"May the grace of our Lord, Jesus Christ, the love of God the Father, and communion of the Holy Spirit be with us all evermore. Amen."

All present joined in the Lord's prayer as the minister repeated it, President Roosevelt's voice being audible at the back of the room.

The service concluded with a simple benediction.

GENERALS MILES, SHAFTER AND OTIS ENTERING THE McKINLEY RESIDENCE AT CANTON.

THE LAST RETURN TO HIS OLD HOME. TAKING THE CASKET OUT OF THE CAR WINDOW AT CANTON.

CHAPTER XXXI.

LYING IN STATE IN BUFFALO.

The funeral services of William McKinley, the man, took place in the Milburn house in Buffalo, Sunday morning, September 15. The funeral of William McKinley, the President, commenced the next afternoon in the official residence of the city where he died.

At the city hall in Buffalo everything was as he, who never denied the people's desire to meet him face to face, and who paid with his life for the self-sacrifice, would have had it. From noon into another day, the reverent thousands upon thousands flowed past his bier, taking a last look on the face they so loved for what it meant to them and their country.

The funeral cortege left the house of President Milburn of the exposition at 11:45 o'clock. Slowly and solemnly, in time to the funeral march, it moved between two huge masses of men, women and children, stretching away two miles and a half to the city hall. Nearly two hours were required to traverse the distance.

Fully 50,000 people saw it pass. They were packed into windows, perched on roofs, massed on verandas, and compressed into solid masses covering the broad sidewalks and grass plots. Most of them stood bare-headed as it passed. Young and old, the strong and the age-bent and the lame faced it with hats in hand, unmindful of wind and rain.

All eyes were on the hearse. President Roosevelt, who rode first in the line, might have claimed some attention for the living if he would. Instead he shrank back in his carriage out of sight. The day belonged to him who had gone, and the new President would have it so.

The Sixty-fifth Regiment New York National Guard band led the line. Behind it were the military escort and a full battalion of soldiers made up of national guardsmen, United States infantry, United States artillery and United States marines. Then came the carriage of President Roosevelt and members of the Cabinet, preceding the hearse. Behind came the line of carriages of friends and associates of the dead President.

The waiting cadences of Chopin's funeral march rose and fell. In the tear-starting productions of that music-famed Pole, the overflowing heart of a nation, mourning the foul work of another Pole, found bitterest expression.

339

The liquid tones of bells attuned came up from the southward to mellow Chopin's funeral cry with a note of hope.

While the military band poured out music the chimes in the belfry of old St. Paul's Cathedral reverently rendered "Abide With Me," "Nearer, My God, to Thee," and then "America."

All night decorators had been at work preparing the city hall. Funeral bunting was draped inside and outside. During the storm of the early morning the exterior decorations were torn down, and some of the bunting became entangled in the machinery of the great clock on the tower. It stopped with the hands pointed to a quarter past two. the hour at which the President had breathed his last on the preceding night.

A block away ropes had been stretched across the streets leading to the city hall, and behind these the crowd was massed in thousands. Its mere weight pushed the ropes out of place, and the police were constantly over-powered in trying to hold the crowd in line against the patient multitude which neither threat of rain nor the storm itself could disturb.

The head of the funeral line reached the city hall a few minutes after noon. The military escort marched down past the main entrance, wheeled into line and came to "present arms" at the moment the storm which had been threatening broke. Rain fell in torrents and belated thunder peals mingled detonations through it.

The carriages carrying President Roosevelt and the Cabinet members rolled up and were discharged. Then the hearse came, and four sergeants of the United States army and four quartermasters from the naval detachment lifted the casket on their shoulders and bore it within, while the band played "Nearer, My God, to Thee."

Directly above the spot where the coffin was to lie there was a dome of black bunting, within which hung straight down above the coffin four American flags, forming with their lower edges a cross which pointed to the four points of the compass.

President Roosevelt and the Cabinet ranged themselves about the spot where the body was to rest. Mr. Roosevelt stood at the foot of the coffin on its right hand, with Secretary Root opposite and facing him. On President Roosevelt's left were Attorney-General Knox, Secretary Long and Secretary Wilson. On Mr. Root's right hand were Postmaster-General Smith, Secretary Hitchcock and Mr. Cortelyou, the President's private secretary.

The casket's upper half was open. The lower half was draped in a flag upon which were masses of red and white roses. The body of the President lay on its back and was clad in a black frock coat, with the left hand resting across the breast. One glance at the face, startlingly changed from its appearance in life, told the story of the suffering which had been endured before death came.

Not a word was said. As soon as the coffin had been arranged, President Roosevelt and Mr. Root, followed by the other secretaries, led the way past the coffin on either side, each glancing for a moment at the dead face. They then passed quickly out of the western entrance. Behind them came Senator Hanna, Senator Fairbanks and about one hundred more men and women who had been waiting in the city hall or who had accompanied the body from the Milburn residence.

President Roosevelt and those who immediately followed him had passed out of the building at eighteen minutes after one o'clock, and there was a slight delay while the guard was posted. At the head of the coffin stood Sergeant Galway of the Seventy-fourth Infantry Regiment of the regular army. Chief Master at Arms Luze of the Indiana stood facing him at the foot with his drawn cutlass at his shoulder. On the south, facing the coffin, stood Sergeant Gunther of the Fourteenth Regiment, and Coburn, a sailor from the Indiana, stood facing him on the north.

The lines approached the eastern entrance from Eagle street on the north and Church street on the south. They were formed by the police, two abreast, and approached the hall in a wide sweeping curve of humanity, which was drawn in constantly at the entrance of the building where the currents joined. Between files of police the stream from the north passed by on the north side of the coffin, while the southern stream flowed by on the south. Both passed quickly out at the western entrance and down the steps, dispersing in various directions.

Nothing was heard in the building but the tread of feet on the marble floor as the crowd passed through without stopping at the rate of about one hundred and sixty a minute. Each individual had time only for a hasty glance as he was urged forward by the police and by those who followed. The plan was so arranged that four persons could pass the coffin, two abreast on each side, at the same moment.

As the afternoon wore on and the lines grew longer at their source, much faster than they were melting away at the hall, the police found it necessary to urge greater haste in order that as many as possible might be admitted.

"Move right along; move right along, now; step lively, please; hurry up; move right up, now," they repeated over and over, at the same time urging the crowd forward with their hands. In spite of their efforts, which necessarily marred to some extent the solemnity of the scene, the crowds outside continued to increase.

The great majority of the crowd was made up of what political orators call the "common people." It was noticed that there were many working-men in the lines, and apparently they were not the least sincere of the mourners. A workingman and his wife and children were the first to see the face of the departed President when the lines commenced to move.

Nothing could more clearly show the hold which William McKinley had on the hearts of the great mass of the people. While he lived they gave him their votes. Dead, they did their all to testify the regard in which they held him. Accustomed to rising early six days in the week, they rose early again on this seventh and took possession of the streets. From break-fast time until afternoon they held their places.

The first woman seen to shed a tear was clad in rusty brown. Her garb, neat and well brushed though it was, and the knotted finger with which she clasped a faded shawl, told of life by hard work. She looked once on the dead face and burst into tears.

Men and women struggled along for hours through the press in stolid patience to press kisses upon the cold glass. Little children were led past weeping as if they had lost a father. G. A. R. men marched by, lifting their hands to their hats in a last military salute to "the major" and the President, who was to them also "commander."

Not by any means all who passed were born under the flag they now call theirs. From the East Side came troops of Poles, denouncing the act of Czolgosz, their countryman in blood. Italians came in troops, their women uncovering shawled heads and dropping tears for the man whose language they probably could not speak. And before and behind through-out the constant stream was the American workingman, bearing himself as if he realized the loss of his best friend.

Among the foremost to reach the coffin was a slender man, poorly dressed, with iron-gray hair and mustache. The little G. A. R. copper button was in his coat lapel. Beside the coffin he leaned over and made a menacing gesture with his hand:

"Curse the man that shot you!" he said.

The police urged him forward, and he went out shaking his head and muttering against the anarchists.

Many men and women brought with them young children, whom they raised in their arms to see and perhaps remember in after life the face of the President. A tattered and grimy bootblack, with his box slung over his shoulder, leading by the hand his sister, smaller but no less grimy than he, filed by, walking on tiptoe to see.

The Indians came in the late afternoon, fifty chiefs from the Pan-American Indian congress, with squaws and papooses. Geronimo, Blue Horse, Flat Iron, Little Wound and Red Shirt led them. Each red man, little or high, carried a white carnation in his hand, which he laid reverently upon the coffin of the "Great Father." Two chubby little Indian girls forgot, and went on, each clasping her flower in a little brown hand.

The storm came again after two o'clock, and with renewed fury. The rain fell in torrents, and was driven by the wind in sheets like small cataracts. But the lines and masses of people waiting for a chance to see their President for a last time never wavered. About half carried umbrellas. They served no purpose except to further drench those who had none, until the wind caught them, turned them inside out and whirled them into the gutters. Hats, women's as well as men's, followed.

By this time the waiting crowds had reached the most cosmopolitan stage. Silk-hatted men and women in automobile coats waited in line with mechanics and women from the factories and stores. All were drenched, and all seemed alike indifferent.

They came through the city hall rotunda with water streaming from their garments, until pools and rivers formed on the marble floor. Great baskets of sawdust had to be brought in and spread to absorb it lest people should fall on the slippery floors.

The officials of the exposition and the representatives of foreign governments commissioned to attend the exposition with exhibits from other countries were in the lines. Soldiers of the regular army, in their blue cape coats, went by, and also policemen off duty, holding their helmets in their hands. National guardsmen with khaki gaiters; colored men, among them James Parker, who figured in the capture of Czolgosz; little girls in their Sunday dresses, with their braided hair over their shoulders; young men, husbands and wives, mothers with their sons or daughters, went by in the never-ending stream.

Many flowers were sent to the house and others were sent to the city hall. Among them was a large wreath of purple asters, with a card on which was written:

"Farewell of Chief Geronimo, Blue Horse, Flat Iron and Red Shirt and the 700 braves of the Indian congress. Like Lincoln and Garfield, President McKinley never abused authority except on the side of mercy. The martyred Great White Chief will stand in memory next to the Savior of mankind. We loved him living, we love him still."

On the other side of the card was the following:

"Geronimo's eulogy. The rainbow of hope is out of the sky. Heavy clouds hang about us. Tears wet the ground of the tepees. The chief of the nation is dead. Farewell."

Flowers were received at the hall also from Helen Miller Gould Tent No. 8, Daughters of Veterans; from the commissioners of Chile to the exposition; from Manuel de Aspiroz, the Mexican Ambassador to the United States, and his family; from the Cuban commissioners to the exposition; from the Mexican commissioners, and from General Porfirio Diaz, President of Mexico.

Monotonously the streams of people flowed past the coffin while twilight fell and darkness gathered. The interior of the city hall was illuminated by electricity, and the streets in the vicinity were brightly lighted. Toward sunset the sky cleared, and there was an immediate increase in the already enormous crowds.

The endurance of the people finally gave out at 11 o'clock at night. At that time practically everybody who sought the opportunity had seen the dead President and the doors were closed. The military guard detailed by order of General Brooke was left in charge of the body.

A death mask of the President's face was made by Eduard L. A. Pausch of Hartford, Conn. Pausch has modeled the features of many of the distinguished men who have died in this country in recent years. The mask is a faithful reproduction of the late President McKinley's features.

CHAPTER XXXII.

THE FUNERAL TRAIN TO WASHINGTON.

From the scene of President McKinley's assassination to the Capital of the nation the hearse of the murdered President made its way. Through almost half a thousand miles, past a hundred towns that had been blessed through his services, between two lines of mourners that massed in unnumbered throngs all the way from Buffalo to Washington, the hurrying train proceeded, anguished mourners within the cars, loving and sorrow-stricken friends without.

President McKinley had left Washington, September 6, 1901, in the full tide of life, in the full flush of hope and power. His cold body, with life extinct, started on the return Monday, September 16, housed in the mournful trappings of woe.

From 7 o'clock in the morning to 8 o'clock at night the solemn progress continued. In the flush of the September dawn the nation's dead was hurried out of the city, which, waving a sad farewell with its one hand, clutched tight his murderer with the other. The roar of mad Niagara sank to a growl of thirsty vengeance reserved for the wretch that remained, and the mists rose up from the deeps of the dead, and bent in gentle majesty to the south as the echo of departing wheels wore away.

Never was such a funeral procession. Never before was a death so causeless, a chief so beloved so pitilessly laid low, and never was humanity startled from universal peace with a grief so sad.

It was a curious journey for the five draped cars, with their engine banked in black. The half hundred attendants—the widow with her friends, the new President with his advisers, the guards and escort making up the visible government of the nation, hurrying from the threshold of woe to the vestibule of a new administration.

No other business occupied the road's attention till this caravan of the dead should pass. Ahead of it ran a pilot engine, insuring against any possible accident. Behind it all business waited till it was far away.

Loving hearts devised new forms of testimony to the fallen chief, and gentle hands discharged the duties that the day imposed. Time and again the track was heaped for rods with all manner of flowers before the on-com-

345

ing train. American Beauty roses were piled above the rails. Glowing asters and gleaming violets alternated with wild flowers and the vivid reds and yellows of autumn leaves. And the iron wheels that whirled the funeral party south cut through the banks of bloom and filled the air with perfume as fragrant as the nation's love.

Schools were dismissed, and little groups of boys and girls stood in silent, puzzled wonder as the train rolled past. At every cross-road from dawn to dark were gathered farmers' teams, with men and women, waiting to pay their silent, tearful tribute to the dead. At every town the flags were held at half-mast, and the streets were crowded with the masses of Americans sincere in their sympathy for the living, profoundly sorrowing for the dead.

There were traces of tears in every face. There were evidences of respect in every attitude. The bells of every village tolled while the flag-draped coffin went hurrying past.

Nothing more pathetic marked the whole procession than the homely badges of black and purple ribbon worn by men in the towns and little cities. There had been no time for the emblems of factory fashioning to reach them, and little rosettes composed by women's hands dotted the bosoms of dresses and the lapels of coats.

Business was suspended. All interest in life was held in abeyance, for the nation's dead was going by.

The one relief to this monotone of woe was furnished by lads in Pennsylvania, who took coins from their slender stores of saving, and laid them on the rails, rescuing them, flattened, when the train had passed. And they will preserve these among their treasures to the end of life.

Down the Susquehanna River the banks seemed lined with watchers, who had assembled for a view, the one tribute possible for them to pay. Upon the opposite side of the track a highway ran, and farmers' homes, fronting it, were draped in mourning, and in their windows displayed the portraits of the President so foully slain, with flags and flowers wreathed into borders, and flashing their testimony of sorrow to those who accompanied the dead.

Shortly after leaving Buffalo Mrs. McKinley was persuaded to lie down, and she rested there undisturbed for hours, her friends watching her continually, and attentive to her every want. She was speechless, simply staring straight before her as if the meaning of this awful blow could not be comprehended. Toward noon she rose, and sat at a window, looking off at the fleeting panorama of hills and fields, and reverent friends who vainly yearned to lighten her sorrow. There were no tears until the train paused in the station at Harrisburg. The crowds had been very dense, and she became conscious that thousands peered intently into the coaches as they passed; so she moved away from the window and still sat silent. There was a moment's wait in the station and then the iron arches of the roof rang with the swelling numbers of the song, "Nearer, My God, To Thee!" The Harrisburg Choral Society, 300 strong, had assembled at the farther wall; and the rolling tide of its melody filled the great structure. It came to the silent little woman in the second coach, so sadly, hopelessly alone; and she bowed her head and wept.

As the train pulled out the Choral Society took up the lines: "My Country, 'Tis of Thee;" and as the sorrowing guardians were hurried away ten thousand voices in the crowd outside the depot and along the streets evidently without prearrangement, joined in that, their funeral anthem:

> "Our Father's God, to Thee,
> Author of Liberty,
> To Thee we sing.
> Long may our land be bright
> With Freedom's holy light—
> Protect us with Thy might,
> Great God, our King!"

Through its wavering melody sounded the note of a bugle. A trumpeter was sounding "Taps."

President Roosevelt, his Cabinet and friends occupied the fourth car, and transacted such business as could not be postponed. Between them and Mrs. McKinley's coach was a combination diner and buffet car; and there the new President went for luncheon at noon. The women who attended Mrs. McKinley brought refreshments to her, and urged her to eat; but she could not. The forward car, a "combination," was occupied by the members of the escort party and a number of correspondents, while in the compartment immediately back of the engine such baggage as was necessary for the party's immediate use was stored.

The last car on the train was an observation car, in the center of which the casket was placed. About it was grouped the sentinels from the army and the navy—whose guardian care was no longer needed; and beside it reposed masses of floral offerings. The car was so arranged that a view of the interior could be had by the crowds that were passed.

At Baltimore the train was reversed, the catafalque car being placed in front, while the others occupied their relative positions in the rear.

Darkness came shortly after the train left Baltimore, and the lights of farm houses in the country still revealed the waiting watchers—always standing, always uncovered, always mutely joining in the universal expression of grief.

Night enveloped the Capital City in its mighty pall as the funeral procession ended. The train pulled into the depot at 8:38. The run from Buffalo had been made in an average of thirty-five miles an hour. The President and his friends alighted. Mrs. McKinley was assisted to her carriage. The stalwart soldiers and sailors gently lifted the casket from its place in the car and carried it through a waiting, silent, tearful crowd, to the hearse at the gates, and it was driven slowly along the streets to the White House.

It was a sad home-coming. Just two weeks before President McKinley, full of life and crowned with all the honors that a successful career could earn, happy in the love of his people and the respect of the world, had gone to visit the Buffalo Exposition; to lend some measure of encouragement to that enterprise, and to see the marvels that had been there assembled. In the midst of them he had fallen. And here, at the end of a fortnight, in the darkness of an autumn night, in the silence of an inexpressible sorrow, his hearse was rolling dully along the avenue, and only the prayers and eulogies and lying in state separated all that was mortal of William McKinley from the unending rest of the grave.

CHAPTER XXXIII.

THE LAST NIGHT IN THE WHITE HOUSE.

Borne upon the shoulders of stalwart representatives of the army and navy, of which he had been Commander-in-Chief for more than four years, all that was mortal of William McKinley, late President of the United States, was returned to the capital of the nation.

As President McKinley left the White House the morning of July 5 for a vacation trip to his home at Canton, O., some of the attachés of the Executive Mansion assembled on the portico to bid him a fond farewell and express their hope for a pleasant trip.

"Take good care of yourselves, boys, until I come back in the fall," was the President's response as he entered his waiting carriage and was driven to the railroad station to take the train for home. These were the last words ever uttered by William McKinley in the shadow of the big white mansion which had been his official residence since March 4, 1897.

He came back in the fall, as he had promised he would, not in the flush of manhood, buoyant in spirits and recuperated from the arduous duties of his official position, but in a narrow, black-cloth-covered casket, around which were draped the colors he had fought to defend when in his teens, and which in maturer years he had seen floating victoriously in every quarter of the globe.

Following his bier as chief mourner came his successor to the Presidency, Theodore Roosevelt, accompanied by the members of his official family and thousands of his countrymen, who mourned in silence his untimely end.

Never before in the history of the capital of this nation has such a scene been witnessed as that presented along the magnificent boulevard known as Pennsylvania avenue. Although it was well-nigh impossible to distinguish anything perfectly in the gloom of the night, mothers brought their children in arms, and stood patiently watching until the cavalcade passed up the avenue and was finally hidden from view in the grounds surrounding the Executive Mansion.

It was a distinguished party which awaited at the Pennsylvania railroad station the home-coming of William McKinley.

Among the first arrivals at the railroad station were Secretary of State

Hay and Secretary Gage of the Treasury department. Both wore upon their high silk hats mourning bands for members of their own families— the Secretary of State for a son and the Secretary of the Treasury for a wife who was one of the most notable figures of the administration now closed.

While waiting the arrival of the funeral train a passenger train pulled into the station from the west, and among those who alighted and pushed his way through the crowd was Senator William E. Mason of Illinois, accompanied by his wife and little ones. As the Senator from Illinois passed through the crowd he was recognized, and amid the hum and buzz of conversation could be distinguished the words: "There goes Senator Mason."

Meanwhile the crowd on the station platform was each second becoming augmented by the arrival of men distinguished in army and navy circles and the walks of civil life. Judson Lyons, Register of the United States Treasury, whose name adorns every bank note of the government, was conspicuous in the throng, not only on account of his towering height and figure but for his color as well, for the successor of General Rosecrans, formerly Register of the Treasury, is a negro.

Nodding plumes of yellow, red, and white, marking the different branches of the army, cavalry, artillery, and infantry, respectively, were conspicuous in the throng, while the gold laced and chapeaued naval officers present reminded the spectator of an army and navy reception night at the White House.

To add to this effect, there was Captain Charles McCauley of the Marine Corps and Captain J. C. Gilmore of the artillery, both of whom had been detailed at the Executive Mansion by President McKinley to assist him in receiving the public at the various receptions held during the gay season when in charge of the State, War, and Navy department here; Sergeant-at-Arms Ransdell of the United States Senate, the bosom friend and companion of the late President Harrison, who appointed him Marshal of the District of Columbia; Acting Secretary of War William Gary Sanger; Colonel Frank Denny, U. S. Marine Corps; Lieutenant Thomas Wood, President McFarland, and Commissioner John W. Ross of the District of Columbia; Chief Wilkie of the U. S. Secret Service; General George H. Harries and the members of the staff of the National Guard of the District of Columbia in full uniform.

Standing at attention in full dress uniform, with swords at their side, stood a dozen sergeants of the Signal Corps of the United States Army, under the command of Captain Charles McKay Saltzman. It was to be their solemn duty to act as body bearers for the President of the United States, relieving the sailors and soldiers who had performed this duty from Buffalo to the Capitol. These body bearers were George H. Kelly, Isaac Hamilton, Frank Gunnard, Harry T. Burlingame, Stephen Bledsoe, Eugene Lazar, Joseph H. Embleton, Harry S. Gribbelle, Charles G. Monroe, William H. Taylor, Thomas A. Davis, and James S. Holmes.

Not a loud word was uttered, and the scene about the station was of a most awe-inspiring and impressive nature as an engine draped with black came slowly puffing into the shed, and instantly all heads were bared. It was the engine drawing the funeral party, and a hush of expectancy pervaded the entire group gathered upon the platform to await its coming. Hardly had the driving wheels ceased to revolve before the body bearers were boarding the front car, which contained the casket and floral tributes, which almost concealed from view the earthly remains of William McKinley. Secretaries Hay and Gage led a mournful procession to the rear car of the train, in which President Roosevelt and the members of the Cabinet were seated.

In deference to the wishes of Mrs. McKinley, the family, and immediate relatives of the President, a passageway was opened for them at the lower end of the platform in order that they might evade the gaze of a curious crowd. Carriages were drawn up awaiting the arrival of the train, and, assisted by Colonel Bingham and Dr. Rixey, Mrs. McKinley was led to a victoria and driven to the White House. She seemed to be bearing up remarkably well under the strain to which she has been subjected, although the lines under her eyes and the haggard expression of the features showed it was only by the greatest exertion of will power that she was being restrained from a collapse.

Abner McKinley and his family occupied the next two carriages, and Mrs. Baer, formerly Miss Mabel McKinley, and her husband, were assigned a carriage to themselves. Mrs. Baer was attired in deep mourning, and it was with difficulty, even with the aid of her crutches, that she could sustain herself sufficiently to traverse the short distance from the train to her carriage.

While this scene was in the focus the members of the Cabinet and guard of honor, composed of army and navy officers, were escorting President Roosevelt from his car to his position in the carriage just behind the hearse which was to convey the body of his predecessor to the executive mansion. Close beside the President walked big George Foster, the secret service agent, who had accompanied President McKinley on nearly all of his trips.

General John R. Brooke walked beside the President on the left, and immediately behind came Secretaries Gage and Hay, walking arm in arm. Five special detectives kept guard over this quartet—Sergeants Clark and Foy of New York, Detective Carroll of Newark, N. J., and Detectives Helan and McNamee of Washington.

These detectives had instructions not to let the President out of their sight until he was safely ensconced in his house, the residence of his brother-in-law, Paymaster W. S. Cowles of the United States Navy, in the fashionable part of Washington. As soon as the President entered his carriage with General Brooke the detectives closed around it and permitted no one to come within twenty feet of its occupant.

Prior to the President entering his carriage there was a delay for a few minutes at the entrance to the baggage-room to permit the remains of President McKinley to be borne through the crowd and placed in the hearse awaiting them. This sable equipage was drawn by six black horses, each animal covered with a heavy black netting, and each horse led by a negro groom in regulation funeral dress.

There was a shuffling of feet as the crowd of distinguished men in attendance upon the President followed his footsteps, which led towards waiting carriages and, surrounded by clattering cavalry and fully equipped infantry, President Roosevelt and the escort left the railroad station and started up Pennsylvania avenue through the lanes of people, who occupied every available inch of room from the curbstone to the building line of the houses against which they pressed.

It was a weird but solemn spectacle that greeted the vision of President Roosevelt and his escort as they rode through the silent streets of the capital to make preparation for the funeral services to be held in the Capitol Building next day. Men, women, and children peered into the darkness in a vain endeavor to ascertain who were the occupants of the carriages, but in this they were disappointed, for darkness threw a veil over the scene from one end of the route to the other.

All that could be seen was the gleam of sabers as the cavalry clattered up the avenue and the gleam of a musket barrel and the glitter of gold lace when an electric light or a gas jet threw some gleams of radiance upon them.

Not a word was uttered during that solemn drive, and Theodore Roosevelt, twenty-sixth President of the United States, was not even visible as he came to take the position which had been filled so ably and efficiently by William McKinley.

It was a different inauguration procession from that in which President Roosevelt participated last March, for while on that occasion there was glad acclaim and exulting shouts of gratified patriots, on this occasion there was silence, somberness, and gloom, painful in its intensity.

And thus Theodore Roosevelt entered the Capitol of the nation to become the first citizen of the greatest republic on earth.

In the east room at the White House, where President McKinley so often was the central figure of noble gatherings, his mortal remains were placed. It was his last night in the place he had made his home for four and one-half years.

Up-stairs the widow occupied the room where she underwent so much suffering and where she was nursed back to health by the devoted husband who now is lost to her for all time.

Except for the immediate family, the guards, and the servants, the executive mansion was deserted, the public retiring and leaving those nearest and dearest to the dead President alone with their grief.

Throughout the day workmen had been busy placing the great east room in condition for the reception of the body of the dead President. That immense room, in which President McKinley had participated in so many public functions, and had taken the hands of thousands of his countrymen, was transformed into a tomb for the time being, and all evidences of past festivities were removed.

It was in this same room that the remains of Lincoln, Garfield, Secretary of State Gresham, and other distinguished public servants rested before final interment. It was also in this magnificent apartment that Nellie Grant was married to Algernon Sartoris of England while her father was President.

As the shades of evening began to fall the guards around the White House were doubled. The gates were closed and policemen were stationed at the various entrances, with positive instructions to allow no one to pass except those on actual duty in an official capacity.

In the meantime the interior of the east room had been robbed of its barren appearance by the placing of a number of potted plants and palms around the room and in the recesses of the windows. In addition to the floral decorations from the Executive greenhouses the tributes from foreign and domestic officials converted the room into a beautiful and fragrant floral bower.

The display of floral tributes deposited in the east room was perhaps never equaled in the history of a public or private funeral in the United States. The predominating emblems were laurel wreaths, but they were so diversified in construction and ornamentation with colored flowers and ribbons that no two pieces were actually alike.

One of the most striking set pieces was an immense shield, appropriately inscribed, and profusely decorated with purple ribbon, from "The American Army in the Philippines." This floral tribute was made up on an order by cable at a cost of over $500. Another striking piece was an immense floral pedestal, surmounted by a floral wreath, standing twelve feet high. This came from the Commissioner of Pensions and his associates in the Pension bureau. There were magnificent wreaths from Mrs. Garret A. Hobart, the wife of the late Vice-President, also one from the government of Costa Rica, one from the President of Costa Rica, Rafael Iglesais.

An immense laurel wreath, decorated with yellow, blue, and red ribbons, came from the Colombian Legation. There was also an immense wreath of orchids inscribed from the Municipality of Havana, Cuba.

And there, sleeping the dreamless sleep of death, beneath a wilderness of blossoms from the loving hands of his countrymen, William McKinley passed his last night in the White House.

CROWDS VIEWING THE REMAINS AT THE
COURT HOUSE, CANTON.

TAKING THE CASKET INTO THE CHURCH AT CANTON.

CHAPTER XXX.V.

FUNERAL SERVICES AND PROCESSION AT WASHINGTON.

At 9 o'clock Tuesday morning, September 17, 1901, the funeral cortege of William McKinley, twenty-fifth President of the United States, third incumbent of the office to fall by an assassin's hand, started from the White House toward the capitol. President Roosevelt, accompanied by his wife and sister, arrived half an hour earlier at the Executive Mansion, and were given seats in the big Red Room. Almost immediately after came former President Cleveland, with Daniel Lamont. Others, notable in the official and social life of the nation, quickly assembled, and the rooms and corridors were filled with a silent, sorrowful throng. Just before 9 o'clock Senator Hanna came into the room. He is visibly aged by the events of the past fortnight. His face seems drawn and pallid, his form is less erect, and all that vigorous, quickly deciding manner seems gone.

Precisely at the hour appointed the big men from the ranks of the Army and the Navy lifted the black casket of him who had been named "Our Well Beloved," and carried for the last time through the doors and down to the waiting hearse. There was on the part of the thousands, both those of the party and the throngs outside, an instant recognition of the contrast between this departure from the White House, and William McKinley's other passings through its doors.

A long line of carriages waited in the streets, and scores of others were massed in the ample grounds at the east front of the mansion. The muffled drums beat the long roll, the military band played "Nearer, My God, to Thee;" and then, as the solemn march began, the mournful strains of the "Dead March from Saul" were borne by the morning breezes over the assembled thousands.

President Roosevelt, with his wife and sister, occupied the first carriage behind the hearse, a band of black crepe bound about his arm. The carriage was drawn by four black horses. Next in order came the carriage of Grover Cleveland, who was accompanied by General John M. Wilson and Robley D. Evans. Following directly came the Justices of the Supreme Court, in their robes of office. Army and navy men, in full uniform, continued the slow moving procession. Representatives of foreign governments in all their trappings of state, followed in order. One carriage was occupied by

Hon. Gerald Lowther, of the British Legation, assigned by a cabled order to personally represent King Edward VII. of England.

Major-General John R. Brooks commanded the entire line, riding a splendid black charger. He was surrounded with his aides, all well mounted.

A cold rain began to fall as the procession started from the White House. It at no time amounted to a heavy shower, but the chilling "drizzle" which marked Mr. McKinley's second inauguration was precisely repeated in this his last progress to the capitol. The flags were limp. The banners were drooping. The wealth of mourning decoration on buildings laid flat against the walls. As the cortege wound down into Pennsylvania avenue it passed between gathered thousands of people who banked the great highway from end to end, and stood in reverent silence while the dead went by.

In that procession were soldiers and sailors from every, service, civic societies, a camp of United Confederate Veterans from Alexandria, Virginia, and a host of miscellaneous organizations. The home of the nation's government awaited the cortege in silent simplicity. A flag, flying at half mast over the marble entrance, was the only sign of mourning. The law decrees that the government buildings in Washington shall not be draped, and they wore no visible sign of the nation's bereavement.

Time and again as the line moved from west to east the notes of that plaintive song, "Nearer, My God, to Thee," rose on the air. At the steps of the capitol a bugle sounded the silver notes of "Church Call." The soldiers and sailors lifted the casket again from the hearse, and carried it with solemn strides up the long flight of marble steps to the open portal, and deposited it on the catafalque directly in the center of the rotunda, beneath the mighty dome which crowns the capitol. The friends and late advisers of the nation's chief, the notable men of the country filed in and grouped themselves to the north of the center. Mrs. McKinley was not present. In her weakened condition it was thought wise to afford her all possible repose, as the trip to Canton will tax all her little store of strength.

A hush as of death fell upon the assembly, and then, beginning softly, but swelling grandly as the hymn progressed, a choir sang Cardinal Newman's touching hymn: "Lead, Kindly Light."

> Lead, kindly light, amid the encircling gloom,
>   Lead thou me on!
> The night is dark, and I am far from home,
>   Lead thou me on!

Keep thou my feet; I do not ask to see
The distant scene—one step's enough for me.
I was not ever thus, nor prayed that thou
    Shouldst lead me on;
I loved to choose and see my path, but now
    Lead thou me on!
I loved the garish day, and, spite of fears,
Pride ruled my will; remember not past years.
So long thy power hath blessed me, sure it still
    Will lead me on;
O'er moor and fen, o'er crag and torrent, till
    The night is gone;
And with the morn those angel faces smile
Which I have loved long since, and lost awhile.

Rev. Dr. Naylor, presiding elder of the Washington District of the Methodist Episcopal church, stood close by the head of the casket, and with folded hands, glanced once around that assembled multitude, then bowed his head. Instantly there was a subdued rustling, a sigh of acquiescence, and every head was bent in reverence. His first words were scarcely heard. Outside the storm had risen, and the rain was driving with an angry roar against the great dome above them. Outside, also, a mighty throng of men and women were massed, insistent on admission, crowding for places sheltered from the rain. Dr. Naylor's prayer seemed echoed in the hearts of those bent in sorrow about the coffin. And this was his prayer:

"O Lord God, our heavenly Father, a bereaved nation cometh to Thee in its deep sorrow! To whom can we go in such an hour as this but to Thee? Thou only art able to comfort and support the afflicted. Death strikes down the tallest and best of men and consequent changes are continually occurring among nations and communities. But we have been taught that Thou art the same yesterday, to-day and forever; that in Thee there is no variableness nor the least shadow of turning. So in the midst of our grief we turn to Thee for help.

"We thank Thee, O Lord, that years ago Thou didst give to this nation a man whose loss we mourn to-day. We thank Thee for the pure and unselfish life he was enabled to live in the midst of so eventful an experience. We thank Thee for the faithful and distinguished services which he was enabled to render to Thee, to our country and to the world. We bless

Thee for such a citizen, for such a lawmaker, for such a governor, for such a President, for such a husband, for such a Christian example and for a friend.

"But, O Lord, we deplore our loss to-day; sincerely implore Thy sanctifying benediction. We pray Thee for that dear one who has been walking by his side through the years, sharing his triumphs and partaking of his sorrows. Give to her all needed sustenance, and the comfort her stricken heart so greatly craves. And under the shadow of this great calamity may she learn as never before the fatherhood of God and the matchless character of his sustaining grace.

"And, O Lord, we sincerely pray for him upon whom the mantle of presidential authority has so suddenly and unexpectedly fallen. Help him to walk worthy the high vocation whereunto he has been called. He needs Thy guiding hand and Thine inspiring spirit continually. May he always present to the nation and to the world divinely illumined judgment a brave heart and an unsullied character.

"Hear our prayer, O Lord, for the official family of the administration, those men who are associated with Thy servant, the President, in the administration of the affairs of government; guide them in all their deliberations to the nation's welfare and the glory of God.

"And now, Lord, we humbly pray for Thy blessing and consolation to come to all the people of our land and nation. Forgive our past shortcomings; our sins of omission as well as our sins of commission. Help us to make the golden rule the standard of our lives, and that we may 'do unto others as we would have them do unto us,' and thus become indeed a people whose God is the Lord.

"These things we humbly ask in the name of Him who taught us when we pray to say: "Our Father which art in Heaven, hallowed be Thy name; Thy kingdom come; Thy will be done on earth as it is in heaven. Give us this day our daily bread, and forgive us our trespasses as we forgive them that trespass against us. And lead us not into temptation, but deliver us from evil, for Thine is the kingdom and the power and glory, forever. Amen.' "

As the bowed heads lifted a sweet voice rose in song. It was Mrs. Thomas C. Noyes, one who had honored the President—as all women honored him—one who had known him well. The words, the air, the pathos of the scene, combined in a wonderful impressiveness.

Not now, but in the coming years
    It may be in the better land,
We'll read the meaning of our tears,
    And there, some time, we'll understand.

CHORUS.

Then trust in God through all thy days;
    Fear not, for He doth hold thy hand;
Though dark the way, still sing and praise;
    Some time, some time, we'll understand.

We'll catch the broken thread again,
    And finish what we here began;
Heav'n will mysteries explain,
    And then, ah, then, we'll understand.

We'll know why clouds instead of sun
    Were over many a cherished plan;
Why song has ceased when scarce begun;
    'Tis there, some time, we'll understand.

Why what we longed for most of all,
    Eludes, so oft, our eager hand;
Why hopes are crushed and castles fall,
    Up there, some time, we'll understand.

God knows the way, He holds the key,
    He guides us with unerring hand.
Some time with tearless eyes we'll see;
    Yes, there, up there, we'll understand.

The venerable Bishop Andrews, the church of which William McKinley had been an almost lifelong member, rose and read the scriptural assurances of life beyond the grave—the blessed assurances that bring such comfort in the hour of grief. Then began the sermon—the funeral oration over the body of his President and his friend.

"Blessed be the God and Father of Our Lord, who of his abundant mercy hath begotten us again unto a lively hope of the resurrection of Christ from the dead, to an inheritance incorruptible, undefiled, and that fadeth not away, reserved in heaven for us who are now, by the power of God through faith unto salvation, ready to be revealed in the last time.

"The services for the dead are fitly and almost of necessity services of religion and of immortal hope. In the presence of the shroud and the coffin and the narrow home, questions concerning intellectual quality, concerning public station, concerning great achievements, sink into comparative insignificance; and questions concerning character and man's relation to the Lord and giver of life, even the life eternal, emerge to our view and impress themselves upon us.

"Character abides. We bring nothing into this world; we can carry nothing out. We ourselves depart with all the accumulations of tendency and habit and quality which the years have given to us. We ask, therefore, even at the grave of the illustrious, not altogether what great achievement they had performed and how they had commended themselves to the memory and affection or respect of the world, but chiefly of what sort they were; what the interior nature of the man was; what were his affinities? Were they with the good, the true, the noble? What his relation to the infinite Lord of the universe and to the compassionate Savior of mankind; what his fitness for that great hereafter to which he had passed?

"And such great questions come to us with moment, even in the hour when we gather around the bier of those whom we profoundly respect and eulogize and whom we tenderly love. In the years to come the days and the months that lie immediately before us will give full utterance as to the high statesmanship and great achievements of the illustrious man whom we mourn to-day. We shall not touch them to-day. The nation already has broken out in its grief and poured its tears, and is still pouring them, over the loss of a loved man. It is well. But we ask this morning of what sort this man is, so that we may perhaps, knowing the moral and spiritual life that is past, be able to shape the far-withdrawing future.

"I think we must all concede that nature and training are—reverently be it said—the inspiration of the Almighty, conspired to conform a man, a man admirable in his moral temper and aims. We none of us can doubt. I think that even by nature he was eminently gifted. The kindly, calm, and equitable temperament, the kindly and generous heart, the love of justice and right, and the tendency toward faith and loyalty to unseen powers and authorities—these things must have been with him from his childhood, from his infancy; but upon them supervened the training for which he was always tenderly thankful and of which even this great nation from sea to sea continually has taken note.

"It was a humble home in which he was born. Narrow conditions were around him, but faith in God had lifted that lowly roof, according to the statement of some great writer, 'up to the very heavens and permitted its inmates to behold the things eternal, immortal, and divine;' and he came under that training.

"It is a beautiful thing that to the end of his life he bent reverently before that mother whose example and teaching and prayer had so fashioned his mind and all his aims. The school came but briefly, and then came to him the church with its ministration of power. He accepted the truth which it taught. He believed in God and in Jesus Christ, through whom God was revealed. He accepted the divine law of the scripture; he based his hope on Jesus Christ, the appointed and only Redeemer of men; and the church, beginning its operation upon his character at an early period of his life, continued even to its close to mold him. He waited attentively upon its administration. He gladly partook with his brethren of the symbols of mysterious passion and redeeming love of the Lord Jesus Christ. He was helpful in all of those beneficences and activities; and from the church, to the close of his life, he received inspiration that lifted him above much of the trouble and weakness incident to our human nature; and, blessings be to God, may we say, in the last final hour they enabled him confidently, tenderly, to say: 'It is his will, not ours, that will be done.'

"Such influences gave to us William McKinley. And what was he? A man of incorruptible personal and political integrity. I suppose no one ever attempted to approach him in the way of a bribe; and we remember with great felicitation at this time for such an example to ourselves that when great financial difficulties and perils encompassed him he determined to deliver all he possessed to his creditors, that there should be no challenge of his perfect honesty in the matter. A man of immaculate purity, shall we say? No stain was upon his escutcheon, no syllable of suspicion was ever heard whispered against his character. He walked in perfect and noble self-control.

"Beyond that this man had somehow wrought in him—I suppose upon the foundation of a very happily constructed nature—a great and generous love of his fellowmen. He believed in men. He had himself been brought up among the common people. He knew their labors, struggles, necessities. He loved them; but I think that beyond that it was to the church and its teachings concerning the fatherhood of God and universal brotherhood of man that he was indebted for that habit of kindness, for that generosity of spirit, that was wrought into his very substance and became him so, though he was of all men most courteous, no one ever supposed but his courtesy was from the heart. It was spontaneous, unaffected, kindly in a most eminent degree.

"What he was in the narrow field of those to whom he was personally attached, I think he was also in the greatness of his comprehensive love toward the race of which he was part.

"Shall I speak a word next of that which I will hardly advert to? The tenderness of that domestic love which has so often been commented upon? I pass it with only that word. I take it that no words can set forth fully the unfaltering kindness and carefulness and upbearing love which belonged to this great man.

"And he was a man who believed in right, who had a profound conviction that the courses of this world must be ordered in accordance with everlasting righteousness, or this world's highest point of good will never be reached; that no nation can expect success in life except as it conforms to the eternal love of the infinite Lord and pass itself in individual and collective activity according to that divine will.

"It was deeply ingrained in him that righteousness was the perfection of any man and any people. Simplicity belonged to him. I need not dwell upon it, and I close the statement of these qualities by saying that underlying all and overreaching all and penetrating all there was a profound loyalty to guard the great king of the universe, the author of all good, the eternal hope of all that trust in him.

"And now, may I say further that it seemed to me that to whatever we may attribute all the illustriousness of this man, all the greatness of his achievements—whatever of that we may attribute to his intellectual character and quality, whatever of it we may attribute to the patient and thorough study which he gave to the various questions thrust upon him for attention, for all his success as a politician, as a statesman, as a man of this great country, those successes were largely due to the moral qualities of which I have spoken. They drew to him the hearts of men everywhere and particularly of those who best knew him. They called to his side helpers in every exigency of his career, so that when his future was at one time likely to have been imperilled and utterly ruined by his financial conditions, they who had resources, for the sake of helping a man who had in him such qualities, came to his side and put him on the high road of additional and larger success.

"His high qualities drew to him the good will of his associates in political life in an eminent degree. They believed in him, felt his kindness, confided in his honesty and in his honor. His qualities even associated with him in kindly relations those who were his political opponents. They made it possible for him to enter that land with which he, as one of the soldiers of the union, had been in some sort at war and to draw closer the tie that was to bind all the parts in one firmer and indissoluble union. They commanded the confidence of the great body of Congress, so that they listened to his plans and accepted kindly, and hopefully, and trustfully, all his declarations.

"His qualities gave him reputation, not in this land alone, but throughout the world, and made it possible for him to minister in the style in which he has within the last two or three years ministered to the welfare and peace of humankind. It was out of the profound depths of his moral and religious character that came the possibilities of that usefulness which we are all glad to attribute to him.

"And will such a man die? Is it possible that he who created, redeemed, transformed, uplifted, illumined such a man will permit him to fall into oblivion? The instincts of morality are in all good men. The divine word of the Scripture leaves us no room for doubt. 'I,' said one whom we trusted, 'am the resurrection and the life. He that believeth in me, though he were dead, yet shall he live, and whosoever liveth and believeth in me, shall never die.'

"Lost to us, but not to his God. Lost from earth, but entered heaven. Lost from these labors, and toils, and perils, but entered into the everlasting peace and ever-advancing progress. Blessed be God, who gives us this hope in the hour of our calamity and enables us to triumph through him who hath redeemed us.

"If there is a personal immortality before him let us also rejoice that there is an immortality and memory in the hearts of a large and ever-growing people, who, through the ages to come, the generations that are yet to be, will look back upon this life, upon its nobility, and purity, and service to humanity and thank God for it.

"The years draw on when his name shall be counted among the illustrious of the earth. William of Orange is not dead. Cromwell is not dead. Washington lives in the hearts and lives of his countrymen. Lincoln, with his infinite sorrow, lives to teach us and lead us on. And McKinley shall summon all statesmen, and all his countrymen, to pure living, nobler aims, sweeter and immortal blessedness."

Again the words and music of that favorite song, "Nearer, my God, to Thee," echoed through the great rotunda, and then the sad audience dispersed. The funeral of another President was ended.

In the midst of the singing Admiral Robley Evans, advancing with silent tread, placed a beautiful blue floral cross at the foot of the casket.

The last notes died away softly, and with uplifted hands the benediction was pronounced by the Rev. Dr. W. H. Chapman, acting pastor of the Metropolitan Church. This ended the religious service.

There was a pause for a few minutes while the ushers cleared the aisles, and the assemblage began to withdraw. First to retire was President Roosevelt, and as he entered so he left, preceded a short distance by Major McCawley and Captain Gilmore, with Colonel Bingham and Captain Cowles almost pressing against him.

The remainder of the company retired in the order in which they entered, the Cabinet members following the President, and after them going the diplomatic corps, the Supreme Court, Senators and Representatives, officers of the army and navy, and officials of less degree.

As soon as the rotunda was cleared of those who had been invited to attend the religious services the bier was prepared for passage out through the west exit.

The people came in double file, one line passing to the right and the other to the left of the casket. Only a hurried glance was permitted to any one, as it was announced that the ceremony would close promptly at 6:30 o'clock. Whenever there was an attempt to linger, especially over the casket, as there was in many instances, the person making it was admonished by the Capitol police to "pass on." When they still remained they were pushed along. In this way about one hundred and thirty people were enabled to view the remains every minute.

CHAPTER XXXV.

LYING IN STATE AT THE CAPITOL.

As soon as the funeral service in the Capitol had concluded, and the audience had dispersed, the guards took their places about the casket, and the big bronze doors of the Capitol were thrown open, and the crowds were admitted. They came in two long lines from both the east and west portals and passed down, one on either side of the catafalque. It was the intention to have those who entered at the east door pass out at the west, and those who came in from the west—from the Pennsylvania avenue side—to leave at the opposite entrance. But the local police arrangements had been very imperfectly provided, and confusion resulted. Had the day been fair probably no untoward circumstances would have marred the solemnity of the occasion. But the storm without added to the discomfort of the crush; and the first two hours of the lying in state made up a scene to be regretted. The crowding at times almost approached the frenzy of a panic. Men were hustled, despite all their struggles. Women and children were thrown down and trampled on. There was no noise, such as usually accompanies a panic in theatres, or on the occasion of a fire, but there was a half-savage exercise of brute force, a dumb insistence on position. And against that frightful pressure human strength was helpless. Men were pressed as with the impetus of engines against stone walls and columns. Women were ground against the sharp angles of granite, or hurled without warning upon the wounding edges of marble.

The force of police provided was wholly inadequate, and for two sad hours the lines that viewed the dead missed the characterization of a mob only because of their evident sympathy.

Men with clothes torn, women with bleeding faces appeared continually in the lines; and back to the south in the rotunda, toward the senate wing, was gathered a constantly increasing company of those who had been injured.

As soon as the faulty condition was discovered those in charge of the funeral ceremonies had called on the police department for a better control; and the reserves were ordered out. Even then it seemed a hopeless time before they could get in position, and restore order in the boundless crowds.

It was the one feature up to that time which had marred the solemn stateliness of the funeral.

As it was, the crowds were simply flung through the bronze doors, and projected to the very side of the casket, where they appeared half hysterical, and wholly lost to the impressive nature of the hour.

Coincident with the restoration of order by the reinforced police, came the ambulances from the Emergency Hospital; and scores were taken away for treatment, while other scores were treated without removal from the rotunda.

After the reserves had taken their places, and had controlled the crowds, a steady, orderly procession came through the doors from 12 o'clock noon until 6 in the evening. In that time more than 30,000 persons passed the casket of their dead chief, and looked for the last time on his pain-marked face.

The appearance of the casket which contained the body of the martyred President was particularly impressive. It was wrapped entirely in a beautiful American flag. Over the top of the casket were laid three groups of flowers, that at the end being a conspicuous sheaf which had been prepared at the express request and under the personal direction of the new President of the United States.

Many beautiful floral designs were grouped around the casket. Conspicuous among them was a massive cushion floral tribute in the form of an army badge from the G. A. R. and offerings from the Loyal Legion and other soldier organizations. General Corbin, now en route home from Manila; General Adna R. Chaffee, and the Commissioners of Porto Rico had floral offerings laid about the bier.

A design of over six feet in diameter composed of galax leaves and American beauty roses, about which was entwined the American flag, came from the Mayor and Council of Richmond, Va. Other tributes came from Mrs. James A. Garfield, widow of another martyred President; Mrs. Garret A. Hobart, Secretaries Hay and Hitchcock, General and Mrs. Miles, Ambassador Porter at Paris, the Argentine, Guatemalan, Costa Rican, and other legations, and the municipality of Havana.

The casket rested exactly beneath the center of the great dome of the Capitol, and surrounding it on all sides were the large historical paintings representing the greatest events of the life of the republic. Above, on the extreme top of the dome, was the beautiful historical painting of the apotheosis of George Washington, while on the floor itself, within easy range of the eye from the center, were statues of Lincoln and Grant, the two great governmental personages of the present generation.

The casket was guarded by details of artillerymen, marines, and sailors, but it was hemmed in by such a distinguished circle of public men as to set it in a proper frame.

The big, black casket was the period at the end of an era. The marble effigies of the great men about it, the canvases on which the features of statesmen and soldiers lived in oil, were but the mute testimonies to a condition which had passed. The pale form, lying in state between moving lines of those who had loved him, was all that earth had left of the man who gathered together the possibilities of the past—who could express the spirit, the effectiveness and the hope of the future.

There was the statue of George Washington, twice a President, once maligned, now half deified. There was John Marshall, once Chief Justice of the United States; once a patriot soldier at Valley Forge; once presiding at the trial of Aaron Burr—whose hand had been raised in a bolder assault; but always the champion of law, the lover of order, the son of republican independence. There hung the portrait of Captain Lawrence—and his dying words carried new courage to the hearts of the mourners: "Don't Give Up the Ship!"

There was Madison, whose seat of government had been driven from the capital when the British assailed the nation in the war of 1812; the man who had watched from the hills to the north the smoke that rose from the burning buildings of the nation.

All the history of the past was bound up in the pictured forms and the marble allegories of that rotunda. And over it all lifted the painted interior of the dome, the apotheosis of that first President, who had been first in war, and first in peace, but who now made room for another beside him in the hearts of his countrymen.

All they had promised, all the nation of the past had hoped for and striven for had been expressed in the administration, had been made possible by the wise statesmanship of this hero who lay still and silent in death below them. And it seemed to the crowds that bent with bared heads as they passed by the coffin that the very death of this great man had made more secure the destiny of the nation.

Outside the storm raged more fiercely, and the people clamored against the savagery of an unguided crowd. Outside the winds were voicing their own requiem, and wailing at the feet of that symbol of liberty which crowns the highest height of the colossal building. And here in the darkened rotunda, where state occasions had signalized the progress of a people from weakness unto strength, from experiment to established systems—forty thousand people—delegates from eighty million of their fellows, touched with reverent fingers the trappings of the dead and moved on to mingle again with the world. While he had lain sick in that fair house of his friend at Buffalo, it had seemed to these thousands that the one voice of the Republic must be:

"Our hearts, our hopes, are all with thee."

Yet as they gazed at the pensive face, as they looked into the countenance which had never feared, had never found a duty too difficult for performing, they added the lines—

"Our hearts, our hopes, our prayers, our tears,
Our faith triumphant o'er our fears,
Are all with thee—are all with thee."

And so they passed out again to the day of gloom, confident that the sunshine of to-morrow would certainly come. And the close of the day left the dead alone with his guards.

A terrible crush, accompanied by a panic, occurred in front of the Capitol while the thousands of people were struggling for a look at the dead President. Fully fifty people were more or less injured and one man lost his life.

Long before the remains had started from the White House the crowd had begun to gather in front of the Capitol building. By the time the great bronze doors of the eastern entrance were swung open the people were massed for acres. A line of police guarded the base of the Capitol steps and gave directions that a double line should be formed as the people should be admitted two abreast. But when the crowd saw that the doors had been opened and that the line had started to go through, there was a general movement to get closer to the point of admittance.

Those in the rear pressed forward and those in the middle, not being able to hold back against the weight, were pressed with greater force against those ahead. Quickly those in front and along the line of ropes were crowded so tightly that they could scarcely breathe.

There were women and children and babies in arms in the press, and soon the section in front of the steps became a fighting mass of humanity.

Men seized small children and held them high over their heads to keep them from being trampled under foot or crushed in the terrible weight which was thrown against them.

A woman was heard to scream and beg for help. The crowd became panic-stricken and women began fainting on every side. An ineffectual squad of mounted police thought to drive back those in the rear and separate the crowd by plunging their horses into the worst of the fray. The result was what might be expected. The panic was increased. The crowd broke all bounds.

The little line of police at the foot of the wide flight of steps was swept down like so many straws. The crowd flowed up the stairs like a mighty flood. One of the mounted officers, goring his horse with his spurs, was carried, horse and all, half way up the steps. Women screamed as they found themselves under the trampling hoofs and men fought to get away.

A colored man at one side whipped out a knife and slashed the rope against which the crowd was pressing. Those in front fell headlong and the rest followed, trampling them under foot.

At the doors of the Capitol rotunda, where the dead President lay in state, the surging was checked. With herculean efforts the capitol police fought off the rising sea of people and closed the gates against them. But quickly they had to be opened in response to the appeal in the name of humanity.

The Capitol police helped to drag the fainting and injured into the building, where they were laid out in rows. Calls were sent to the hospitals and surgeons were sent in an ambulance. The Capitol was the only refuge for those who had been borne down in the rush, and the victims were passed over the heads of the crowd and taken in at the doors.

The committee-rooms were pressed into service and women were taken to them and attended by the doctors. Ambulances drove up, but could not penetrate the dense crowd. Colonel Dan Ransdell, sergeant-at-arms of the Senate, arrived on the scene and gave orders that the doors be thrown wide open. This, he perceived, was the only way the congestion could be relieved. It was growing worse at every moment.

The crowd broke in when the obstructions were removed and in a moment the rotunda was filled and packed. Then the Capitol police hurried the people through and out the other side.

Meantime the trouble in front had been growing worse rather than better. Men and women fought like beasts to get out of the suffocating crush. Clothing was torn; hats, coats, umbrellas, neckties, women's silk waists and light summer gowns were torn and scattered in every direction. The mounted police charged about the outskirts of the crowd adding to the excitement. Some colored men at the western edge got into a fight and whipped out razors, which were brandished about and several were severely cut.

The ambulances dashed about clanging their bells and adding to the turmoil. They made hurried trips to the hospitals carrying the senseless and bleeding. Often they carried as many as half a dozen at a time. The police appealed to the crowd to fall back, but it was like talking to the ocean.

Fearing that the disorder would spread to the rotunda and that the remains of the President might be endangered the Capitol police, under the command of Captain McGrew, determined again to close the doors. This was accomplished only after the greatest efforts. The people within were then driven out on the western side and the stairways and halls were also thrown open to facilitate their exit.

A force of police on foot was hurried to the rescue and the crowd was charged from the sides and driven back toward the east again. This relieved the pressure about the steps and gradually order was restored. Then the officers insisted that the people be formed into double line and the space about the entrance was cleared. By two o'clock the line was passing through the rotunda again in quiet and decent fashion.

People who have witnessed similar gatherings at the Capitol express wonder that there have not been panics and crushes before. The police of Washington seem to have little idea of handling large crowds. At inauguration times the only reason there has not been trouble is that the exercises have been held in the open air. The crowds which come together are permitted to mass over large areas without openings and passageways through which the women and others may escape in case they desire to get away.

The management of this part of the programme was under the charge of the War Department, and earlier in the day there was a company of soldiers on duty keeping the crowd within bounds and under control. But this company was withdrawn and the rest was left to the city officers, who claim that the force was insufficient for the occasion.

When the people had had an opportunity to view the remains of their beloved President, the body was taken to the depot, and between eight and nine o'clock in the evening the funeral train departed for Canton.

McKINLEY'S GUARD IN ADVANCE OF HEARSE, CANTON.

PLACING THE BODY IN THE VAULT   AT WESTLAWN CEMETERY, CANTON.

CHAPTER XXXVI.

THE ASSASSIN ARRAIGNED.

At the midhour, when the people were filing past the casket that held all that was mortal of the late President of the United States, in the rotunda of the capitol at Washington, Leon Czolgosz, his assassin, was being arraigned for trial in the court room at Buffalo.

"Are you guilty, or not guilty?" was the question which the Law asked of him.

Whatever he was, whatever he had done, the public of the nation was too great to visit upon him the summary vengeance his awful act so richly merited.

Society is better than Czolgosz thought it to be. If it had been the monster he pictured, if it had been the unreasoning and unjust force he had been taught, and which his mad act showed that he believed, that man would have been turned loose from the jail in Buffalo, and the society he condemned would have had its will with him. And the mangled fragments of the Third Assassin would have borne mute testimony to the truth--as well, perhaps, as the justice—of the estimate which he placed upon it.

But instead of that, society gave him all the forms of trial, all the possibilities of defense.

He had the assistance of learned counsel. He might well be sure that all that his most devoted friend could say in wisdom for his defense will be brought forward on his trial. He was not condemned unheard. He was placed with hands unbound in the presence of a sedate tribunal—of one of the tribunals which all the organs of his creed had been maligning in their every issue; and there he was asked:

"Are you guilty, or not quilty?"

District Attorney Penney almost shouted the words at Leon Czolgosz, sitting in the county courtroom at 3 o'clock this afternoon. The assassin did not even turn his eyes toward his questioner. Two hundred auditors watched him, listening for his answer, but he did not look at any of them, and his unshaven lips were silent. He stared at the floor, and shunned the eyes of his fellow creatures.

The assassin, arrayed in clean linen for the first time since he shot the

President, sat sullen before the court while the charges were being read. He looked no man in the eye. Sometimes his lips moved nervously, as if he would speak. But he only moistened them with his tongue, and with groveling eyes sat stolid and voiceless.

"Are you guilty? Answer yes or no!" thundered the district attorney, but the fair-haired monster in the chair paid no heed.

"Do you understand what has been read?" asked Mr. Penney.

For an instant the skulking glance of the assassin fixed itself upon the lawyer's face. An immediate hush fell upon the audience. The assassin leaned forward in his chair, then dropped his eyes, then leaned back in silence.

"You have been indicted for murder in the first degree," said Mr. Penney.

Czolgosz's eyes wandered toward the ceiling for a second, then to the floor. Then he shifted half way round in his chair and sat mute in the face of his accuser.

Judge Loren L. Lewis, former justice of the Supreme Court, who had been assigned to the defense of the assassin by Judge Edward K. Emery, then arose and addressed the court. It was at once apparent that the duty was distasteful, but Mr. Lewis entered a plea of "Not Guilty."

He asked permission to reserve the right to withdraw the plea, enter a special plea, or withdraw the demurrer if, after consultation with Judge Titus, also assigned to the case, it was decided to decline the assignment. Judge Titus being in Milwaukee, Mr. Lewis said that it was impossible to enter further into the case and, therefore, he informally offered the plea of not guilty.

Attorney Lewis then told the court that he had called upon the prisoner, but had been met with a stubborn refusal to discuss the case. Czolgosz would not even admit that he wished the services of counsel. Mr. Lewis asked the court for permission to introduce alienists to examine into the prisoner's mental condition, as this step had already been taken by the attorneys for the people. He mentioned incidentally that he was sorry his name had been connected with the case, but that as a lawyer and an officer of the court he felt himself obligated to carry out its wishes.

Mr. Penney next gave notice that he would move to have the trial transferred to the Supreme Court, and would ask notice of it for next Monday. Czolgosz's attorney then said that he knew of no reason why his client should not be ready Monday, but Judge Emery upon request agreed not to enter the order till Mr. Titus, associate counsel for Czolgosz, returns from Milwaukee.

Mr. Lewis' request to be permitted to introduce alienists gave rise to the prevalent belief that the defense will be built upon the theory of insanity.

At the close of Attorney Lewis' address Judge Emery said:

"Remove the prisoner."

He was quickly handcuffed. There was a rush of spectators toward the stairway leading to the tunnel that connects the courthouse with the jail. Czolgosz, the assassin, now manacled and hustled along, passed within a lane of staring citizens.

His dirty sleeve brushed against the drapery of black that enwrapped the pillars of the halls and stairs as he descended. Above his head, as he passed downward into the tunnel, the black encinctured portrait of the martyred President looked down upon his frowzy head as he went. But he did not look up. Surrounded by detectives, mute, sullen and shambling, he shuffled down the stone stairway.

Then a low hiss, subdued but ominous, rose from the watching crowd. It swelled and echoed down the squalid passageway as the murderer slunk away and passed back to the jail, which is connected by a dark subway under Delaware avenue with the courthouse.

It was the opinion of those who saw Czolgosz to-day that he is shamming insanity. Since his arrest he has made no rational request, except that he be shaved. Chief of Detectives Cusack said "No," and the murderer came into court to-day with a ten days' growth of beard that made him look disheveled and dirty.

"He gets no razor while he is my prisoner," explained Cusack. "That would be too easy."

The audience which assembled in court to witness Czolgosz's arraignment to-day was not as large as was expected. Few believed that Judges Titus and Lewis would consent to serve in behalf of the accused assassin. Both the lawyers assigned to the case by Judge Emery are high in their profession, and it is well known that they are mortified and annoyed by the assignment. However, the law requires that the court's behest be followed, and it is probable that the attorneys named will carry out the instructions of Judge Emery.

There is something in the family history of the assassin which sheds a baleful light on the acts of the present, and they were revealed in the very hour when he was standing trial for his life in Buffalo.

There was a time when the father of this young man took the law into his own hands. And this is the story of it:

The elder Czolgosz was one of the colonists in Presque Isle County, ruled over by Henry Molitor, who was an illegitimate son of King Louis of Wurtemberg, and who fled from Germany under sentence of death.

Stung to desperation by King Molitor's tyrannies and vice, a band of colonists poured a volley of shots through the window of the company store on August 16, 1876, killing Molitor.

The principal actors in this tragedy, of whom the elder Czolgosz was one, were sentenced to prison for life, but were subsequently pardoned. Amid such surroundings Assassin Czolgosz was born and reared.

All that occurred twenty-five years ago. It could have had no influence on the life of the lad, if, indeed, he had then been born. But it in some degree shows the strain of blood in the family, and in some measure accounts for the stolid silence in which that young man sits when, for murder most foul, he is called before the bar of the people.

Following is the formal true bill returned by the grand jury of Erie County, New York, against Leon F. Czolgosz, the assassin of the late President McKinley:

The people of the State of New York, entered against Leon F. Czolgosz, alias Fred Nieman.

The grand jury of the County of Erie, by this indictment, accuse Leon F. Czolgosz, alias Fred Nieman, of the crime of murder in the first degree.

That the said Leon F. Czolgosz, alias Fred Nieman, on the sixth day of September, in the year of our Lord one thousand nine hundred and one, at the City of Buffalo, in the County of Erie, with force and arms in and upon one William McKinley, in the peace of the people of the State of New York, then and there being, willfully, feloniously and from a deliberate and premeditated design to effect the death of said William McKinley, did make an assault, and the said Leon F. Czolgosz, alias Fred Nieman, then and there willfully, feloniously and from a deliberate and premeditated design to effect the death of the said William McKinley, did shoot off and discharge to, at, against and upon the said William McKinley a certain pistol and firearm, then and there charged and loaded with gunpowder and leaden bullets, and the said Leon F. Czolgosz, alias Fred Nieman, with the leaden bullets aforesaid, out of the pistol and firearm aforesaid, then and there by force of the gunpowder aforesaid, shot off, sent forth and discharged, him, the said Leon

F. Czolgosz, then and there feloniously, willfully and with a deliberate and premeditated design to effect the death of the said William McKinley, did strike, penetrate and wound, giving unto him, the said William McKinley, then and there with the leaden bullets aforesaid so as aforesaid discharged, sent forth and shot out of the pistol and firearm aforesaid, by the said Leon F. Czolgosz, alias Fred Nieman, in and upon the stomach, abdomen and body of the said William McKinley, one mortal wound, of which said mortal wound he, the said William McKinley, from the sixth day of September, in the year aforesaid, until the fourteenth day of September, in the same year aforesaid, at the city and county aforesaid, did languish, and, languishing, did live, on which said last-mentioned day he, the said William McKinley, at the city and county aforesaid, of the said mortal wound, did die; contrary to the form of the statute in such case made and provided, and against the peace of the people of the State of New York and their dignity.

Second Count—And the grand jury of the County of Erie aforesaid by this indictment do further accuse the said Leon F. Czolgosz, alias Fred Nieman, of the crime of murder in the first degree, committed as follows, to-wit:

That on the sixth day of September, in the year of our Lord one thousand nine hundred and one, at the City of Buffalo, and in the County of Erie, the said Leon F. Czolgosz, alias Fred Nieman, in and upon the body of one William McKinley, in the peace of the people of the State of New York to and there being willfully, feloniously and of his malice aforethought, did make an assault, and a certain pistol then and there charged with gunpowder and one leaden bullet, which he, the said Leon F. Czolgosz, alias Fred Nieman, in his right hand then and there had, and held to, at, against and upon the said William McKinley, then and there willfully, feloniously and of his malice aforethought, did shoot off and discharge, and the said Leon F. Czolgosz, alias Fred Nieman, with the leaden bullet aforesaid, then and there by the force of the gunpowder aforesaid shot off, sent forth and discharged as aforesaid, him, the said William McKinley, in and upon the stomach, abdomen and body of him, the said William McKinley, then and there willfully, feloniously and of his malice aforethought, did strike, penetrate and wound, giving unto him, the said William McKinley, then and there with the leaden bullet aforesaid, so as aforesaid discharged, sent forth and shot out of the pistol aforesaid, in and upon the stomach, abdomen and body of him, the said William McKinley, one mortal wound, of which said mortal wound he, the said William McKinley, from the said sixth day of September, in the year aforesaid, at the city and county aforesaid, did languish, and, languishing, did live; on which said last-mentioned day he, the said William McKinley, at the city and county aforesaid, of the said mortal wound, did die.

And so the grand jury aforesaid do say that the said Leon F. Czolgosz, alias Fred Nieman, him the said William McKinley, in the manner and form and by the means aforesaid, did kill and murder against the form of the statute in such case made and provided and against the peace of the people of the State of New York and their dignity.

(Signed.)   THOMAS PENNEY,
                          District Attorney of Erie County.

CHAPTER XXXVII.

THE SAD JOURNEY TO CANTON.

The funeral train bearing the remains of President McKinley crossed the west line of Pennsylvania and entered his home State and his home Congressional District at 10 o'clock a. m., Wednesday, September 18, 1901.

This is the district he represented for fourteen years in the halls of Congress. Many who had known the President personally, who had shaken his hand and gazed into his genial face, lined the tracks to do honor to all that remained on earth of their neighbor, friend and chief. From the State line to Canton, the President's home, the line of mourners was almost continuous. Although a stirring depth of feeling had been manifested as the train passed through other States of the Union with its burden, nowhere was poignant grief so evident as it was during the sad journey through the President's home State.

It is the second time the State of Ohio has been called upon to pay homage to the ashes of one of its sons, elevated to the Presidency and then stricken by an assassin's bullet in the prime of his career.

The mustering of popular sentiment was awe-inspiring, both because of the numerical strength of the mourners and the intensity of feeling shown. In every sense was the trip of the President's body to its last resting place memorable. Miles upon miles of humanity were passed, thousands upon thousands of heads were bared. Hundreds upon hundreds of crape-tied flags were displayed, while, in the distance, the emblem of the nation was seen at half-mast upon the schoolhouse or other public building.

Company upon company of State militia presented arms, while peal upon peal of the death knell came from church and courthouse bells. In all there was not a smile seen from the train, and the ears of President Roosevelt and Mrs. McKinley were not jarred by the sound of cheers or unseemly shouts of acclaim. The thousands of school children, lined up near the track, maintained a silence as profound, as sympathetic and as reverent as their elders, who felt more deeply.

Through Maryland and Pennsylvania, where the outlines of black mountains frowned dimly upon the train as it passed in the night, bonfires were seen where they had been lit to keep the watchers awake in their night vigil.

The flames lit up the sides of the funeral train and cast flickering shadows against the sides of the great hills. In the towns at night the torches lit up the anxious, sympathetic faces of the mourners, who had lost sleep and braved the chill so as to have a brief look at the train which was hurrying to the President's burial ground.

An entire regiment of the State troops was ranked along the tracks at Pittsburg near the station. No stop was made at the big sooty city. Against one of the hills were placed several hundred girls in the form of a flag. The long railroad bridge over the Allegheny was solid with men and boys, whose coats almost touched the train as it passed through.

From Pittsburg the train followed the Ohio river for miles. Old river steamboats blew sorrowful, long-drawn-out salutes to the passing train. Flags upon them were at half-mast.

On the shores of West Virginia opposite there were crowds assembled who saw the train speed by in the distance. Many of the towns on the banks of the Ohio consisted of long strings of houses in the gulch. Some of the towns containing only a few thousand inhabitants stretched along for a great distance. All the people were gathered at the track, both from the towns and the country sides for miles around. Doorsteps of every house were filled with watchers, the old folks' faces were seen gazing through the windows and the roof tops were thronged.

At a country cross-road, where there was not a house in sight, several score of men, women and children were gathered. The buggies and farm wagons a little distance away showed they had come from a distance. Their horses were munching in their feed bags, unaware of what was the mournful occasion of their day's journey.

East Palestine, the first Ohio station passed by the train, appeared to be a little village nestled in between two great hills. There were enough people scattered at the tracks, however, to warrant the presumption that it was a city of considerable importance.

From early dawn, when the first rays of the sun came shimmering through the Allegheny mists, the country through which the McKinley funeral train passed seemed alive with waiting people. As the train was later than its schedule the probabilities were that many thousands lined up along the track had been waiting for almost an hour for the fleeting glimpse of the cars accompanying the murdered President's body to its last resting place.

Steel workers, with their dinner pails in their hands, ran the risk of being late at the mills in order to pay their last homage to the dead. It was at the steel towns, just east of Pittsburg, that the largest early crowds lined the tracks.

Between and east of the mill towns was the open mountain country interspersed with an occasional cluster of houses near coal mines or oil wells. Even in the open country as early as 6 a. m. there were people gathered at the cross-roads or leaning against farm fences.

Faces were seen peering through, up and down windows of houses situated near the tracks. In railroad yards hundreds were crowded on top of cars so as to obtain a view as the sections of the Presidential train picked their way through the maze of tracks. Women and girls as well as men and boys were eager to see the cars go by.

In the railroad cars in Pitcairn, a few miles east of Pittsburg, hundreds of factory girls were lined up. It was 8:35 a. m. when the train passed through Pitcairn, so most of the girls with lunch boxes under their arms must have been quite late to work, all for the sake of the few seconds' look at the train which brought so close to them the victim of the anarchist's bullet and his successor, President Roosevelt.

Young women who were not shop girls were there, too, evidently having come from the most exclusive residence districts of the little city, trudging through the rough tracks to obtain a brief look.

Away from the crowds at the towns solitary watchers were passed. Engineers and firemen of passing trains leaned far out of their cab windows when the train approached. Boys and girls, perched high on rocky crags, remained in their points of vantage to see the train fly past.

As the train neared Pittsburg it passed between a continuous line of men and women, boys and girls, miles long.

There was hardly a space of a dozen feet that was not filled. On the sides and tops of the near-by foothills colored specks told of the bright dresses of women and girls, who were watching the entrance of the long tunnel in Pittsburg, which was like a human archway, so many persons of all ages and sexes were crowded around and above the black opening.

One enterprising lad was high on a church steeple and waved his hat. The viaducts were simply jammed with thousands of human beings. The high tops of the iron girders were covered with boys, while the vertical steel pillars supported venturesome climbers. Windows of mills and factories, where employes were busy a moment before, were crowded with eager faces as the train drew near.

From beyond Braddock, which is twelve miles from Pittsburg, the continuous and mournful ovation began and continued almost in a solid line until the train was miles out of the Smoky City.

On top of a carload of stone in Pittsburg were about a hundred girls, and they presented a most picturesque appearance. Although the crowds were far greater than ever greeted any President of the United States alive, not a smile was seen, not a cheer was heard. The train passed between the walls of solemn-visaged humanity miles long.

The sun burst through the smoky pall at intervals and lit up the bright colors of the women's dresses with an indescribable effect. Although the dresses were bright, the faces were not. They were evidently filled with sympathy for the dead President and Mrs. McKinley, and with execration of the assassin whose foul deed was the cause of the present sad demonstration.

Thousands upon thousands of bared heads of the men as seen from the train windows bore evidence of their reverence for the ashes of their President, while the grim set of their countenances bespoke little of the quality of mercy for the murderous anarchist.

Grassy terraces covered with a bright green carpet were dotted with the pink, red and blue dresses of the women and girls, presenting in the bright sunshine a wonderful effect. The crowds thickened as the depot was approached until every street was jammed and every available space filled hundreds deep.

As the train sped through the Ohio hills the country smiled with glowing golden rod as if to remind those on the train that the simple blossom was a favorite with the late President. The mowed fields were as green as if the summer were young instead of at its close.

Gorgeous red of the sumac and the russet brown of the ivy were the only colors to relieve the green of the woods. The aspect of the land was pleasant as if the honored son of Ohio were being welcomed to his last home-coming by the earth which was to receive him so soon. A sprinkling of clouds tempered the rays of the sun and relieved its glare, making it an ideal day for rejoicing, rather than gloom.

Smiling as were the elements, however, their gladsome joy was not reflected in the countenances of the fellow-citizens of the departed Ohioan. Had the sky been somber as night and the earth as desolate as the desert the countenances of those thousands of human beings assembled along the route could not have been gloomier.

One noticeable feature of the crowds was that so many people were attired in their Sunday best. These had arrayed themselves as for a funeral, the same as if some member of their own family was to be buried, and all for the sake of the mere glimpse of the presidential train and for the privilege of paying a momentary mute homage to the memory of the illustrious dead.

In other days Canton has been clothed in a gay garb of color, bands have played stirringly, richly attired women have smiled and men have shouted for William McKinley. But those were happier days than this, the occasion of the home-coming of a guide, friend and neighbor who, having climbed the ladder of fame, fell before the assassin's bullet and died in the arms of his country.

In all the little city which the dead President loved there was hardly a structure that bore no badge of sorrow. In Tuscarawas street, from one end to the other, business houses were hung heavy with crape and at intervals huge arches, draped and festooned in mourning colors, spanned the route of the procession from the train to the county courthouse.

One of the arches was in front of the Canton high school, half a block from McKinley avenue. The school was draped, and in every window was a black-bordered portrait of the late President. In this thoroughfare, too, are two large churches, one of which was regularly attended by Major McKinley, the First Methodist Episcopal, at Cleveland avenue, a block from the courthouse. At each corner of the edifice and above the big cathedral windows were broad draperies deftly looped, each bearing a large white rosette. The other church, the First Presbyterian, was similarly adorned.

The courthouse, the scene of the lying in state, was a mass of sable hue. At the entrance, between the two big doors, was a tablet wrought in crape and upon the cloth shield was emblazoned in white the utterance of the President when told that he must die:

"It is God's way. His will, not ours, be done."

In front of the courthouse was another massive arch.

Canton was astir with break of day, such residents as had not displayed badges and draperies of mourning performing the task that morning. At Nemicella Park the soldiers of Troop A of Cleveland and the militia of various parts of the State were busy preparing to escort the distinguished dead up Tuscarawas street.

On every corner in the downtown districts boys and men were shouting out "Official badges here" and selling pictures of the dead President.

Before 8 o'clock the rotunda of the courthouse had been prepared for the reception of the body. With the exception of dainty white streamers from the chandeliers there was no trace of white in the large apartment wherein the public should have a last look upon the face of the departed executive. The walls and ceilings were covered with black cloth looped here and there from the ornamental pillars with streamers and rosettes of the same color. From each chandelier was suspended a small American flag, a larger one fluttering just above the catafalque.

Three hours before the funeral train was scheduled to arrive more than a thousand men and women had gathered at Courthouse square and hundreds of others had congregated in the vicinity of the railway depot, each anxious to be as near the casket as possible when it was taken from the car Pacific.

At the McKinley home itself, almost the only residence in Canton that bore no trace of mourning, was another throng, and there was not a door or window that had not been peered at most assiduously by curious visitors and equally curious residents of the city.

Every train brought crowds of visitors, come to witness and take a sorrowful share in the last rites. Every hotel was full to overflowing, four or five persons occupying a room scarcely large enough for two, and halls and parlors had been filled with cots. Even these brought prices as high as would procure one of the best rooms in a metropolitan hotel.

Complete plans could not be made until after the arrival of the funeral train. It had been the intention to have the body lie in state until evening and then remove it to the McKinley home in North Market street, but Mrs. McKinley objected, asserting that she could not endure the thought of having her husband's body disturbed.

Above the high steps and over the main entrance to the courthouse hung a painting of Maj. McKinley twenty feet square. It had a white border and made a very effective piece against the broad expanse of black that obscured all the first part of the second story of the structure. The most effective arch in the city was that in front of the high school. This was erected by the pupils of the public schools. It was square on top and bore on either side a picture of the dead President. On the left of each picture was the legend "We loved him," and on the right "He loved us."

On either support was a large card bearing this: "Canton Public Schools."

CHAPTER XXXVIII.

CANTON BATHED IN TEARS.

The funeral train proper, bearing the body of President McKinley, arrived at 12 o'clock. It was met by Judge Day, at the head of the local reception committee, while assembled about the station was the entire militia of the State.

Mrs. McKinley, weeping piteously, was helped from the train by Dr. Rixey and Abner McKinley and conducted to a carriage.

The body was then lifted from the catafalque car and carried on the shoulders of the bodybearers through a pathway formed by President Roosevelt and his cabinet to the waiting hearse. The surrounding soldiers were at present arms and bugles sounded taps.

The President and cabinet then entered carriages. They were followed by the guard of honor, headed by Admiral Dewey and General Miles in full uniform, and the sad procession then moved up Tenth street in the direction of the courthouse, where the body was to lie in state. Soldiers at intervals all the way kept back the immense crowds which thronged the streets. The procession passed all the way beneath big arches draped with black.

President Roosevelt and the members of the cabinet were the first to pass by the bier, followed by the highest officers of the army and navy, Senator Hanna and many others high in public life.

Later the public was admitted to the chamber and thousands viewed the body. Mrs. McKinley and the relatives did not go to the courthouse. She stood the trip fairly well, and soon after arriving went to sleep in the old home.

Mrs. McKinley was almost the first to leave the train. She leaned heavily on the arm of Abner McKinley and was supported on the other side by Dr. Rixey. She walked slowly toward the carriage prepared for her and was taken to the home of which she has been mistress for so many years. There was not a person of the hundreds who saw her at the depot but who knew her. Her sweet face was not visible through the heavy black of her mourning veil, but her frail form and bearing made her instantly recognized by those assembled.

A sublime hush fell upon all. There were scores of women present and

387

all were in tears. It was a great, silent outpouring of deep sympathy for the crushed soul of their beloved neighbor.

President Roosevelt and the cabinet left their car in the opposite direction and took their places in the closed carriages for the funeral procession. The great throng regarded them respectfully. For five years those gathered here had annually received as President of the United States their fellow townsman. The sorrow of the citizens of Canton was yet too poignant to permit of the expression of any other emotion than grief. Eight artillerymen and eight soldiers slowly trod down the steps of the Pacific, the car in which the President's body rested. A passing cloud which had cast its kindly shade upon the dolorous form of the President's widow now withdrew from the face of the sun so as to permit the warming rays to rest upon the casket of the dead President.

A window was raised toward the rear of the car, the same window through which the body had been passed thrice before. The opening looked very small. Eight of the guards, four bluejackets and four red-striped sergeants of artillery, stood below to receive the heavy burden. A moment later the end of the coffin, draped with the red, white and blue of its silken covering, protruded. A few of the onlookers had not thought it necessary to remove their hats, they had been so absorbed in the incoming of the train. Their heads were bared instantly. The eight soldiers and sailors received the great weight on their shoulders. They were sturdy men, but their limbs trembled under the strain.

Preceded by Judge Day and other members of the reception committee, the coffin was borne the whole length of the station platform, several hundred feet. The militia surrounding the station stood at present arms. At the end of the platform was the hearse chosen to carry the corpse in the procession to the courthouse.

"Present arms!" came the command from the sergeant of hussars opposite the hearse. Magnificently caparisoned in all the trappings of their full dress, Troop A of the Cleveland Hussars had been chosen to precede the hearse in the procession.

At the call one hundred swords were unsheathed and held pointing upward from the broad bosoms of the cavalrymen. The bright blades, freshly burnished for the occasion, flashed the sunlight like white fire. The gold lace shone, and the bearskin caps, towering above the erect heads of the hussars, added to the martial effect.

In the attitude of present, like a hundred equestrian statues, the hussars remained motionless until the casket had been placed within the hearse. If a horse moved its foot or whisked a fly from its sides the motion was not apparent. The air was still, the crowd was still, the engine at the head of the train was still, and the intense silence pervaded the entire surroundings.

Heartrending beyond the power of pen to describe were the scenes at the side of the bier while the simple folk of Canton walked slowly by in two single files. The sorrow of those who knew the President was too intense for utterance, but was so full it burst the bounds of control over the emotions. Rough workingmen trembled from head to foot and their chests heaved with emotion, as great tears rolled down their faces. The ghastly appearance of President McKinley's face, which was blue and thin, far more discolored than it was when the body lay in state in Buffalo, made the grief more poignant.

It seemed as though none who had known him in his genial vigor as their fellow townsman and neighbor could see that discolored face, the result of the assassin's deadly work, without bursting into tears.

A farmer of 80, old, bent and weather-beaten, tottered in the line as he wound his decrepit way through the black corridor to the bier. When he saw the pinched, drawn face he placed his great gnarled hands to his face and wept as no heart-broken child could weep. He was bowed and broken when he entered the darkened hall and his step was shaky. When he left his shaggy white head was bowed lower, his spirit seemed broken almost to the point of leaving his aged frame and his step was a staggering shuffle. He was the impersonation of abject, venerable grief.

The sight had been throughout profoundly impressive.

Up the street soldiers at intervals of ten feet with difficulty restrained the solid wall of people. Canton had suddenly become a city of 100,000, and the entire population was in the streets. The station itself was cleared, a company of soldiers of the Eighth Ohio from Worcester keeping the platform clear. Opposite, over the heads of acres of people, on the wall of a big manufacturing establishment, was an enormous shield thirty feet high, with McKinley's black-bordered picture in the center. The local committee, headed by ex-Secretary of State William R. Day and Judge Grant, was on the platform.

All about were the black symbols of mourning. The approach of the train was unheralded. No whistle was blown, no bell was rung. In absolute silence it rolled into the station. Even the black-hooded locomotive gave no sound. There was no panting of exhaust pipes. The energy that brought it seemed to have been absolutely expended.　At the mere sight of the train the people who had been waiting there for hours were greatly affected.　Women sobbed and men wept.

For a full minute after it had stopped no one appeared.　Judge Day and his committee moved slowly down the platform in front of the line of soldiers to the catafalque car and waited.　Colonel Bingham, the President's aid, then gave directions for the removal of the casket from the car.　The coffin was too large to be taken through the door and a broad window at the side was unscrewed and removed.

While this was going on the floral pieces inside were carefully lifted out and placed upon the ground at the side of the track.　When all was ready the soldiers and sailors who had accompanied the body all the way from Buffalo emerged from the car and took up their places.　The soldiers trailed their arms and the sailors held their drawn cutlasses at their sides.　Only the body-bearers were bareheaded and unarmed.

Meantime President Roosevelt, with his brother-in-law, Captain Cowles of the navy, in full uniform, at his side, had descended from the car ahead of that occupied by Mrs. McKinley.　The members of the Cabinet, excepting Secretary of State Hay and Secretary of the Navy Long, were present. Secretary Cortelyou, Governor Nash, Lieutenant-Governor Caldwell and Judge Marshall J. Williams of the Supreme Court, representing the three branches of the State government of Ohio, followed President Roosevelt from the train.

The President was met by Judge Grant of the Reception Committee. and the official party then moved to the west of the station, where they formed in line, with the President at the head. All were uncovered.

With the body placed in the hearse, the bugle note sounded again and the hundred swords were sheathed.　The hundred bright steels faced to the right, and with slow step the men advanced to take the position of honor before the hearse.　At the given signal the soft notes of "Nearer, My God, To Thee," swelled up from the military band.　The horses kept the slow step perfectly.　The two drivers of the hearse, who had kept their heads bared reverently, replaced their hats and gave the sign to the black horses which were to draw the catafalque.

The two steeds stepped forward and the funeral procession was in motion.　At that moment the power plant of the Canton Electric Light Company was started.　A mournful whir broke upon every ear.　It was like the dirge note of a Scotch bag-pipe.　It fitted in with the notes of the President's

DISPLAY OF FLOWERS IN FRONT OF RECEIVING VAULT, WESTLAWN CEMETERY, CANTON, OHIO.

U. S. SENATE PASSING THE SPANISH WAR APPROPRIATION OF $50,000,000.

hymn perfectly, as if the ancient pipers of the clan of the McKinleys were sounding the dirge for their chieftain.

Save the plaintive whir of the electric motor, the gentle notes of the hymn and the slow and mournful click of the horses' hoofs upon the brick pavement all was silence. For the first time in over thirty years William McKinley passed through the familiar streets of Canton and there was silence.

With bared heads and tearful eyes the dense throngs that lined Cherry, Tuscarawas and Market streets observed with restless eagerness the progress of the funeral procession to the court-house. It was three-quarters of an hour after the column moved that the casket was carried into the somber rotunda of the big public building, and in that time thousands of women sobbed and men wept.

Following the President's carriage were carriages containing members of the Cabinet, after whom came the diplomats and citizens. It was nearly 1 o'clock when the President reached the court-house. He waited until the casket had been borne inside and placed on the catafalque. Then, attended by Commander Cowles and the members of the Cabinet, the Executive entered the rotunda, passed by the body of the illustrious dead, bowed low a moment over the face of his predecessor and left the building.

With the Commodore he went direct to the residence of Mrs. George H. Harter, 933 North Market street, where he took luncheon. After the President came the Cabinet members, Secretary Root leading, and then the military guard of honor and the diplomatic corps in turn. Ten minutes later the public was admitted in two columns, one passing on each side of the casket.

The decorations of the rotunda were exceedingly impressive. A striking conceit of the artist consisted of three chairs, all covered with crape. They represent the chairs of state left vacant by the tragic deaths of Lincoln, Garfield and the statesman mourned to-day. At the head of the casket stands a Knight Templar, at the foot a member of the Ohio militia, while the sides are guarded respectively by a regular army soldier and a marine.

Meantime Admiral Dewey, General Miles and the other high officers of the army and navy, who composed the guard of honor, had moved around the east side of the station. They also entered carriages and took their place in the larger procession that was now forming. All were attired in the full uniform of their ranks. They were fairly ablaze with gold lace.

The shrill notes of the bugle had given the first sign to the waiting multitude outside the station that the casket was approaching. Instantly the long lines of soldiers became rigid, standing at present arms. The black horses of the Cleveland Troop, immediately facing the station, stood motionless, their riders with sabers lowered. Slowly through the entrance came the stalwart soldiers and sailors, with solemn tread, bearing aloft the flag-covered coffin of the man this city loved so well. As it came into view a great sigh went up from the dense throng.

Immediately following the mounted troops came the hearse bearing its flag-covered burden. This was the sight that sent a hush along the dense, long lines of humanity stretching for a mile away to the court-house. As the casket passed every head was bowed and every face evidenced the great personal grief which had come upon the community.

CHAPTER XXXIX.

FUNERAL SERVICES IN ALL CHURCHES.

While funeral services were being held over the remains of President McKinley on the Sunday after his death, every church edifice in the whole nation was the scene of a similar service. Without regard to sect or creed, without regard to location, far or near, high or low, in cathedral and in chapel, the words of preacher and the heartfelt sympathy of people rose in united worship to the God whom William McKinley had worshiped.

Services in the Metropolitan Methodist Church at Washington, of which President McKinley was a member and constant attendant when at Washington, were of an unusually impressive character.

The congregation present tested the capacity of the building, many persons being compelled to stand. Drapings of black covered the President's pew, and these sombre habiliments of woe covered the pulpit, partly made of olive wood from Jerusalem. During the service the choir sang "Lead, Kindly Light," and "Nearer, My God, to Thee," favorites of the dead President, the vast congregation joining in both selections. Rev. Dr. F. M. Bristol, the pastor, was in Europe; but Rev. W. H. Chapman delivered the sermon, taking his text from Jeremiah, "Judah mourneth." In the course of his remarks Dr. Chapman said:

"No safer, purer man than William McKinley has ever presided over this great republic and no man was ever more admired. Adorned was he with the highest and noblest virtues, which gave dignity and force to his character and moral beauty to his life. He was a Christian man and exemplified in his daily life the sublime principles of Christianity. From early manhood he had been identified with the Christian church, with that branch which we represent. It was the church of his mother, the church in which he had been trained from childhood, that he had received lessons which added to those imparted to him by his maternal parent laid the foundation for that solid, symmetrical character which he attained and for which he was distinguished.

"Christianity nobly sustained him during his illness, enabling him to endure calmly and submissively. In his quiet moments, with eyes closed but not asleep, he said, 'Nearer, my God, to Thee.' To his beloved companion who had trod with him for many years the path of life, bending over him with tearful eyes and throbbing heart, near the parting hour, he said 'Not our will, but God's will be done,' meaning 'be resigned but trustful; leave all with the Lord and it shall be well with thee when I am gone.' How peaceful and resigned he went into the valley, covered with splendid sunshine and found rest from his labors! He has left behind him, to his kindred and to us the rich legacy of a splendid character and an unsullied record. A life that says to others: 'This is the way. Walk in it, the way that leads to moral wealth, far above all material wealth, and which leads at last to heaven and to God.'

"We shall miss him in this sanctuary and look no more upon him in yonder pew devotional in worship and listening attentively to the precious word as if indeed it were manna to his soul and a refreshing stream from the fountain of life. But he worshiped today in the temple not made with hands, with many of those with whom he was wont to worship in the church below. May we all imitate his example, emulate his virtues and at the last be counted worthy of a place with him in the kingdom of heaven."

Rev. Dr. Frank W. Gunsaulus, of the Central Church, at Chicago, used these words:

"The awful feature of this calamity is undisguised in the fact that it is a stroke against the enterprise of government, which is the noblest enterprise undertaken by man. It was a dagger thrust at the heart of civilization. It makes it all the more horrible and helps us to see the ghastly features of anarchy more truly when we reflect that the wound which it opened was through the now stilled heart of a man at once so loving, so loved and so lovable as the President. To so dishearten the whole of Christendom in its efforts toward public order, that wretch had to pierce through one of the fairest and sweetest lives the world has known. And it was this tender and noble man who believed so profoundly in the safety of free government. When anarchists were loud in 1893 the now silent orator eloquently said: 'With patriotism in our hearts and the flag of our country in our hands there is no danger of anarchy.' It is a frightful thing to believe that this confidence has been at all shaken, and it is the instant demand of our religion and our education that somehow they shall be made able to put patriotism into the hearts of the alien peoples and to get them to take hold sympathetically of our flag and love it, so that anarchy may be impossible. William McKinley's kindly heart and generous spirit, his enormous public services, resulting in countless benefits to the poor man, his unswerving devotion to the principle that no minority is without rights, his purity and power are permanent forces and realities which have been exalted upon an altar of martyrdom. The assassin supposed he could slay them from the high and heavenly place in which the citizens of the republic behold them. They will organize into a knightly personality and William McKinley will be the slayer of anarchy in America. From this time forward, whatever makes for anarchy must hide its treacherous face away from the light of him whom we loved. Slanderous lies as to the motives and character of those whom the nation has trusted with the reins of government, the vulgarity of newly acquired wealth which seems often to flaunt itself in the face of human need, the wild ravings of men who have no idea of loyalty to government and law, the thoughtless debate of theologians who have forgotten the simple dictates of Christian religion and the Godless enemies of public justice, all writhe away like serpents smitten with intolerable light as we think of the awful price we have paid and ever must pay if we fail to do our duty in upholding the flag and making it a symbol as sacred and as just as the cross of Christ. William McKinley has entered into the Holy of Holies bearing out sins. Let us awake to newness of life."

At St. Patrick's Cathedral in New York Archbishop Corrigan was too much moved to deliver the sermon, but throughout the sermon by Father Lavelle he knelt in prayer. Father Lavelle devoted his entire sermon to the life of President McKinley, and his words received the closest attention. He first read the open letter of the Archbishop to the clergy in his diocese asking for prayers for the late President, praising the latter's virtues and condemning anarchy.

"These words of our Archbishop," he added, "express as complete as words can the sentiment of the American people in general and the Catholics as well on this day of national sorrow. I say as well as words can, because on occasions of this kind the very best words seem hollow and meaningless compared with the depth and vast significance that stirs the heart of the nation, William McKinley was one whose name, even if misfortune had not overtaken him, would have gone down to posterity as one of the greatest Presidents of the United States. This is conceded by all, those who opposed him politically as well. He was really the idol of the nation. We all voted for him either directly or indirectly. If we voted for his opponent we did so for the principle, not for the man, as no one had a better character than William McKinley.

"He was a statesman who has left an indelible impression upon the history of this country and of the world, and before he was President the name of William McKinley was better known outside of the United States and throughout the world than any other American. He was a man of large faith in God and of deep religious sense. He was devoid of bigotry. During two summers spent away from Washington he spent his vacation at Lake Champlain, in the immediate vicinity of the Catholic Summer School, and the courtesy and kindliness he showed was such as to bring him nearer to the hearts of all people there and make him seem as if he was one of them.

" 'Justice will be done.' That was the principal guiding star of his life; the aim and object that spurred him on to his duty. Well does he deserve a nation's tears and gratitude. Does it not seem strange that a life so noble, a life without stain, at which the voice of calumny was never once lifted, should find an enemy capable of destroying the vital spark?"

Father Lavelle then referred to anarchism and to the writings of Pope Leo XIII on the subject. At this time Archbishop Corrigan showed his deep emotion and kept his handkerchief pressed to his eyes for some time. In speaking of anarchists the Rev. Mr. Lavelle said:

"These misguided creatures sometimes pretend to find a root of their false doctrines in the Scriptures themselves. Anarchy is as impossible as that five is equal to two. We trace the beginning of this inequality in God Himself. In our family, where the father and mother must be the head, this man, the anarchist, gets over the difficulty by destroying the family. If we wish to prevent a renewal of the calamity which we mourn to-day it is only through stronger faith in God. That is the bulwark of society and of this nation. You have noticed in the morning papers that the new President has issued a proclamation, asking the people to assemble in their places of worship on next Thursday and pray for our illustrious dead. In accordance with that proclamation our reverend Archbishop has set aside that day for services in this diocese. A special mass will be held in the Cathedral at 10 o'clock, and I beg all of you who can to come and pray with your hearts for this noble, true man, whom we have lost.

"May we come to that service with the thought that the holy sacrifice may go up to God, asking for new strength for our people and for the unblemished hero who has gone—asking for the new President strength, health and God's spirit, so that they may aid him in the proper discharge of his duties, and that never again in our history may we find that the head of our nation has been laid low by anarchy, jealousy or any other passion."

Time and again through the service, when the speaker's words touched upon the beauties of President McKinley's life, the Archbishop was seen to bow his head in tears, while great sobs choked his frame.

One of the notable incidents of the day was Rev. F. D. Powers' sermon at the Vermont Avenue Christian church in Washington. He it was who conducted the funeral services over the body of President Garfield, in the rotunda of the capitol, twenty years ago. He chose as his text the words of Christ to Peter in the garden of Gethsemane: "The cup which my Father gave me, shall I not drink it?" He said in part:

"Our beloved Christian President, in the terrible moment when the blow was struck, said: 'Do him no harm; he does not know what he is doing.' How true and wise and just and Christlike! And when he resigned himself to the faithful surgeons with that faith and majestic courage and magnificent simplicity that marked his character of life throughout, he said: 'Our Father who art in heaven, hallowed be Thy name; Thy kingdom come; Thy will be done,' and passed into unconsciousness with those last words on his lips. Hear him, as all the glory of this world fades above his vision and the gates of the unseen are swinging wide, when he breathed the hymn, 'Nearer, my God, to Thee, nearer to Thee.' Hear him as the last farewell is taken: 'It is God's way. His will be done.' How he speaks to the nation! How he speaks to the ages! God holds the cup, and the draught is wholesome and needful. God help us to be ready, as he was! Death is a friend of ours, and we must be ever ready to entertain him. God make us strong in Him who said: 'I am the resurrection and the life.' "

Historic Trinity church, in New York, was crowded with worshippers. Rev. Morgan Dix, the pastor, is a son of that stern old Governor John A. Dix, who in an earlier day sounded the note of a vigorous policy: "If any man hauls down the American flag, shoot him on the spot."

Dr. Dix, before a congregation that filled every available seat and overflowed in the aisles, delivered a sermon that was a eulogy of the virtues and statesmanship of the late President, William McKinley. After denouncing the crime Dr. Dix severely arraigned anarchy as a danger which would destroy modern civilization, and recommended that action be taken to suppress it. In the liturgical part of the service which preceded the sermon the President's favorite hymn, "Lead, Kindly Light," was sung. Dr. Dix spoke in part as follows:

"Men and brethren, eye to eye, hand to hand, heart to heart, we face each other now crying, 'Woe is me!' Woe for the common grief, woe worth the day and the tidings which it brings of destruction, desolation, death and violence lording it over us all! We are one in our distress at the last calamity and national affliction, in horror at an unspeakable crime. And so suddenly has the blow been dealt that there has been no time to search for the words which one might wish to speak. Two things surely are filling our thoughts today. We are looking at the man; we are looking at the crime. As for the man, his warmest friends, his greatest admirers, could have asked for him no more brilliant apotheosis. Estimates have varied of him, his ability, his work. But millions have been praying as men seldom pray that his life might be precious in the sight of God; and far beyond our borders, and widely through foreign lands, others innumerable, our brethren in a common humanity, have been on their knees pleading for his life. This tells the story of his character, his acts, his greatness; the general consent of the wide world, from which there can be no appeal.

"Our President was a great man in the highest sense in which that adjective can be applied. I am not speaking as a publicist, nor analyzing a political career; there is room for difference of judgment there; but there are other matters upon which we are all agreed. What is it to find in the highest place among us a man devout and faithful in his Christian profession, modest, calm, capable; a pattern of the domestic virtues, an example of right living? Has not the public, the great American nation, taken in the beauty first of that good, honest, loyal life? Is it not for this that the man has been beloved and mourned throughout our families and our homes?

What makes the Christian gentleman to begin with but simplicity and sincerity of life, courteous manners, dislike of pride and ostentation, abhorrence of display and vulgar show? So have we thought first of this man, and then we have followed his life through its varied phases. We have seen the quiet student, the soldier, the legislator, the executive officer; and, looking on, our admiration has grown more and more. We have seen him chosen by a vast popular movement to be the chief magistrate of the nation; we have scanned his conduct and acts during four years, among the most critical in the nation's history, and as the result of such scrutiny in the broadest light that could be thrown upon his path, and under the severest criticism to which a public man can be subjected, we have seen him re-elected to his great office by a larger vote than ever amid the acclamation of the people and to the confusion of his adversaries.

"All this we have seen. And then we have said: 'In this system of ours we do not ask for a man who shall make and control, but for a man who shall wisely guide, oversee, direct; a man who catches the spirit of the age, who knows the signs of the times, who interprets movements, and in his sound judgment shapes their course.' Looking at the last four years, more full of vital issues to the nation than any since the days of Abraham Lincoln, we have seen wonderful things. A nation passing on from small to great, from narrow places to broad, the horizon enlarging all the while, the nation attaining its majority, the world looking on with amazement, great questions put and answered well, great principles settled, great deeds done for freedom and clarifying of evil, and instruction in sound views of government; one great, grand, forward, upward movement, dazzling the eyes and charming the senses and kindling hope. And at the head of all this a man—not as if he were the author of these things, but certainly the wise, prudent, earnest leader; such a leader as Providence, we believe, must have raised for that particular work and inclined us to put in that position. That was the man.

"And up to Friday, September 6, that was the scene presented by our happy and highly favored land—a land blessed and contented, at peace and secure; never before so prosperous, never yet so honored abroad, never yet so hopeful, so confident; marching on its splendid path to greater things. And always at the head that good citizen, that earnest patriot, that wise head, that warm, affectionate heart, that friendly, fearless instance of the best that our American civilization has yet brought forth to help and cheer; trusted by a great people; strong, able, healthful, with his friends about him and the light of coming years in front. That was the fate of the people, and that was their will, and according to all ideas the will of the people is the law of the land, and he who gainsays is the enemy of the sovereign people. So stood matters a week ago last Friday.

"And now what shall we say?

"The crime; what was it? That high treason against the sovereign people of these United States? Let us compare crime with crime, and we shall see in this the worst of all we have ever known, the worst, the most outrageous ever committed in this land."

After reviewing the assassination of Garfield and Lincoln, Dr. Dix continued:

"But there was worse to come. And it has come. Something else; something new among us; not new elsewhere, alas! but new in this land supposed to be a land of freemen, the refuge for the oppressed, the home of the higher and better civilization. Right in the path on which the great nation is advancing stands the most horrid spectre by which social order has yet been confronted. A shadow has fallen on the road, blacker than any shadow of death. Be the individual who he may that happens to represent this new foe, he is of very little consequence compared with the motive which inspired his act. This spectre to-day announced as its aim and end the total destruction of modern civilization, the overthrow of all law, of all governments, of restraint of any kind on the private individual will. And the fatal blow of Friday, September 6, was dealt at the Chief Magistrate of the United States by a believer in that system and in exact accordance with its well-known principles.

"And that lends the real horror to the act and gives its double horror to the crime. It is not a crime like other crimes; it is not one with which we are familiar. And our hearts sink at the thought that we are now at length face to face with this infernal propaganda, and have felt in the merciless butchery of our great and good President the first taste of more to come, unless God grants the wisdom and teaches the way to defend our lives.

"Next to the anguish of the hour which has made strong men weep like children and melted hearts at the cruel desolation of a pure and loving home comes the dread engendered of a doubt as to the will and power of the nation to save its own life; whether there is force enough among us to rise and lay strong hold on this monster now distinctly revealed and upon us, in the murderous attack on the noblest and best in the land. Already we are beginning to hear it said that the people are rallying from the blow; that the first alarm is over; that all are recovering courage; that finance will soon flow again in its usual channels; that we shall go forward once more in the pursuit of arts and the ordinary vocations of the time. Yes, all this is well, but will the nation fail to act as a great nation should, to deal as it ought to do with the most deadly foe that it has or ever can have? For if this foe prevails, the nation, the state, the law, the government will disappear forever and ever. Are we to forget what has thrown us into this present mourning and these tears? Are we to lapse into a fatal apathy, and let the preaching of murder and inciting to murder and the applauding of murder go on as before? Are the laws still to protect the very persons who hate and detest them and are banded together for the overthrow of society? It seems to me that the most solemn issue of the hour is as to what we have to do who remain—whether we are equal to the occasion. Are we now to fall back before this enemy, the last and most dangerous we have ever encountered or ever shall, and let things drift from bad to worse, in new instances of a passion which spares not one life that stands in its way?

"There is a great deal to be said of the national sins which have led to such national judgments as we have felt and are feeling now; of the falling away from religious standards, of the loss of faith, of growing luxury and sin, of the decline in morals and piety which invite the judgments of heaven; of the indifference to law, the loss of respect for authority, the habit of railing at and writing on public men and telling lies about them, such as that gross one heard not long ago that our President was a traitor and would fain overthrow our republican and democratic government—for these things there will be time to speak later, but to-day I cannot speak of more than these two—the man and the crime.

"And so leave we the beloved and honored President to his rest and his future glory; for certainly his name will shine magnificently among those of the greatest of the lives immortal—with those of Washington and Lincoln; great for the way in which he guided the country through a mighty crisis in its fortunes; great in his closing words; great in his constant thought for others; great in his submission to the will of God—greatest perhaps in that deathbed scene, so perfectly accordant with the precepts of the Gospel and the example of his Savior." (Here Dr. Dix became so affected that he sobbed audibly.)

The Rev. Dr. Dix made the announcement that on Thursday, the day of the funeral, a Litany service would be held at noon, and that another service would be held in the afternoon of the same day, when the offices of the dead would be read.

The foregoing expressions are given as expressing the general tone of the sermons delivered in all of the churches, from the stately cathedrals of the great cities, to the humble little frame or log buildings in remote communities.

CHAPTER XL.

CANTON'S FAREWELL TO McKINLEY.

William McKinley had come home for the last time.

At Buffalo, at Washington and throughout the hundreds of miles between, the nation had mourned the dead President. The city and state which gave him to the nation now knelt and wept for him. For a decade and more his life had been the greatest fact in their history. To say Ohio or Canton was to say McKinley.

Two weeks before he left them in the full tide of health and strength, followed by the cheers of his neighbors, who felt themselves honored in him, their President. And now he was brought back dead. He whose life was all of kindness and love had been stricken by the hand of an assassin. That thought added a bitter drop to the cup of woe which his city and state now drinks.

Canton had done its utmost a score of times in honor of William McKinley. The demonstration as he came home with the representatives of a sorrowing nation and of sympathizing peoples in his funeral train rolled them all up into one supreme testimonial.

Imagine the picture. The city robed in black. Places of business are closed and draped. Crepe from public buildings and on private houses where death has never entered. Arches of mourning span the street. Flags looped with crepe and great banners of black and white wave overhead. The business block which bears his name, the old law office where he worked, are wrapped in mourning. The multitude is silent in the streets with loops of crepe on arms and shoulders.

The courthouse, scene of his early struggles as a lawyer, has been transformed, as it were, into a huge funeral crypt, swathed in the garb of sorrow from sill to tower peak. Across the front, shining in letters of gold against the somber background, is inscribed President McKinley's last message to those he loved: "It is God's way; His will, not ours, be done."

There the stricken President's body lay all day guarded by soldiers of the state and nation, only one step from the tomb, while his old friends and neighbors, companions of his early struggles and his later triumphs, streamed by for one last look at his face.

For one night he rested under the cottage roof whence he went to the highest seat in the nation.

The scenes along the last stage of President McKinley's progress toward the grave duplicated those which accompanied his funeral train from Buffalo to Washington. Most of the journey from Washington to this city was by night. It made no difference to the people who sought the last chance to show their regard for the lamented President.

The funeral train slipped out of Washington at 8:20 o'clock, leaving an uncovered multitude behind. At Baltimore thousands were in waiting. The train stopped only long enough to change engines and then started northward.

All along the way railroad operations were suspended. Not a bell rang, not a whistle blew, not a wheel turned. It was as if the whole world knelt in the presence of the nation's dead.

Throughout the night the train passed between a constant line of camp fires through the valleys and among the hills of Pennsylvania. As the black draped engine approached the gathered people rose, and by the flickering of their camp fires they could be seen and heard standing with bared heads and singing "Nearer, My God, to Thee."

Gangs of miners came up from the shaft on dozens of hillsides, their lamps gleaming through the night as they stood caps in hand to show their regard for a statesman who was ever their friend.

Solitary track walkers turned aside and uncovered. That was the supreme evidence of reverential honor. When one man does that in the isolation and darkness of the night he does it because it expresses what is in his heart.

At Harrisburg 20,000 people remained in the street around the railroad station until long after midnight. Then the train plunged into the Juniata valley and commenced its long climb over the mountains. And still camp fires glowed beside the track and still voices were raised throughout the night in that old hymn which has become a nation's funeral chant.

Half the population of Johnstown, the first of the great steel manufacturing centers through which the train passed, was at the track and a company of local militia stood drawn up at attention. Four women with uplifted hands knelt on the station platform. From the smoke-covered city came the sound of the church bells tolling out the universal sorrow as the train slowed down that the people might better see the impressive spectacle within the observation car—the casket with its burden of flowers, the two grim, armed sentries on guard, "one at the head and the other at the foot."

Those in the Canton reception committee rode as if to the funeral of one their own kin. They had known William McKinley and worked with him in business and official and social life for years. They loved him as a brother, and as a brother they mourned his death.

Some of them gave way utterly to their emotions and wept like children. A notable example was Judge Isaac H. Taylor. He had served in Congress with Mr. McKinley when they represented adjoining districts. Away back in the '80s, when the Congressional map of Ohio was remade, the counties in which they lived were thrown into the same district. Both had hosts of friends. Both wanted to go back to Congress. The district was nearly evenly divided between them. If the contest for the nomination in the new district had gone to the point such political rivalries usually reach, both might have had to give way to a new man.

In that contingency Judge Taylor had the eye of the prophet and a breast full of admiration for his rival. He went to him and said:

"Major, I think I am as good a lawyer as you are, and I know that you are a better Congressman than I am. This district needs you in Washington and it can get along without me. If I can't get on the bench I can make a living practicing law. You must take this nomination. My friends will be for you."

That action by Judge Taylor, so much do great events hang upon seeming trivialities, sent Mr. McKinley back to Washington to continue his career in the public service, and mayhap it made him President of the United States. Judge Taylor may have been thinking of this today when the funeral cortege passed through the streets of Canton. More likely he was thinking of the qualities of the man for whom he had sacrificed his own ambitions. He wept bitterly, and, turning to his friends, said: "We have lost the best man I ever knew."

Through Tenth street and then to Cherry and Tuscarawas the solemn pageant moved between solid masses of people, banked from curb to store front, crowding the house tops and filling every window. Turning into Market street, the main thoroughfare of the city, the procession moved under great curtains of mourning, strung from building to building across the street every hundred feet.

The line moved to the music of "Nearer, My God, to Thee," played as a funeral march. Except for the gentle notes of the old hymn it moved through absolute silence. Every hat was off. Every head was reverently bent. In the intervals of the music one could hear the soft footfalls of the moving soldiers, so completely did silence envelop the scene.

The funeral march finally led through the public square, where Mr. McKinley had addressed his fellow citizens times almost without number on those issues and principles which made him President. Other times without number the people had gathered by thousands in that same square in his honor. To-day the old courthouse clock looked down upon the same spot and upon the same people as in other days, its hand stopped at fifteen minutes after two, the hour at which the President died, a silent reminder of God's way.

As the head of the procession reached the great square the military ranks swung about, forming solid fronts facing the approaching hearse. As it was driven to the curb the bearers stepped from the places alongside and again took up their burden. Before the eyes of the vast concourse filling the square the casket was tenderly raised and borne up the wide stone steps of the courthouse. The strains of "Nearer, My God, to Thee" were still sounding as the flag-draped coffin was taken to the main corridor of the building.

The interior of the corridor was a mass of black. There, as elsewhere, the people of Canton seemed to find much relief for their feelings by exhausting the possibilities of outward expressions of sorrow. From front to rear of the building inside there was not visible one square inch of bare wall. The vault of blackness typified the dark void in Canton's heart. Opposite the head of the casket upon a raised platform stood three chairs clothed in black, symbolizing the vacant places of the three martyred Presidents, Lincoln, Garfield and McKinley.

The President's casket was guarded, as always since he died, by picked men of the army and navy. An additional guard of honor was supplied in this instance by Canton Commandery Knights Templar, to which President McKinley belonged.

When word was given that all was ready for the last public farewell, President Roosevelt, followed by his Cabinet, stepped into the hall. He glanced down as he reached the casket, halted for a moment, and went on with set face. The members of the Cabinet followed him one by one.

The officers of the army and navy, headed by General Miles, General Otis and General Brooke, came next. Objection was made by some of the army officials to the bright light shed by the electric globes full in the face of the President, and a desire was expressed that it should be dimmed.

The chandelier was too high to reach, and a delay of fully ten minutes ensued while a hunt was made for a chair. The light at the base of the chandelier was then extinguished and other electric light globes on the chandelier turned off. The result was a decided advantage. The light, while being ample, was much softer and more in keeping with the occasion.

Four detachments of militia then marched into the hall and were drawn up in a line reaching from the entrance on the south to the bier. Another line stretched from the bier to the place where the hall diverged, and down each side hall were other lines. Strict orders were given to see that there was no delay in the crowd as it passed out of the building.

When everything was ready for the public to enter, Joseph Saxton, uncle of Mrs. McKinley, an aged man bowed deeply with the weight of years, entered from the east hall and passed up to the casket. He stood for fully two minutes gazing into the face of his distinguished kinsman. He then passed slowly down the hall, his head bowed low, his lips twitching convulsively.

A few final details were arranged and then the door was opened to the public. Two little girls were the first to approach the casket. Directly behind them was a tall powerful man with a red mustache. As he gazed into the casket he caught his breath in a quick sharp sob that was audible in every part of the hallway. He then gave way entirely, and, weeping bitterly, passed out.

For five hours the old friends and neighbors of the stricken chieftain marched by in two constant streams, fed by a river of men and women and children, which stretched away through the city for nearly a mile. These were no mere curiosity seekers, eager to see how a dead President looked. They were men and women who knew and loved him and children who planned in their youthful dreams to emulate him.

Tears came unbidden to wet the bier. Perhaps it was the great change that had come upon the countenance which moved them more than the sight of the familiar features. The signs of discoloration which appeared upon the brow and cheeks yesterday at the state ceremonial in the rotunda of the capital at Washington had deepened and the lips had become livid.

One of the first men in the line was an old farmer from the lower end of Stark County. He paused beside the casket and burst into tears. "His kindness and his counsel saved a boy of mine," the old man murmured half in apology to the guards as he tottered out of the building.

Old soldiers who had served with the "major," as they called him,

ABRAHAM LINCOLN.

JAMES A. GARFIELD.

stumped by with limping feet on wooden legs and on crutches. Poor men and poor women whom he had helped when they needed help, and without anybody being the wiser, dropped flowers on the pall. One old soldier broke through the line a second time for another look.

"I went to the war with him," the old man said, "and I would not have come back but for him. He saw that I wasn't forgotten in the hospital." The apology was enough to excuse the old man's breach of the rules in the eyes of the guard.

A little girl came along. She stopped long enough to press a kiss upon the glass above the dead face and then ran from the building with streaming eyes. One of the guards thought he saw her drop something and looked. He found it hidden away among the costly wreaths and clusters of roses and immortelles and almost priceless orchids. It was a little cluster of common, late blooming garden flowers, and to it was tied with a piece of thread a note written in a cramped childish hand:

DEAR MR. M'KINLEY: I wish I could send you some prettier flowers, but these are all I have. I am sorry you got shot.
KATIE LEE.

That guard had a spark of poetry in his soul. He picked up the modest little bunch of flowers and tenderly laid it across a cluster of orchids.

"I thought I saw the President smile," he said when he told a comrade.

The line continued to form, to swing by, and to melt away until the sun went down. Its characteristics changed with each minute. Men who manage great business enterprises and men who make the politics of this state walked side by side with the miner, the factory hand, the farmer and the laborer. But a single dominant characteristic made them as one. Every face bore the mark of sorrow, and in most eyes were the traces of tears.

Late in the afternoon an aged man leaning upon two crutches, which he managed with difficulty, appeared at the door through which the people were making their exit. He asked the sentry to allow him to enter, and when the soldier refused, saying he had received orders to allow nobody through that door, the old man stood back the picture of woe. In a short time he again asked the young sentry in pleading tones to allow him entrance through the doorway, saying that in his feeble condition he was not able to stand in the line which at that time was extending fully a mile from the entrance.

"I fought in his regiment during the war," he said, "and I just want to lay this flag on his coffin and then keep it as a reminder of the time I saw him last."

"Take it in," said the sentry, the catch of a sob in his bronzed throat; and the veteran hobbled into the hall. When he got inside he had more trouble, and was compelled to explain his errand several times. Finally the line passing the coffin was stopped long enough to allow the old man to step to its side for a glance into the coffin and to lay his tiny flag on its glass front. Then he turned back with the crowd, hugging the now sanctified flag tightly beneath his coat.

At one time a group of schoolgirls approached the casket. There were six of them and they came three abreast. One in the forward row leaned over for a look, and, gently disengaging from the bosom of her dress a scarlet geranium, laid it gently on the top of the wreaths that rested there. The others followed her example, and although the sentries had orders to permit nobody to place anything upon the coffin or to touch the floral offerings that were already there the little tributes of the girls were allowed to remain.

All through the afternoon the crowd passed the catafalque approximately at the rate of 100 every minute, making in the five hours in which the body lay in state a total of 30,000 people, practically a number equal to the actual population of Canton. When the doors were closed at 6 o'clock the line, four abreast, stretched fully one mile from the courthouse, and people were still coming from the side streets to take their places in line.

Twilight had come as the guard and escort were formed to remove the casket to the McKinley cottage. The streets were still thronged. Amid silence that played upon the heart as the shades of night were drawn closer the casket was carried from the courthouse for the last journey of William McKinley to the little cottage, where the greatest fortune that can come to any man should come to him.

The Grand Army post of the city acted as escort. Most of these old soldiers had served in the war with him in the Twenty-third Ohio. The heaviness of personal grief was in their footsteps as they marched away.

There was no ceremony at the McKinley cottage. The casket was borne within and laid in the little front parlor from which the nation had called its chosen chief five years ago.

Mrs. McKinley was in her room when the body came. Her anguish broke out afresh on this reminder that all which had taken place there was at an end and that, worst of all, he who had wrapped her life in tenderness, who had been through many years more than husband, than father, in his care for her weakness, was now cold in death.

Friends hastened to her side and did the little which friends can do at such a time. All others were excluded. Guards were quickly thrown about the house. Darkness fell, and for the last time Mrs. McKinley was left alone with her dead.

The following day, city and state followed the mortal remains of their great son to the tomb. Other cities by their chiefs, other states by their governors, offered sympathy to their sister. All of the mournful pomp and circumstance which the devoted regard of his friends and people could throw around the occasion followed to the grave, and the life of William McKinley was history.

The funeral services began at 1:30 p. m. at the First Methodist Episcopal Church, of which the martyred President was a communicant and trustee. They were brief, by the expressed wish of the family.

Rev. O. R. Milligan, pastor of the First Presbyterian Church, in which President and Mrs. McKinley were married thirty years ago, made the opening prayer. Dr. John Hall of the Trinity Lutheran Church made the first scriptural reading and Dr. E. P. Herbruck of the Trinity Reformed Church the second. Dr. C. E. Manchester, pastor of the late President's church, delivered the only address. A quartet sang "Beautiful Isle of Some-where," and another quartet rendered Cardinal Newman's hymn, "Lead, Kindly Light."

An imposing procession, consisting of many of the G. A. R. posts in the state, the National Guard of Ohio, details of regulars from all branches of the service, fraternal, social and civic organizations and representatives of commercial bodies from all over the country, the governors of several states with their staffs, the House and Senate of the United States and the cabinet and President of the United States followed the remains to Westlawn Cemetery.

Strange as it may seem, the only house in all that sorrow-stricken city without a touch of mourning drapery was the old McKinley cottage. The blinds were drawn, but there was no outward token of the blow that had robbed it of its most precious possession. The flowers bloomed on the lawn as they did two weeks ago. There was not even a bow of crape upon the door when the stricken widow was carried through it into the darkened home by Abner McKinley and Dr. Rixey. Only the hitching post at the curb in front of the residence had been swathed in black by the citizens in order that it might conform to the general scheme of mourning decoration that had been adopted.

President Roosevelt, at the home of Mrs. William Harter, kept himself from all visitors except intimate personal friends all day. He felt keenly the position into which he had been thrust by fate in the form of an assassin's bullet. He was much pained by the unseemly cheering which greeted the funeral train at Washington.

The President was closely guarded at night. He did not like it, but he was forced to submit. Detachments of state militia were posted at the Harter home, and sentries paced under the windows on all sides of the house. They also kept guard at the McKinley cottage, where the dead President lay.

In that cottage, as the hour of midnight approached, one of the most dramatic scenes of the whole sad event transpired. Mrs. McKinley had asked to be taken for a moment to the room where her dead husband lay. She wished, for the moment, that every one, even the guards, be removed. She was for the time entirely calm, and she longed for just one precious season of silent communion at the side of him who had been her life, her love, for more than thirty years.

So they led her to the room where lights subdued revealed but dimly the details of those decorations about the bier. They watched her, for the frail body had suffered so keenly, the hold on life seemed so light, that they dare not leave her utterly. But in the room she was alone. They had placed a chair near the casket, and there she sat, looking from dry, puzzled eyes at the square, black bulk which held the form of her girlhood's lover. The thin, white hands were clasped in her lap, the face—pain-refined from twenty years of trial—was bent slightly forward, and she seemed questioning that mighty fact.

She was entirely calm, and her attendants, keeping vigil from the darkened hall, felt the grip of her mighty, unspoken sorrow, as she sought in the night for a touch of that vanished hand, for a glimpse of a day that was dead.

CHAPTER XLI.

McKINLEY LAID AT REST.

The mortal remains of President McKinley are at rest. For six days and through hundreds of miles a sorrowing nation has followed his bier. Now the last look has been taken, the last farewells have been said. The last salute to a dead President has echoed above his head.

His body was laid for the moment in the little cemetery of Canton, guarded by soldiers of the flag he loved so well, until it shall be placed beside the mother and other dear ones who departed before him. There the people who loved and honored him will raise a monument to his name and make of his grave a shrine.

But his highest monument must ever remain in the hearts of his countrymen. A mourning people raises its head from the dust and goes forward encouraged and guided by the life he lived.

Gray and somber dawned the morning of the entombment. There was a chill in the air indicating that nature was in full harmony with the multitudes who were here to see. It was just twenty years to the day since the death of James A. Garfield, the second martyred President, and many remembered that fact and were still further depressed.

Before the sun had been able to pierce its way through the clouds, infantry, cavalry and artillery were moving in the direction of the McKinley home. Long before 9 o'clock five thousand members of the Ohio National Guard were in position, some assisting in guarding the streets, others ready to take part in the funeral procession. Regulars were there in great numbers. Sailors and marines were out. Civic bodies were formed.

Entrance to the church was by card. Although the public knew this, all hoped against hope that by some chance they could force their way into the edifice. Hours before the doors were opened long lines were formed by the holders of cards, and back of them were thousands who were willing to stand in the chill air on a single chance that enough room might be spared for them to squeeze in.

The same eight stalwart soldiers and marines who had carried the coffin when it had been previously moved, shouldered it and bore it down the steps, down the path through the yard, with its beautiful lawn and flower-beds gay with the blossoms of the late summer, out to the waiting hearse. The casket was draped in the flag that William McKinley had fought to maintain as that of an undivided country. About the coffin flowers were massed in such quantities as to fill the hearse.

A signal was given and the forward move began. Thayer's military band led the way behind the police guard. As the hearse moved the familiar strains of "Nearer, My God, to Thee" were sounded. The music was soft and sweet, barely loud enough to be heard a block away.

The strains of "Lead, Kindly Light" announced the approach to the church, and a hush fell upon the struggling throng. The cavalry escort slowly swung into Tuscarawas street at the head of the funeral line, with the bugles silent and all orders given by signs. The cavalrymen formed three sides of a hollow square opposite the church doors, brought their swords to the position of "present arms" and sat like statues.

The great organ inside the church was waked by the first faint ripple of music from the street, which quivered through the black-draped doors, and commenced to breathe softly through the auditorium the solemn notes of Beethoven's funeral march.

Four girls rose and joined their voices to the beautiful melody of the beautiful song, "Beautiful Isle of Somewhere." It was like an answer to complaining hearts as it ran:

> Somewhere the sun is shining;
>> Somewhere the song birds dwell;
> Hush, then, thy sad repining;
>> God lives and all is well.

> Somewhere, somewhere,
>> Beautiful Isle of Somewhere;
> Land of the true, where we live anew;
>> Beautiful Isle of Somewhere.

> Somewhere the load is lifted,
>> Close by an open gate;
> Somewhere the clouds are rifted;
>> Somewhere the angels wait.

Somewhere, somewhere,
Beautiful Isle of Somewhere,
Land of the true, where we live anew;
Beautiful Isle of Somewhere.

Rev. O. B. Milligan, pastor of the First Presbyterian Church, led in prayer. In these words he asked for Divine light on a way out of the shadow cast upon the nation, and especially for heavenly assistance for Mrs. McKinley in her great sorrow.

Everybody in the church joined in the Lord's prayer, Rev. Dr. John A. Hall, pastor of Trinity Lutheran Church, then read from the scriptures the Nineteenth Psalm, to which President McKinley was accustomed to turn for comfort when his heart was heavy. Rev. E. P. Herbruck, pastor of Trinity Reformed Church, also read from the scriptures, selecting the fifteenth chapter of the first epistle to the Corinthians, verses 41 to 58.

The quartet again arose and sang Cardinal Newman's grand hymn, "Lead, Kindly Light," the beautiful words floating through all the church.

Rev. Dr. C. E. Manchester, pastor of the First Methodist Episcopal Church of Canton, then delivered the funeral sermon.

"Our President is dead. The silver cord is loosed, the golden bowl is broken, the pitcher is broken at the fountain, the wheel broken at the cistern, the mourners go about the streets.

"One voice is heard, a wail of sorrow from all the land, for the beauty of Israel is slain upon the high places. How are the mighty fallen! I am distressed for thee, my brother. Very pleasant hast thou been unto me. Our President is dead.

"We can hardly believe it. We had hoped and prayed and it seemed that our hopes were to be realized and our prayers answered when the emotion of joy was changed to one of grave apprehension. Still we waited, for we said, 'It may be that God will be gracious and merciful unto us.' It seemed to us that it must be His will to spare the life of one so well beloved and so much needed.

"Thus, alternating between hope and fear, the weary hours passed on. Then came the tidings of defeated sciences, of the failure of love and prayer to hold its object to the earth. We seemed to hear the faintly muttered words: 'Good-by all, good-by. It's God's way. His will be done,' and then, 'Nearer, My God, to Thee.'

"So, nestling nearer to his God, he passed out into unconsciousness, skirted the dark shores of the sea of death for a time and then passed on to be at rest. His great heart had ceased to beat. Our hearts are heavy with sorrow.

> "A voice is heard on earth of kinsfolk weeping
>   The loss of one they love;
> But he has gone where the redeemed are keeping
>   A festival above.
>
> "The mourners throng the ways and from the steeple
>   The funeral bells toll slow;
> But on the golden streets the holy people
>   Are passing to and fro.
>
> "And saying as they meet, 'Rejoice.
>   Another,
>   Long waited for is come.
> The Savior's heart is glad, a younger
>   Brother
> Has reached the Father's home.'"

"The cause of this universal mourning is to be found in the man himself. The inspired penman's picture of Jonathan, likening him unto the 'Beauty of Israel,' could not be more appropriately employed than in chanting the lament of our fallen chieftain. It does no violence to human speech, nor is it fulsome eulogy, to speak thus of him, for who that has seen his stately bearing, his grace and manliness of demeanor, his kindliness of aspect, but gives assent to this description of him.

"It was characteristic of our beloved President that men met him only to love him. They might indeed differ with him, but in the presence of such dignity of character and grace of manner none could fail to love the man. The people confided in him, believed in him. It was said of Lincoln that probably no man since the days of Washington was ever so deeply imbedded and enshrined in the hearts of the people, but it is true of McKinley in a larger sense. Industrial and social conditions are such that he was, even more than his predecessors, the friend of the whole people.

"A touching scene was enacted in this church last Sunday night. The services had closed. The worshipers were gone to their homes. Only a few lingered to discuss the sad event that brings us together to-day. Three men in working garb, of a foreign race and unfamiliar tongue, entered the room. They approached the altar, kneeling before it and before his picture.

Their lips moved as if in prayer, while tears furrowed their cheeks. They may have been thinking of their own King Humbert and of his untimely death. Their emotion was eloquent, eloquent beyond speech, and it bore testimony to their appreciation of manly friendship and of honest worth.

"It is a glorious thing to be able to say in this presence, with our illustrious dead before us, that he never betrayed the confidence of his countrymen. Not for personal gain or pre-eminence would he mar the beauty of his soul. He kept it clean and white before God and man, and his hands were unsullied by bribes. 'His eyes looked right on, and his eyelids looked straight before him.'

"He was sincere, plain and honest, just, benevolent and kind. He never disappointed those who believed in him, but measured up to every duty, and met every responsibility in life grandly and unflinchingly.

"Not only was our President brave, heroic and honest; he was as gallant a knight as ever rode the lists for his lady love in the days when knighthood was in flower. It is but a few weeks since the nation looked on with tear-dimmed eyes as it saw with what tender conjugal devotion he sat at the bed-side of his beloved wife, when all feared that a fatal illness was upon her. No public clamor that he might show himself to the populace, no demand of a social function, was sufficient to draw the lover from the bedside of his wife. He watched and waited while we all prayed—and she lived.

"This sweet and tender story all the world knows, and the world knows that his whole life had run in this one groove of love. It was a strong arm that she leaned upon, and it never failed her. Her smile was more to him than the plaudits of the multitude, and for her greeting his acknowledgments of them must wait. After receiving the fatal wound his first thought was that the terrible news might be broken gently to her.

"May God in this deep hour of sorrow comfort her. May His grace be greater than her anguish. May the widow's God be her God.

"Another beauty in the character of our President that was a chaplet of grace about his neck was that he was a Christian. In the broadest, noblest sense of the word that was true. His confidence in God was strong and unwavering. It held him steady in many a storm where others were driven before the wind and tossed. He believed in the fatherhood of God and in His sovereignty.

"His faith in the gospel of Christ was deep and abiding. He had no patience with any other theme of pulpit discourse. 'Christ and Him crucified' was to his mind the only panacea for the world's disorders. He believed it to be the supreme duty of the Christian minister to preach the word. He said 'We do not look for great business men to enter the pulpit, but for great preachers.'

"It is well known that his godly mother had hoped for him that he would become a minister of the gospel and that she believed it to be the highest vocation in life. It was not, however, his mother's faith that made him a Christian. He had gained in early life a personal knowledge of Jesus which guided him in the performance of greater duties and vaster than have been the lot of any other American President. He said at one time, while bearing heavy burdens, that he could not discharge the daily duties of his life but for the fact that he had faith in God.

"William McKinley believed in prayer, in the beauty of it, in the potency of it. Its language was not unfamiliar to him, and his public addresses not infrequently evinced the fact. It was perfectly consistent with his lifelong convictions and his personal experiences that he should say at the first critical moment after the assassination approached, 'Thy kingdom come; Thy will be done.' He lived grandly; it was fitting that he should die grandly. And now that the majesty of death has touched and calmed him, we find that in his supreme moment he was still a conqueror.

"My friends and countrymen, with what language shall I attempt to give expression to the deep horror of our souls as I speak of the cause of his death? When we consider the magnitude of the crime that has plunged the country and the world into unutterable grief, we are not surprised that one nationality after another has hastened to repudiate the dreadful act.

"This gentle spirit, who hated no one, to whom every man was a brother, was suddenly smitten by the cruel hand of an assassin, and that, too, while in the very act of extending a kind and generous greeting to one who approached him under the sacred guise of friendship. Could the assailant have realized how awful was the act he was about to perform, how utterly heartless the deed, methinks he would have stayed his hand at the very threshold of it.

"In all the coming years men will seek in vain to fathom the enormity of that crime. Had this man who fell been a despot, a tyrant, an oppressor, an insane frenzy to rid the world of him might have sought excuse; but it was the people's friend who fell when William McKinley received the fatal wound.

"Himself a son of toil, his sympathies were with the toiler. No one who has seen the matchless grace and perfect ease with which he greeted such can ever doubt that his heart was in his open hand. Every heart throb was for his countrymen.

"That his life should be sacrificed at such a time, just when there was abundant peace, when all the Americans were rejoicing together, is one of the inscrutable mysteries of Providence. Like many others, it must be left for future revelations to explain.

"In the midst of our sorrow we have much to console us. He lived to see his nation greater than ever before. All sectional lines are blotted out. There is no South, no North, no East, no West. Washington saw the beginning of our national life. Lincoln passed through the night of our history and saw the dawn. McKinley beheld his country in the splendor of its noon. Truly, he died in the fullness of his fame.

"With Paul he could say, and with equal truthfulness, 'I am now ready to be offered.' The work assigned him had been well done. The nation was at peace. We had fairly entered upon an era of unparalleled prosperity. Our revenues were generous. Our standing among the nations was secure. Our President was safely enshrined in the affections of a united people.

"It was not at him that the fatal shot was fired, but at the very life of the government. His offering was vicarious. It was blood poured upon the altar of human liberty. In view of these things we are not surprised to hear from one who was present when this great soul passed away that he never before saw a death so peaceful, or a dying man so crowned with grandeur.

"Let us turn now to a brief consideration of some of the lessons that we are to learn from this sad event. The first one that will occur to us all is the old, old lesson that 'in the midst of life we are in death.' 'Man goeth forth to his work and to his labor until the evening.' 'He fleeth as it were a shadow and never continueth in one stay.'

"Our President went forth in the fullness of his strength, in his manly beauty, and was suddenly smitten by the hand that brought death with it. None of us can tell what a day may bring forth. Let us therefore remember that 'no man liveth to himself and none of us dieth to himself.' 'May each day's close see each day's duty done.'

"Another great lesson that we should heed is the vanity of mere earthly greatness. In the presence of the Dread Messenger how small are all the trappings of wealth and distinctions of rank and power. I beseech you, seek Him who said, 'I am the resurrection and the life; he that believeth in Me, though he were dead, yet shall he live; and whosoever liveth and believeth in Me shall never die.' There is but one Savior for the sinsick and the weary. I entreat you, find Him, as our brother found Him.

"But our last words must be spoken. Little more than four years ago we bade him good-by as he went to assume the great responsibilities to which the nation had called him. His last words as he left us were:

"'Nothing could give me greater pleasure than this farewell greeting—this evidence of your friendship and sympathy, your good will, and I am sure the prayers of all the people with whom I have lived so long and whose confidence and esteem are dearer to me than any other earthly honors.

"'To all of us the future is as a sealed book, but if I can, by official act or administration or utterance, in any degree add to the prosperity and unity of our beloved country, and the advancement and well-being of our splendid citizenship, I will devote the best and most unselfish efforts of my life to that end. With this thought uppermost in my mind, I reluctantly take leave of my friends and neighbors, cherishing in my heart the sweetest memories and thoughts of my old home—my home now—and I trust my home hereafter so long as I shall live.'

"We hoped, with him, that when his work was done, freed from the burdens of his great office, crowned with the affections of a happy people, he might be permitted to close his earthly life in the home he loved. He has indeed returned to us, but how? Borne to the strains of 'Nearer, My God, to Thee,' and placed where he first began life's struggle, that the people might look and weep over so sad a home-coming.

"But it was a triumphal march. How vast the procession. The nation rose, stood with uncovered head. The people of the land are chief mourners. The nations of the earth weep with them. But, oh, what a victory! I do not ask you in the heat of public address, but in the calm moments of mature reflection, what other man ever had such high honors bestowed upon him and by so many people? What pageant has equaled this that we look upon to-night?

"We gave him to the nation but a little more than four years ago. He went out with the light of the morning upon his brow, but with his task set, and the purpose to complete it. We take him back a mighty conqueror.

> "'The churchyard where his children rest,
> The quiet spot that suits him best;
> There shall his grave be made,
> And there his bones be laid.
> And there his countrymen shall come,
> With memory proud, with pity dumb,
> And strangers far and near,

For many and many a year,
For many and many an age,
While history on her ample page
The virtues shall enroll
Of that paternal soul.' "

Venerable Bishop I. W. Joyce of Minneapolis then led in brief prayer. He had been conducting the East Ohio Methodist Episcopal conference at New Philadelphia when the President died. The conference adjourned, and Bishop Joyce and his cabinet have been ever since at the disposal of the friends of the President. He especially remembered President Roosevelt in his petition this afternoon.

The choir then sang "Nearer, My God, to Thee," at first softly, and then rising into the passionate declaration, "Still all my song shall be." It was as if the whole nation were being brought closer to the great white throne by the sacrifice of their President's life.

Rev. Father Edward J. Vattmann of Chicago pronounced the benediction. He is chaplain of the United States Army at Fort Sheridan.

It was after 3 o'clock when the silent and anxious throngs outside the church saw the solemn pageant reappear through the church doors. A more impressive sight than the cortege of the President from the church to the cemetery has seldom been witnessed in this country. Nominally it was a private funeral. Actually it was a national demonstration. More than 12,000 marching men were in line. About 6,000 were the citizen soldiery of Ohio. The others were old soldiers and members of civic and fraternal organizations from all quarters of the state.

The head of the cortege arrived at Westlawn Cemetery at 3:30 o'clock. The roadway from the gate to the receiving vault was carpeted with flowers. Geraniums, carnations, sweet peas and roses had been strewn in great profusion. The old soldiers who had marched the weary march to honor their old comrade a last time could not forego the chance to take away a fragrant souvenir of his earthly end. One by one they stooped to gather a flower, and when they had passed the roadway it was almost bare.

The funeral car reached the cemetery gates at 4 o'clock. From the hilltop the President's salute of twenty-one guns, fired at intervals of one minute, announced its coming. The military guards came to a "present" with a snap as the funeral car approached for the last scene in the life and death of William McKinley—a scene beautiful and impressive as his life had been.

After the arrival of the casket there was a moment's pause as Colonel Bingham looked to see that all was in readiness. He then looked toward Bishop Joyce, who read the burial service of the Methodist church, slowly but in a voice that could be heard distinctly by all who were grouped about the vault. Instantly from the eight buglers rang out the notes of the soldier's last call, "taps."

With bared heads the President and members of the cabinet, who were followed by the officers of the army and navy, stood on each side of the walk, the lines reaching just to the edge of the roadway. Within a minute after the formation of the lines, the funeral car came up to the walk. The casket was gently lifted from the hearse, and borne to the floor of the vault, where it was rested upon the catafalque.

The last of the procession passed the bier at 5:45 o'clock, and then orders were given by Captain Riddle that the cemetery be cleared. This was quickly done, and the President was left in the care of his guard of honor. The first sentry to be posted in a tour of guard duty before the doorway was Private Otto White of Company C, Fourteenth Infantry, whose home is in Genoa, Ohio.

The vault gates closed with a hollow clang as the soldiers took up the weary round of sentry duty in the lonely cemetery. Two miles away, in the cottage so lately the home of a President, a heart-broken widow wrestled with her grief.

And the funeral of William McKinley was over.

CHAPTER XLII.

NATION OBSERVES BURIAL DAY.

When King David lay dead, at the threshold of Judah's mighty era, the Bible tells us "There was sorrow in the cities."

That, better than any other language that could be employed, describes the state of affairs in the United States of America when the body of the dead President lay in state in the town which had been his home on the day of his burial. Every city in the land chose its own methods of expressing the grief that was felt, but all united, at the selfsame hour, to express in the several ways the grief that was felt for the nation's bereavement.

In Canton, of course, the expression of sorrow was profound. Nothing else occupied the attention or the time of any one within the gates of the city but that one great, overpowering subject.

In Washington all the many public offices of the government were closed, and the army of employes gave the day to sorrowing for the dead. There were services in nearly all of the churches. Theaters were closed. No places of amusement admitted frequenters. The storm-drenched draperies of woe that had been spread so lavishly on the day the remains of the President arrived from Buffalo, gave a drearier aspect to the silent and sorrowing city. There was little travel. Street cars nearly vacant hummed unchecked through the streets. Galleries and points usually sought by visitors were left quite abandoned. Even the great Washington Monument had fewer visitors than on any day since President Garfield lay in state in the White House.

In Chicago there were services in the Auditorium, presided over by some of the foremost citizens, and addressed by orators of note throughout the nation. A multitude of social organizations joined in a monster parade. It was a general holiday, and workmen laid down the tools of their craft, and postponed activity and wage-earning till the body of the dead should be at rest. Naval veterans from the war with Spain formed a compact phalanx and marched for the last time in honor of him who had been their chief.

In New Orleans a general holiday also was decreed, and schools were closed; shops were deserted; the activity of the city was still. It has been described as nearly approaching those distressful days when the fear of the plague had laid a silencing hand on the industries of the town. There was no fear in the present case. But the pall of a sorrow was great enough to palsy all movement. President McKinley had endeared himself to the people of the South as no other President had done since the civil war. His trip across the continent last May was of the greatest benefit to his fame and popularity in the South. It was realized that here was a man who was President of the whole United States, and that he held those in that section of the country as close to his heart and his hope as the people of any other section.

In San Francisco a service was held in the City Hall, addressed by a number of the prominent citizens. It was here that Mrs. McKinley was taken ill when the Presidential party was on its journey across the country; and it was here that President McKinley gave that great evidence of his devotion to his wife. It disarranged the plans of the people who had the trip in charge, and of the managers of the fair at which he was to have appeared. But above and beyond all desire for profit was their recognition of the generous and noble qualities of the man. And they paid their heartfelt tribute to the departed.

In Montreal, Canada, the provincial synod of the Anglican Church held a memorial service in Christ Church cathedral in honor of the memory of President McKinley. The Duke of York, who was in the city at the time, attended the service, and gave every evidence of that grief which he had at other times expressed. It had been the intention of the city authorities of Montreal to give a series of fetes in honor of the Duke and the Duchess, as has been the custom in most of the cities which they have visited in the course of their tour about the world, forming the better acquaintance of the subjects of the English King. But these plans were abandoned, although a large sum of money had already been expended. Neither the Duke nor his wife wished to proceed with the festivities.

London was a city of sorrow. The recent death of the Queen had called forth expressions of sorrow from President McKinley and the people of the United States which had touched a very tender chord in the nature of the Englishmen. And they were grieved beyond expression at the disaster that had befallen the Republic. They devoted the day to a special service in Westminster Abbey, a rare performance indeed. Portraits of President McKinley were displayed in all the shop windows, and were freely sold on the streets. All the papers of the British capital printed expressions

PRESIDENT LINCOLN AND HIS CABINET.

of sorrow and of appreciation of the good qualities of the man who had passed away, and all expressed the hope that the nation would be comforted in its grief. One of the most touching features of their publications was the tone of sympathy for Mrs. McKinley. There was a pathos about these words which keenly recalled the late bereavement of the nation of Victoria.

Funeral services were held in far-away Manila. All the government offices were closed, and the buildings were draped in black. There was a peculiar sadness in the crowds that passed up and down the streets. Most business houses were closed for half the day, some for the entire day. Among the expressions of sorrow sent from Manila was one from Emilio Aguinaldo. He declared President McKinley a noble enemy, and a valued friend, and for the good of all the people under the flag of the Republic he could not but look on the death of such a man, particularly in such a manner, as an unparalleled calamity. He gave utterance to the most vigorous condemnation of the dastardly act which cost the President his life.

And so, from the rising to the setting of the sun, "there was sorrow in the cities." It was not in the big cities alone. Wherever communities had been gathered, there was sorrow, and the effort to express the grief that was universal throughout the nation. Churches were filled with communicants and friends. Men and women who had not been in the habit of attending divine services made this the occasion when they paid their tribute of respect to the memory of a great man fallen. Pastors and orators employed their best talents in extolling the virtues of the dead, and holding out hope to the living.

And not even in the cities—large or small—was the grief monopolized. There was not a farm house, perhaps, in the land where grief was absent. In those hours when the service was being conducted over the bier of the martyred President in Canton, there was a bowing of heads throughout every part of the land. The beneficent results of the public labors of this man had reached to the farthest home, and the fame of his loyal manhood had penetrated all hearts. He was loved and honored and mourned. And the nation paused at the brink of his grave, in body or in spirit, whether they stood in the city he had called his home, and whether they held to their places at any other point in the broad land.

The sorrow of the cities bathed all the land in tears.

Of all the tributes paid to the memory of the dead President, none approached in majesty and impressiveness that utter abandonment of all occupation for the moments when the burial was actually taking place. For five minutes, from 2:30 to 2:35, there was absolute rest throughout the nation. That was the time when the body of the murdered President was being lifted to its last final repose.

And from the Atlantic to the Pacific, not a wheel turned for those five minutes.

For the space of five minutes every train in the country was stopped, and held motionless. Engineers, firemen, conductors and crews paused for that period in their occupation, turned devoutly to the little town where the last sad rites were being performed, and sent their thoughts out to the hovering spirit of the man who had fallen.

Labor in shop, in store, on farm, in mill—everywhere—had ceased.

That stopping of America, that pause of the United States, that wait of every citizen while the body of one dead was lowered to the tomb, is a mightier miracle than that which marked the last victory of Judea's leader.

Five minutes taken out of life! Five minutes snatched from activity, lost to productive effort, subtracted from material struggle! It is an amazing thing in the most energetic, the most thrifty nation on the face of the earth.

And yet that five minutes, stricken from the total money value of the day, brought in return a sense of tenderness, of fraternity with all the other millions waiting, bowed and reverent, which nothing else could have produced. That five minutes was the best investment that busy lives could make. It brought them nearer to the ideal life that had been ended. It helped to impress upon them the value of his splendid example. It gave them a better confidence in the citizenship of America. It enacted anew the law of love, and blessed with its swift ministrations the purer patriotism for which this man of the people, this believer in God had stood as a representative.

Silence and tears for the noble victim of malignant hate; new resolves for the upholding of law and the extension of real liberty; unbounded faith in the stability of our republican institutions; an impressive warning to the foes of order—such was the day's meaning to every loyal American citizen.

Eighty millions of people gathered about six feet by two of hallowed earth! That is the spectacle bought at a price so matchless.

CHAPTER XLIII.

ASSASSINATIONS OF LINCOLN AND GARFIELD.

There had been a long and fratricidal war, the most pitiful that has ever occurred in the history of the world, or even that of heaven, described by Milton. For in the latter the rebellious ones were urged on by envy and utter wickedness, with no thought of right on their side, and their end was "outer darkness." In the Civil War between the States, both sides fought for what they deemed the right, and the patriotism of both was as pure as mother love.

Born of the one side and nurtured by the other, Abraham Lincoln loved both alike, but the logic of events and the uncontrollable influences of environment made him the President and partisan of the Union, the head and director of a stern, relentless, cruel and long-continued war, for the preservation of that Union's integrity on one side, for independence and the strong claim of "States rights" on the other.

There had been marches and battles, sufferings unspeakable, misery, sorrow, death, destruction, all the woes of war, on both sides, four long, dark years, and through it all steadfast in duty, earnest and honest, Abraham Lincoln, President of the United States, with a heart as great as God giveth, and an intelligence as high as heaven, had, with kindly face and even temper, borne through it his burden of responsibility and his soul sorrow in it all.

The end of the war had come, and the great, good man, who had thousands of times earned the satisfaction and sweet peace that should have come to him and been to him a living joy, was, at the moment of his worthy triumph of that which was to prove best for all, laid low in death, at the hands of a monomaniac, an irresponsible, unfortunate enemy to both causes and to himself.

The nation mourned; even Lincoln's enemies condemned the deed, and from that day to this there has been a deep regret in the heart of that generation, and the generation that has succeeded, that Lincoln did not live to see the great good that he had wrought. Yet in the finitude of human understanding we may not have fully felt that Jehovah's wisdom called him to the higher and broader sphere of heaven that he might in a more exalted and perfect manner enjoy the results of his great work.

But Lincoln lived to see the dawn of peace. When he came to deliver his second inaugural address the way was clear, but in that splendid effort there was not a note of victory; there was no exultation over a fallen foe. It breathed but the spirit of brotherly love and the incense of prayerful hopes.

"With malice toward none, with charity for all, with firmness in the right as God gives us to see the right, let us finish the work we are in, to bind up the nation's wounds, to care for him who shall have borne the battle, and for his widow and his orphans, to do all which may achieve and cherish a just and lasting peace among ourselves and with all nations." This was the word and spirit of his way in all the trying time. He went down to death with that flowing from his soul and as a benediction to the people, the republic and its institutions.

It was not long after this beautiful message that General Lee gave up his stronghold at Richmond, departing with about half of his original army, and that closely pursued by the victorious hosts led by General Grant. The army in blue overtook the gray remnant at Appomattox, and there one April day, amid its sunshine and showers, its smiles and its tears, War's sable plume bowed before the white banner of Peace, and Lincoln's great mission had been performed.

The flag of the Union had once more become the flag of all the country, and in this condition of affair- President Lincoln visited Richmond and the final scenes of the mighty conflict and then returned to Washington to begin his new work of "binding up the nation's wounds."

He had now reached the climax of his career and had touched the highest point of his greatness. His great task was done and the heavy burden that had so long worn upon his heart had been lifted off and carried away. Then, when the whole nation was rejoicing over the return of peace, the Saviour of the Union was stricken down by the hand of an assassin.

From early youth, Mr. Lincoln had been followed by presentiments that he would die a violent death, or that his final days would be marked by some great tragic event. And yet from the time of his first election to the Presidency it had been an unsuccessful task upon the part of his closest friends to endeavor to make him understand that he was in constant danger of assassination; for, notwithstanding his presentiments, he always laughed at their fears in that direction, in his splendid courage.

During the summer months he lived at the Soldiers' Home, some miles from Washington, and frequently made the trip between the White House and the Home, unguarded and without escort. Secretary of War Stanton and Ward Lamon, Marshal of the District of Columbia, were in a constant state of alarm over this unnecessary exposure of the President to the danger of assassination. They frequently warned him and provided suitable bodyguards to attend him. But Lincoln as constantly gave the guards the slip, and, mounting his favorite saddle-horse, would set out alone, and often after dark, for the lone ride to his place of rest.

One night, while thus riding, a would-be assassin fired on him from ambush, the bullet passing through his famous high hat. But Lincoln never would admit that the shot had been fired to kill him. He persisted in attributing the incident to an accident, and begged his friends to forget it and say nothing concerning it.

Now that all the circumstances are known as to the assassination, it has been made plain that there was a deep-laid and well-conceived plot to kill President Lincoln long before the crime was actually committed.

When Lincoln was delivering his second inaugural address, on the steps of the Capitol, an excited individual attempted to force his way through the guards in the building to get on the platform with the President. It was afterward learned that this man was John Wilkes Booth, who was afterward more successful in his assassin intent. On the night of April 14, 1865, at Ford's Theater, Washington, the assassin accomplished his terrible purpose.

The manager of that theater had invited the President to witness a performance of a new play, "Our American Cousin," in which the then famous actress, Laura Keane, was playing. Lincoln was peculiarly fond of the theater. It was his most satisfactory source of relaxation from the burdens and anxieties of his life. He particularly delighted in Shakespeare's plays and never lost a reasonable opportunity to witness their worthy presentation. Mrs. Lincoln was even more fond of the drama, and was less discriminating in her choice as to plays.

As "Our American Cousin" was a new play, the President was not specially anxious to see it, but as Mrs. Lincoln was very much inclined to attend, her husband consented and accepted the invitation.

General Grant was in Washington at the time, and as he was extremely anxious about the personal safety of the President, he reported every day regularly at the White House. Thus the General and Mrs. Grant had been invited by the President to accompany him and Mrs. Lincoln on this occasion, and Grant had accepted, but at the moment while the General and the President were talking on the subject, a message came from Mrs. Grant to the effect that she wished to leave Washington that evening to visit her daughter in Burlington. General Grant thereupon made his excuses to the President and went his way to accompany his wife to the railway station. It afterwards became known that it was part of the plot to assassinate General Grant also, and but for the fortunate departure of Mrs. Grant from Washington, the great commander would have fallen with his illustrious chief.

General Grant afterward remarked that as he and Mrs. Grant were riding along Pennsylvania avenue to the railway station, a horseman rode rapidly by them, but wheeled his horse and came back, peering into the carriage as he passed.

Mrs. Grant, at the time, said to the General: "That is the very man who sat near us at luncheon to-day, and tried to overhear our conversation. He was so rude, you remember, as to cause us to leave the dining-room. Here he is again, riding after us."

General Grant attributed the actions of the man to idle curiosity, but learned afterward that the man was John Wilkes Booth.

It has been suggested that the probable reason for Lincoln's disinclination to attend the theater on that fatal night was something of a promise that he had made to his friend and bodyguard, who had once been his law partner, Ward Lamon, then Marshal of the District of Columbia.

Two days previous Lincoln had sent Lamon to Richmond on business connected with the call of a convention to discuss reconstruction. Before his departure, Lamon had held an interview with Mr. Usher, Secretary of the Interior, in which he had requested the Secretary to endeavor to persuade the President to be more cautious as to his personal safety, and to go out as little as possible while Lamon was absent. Together they called upon the President, and Lamon preferred his request for the promise.

"I think I can venture to say I will," was the reply. "What is it?"

"Promise me that you will not go out, after night, while I am gone," said Lamon, "particularly to the theater."

President Lincoln turned to Secretary Usher and said: "Usher, this boy is a monomaniac on the subject of my safety. I can hear him or hear of him being around at all times in the night, to prevent somebody from murdering me. He thinks I shall be killed, and we think he is going crazy. What does any one want to assassinate me for? If any one wants to do so, he can do it any day or night, if he is ready to give his life for mine. It is nonsense."

The Secretary, however, insisted that it would be well to heed Lamon's warning, as he was thrown, all the time, among persons from whom he had better opportunities to know concerning such matters, than any one else.

"Well," said the President to the Marshal, "I promise to do the best I can toward it."

The assassination of President Lincoln was most carefully planned, even to the smallest detail. The box set apart for the President's party was a double one, in the second tier, and at the left of the stage. It had two doors with spring locks, but Booth had loosened the screws with which the locks were fastened, so that it was impossible to secure them from the inside. In one door he had made a gimlet hole, in order to be able to see what was going on inside.

An employe of the theater, named Spangler, who was an accomplice of the assassin, had even gone so far as to arrange the seats in the box to suit the purpose of the assassin.

On that eventful night the body of the theater was densely crowded with people. The presidential party arrived a few minutes after nine o'clock and was composed of the President and Mrs. Lincoln, Miss Harris and Mayor Rathbone, daughter and step-son of Senator Harris of New York, and the vast audience arose and cheered as the President was ushered to his box.

Booth, the assassin, came into the theater about ten o'clock, and being a well-known actor, of influence in his circle, could easily take unusual liberties about the theater.

He had not only planned to kill the President, but had also made excellent arrangements to escape into Maryland. A swift horse, saddled, bridled and ready for the venturesome race, was in waiting at the rear of the theater. For a few minutes the assassin pretended to be interested in the play, and then he gradually made his way around the back of the seats in the second tier to the door of the President's box.

Before reaching that point, however, he was halted by a messenger of the President, who had been stationed at the end of the passage leading to the boxes to prevent the intrusion of unwelcome persons. To this man Booth delivered a card purporting to be a message from the President to the effect that he had sent for the bearer. Thus Booth was permitted to enter.

Inside the passageway leading to the boxes the assassin closed the outer door and secured it with a bar that had been provided for the occasion. Thus it became impossible for any one on the outside to follow the assassin by means immediately at hand. Booth quickly entered the box by the right hand door to where the President was sitting in the left hand corner, nearest the audience and in an easy armchair. He was leaning on one hand and held with the other a fold of the drapery. He, with the others, was intently watching the performance on the stage, and a pleasant smile was on his face.

In the right hand the assassin carried a small, silver-mounted derringer pistol and in his left a long-bladed double-edged dagger. The pistol he placed behind the President's left ear and fired, and at the report the victim bent slightly forward, his eyes closed, but in every other respect his attitude remained unchanged.

The report of the pistol startled Major Rathbone, who sprang to his feet and grappled with the assassin, who was then about six feet away from the President. Booth escaped from the grasp of Major Rathbone and throwing down the pistol struck at Rathbone with the dagger, inflicting a severe wound. The assassin then placed his hand lightly on the railing of the box and vaulted to the stage, eight or ten feet below.

The President's box had been heavily draped with a large flag of the Union, and in jumping Booth's spurs caught in the folds of the flag, which was carried with him, and as he fell heavily his ankle was sprained, an incident that more than anything else led to his capture and death.

The assassin, as he arose, walked, without sign of pain, and theatrically, across the stage, and as he did so turned to the audience, flourished his dagger and exclaimed, "Sic semper tyrannis!" adding, "The South is avenged!"

The audience was stunned for the moment with horror, and seemed incapable of action, excepting one man, a lawyer named Stuart. He instantly comprehended the situation and leaping to the stage attempted the capture of the assassin, but Booth, being familiar with the arrangement of the stage, eluded his pursuer by darting out through one of the stage entrances to a rear door, where the horse stood, held in readiness for him, and vaulting into the saddle, dashed away, taking a street leading into Virginia.

Miss Keane rushed to the President's box with water and stimulants, and medical aid was quickly at hand.

The full import of the act dawned upon the audience and it realized the tragedy, then followed a scene such as has never been witnessed in any other public gathering. Women wept, shrieked and fainted, men raved and swore, and horror was depicted upon every face. Before the audience could emerge from the theater horsemen were dashing through the streets, and the telegraph was carrying the details of the awful tragedy to all the world.

The assassin's bullet did not produce instant death, but the President never again became conscious. He was carried to a house opposite the theater, where he died the next morning. In the meantime the authorities had become aware of the wide-reaching conspiracy, and the capital was in a state of terror.

On the night of the assassination of Lincoln, Secretary of State Seward was attacked, though in bed with a broken arm, by Booth's fellow-conspirators and badly wounded.

The assassins had also planned to take the lives of Vice-President Johnson and Secretary Stanton. Booth had called on Vice-President Johnson the day before, and not finding him, had left a card.

Secretary Stanton acted with his usual promptness and courage, and though acting as President during the period of excitement, he directed the plans for the capture of Booth.

After President Lincoln had been taken to the house where he died, he was at once divested of his clothing by the surgeons in attendance.

Surgeon-General Barnes presiding, examined the wound, and it was at once seen that he could not possibly survive many hours. The ball had entered on the left side of the head, behind the left ear, and three inches from it. Its course was obliquely forward, traversing the brain, and lodging just behind the right eye. The President was at once surrounded by the prominent officers of the government. Mrs. Lincoln, overcome with emotion, was led from the theater to the house where her husband lay. Secretary McCullough, Attorney-General Speed, Secretary Welles, Senator Sumner, and other distinguished gentlemen, remained in the room through the night.

When first brought into the house the President's breathing was regular, but difficult. This continued throughout the night, he giving, with occasional exceptions, no indications of suffering, and remaining, with closed eyes, perfectly unconscious. At about seven in the morning his breathing became more difficult, and was interrupted at intervals sometimes for so long a time that he was supposed to be dead. At twenty-two minutes past seven he ceased breathing, and thus expired. There was no convulsive action, no rattling in the throat, no appearance of suffering of any kind— none of the symptoms which ordinarily attend dissolution and add to its terrors. From the instant he was struck by the ball of the assassin, he had not given the slightest indication that he was conscious of anything that occurred around him.

The news that the President had been shot spread at once through the town, and was instantly followed by tidings of a murderous assault, still more terrible in its details, upon the Secretary of State. Some days previously Mr. Seward had been thrown from his carriage, and seriously injured. His right arm was broken above the elbow, his jaw was fractured, and his whole system seriously shattered. For nearly a fortnight he had been confined to his bed, unable to swallow anything but liquids, and reduced, by pain and this enforced abstinence, to a state of extreme debility. His room was on the third floor of his residence in Madison Place, fronting on President Square, and the bed on which he lay stood opposite the door by which the room was entered, and about ten feet from it. At a few minutes past ten—within five minutes of the time when the President was shot—a man, proved afterwards to be Lewis Payne Powell, generally known as Payne, rang at the door of Mr. Seward's residence, and said to the colored lad who opened it that he had some medicines prescribed for Mr. Seward by Dr. Verdi, his family physician, which he must deliver in person. The lad said that no one could go up to Mr. Seward's room; but Payne pushed him aside and rushed up stairs. He had reached the third floor, and was about to enter Mr. Seward's room, when he was confronted by Mr. Frederick W. Seward, the Secretary's son, to whom he made the same statement of his errand. He was refused admission, when he drew a pistol and snapped it at Frederick without effect; he then struck him with it upon the head twice, with such force as to break the pistol and prostrate his victim, fracturing his skull. Hearing the noise, Miss Fannie Seward, who was in her father's room, opened the door, into which Payne instantly rushed, and, drawing a bowie-knife, threw himself upon the bed, and made three powerful stabs at the throat of Mr. Seward, who had raised himself up at the first alarm, and who instantly divined the real nature and intention of the assault. Each blow inflicted a terrible wound, but, before the assassin could deal another, he was seized around the body by an invalid soldier named Robinson, who was in attendance as nurse, and who strove to drag the murderer from his victim. Payne at once struck at Robinson and inflicted upon him several serious wounds, but did not succeed in freeing himself from his grasp. Mr. Seward, the instant his murderer's attention was withdrawn from him, threw himself off the bed at the farther side; and Payne, finding that his victim was thus beyond his reach, broke away from Robinson, and rushed to the door. The colored lad in the lower hall had run into the street for help, and Miss Fannie Seward shouted "Murder!" from the upper window. The assassin, on reaching the upper hall, met Major Augustus Seward, another son of the Secretary, whom he struck with his dagger, and on the stairs encountered Mr. Hansell, one of the Secretary's attendants, whom he stabbed in the back. Forcing his way through all these obstacles, he rushed down the stairs, and finding, to his surprise, no one there to oppose his progress, he passed out at the front door, mounted a horse he had left standing in front of the house, and rode leisurely away.

When the news of this appalling tragedy spread through the city, it carried consternation to every heart. Treading close on the heels of the President's murder—perpetrated, indeed, at the same instant—it was instinctively felt to be the work of a conspiracy, secret, remorseless, and terrible. The Secretary of War, Mr. Stanton, had left Mr. Seward's bedside not twenty minutes before the assault, and was in his private chamber, preparing to retire, when a messenger brought tidings of the tragedy, and summoned his instant attendance. On his way to Mr. Seward's house, Mr. Stanton heard of the simultaneous murder of the President, and instantly felt that the Government was enveloped in the meshes of a conspiracy, whose agents were unknown, and which was all the more terrible for the darkness and mystery in which it moved. Orders were instantly given to close all drinking-shops and all places of public resort in the city, guards were stationed at every point, and all possible precautions were taken for the safety of the Vice-President and other prominent Government officials. A vague terror brooded over the population of the town. Men whispered to each other as they met, in the gloom of midnight, and the deeper gloom of the shadowy crime which surrounded them. Presently, passionate indignation replaced this paralysis of the public heart, and, but for the precautions adopted on the instant by the Government, the public vengeance would have been wreaked upon the rebels confined in the Old Capitol Prison. All these feelings, however, gradually subsided, and gave way to a feeling of intense anxiety for the life of the President. Crowds of people assembled in the neighborhood of the house where the dying martyr lay, eager for tidings of his condition, throughout the night; and when, early in the morning, it was announced that he was dead, a feeling of solemn awe filled every heart, and sat, a brooding grief, upon every face.

And so it was through all the length and breadth of the land. In every State, in every town, in every household, there was a dull and bitter agony, as the telegraph bore tidings of the awful deed. Everywhere throughout the Union, the public heart, bounding with exultation at the triumphant close of the great war, and ready to celebrate with a mighty joy the return of peace, stood still with a sacred terror, as it was smitten by the terrible tidings from the capital of the Nation. In the great cities of the land all business instantly stopped—no man had the heart to think of gain—flags drooped half-mast from every winged messenger of the sea, from every church spire, from every tree of liberty, and from every public building. Masses of the people came together by a spontaneous impulse, to look in each other's faces, as if they could read there some hint of the meaning of these dreadful deeds—some omen of the country's fate. Thousands upon thousands, drawn by a common feeling, crowded around every place of public resort, and listened eagerly to whatever any public speaker chose to say. Wall street, in New York, was thronged by a vast multitude of men, to whom eminent public officials addressed words of sympathy and of hope. Gradually as the day wore on, emblems of mourning were hung from the windows of every house throughout the town, and before the sun had set every city, throughout the length and breadth of the land, to which tidings of the great calamity had been borne by the telegraph, was enshrouded in the shadow of the national grief. On the next day, which was Sunday, every pulpit resounded with eloquent eulogies of the murdered President, and with such comments on his death as faith in an overruling Providence alone could prompt. The whole country was plunged into profound grief—and none deplored the crime which had deprived the Nation of its head with more sincerity than those who had been involved in the guilt of the rebellion, and who had just begun to appreciate those merciful and forgiving elements in Mr. Lincoln's character, whose exercise they themselves would need so soon.

Immediately after his death, the body of the President was removed to the Executive Mansion, embalmed, and placed in the Green Room, which had been prepared by suitable emblems of mourning for its reception. Near the center of the room stood the grand catafalque four feet high, upon which rested the mahogany coffin, covered with flowers—the last sad offerings of affection—in which the body was placed for its final rest.

The conspiracy to assassinate President Lincoln involved altogether twenty-five people. Among the number captured and tried were David C. Herold, G. W. Atzerodt, Louis Payne, Edward Spangler, Michael O'Loughlin, Samuel Arnold, Mrs. Surratt and Dr. Samuel Mudd. Dr.

Mudd was deported to the Dry Tortugas. While there an epidemic of yellow fever broke out and he rendered such good service that he was granted a pardon and died some years ago in Maryland.

John Surratt, the son of the woman who was hanged, made his escape to Italy, where he became one of the Papal guards in the Vatican at Rome. His presence there was discovered by Archbishop Hughes, and although there were no extradition laws to cover the case, the Italian Government gave him up to the United States authorities.

He had two trials. At the first the jury disagreed; the long delay before his second trial allowed him to escape by pleading the statute of limitation. Spangler and O'Loughlin were sent to the Dry Tortugas and served their time.

Ford, the owner of the theater in which the President was assassinated, was a Southern sympathizer, and when he attempted to reopen his theater, after the great national tragedy, Secretary Stanton refused to allow it. The Government afterward bought the property and turned it into a national museum.

Booth, the arch-conspirator, accompanied by David C. Herold, finally made his way into Maryland, where, eleven days after the assassination, the two were discovered in a barn. Herold surrendered, but Booth, who refused to be taken alive, was shot and killed by Boston Corbett, a sergeant of cavalry.

ASSASSINATION OF GARFIELD.

In this fair republic of ours, a fabric of government strong in structure, superb and imposing, chaste and grand; a temple whose real devotees are true-hearted patriots, there has not been one who has more perfectly exemplified the possibilities of American youth than James Abram Garfield, child of penury, farmer boy, canal-boat lad, student, teacher, statesman, soldier, President, martyr. In all, true and brave, endowed with the royalty of right manhood, that was becoming as a sovereign citizen, a pattern and a patriot.

He won his way, almost from babyhood to the most exalted place in the nation, by conscientious and industrious work, purity of purpose, carefulness of character, guided, at every moment, by simple rules of truth and honor.

His heritage was that of every healthy boy in the United States, stronger than money, fairer than influence, better than brilliancy, more potent than genius.

Determination to rise, steadfastness of purpose, well-directed common-sense, commendable ambition. These were the factors that made the man, whose unsullied name is graven high in the history of the republic, and whose life was a satisfaction to himself, his associates and his people. Exalted without ostentation, great without conceit, helpful to his family, his friends, his race, his country and himself, blessed of God, the beginning and end of a benediction.

His death was an accident of fate.

Saturday, July 2, 1881, was a fair, hot midsummer day. The inmates of the White House were astir early. The President was going to Massachusetts to attend the commencement exercises at his old college at Williamstown, and afterward to take a holiday jaunt through New England, accompanied by several members of the Cabinet and other friends. His wife, who was at Long Branch, New Jersey, just recovering from a severe attack of malarial fever, was to join him at New York. He had looked forward with almost boyish delight to his trip, and was in high spirits as he and Secretary Blaine drove off to the railway station.

There was no crowd about. Most of those who were to take the train had already gone on board. Among the few persons in the waiting-room was a slender, middle-aged man, who walked up and down rather nervously, occasionally looking out of the door as if expecting some one. There was nothing about him to attract special notice, and no one paid much attention to him. When President Garfield and Mr. Blaine entered, he drew back, took a heavy revolver from his pocket, and, taking deliberate aim, fired. The ball struck the President on the shoulder. He turned, surprised, to see who had shot him. The assassin recocked his revolver and fired again, and then turned to flee. The President fell to the floor, the blood gushing from a wound in his side.

In a moment all was confusion and horror. Secretary Blaine sprang after the assassin, but, seeing that he was caught, turned again to the President. The shock had been great, and he was very pale. A mattress was brought, his tall form was lifted tenderly into an ambulance, and he was swiftly borne to the Executive Mansion. His first thought was for his wife—the beloved wife of his youth, just recovering from sickness, expecting in a few hours to meet him. How would she bear the tidings of this blow?

"Rockwell," he said, faintly, to a friend, "I want you to send a message to 'Crete'" (the pet name for his wife, Lucretia). "Tell her I am seriously hurt —how seriously I cannot yet say. I am myself, and hope she will come to me soon. I send my love to her." During the dictation of the dispatch, Dr. Bliss and several other physicians arrived. A hasty inspection demonstrated that the President was terribly wounded.

A swift train brought Mrs. Garfield to her husband's side that evening. The persons present in the sick-room retired to allow Mrs. Garfield to meet her husband alone, as he had requested. They remained together only five minutes; but the effect of this brief interview was soon seen in the rallying of the almost dying man. At the end of that time the doctors were again admitted, and then began the long struggle for life, with its fluctuations between hope and dread, which lasted for almost three months. Just after Mrs. Garfield's arrival there was a sudden collapse which seemed to be the end, and the family of the President were hastily summoned to his bedside; but, to the surprise of every one, the crisis passed, and for three weeks he seemed to improve. Then came a turn for the worse, and from that time the President lost ground. The hot summer days, hard to bear even for those in full health, wasted and weakened him terribly. He sank steadily; and it was seen that unless relief from the intense heat could be had, he would inevitably die within a few days. It was decided to remove him to Elberon, on the ocean shore, near Long Branch, New Jersey; and on September 7th, accompanied by his family and the members of the Cabinet, he was borne by a swift special train northward to the seaside. A summer cottage had been offered for his use, and there for two anxious weeks lay the man who, it may be truly said, had become

> "The pillar of a people's hope,
> The center of a world's desire."

The cooling breezes of the seaside brought some relief, and the change no doubt prolonged his life; but it could not be saved. In the night of September 19th, almost without warning, the end came; the feeble flame of life, so anxiously watched and cherished, flickered a moment, and then went out in the darkness.

During the long, sultry days of that anxious summer, for many hours of the day and night, throughout all the land, wherever there was a newspaper or a telegraph office, about such places stood groups of people, measured in numbers by the degree of population, waiting and watching eagerly for the slips of paper which from time to time were posted in a conspicuous place on the front of the building. In the intervals they would gather in little knots and talk together in low tones. To one who did not know what had happened on July 2d, it would have been hard to guess what gathered these waiting crowds, day after day, throughout the land. With intense, foreboding suspense fifty millions of people were watching for the news from the bedside of the

President of the United States, who had been stricken down by the bullet of the assassin. Who that lived through that long summer can forget those anxious days and nights? And when at last the brave struggle for life was ended, and the silent form was borne from the seaside to rest on the shores of Lake Erie, who can forget the solemn hush which seemed to prevail everywhere as the tomb opened to receive all that was mortal of the beloved President, James A. Garfield?

The President's body was borne back to Washington, where it lay in state, viewed by great throngs of mourning people; then it was taken westward to Cleveland, and laid in the tomb by the shores of Lake Erie, almost in sight of his old home. The journey was one long funeral pageant. For almost the entire distance the railway tracks were lined with crowds of people, who, with uncovered heads, stood in reverent silence as the train passed. Not since the day when that other dead President, the great Lincoln, was borne to his last resting place, had such an assembly been gathered; and the love and grief which followed Garfield to his grave are the best tribute to the worth of his character.

Five months later, in the hall of the House of Representatives at Washington, amid such a throng as that chamber has seldom seen, Secretary Blaine delivered his eulogy of the dead President; and from that splendid and pathetic address we take the concluding words, which will fitly close this brief sketch:

"As the end drew near, his early craving for the sea returned. The stately mansion of power had been to him the wearisome hospital of pain, and he begged to be taken from its prison walls, from its oppressive, stifling air, from its homelessness and hopelessness. Gently, silently, the love of a great people bore the pale sufferer to the longed-for healing of the sea, to live or to die, as God should will, within sight of its heaving billows, within sound of its manifold voices. With wan, fevered face tenderly lifted to the cooling breeze, he looked out wistfully upon the ocean's changing wonders; on its fair sails, whitening in the morning light; on its restless waves, rolling shoreward to break and die beneath the noonday sun; on the red clouds of evening, arching low to the horizon; on the serene and shining pathway of the stars. Let us think that his dying eyes read a mystic meaning which only the rapt and parting soul may know. Let us believe that in the silence of the receding world he heard the great waves breaking on a further shore, and felt already upon his wasted brow the breath of the eternal morning."